Toward the
SCIENTIFIC STUDY
of HISTORY

Toward the SCIENTIFIC STUDY of HISTORY

Selected Essays

of LEE BENSON

J. B. LIPPINCOTT COMPANY

Philadelphia   New York   Toronto

Paperbound: ISBN-0-397-47223-4
Clothbound: ISBN-0-397-47265-X

Library of Congress Catalog Card Number: 73-161415

Printed in the United States of America

Cover and interior design by Robert C. Digges

FOR
PAUL LAZARSFELD
AND
ERNEST NAGEL

who helped me to see the logic
of trying to contribute to
"the logic of social inquiry"

ACKNOWLEDGMENTS

WITH one exception, the essays in this volume have been previously published. The exception is an essay written in 1971, "Explanations of American Civil War Causation: A Critical Assessment and a Modest Proposal to Reorient and Reorganize the Social Sciences." Other than corrections of typographical errors and minor stylistic lapses, the essays have been reprinted unchanged and in chronological order of publication. I have done so to suggest the development of my ideas, as well as to suggest how they were affected by developments in historiography in particular and social science in general. I am grateful to the original publishers for permission to reprint:

"Research Problems in American Political Historiography," in Mirra Komarovsky, ed., *Common Frontiers of the Social Sciences* (Free Press: Glencoe, Ill., 1957), 113-183, 418-421.

"Causation and the American Civil War," *History and Theory*, 1:163-175 (1961).

"Quantification, Scientific History, and Scholarly Innovation," *AHA Newsletter*, 4:11-16 (June, 1966).

"An Approach to the Scientific Study of Past Public Opinion," *Public Opinion Quarterly*, 31:522-567 (Winter 1967).

"The Empirical and Statistical Basis for Comparative Analyses of Historical Change," in Stein Rokkan, ed., *Comparative Research Across Cultures and Nations* (Mouton:Paris, 1968), 129-139.

"The Historian as Mythmaker: Turner and the Closed Frontier," in David M. Ellis, ed., *The Frontier in American Development: Essays in Honor of Paul Wallace Gates* (Cornell University Press: Ithaca, N.Y., 1969), 3-19.

"Middle Period Historiography: What Is to be Done?", in George Billias and Gerald Grob, eds., *American History: Retrospect and Prospect* (Free Press: New York, 1971), 154-190.

Table of
CONTENTS

It is not possible to run a course aright when the goal itself is not rightly placed. The true and lawful goal of the sciences is none other than this: that human life be endowed with new discoveries and powers.

Francis Bacon, *Novum Organum*

[My work on physics] caused me to see that it is possible to attain knowledge which is very useful in life, and that, instead of that speculative philosophy which is taught in the schools, we may find a practical philosophy by means of which, knowing the force and the action of fire, water, air, the stars, heavens and all other bodies that environ us, as distinctly as we know the different crafts of our artisans, we can in the same way employ them in all those uses to which they are adapted, and thus render ourselves the masters and possessors of nature . . . . I [decided] to beg all well inclined persons to proceed further by contributing . . . to experiments and communicating them to the public . . . in order that the last should commence where the preceding had left off and thus by joining together the lives and labors of many, we should collectively proceed much further than anyone in particular could succeed in doing.

René Descartes, "The Discourse on Method"

INTRODUCTION

TELL me, Daddy. What is the use of history?"

That is how Marc Bloch began his celebrated book on *The Historian's Craft*. We might, however, change his son's question to: "What are the *uses* of history?"

When we reformulate Bloch's question, we can see more clearly that the study of past human behavior has multiple—and radically different—uses. And when we see *that* clearly, we can more easily free ourselves of the traditional delusion that the study of past human behavior constitutes, or should constitute, a single discipline.

To achieve radically different goals, it seems reasonable to believe, scholars must develop different types of orientation and different types of training and organization. That belief, at any rate, informs all the essays assembled in this volume—although I only came to that realization after I had assembled them and began to write this introduction.

From the outset, I have recognized that my work rested on two assumptions: 1) Past human behavior can be studied scientifically. 2) The scientific study of past human behavior is indispensable to the scientific study of human behavior, past and present. No scientific historiography, no powerful social science.

What was not clear to me at the outset of my work, however, was why a *genuinely* scientific historiography, as differentiated from a *nominally* scientific historiography, had not been developed. That question, and its activist corollary, "What can be done to develop a genuinely scientific historiography?", are the basic questions to which, in one way or another, all the essays in this volume are addressed. My answers, however, as readers will note, have changed somewhat over time.

That my answers still are not *the* answers to the questions posed above hardly needs saying. But as a perennial optimist "left over from the late-eighteenth century" (to quote a friend's characterization), I should like to think that the essays tend to give progressively better answers to them. In any event, in the last and most ambitious essay, I have directly tried to answer the two questions around which this volume can reasonably be said to be organized: 1) Why haven't scholars developed a genuinely scientific historiography? 2) What can scholars do to develop a genuinely scientific historiograpy?

1 RESEARCH PROBLEMS in AMERICAN POLITICAL HISTORIOGRAPHY

I. Introduction

AN American historian's lot is not an easy one. His beat is a country of continental proportions, peopled by an incredible number of intermingled ethnic and religious groups physically and socially mobile to an unparalleled degree. Moreover, it is a country settled at different times and in different ways. The economy and its resource patterns have been, and are, extraordinarily diverse and dynamic. Small wonder that of the making of "new" interpretations there is no end. Probably one major reason for the rapid fluctuations and relative lack of consensus characterizing our historiography is the difficulty inherent in explaining American political development. In the absence of a well-defined common methodology, and the presence of a near-universal dependence upon impressionistic techniques and data, one might reasonably expect to find that different frames of reference, training, interests, access to data, etc., result in a splendid profusion of varying interpretations. Such expectations are satisfied by a survey of the literature of American political history. If it does nothing more, a survey of this kind demonstrates that among historians—if nowhere else—"rugged individualism" still holds forth.[1]

Scholarly initiative and independent-mindedness can only be applauded. But it is suggested here that fluctuating views and lack of consensus among political historians are best attributed to other factors. For example, presidential elections have tended to be the major foci of American political history; usually, they also have been taken, in some degree at least, as measures of economic, social, cultural, religious, and other developments. Setting aside the basic theoretical question of whether such an orientation is really desirable, it seems correct to assert that historians *do not yet have available the systematic data necessary to begin to interpret voting behavior, nor the methodological techniques to handle such data were they available.* (The terms, "systematic data" and "systematic methods," will be defined below.) In effect, historians are called upon to answer the "why" of American presidential elections without knowing the "what" and the "who." That is, historians do not now have available to them, in meaningful and easily workable form, the basic election statistics over time and space, nor anything but the scantiest verified data on who (what groups) voted for whom, when.[2] *It is the central proposition of this study that historians, therefore, have found it extremely difficult to function as historians and view political developments in long-term perspective. Instead, each election is usually treated as a separate phenomenon, and interpretations of voting behavior at one time do not rest upon detailed comparison with voting behavior over time and space.* As will be emphasized below, this *ahistorical* tendency is not attributed to the failings of individuals; on the contrary, it is believed to reflect the

1. The study has been prepared under the joint direction of Professors Paul Lazarsfeld of the Columbia University Planning Project for Advanced Training in Social Research and Seymour Lipset of the Columbia Committee Conducting a Propositional Inventory of Political Behavior. Both advisers have contributed much to the final result, but I am particularly grateful to Professor Lazarsfeld for searching criticisms and fruitful suggestions. It need hardly be added that neither adviser should be held responsible for any shortcomings.

I am indebted to Thomas C. Cochran of the University of Pennsylvania, Manning J. Dauer of the University of Florida, and James C. Malin of the University of Kansas for calling my attention to errors and questionable formulations in an earlier draft.

difficulties confronting all students of political behavior in the United States.

Primarily, the study is designed to focus attention upon problems of interpretation which result from lack of detailed voting data over time and space, and from the present unsystematic techniques of handling available data. It also discusses a tentative method *to identify potentially verifiable hypotheses* originally derived from impressionistic research, and, conversely, one which can be carried further *to formulate potentially verifiable hypotheses.* The concept, "potentially verifiable," will be considered later.

For our purposes the problems of securing access to contemporary source materials and acquiring historical perspective are irrelevant. As employed here, the time dimension essentially connotes the *process* of charting, analyzing, and relating the chronological distribution of events. But, if the requisite data is available, it is also possible to handle similarly the spatial distribution of phenomena at any given moment in time. Combining the two dimensions, that is, studying both the chronological and spatial distribution of phenomena, permits one to obtain a far closer approximation to reality than if either dimension is employed alone. To make the study really dynamic, however, it is necessary to introduce the rate dimension, or the dimension which measures the *pace* of events as well as their chronological and spatial distribution.[3] Basically a function of the time dimension, the rate

2. Subsequent to the completion of the present study, W. Dean Burnham's compilation of national election statistics was published. *Presidential Ballots, 1836-1892* (Baltimore: Johns Hopkins Press, 1955), is a praiseworthy example of scholarly resourcefulness and diligence. By presenting the raw voting statistics for American presidential elections in the nineteenth century, it makes a basic contribution to political historiography. It neatly supplements the pioneering works of Edgar E. Robinson, *The Presidential Vote: 1896-1932* (Stanford, Calif.: Stanford University Press, 1934), and *They Voted for Roosevelt, the presidential vote, 1932-1944* (Stanford, Calif.: Stanford University Press, 1947). The publication of Mr. Burnham's volume increases the likelihood that some day we shall have verified statements of who voted for whom, when. When this indispensable task is accomplished, it will then be possible to tackle the more difficult questions involved in *explaining* American voting behavior.

3. Although the concepts employed here differ somewhat from those developed by Derwent Whittlesey, see his stimulating paper, "The Horizons of Geography," in *Annals of the Association of American Geographers,* 35:1-36 (1945).

measure is important enough in its own right to warrant separate demarcation. One might know that certain phenomena almost uniformly succeed other phenomena, but the historical processes of development would differ significantly if the rate of succession varied from place to place.

Under ideal conditions, the historian, fully armed, can be expected to carry out his explorations in three dimensions. He is able to study the unfolding of events over time, their distribution over space, and their *relative rate over both time and space*. But conditions are rarely ideal and in practice more or less of his time and resources are given to one or the other dimensions according to the nature and accessibility of source materials, the kind of questions for which answers are sought, and the degree of precision desired. Sections II to IV analyze some problems involved in effectively using the three historical dimensions to evaluate *generalized explanations* of American voting behavior. Section V deals with that type of hypothesis which does identify *specific voting groups* or *specific causal factors,* or both. Generalized explanations are considered to be those which do not single out a clearly defined voting group as responsive to a particular causal factor (or set of factors). Instead, that factor is made the determinant of voting behavior in general and voters are relatively undifferentiated along group lines.

Systematic Methods and Potentially Verifiable Hypotheses.   Perhaps the chief criterion distinguishing systematic methods from those employed in impressionistic research is that they yield data which can be represented *quantitatively*. In this connection it may be useful to note that any statement connoting some form of measurement logically can be viewed as quantitative in nature. When historians cite "typical" newspaper editorials and the beliefs of "representative men," or when they use terms such as "significant," "widespread," "growing," "intense," in effect they are making quantitative statements. Though the problem is outside the present study's scope, it seems pertinent to suggest that systematic methods can be used to convert into direct quantitative form many types of historical data not usually regarded as capable of such representation.

But quantification is not the only criterion of systematic methodology. Another criterion is that the data are compiled, classified, and analyzed *comprehensively and rigorously*, not partially or in unstandardized fashion. Finally, systematic methods yield *objective* data, i.e., data which experts can agree are factually correct and unambiguous in meaning, whether or not they agree in their interpretations of those data or share the same frame of reference.

Perhaps the best perspective for the reader to adopt is that the study is basically designed to raise questions, call attention to research problems in political history, and serve as a springboard for their discussion. It does not report the results of intensive research in political history based upon primary or secondary sources, nor does it do more than sketch in rough outline a methodological procedure to facilitate research in political history. But in order to demonstrate the need for such a procedure, as well as the possibility of its attainment, the study analyzes conclusions reached by qualified scholars concerning a variety of significant political contests.

Understandably, because the data concerning spatial distribution of voting behavior over time are not available in manageable form, historians have tended to treat each election in isolated fashion. This observation applies even to presidential contests where national and state totals at least are not difficult to ascertain; when historians deal with congressional results for the country at large, or state and local elections, their problem regarding statistics is much greater. Yet it is almost axiomatic that without the voting data for elections on *all levels*, interpretations of American elections on any *one level* cannot be regarded as comprehensive.

That the inadequacies of available quantitative data severely handicap historians in interpreting elections can be seen from the examples which follow. In one form or another they show the same basic pattern: voting determinants are deduced from impressionistic research and little attempt is made to specify the conditions under which they operate, or the type of data necessary to establish that they actually are the voting determinants in a given election. Prominent historians and highly regarded works have been deliberately chosen to point up the representative quality of these examples, as well as to demonstrate a variety of interpretative problems. But the choice of particular hypotheses for examination *was not* based upon an evaluation of their intrinsic significance, nor the importance attached to them by their authors. The hypotheses were selected because their formulations permit unambiguous evaluation, because they reflect the impressionistic approach long dominant in American political historiography, and because they fit in with the structural design of this study. I trust that the tone of the analysis is nonpolemical and therefore consonant with its purpose. Employment of the case method, it is anticipated, will focus attention upon some basic historiographic problems rather than upon specific elections and interpretations of them.

Because the analysis focuses upon secondary works which treat a wide range of complex developments, data is marshalled in a manner designed to evaluate hypotheses or propositions already stated to be valid or proven. But the preliminary results of research now in progress indicate that the technique can also be applied to the *formulation* of hypotheses when the requisite systematic data is collected, analyzed, and organized into easily-worked categories.

Time, Space, and Rate Dimensions.   In their explorations, historians are limited to three dimensions: time, space, and rate. Though no meaningful inquiry into human behavior can really dispense with the time dimension, until now the historian has been distinguished from workers in other disciplines by his unique emphasis upon the chronological order of events. But emphasis on the recording, analysis, and relationship of events over time hardly means that the more removed the investigation is from the present moment the more "historical" it is. Studies of ancient Egypt can be fundamentally "unhistorical," and studies of contemporary phenomena might be historical in the best sense of that much abused word.

Several examples may clarify the distinction made above between systematic and impressionistic methods. Obviously, voting statistics compiled by any method represent quantification, but voting statistics can be obtained and used either systematically or impressionistically with remarkably different results.

In terms of the *space dimension* available to historians, an example of nonsystematic or impressionistic use of data would be to offer the election results in one state as evidence for a generalized hypothesis concerning the national outcome without reference to the results in all other units *within that category*, i.e., without reference to all other states. Another example of nonsystematic use of spatial data: focusing attention solely on the voting behavior of an ethnic group (or economic class) in one section of the country and then citing these statistics as demonstration of a hypothesis concerning that group's voting behavior throughout the country. In terms of the historian's *time dimension*, a nonsystematic use of data would be to compile and analyze the voting statistics in one election without adequate reference to like statistics for previous and subsquent elections.

Systematic data concerning voting behavior, therefore, means that statistics are not considered in haphazard isolation but are compiled, organized, and analyzed in relation *to all other data in the same category, both spatially and chronologically.* The nature of the problem and the degree of precision desired determines the adequacy of the spatial and chronological categories utilized, i.e., nation, states, counties, townships, one or more elections before and after the campaign under analysis, etc. What is central to the definition is the *inclusiveness* of the voting statistics cited irrespective of the kind of unit employed, and their statement in at least a minimum historical time setting.

Employing techniques which yield systematic data, the present study attempts to demonstrate a tentative, crude working procedure for the analysis of propositions concerning American political history. Such a procedure is particularly necessary if one desires to inventory the propositional content of the vast amount of existing impressionistic literature. Clearly, judgments concerning the validity of propositions supported by impressionistic data must necessarily be impressionistic unless some systematic method is employed as a measuring device. However, it must be stressed that this procedure does not pretend to "prove" a hypothesis, it merely seeks to establish a hypothesis as "potentially verifiable" in the light of one type of systematic data.

The procedure employed in this monograph to identify a potentially verifiable hypothesis is to distinguish between its factual and interpretative elements, define its terms fairly precisely, develop at least some of its logical implications, and stipulate a certain set of systematic data which it must satisfy. Because the studies analyzed here deal with American presidential elections, the primary test is to state the hypothesis' claims in terms of the systematic data most pertinent to it, i.e., the statistics of voting behavior. If the hypothesis fails to satisfy those stipulations when the pertinent voting statistics are made available and subjected to close analysis, it either must be reformulated or held to be demonstrably invalid. *That is, for our purposes, a potentially verifiable hypothesis is one consonant with the statistics of voting behavior, systematically collected, organized, and analyzed.* In the present monograph, testing will not go beyond a systematic analysis of pertinent voting statistics. But that operation might be clarified by noting that the likelihood of verifying a hypothesis is increased if additional kinds of data are stipulated and their satisfaction demonstrated.

It is a key proposition of this study that no interpretation of an election outcome can begin to be verified until the description of what happened is translated into who (voting groups) caused it to happen. The term, "who," refers to any characteristic distinguishing certain voters from other voters. The distinguishing characteristic can range from full socioeconomic descriptions to the extremely specialized case of voters who listened to a particular campaign address. That is, even a systematic descriptive statement of party victory or defeat, gain or loss, etc., does not permit interpretation. We must designate explicitly the group, or groups of voters, affected by an issue, or set of issues—let us say, past political corruption—before we can systematically marshal voting statistics and other data to support our interpretation of what happened. In other words, using the time dimension, this question must be answered before we can proceed: "Who voted for whom, when?" Broadly speaking, distinguishing features can be of two types: *group characteristics* of particular voters (religion, economic class, ethnic origins, urban-rural, socioeconomic status, etc.); or *operative conditions* in a certain place at a certain time (economic depression, heightened sectional conflicts, intense religious or ethnic antagonisms, etc.), without direct reference to the group characteristics of voters living in that area. It is also possible to combine the two types of distinguishing features so as to specify the different responses of particular groups of voters (e.g., "Yankees" and Irish-Americans) living in areas affected by certain conditions (e.g., low socioeconomic-status districts in an area experiencing economic depression). Subject to the number of variables introduced, combinations of the two broad types of distinguishing features can be devised to achieve greater precision.

The *group characteristics* and *operative conditions types* of distinction have at least one feature in common. They enable us to make some specification concerning *differentiated* patterns of voting behavior which are subject to systematic verification. For example, if in our hypothetical study the Republicans were the party in power, we might claim that as a result of the corruption issue Yankees *generally* were "less Republican than usual," Irish-Americans *generally* were "as Republican as usual." We could then go on to make more precise claims: Yankees in both high and low socioeconomic-status areas experiencing depression were "*much less* Republican than usual," Irish-Americans were "less Republican than usual" only in depressed, low socioeconomic-status areas, Yankees in both high and low socioeconomic-status areas enjoying *prosperity* were "less Republican than usual," etc.

Possible Contributions of Systematic Research Methods to Political Historiography.   Perhaps another useful preliminary to the concrete case studies presented below is to discuss briefly some of the contributions systematic research methods might make to political historiography. Stated in oversimplified terms, let us consider a hypothesis which claims that the nomination of a candidate possessed of a blemished political past led to sharp departures from normal voting patterns in a certain presidential election. Though his nomination by the party long entrenched in power is stated to be the *direct causal factor*, the *basic condition* shaping the election outcome is held to be a widespread, deeply-felt conviction that his party's growing corruption made a political change imperative.

Assuming the hypothesis to be valid, a difficult problem must be faced at the outset. How can we go about *establishing* its validity so that experts will attach a *substantial* degree of credence to it? (*Substantial* is deliberately not defined more precisely here. It only implies a greater degree of credibility for one hypothesis than for any other suggested as an explanation of the same phenomenon.) What is necessary is to marshal systematic data supporting the hypothesis' claims concerning both the basic condition governing the election and the causal factor directly determining voting behavior. In the first instance, in line with the discussion above, it is necessary to demonstrate that the hypothesis is consonant with the systematic data derived from voting statistics.

But before we can begin to marshal the requisite data it is necessary to reformulate the hypothesis. As it stands it is too general. Among other things, we cannot tell as yet what stipulations the voting data must satisfy for the hypothesis to be potentially verifiable. The direct causal factor can be taken as a case in point, i.e., a particular candidate's nomination by the party in power. Obviously, we are not required to show that *every vote* cast in the election was determined by his candidacy. Equally obvious, we do not have to show his candidacy to have been the *sole* determinant of any *single* vote. But the hypothesis does require us to make some explicit statement subject to verification. Merely asserting that the candidate cost his party enough votes to lose the election puts the problem in so general a form as to prevent demonstration that he cost them any votes.

Depending upon the degree of precision and persuasion sought, it is necessary to state the *number* and *kind* of voters who decided to vote against the party in power, to a greater or lesser extent, because its candidate was suspect. Moreover, it is not enough to say that certain votes were determined by his nomination. To carry conviction the hypothesis must offer some explanation of why those votes were affected adversely from his party's viewpoint, and why *others were not.* Again, no implication is intended that the hypothesis must account for all voting decisions in the election or assign an exact weight to a causal factor as a determinant of any single vote. But it is worth repeating that the hypothesis' verification requires us to provide systematic data supporting our interpretation of two different kinds of voting behavior; voters who were sufficiently disturbed by the nomination of a suspect candidate to express their dissatisfaction at the polls, and voters who were not affected. Nonetheless, though the problem now is somewhat more clearly defined, we still have not indicated how to go about securing the requisite data.

Implicit in these claims is the premise that Yankees as a group were historically more responsive than Irish-Americans to the issue of corruption; a premise which would require demonstration for the hypothesis to be verified. Moreover, although these claims specify certain *operative conditions* and nonethnic *group characteristics* as increasing or decreasing the impact of corruption upon voting behavior, they also hold that "Yankees" as a group were demonstrably more responsive to the issue in the particular election studied.

Granted our ability to employ systematic methods to compile the data and construct the indexes implicit in the factual claims made above concerning voting performance, they can be demonstrated to be valid or invalid. Obviously, such demonstrations would not "prove" the causal inferences but their consonance with the systematic data of voting performance would give some credence to them. Having identified "Yankees" as a group responsive to the corruption issue in a given election, and having demonstrated their actual voting performance to be consonant with that interpretation, we could then attempt to present other supporting data. *In sum, only after we have stated and demonstrated who voted for whom, when, can we tackle the far more complex problem of establishing why they did so.*

Though anything but easy in reality, the process of specifying differentiated types of voting behavior patterns is simple compared to that involved in assigning *relative weight* to a given causal factor as a determinant of voting behavior. Probably few historians mean to contend that a *single* factor is the *sole* determinant in any election, despite the fact that their terminology frequently lends itself to that conclusion. Thus two separate but interrelated types of problems exist: how to assign different weights to more than one causal factor, and how to assign *different* weights to the *same* causal factor according to the distinguishing features of voters, i.e., *group characteristics* and *operative conditions.* For example, to use the example above, how much weight should be assigned to an anticorruption campaign in determining its impact upon "Yankees" of high and low socioeconomic status, in areas experiencing depression, and in those enjoying prosperity?

Hopefully, introduction of the additional problem of assigning relative weights to causal factors has clarified the proposition that the voting groups affected by given causal factors must be designated explicitly before interpretation can begin. Because it raises extremely complicated and difficult questions, it seems best to reserve discussion of the problem of assigning relative weights to causal factors for another methodological study now in progress.

II. Generalized Interpretation Analyzed in Terms of Time, Space, and Rate Dimensions

The election of 1884 put a Democrat in the White House for the first time since the Civil War and various historical explanations have been offered for Grover Cleveland's hairbreadth victory over James Blaine. Not surprisingly, the closeness of the election has been used to reinforce the doctrines of that "fortuitous" school of history which minimizes the possibility of discovering causal patterns in human behavior. Since various "accidental" factors of that campaign usually have been pointed to as determinants of the final result, the conclusion could be drawn that sheer chance was responsible for Blaine's defeat. But Allan Nevins, in his Pulitzer Prize biography of Cleveland, attempted to reformulate the problem in such a manner as to place "accidents" and petty factors in perspective, and thereby dispose of the fortuitous explanation. Discussing the situation in New York, the one "close state" whose electoral votes could have decided the outcome in favor of either candidate, Nevins dismissed the charge that Democratic fraud cost Blaine the election:

> The whole cry of fraud like the charges of mismanagement shortly [thereafter] brought against Chairman Elkins and Jones [Republican campaign managers], was essentially an effort to obscure the real cause of Blaine's failure. The vote cast in Republican districts for St. John [Prohibitionist]; the rain that kept rural Republicans at home; the loss of more than 2,000 Republican votes in Conkling's [Republican rival of Blaine] home, Oneida County; the Burchard alliteration [Rum, Romanism, and Rebellion] —these all counted. But the great central

explanation of the defeat was simply that Blaine was morally suspect.[4]

In effect, what Nevins did was to set down the *basic condition* under which accidental factors operated to cause Blaine's defeat. They "counted" only because Blaine was morally suspect, otherwise their effect would have been unimportant. Whether his interpretation is correct or not, it is not too much to say that Nevins persuasively disposed of the fortuitous explanation the moment he reformulated the problem. Clearly, rain in the rural districts, Republican desertions to minor parties, politically embarrassing oratorical slips just before election day, all would have been insignificant in the 1896 campaign, for example, when more basic issues were sharply drawn between the two parties and the Republican plurality in New York state was over 250,000. In all likelihood, under those circumstances similar campaign "accidents" would have had little influence in determining any but a small number of votes. In any event, the number of votes "accidentally" determined in 1884 hardly would have dented the Republican plurality of 1896.

Stated in other terms, the significant question posed by the 1884 election is not whether chance factors affected the small number of ballots which were enough to give the Democrats the winning electoral votes. Narrowly conceived, this may be a "correct" explanation of the 1884 election. Seen in meaningful perspective it is a gross distortion because chance factors are made out to be of major importance in accounting for voting behavior, whereas, at best, they affected a minute percentage of the total vote either in New York or the nation at large. The significant question is the very reverse of whether or not accidental developments determined a small number of votes. *Why was the outcome so close, why were chance factors of any significance in the election of 1884?*

To begin with, let us assume that Nevins's hypothesis is verifiable and restate it as presented in his two chapters dealing with the 1884 campaign:

---

4. Allan Nevins, *Grover Cleveland* (New York: Dodd, Mead Company, 1947 printing), p. 187.

The great central explanation of Blaine's defeat is that he was morally suspect because of unethical conduct in public office. At that particular time in American history *men all throughout the nation were in revolt against the entire system of government by special favor of which Blaine was simply the emblem. Under those conditions, the national contest became so close that a Democrat was elected president because of accidental factors.* But accidents determined the outcome only in the sense that the nomination of Blaine created a situation in which the election could turn on the relatively insignificant number of votes they directly influenced.[5]

To support the hypothesis' claims that no issues were of major significance except the public integrity of the major party candidates, stress was given to the neat manner in which one of Cleveland's supporters summed up the "real issue" of the campaign:

> We are told (he said) that Mr. Blaine has been delinquent in office but blameless in private life, while Mr. Cleveland has been a model of official integrity, but culpable in his personal relations [fathered an illegitimate child]. We should therefore elect Mr. Cleveland to the public office which he is so well qualified to fill, and remand Mr. Blaine to the private station which he is so admirably fitted to adorn.[6]

In assessing the relative weight assigned to Blaine's integrity as a determinant of voting behavior, no attempt is made here to interpret strictly the description, "real issue." A reasonable interpretation would be that in general, among groups and in areas where the Republican party percentage declined, Blaine's candidacy operated as a significant determinant of that change. It would not be expected to have acted with equal effect everywhere, but, according to our hypothesis, it must be shown to have acted generally, and to a greater extent than any other factor. To demonstrate the impact of Blaine's candidacy, therefore, it must be demonstrated that some measurable pattern of changed Republican strength actually exists. We must also specify the

---

5. *Ibid.*, pp. 145-188, 190.
6. *Ibid.*; pp. 166-167. However, five other "special factors" affecting voting behavior were named "apart from the dominant issue of Blaine's integrity ..." *Ibid.*, pp. 169-175.

group characteristics or the *operative conditions* which can be shown to have been associated with Republican percentage declines resulting from Blaine's candidacy.

Questions of this order need to be posed: Did Blaine's candidacy merely result in a slight percentage decline in a few normally closely balanced states, or was there a nationwide Republican percentage decline of considerable proportions? Which, if any, distinguishable groups of voters were influenced by charges against his public integrity? Under what conditions, if any, did voters in specific areas become receptive to such charges? In other words, the hypothesis must make some explicit statement concerning who (i.e., voters by group or area, or both) cast less than normal Republican votes because of Blaine, *and why they did so and other voters did not.*

Both the generalized nature of the causal factor and the stress given it as the "real issue" in the campaign are sufficient to negate the possbility that it could have been operative only in one state, or a few states. If it were the real issue in the nation, why, for example, should Blaine's integrity have been a determinant of voting behavior only in New York state? To make such a claim, one would have to provide detailed, verifiable evidence that though it was the real issue everywhere, Blaine's questioned integrity was a significant voting determinant only in New York because of group characteristics or operative conditions, or some combination thereof, peculiar to that state. Moreover, it is not necessary to rely solely upon logical argument. Two full chapters are given to the 1884 campaign in the book from which the hypothesis is drawn and they make it abundantly clear that the "morally suspect" explanation is not confined to New York but is applicable to the nation at large. Those chapters maintain that the impact of Blaine's nomination was not only widespread but considerable. It is described as the single, most important factor causing marked Republican losses throughout the country. The extensive quotations strung together below are from different pages but are in context and provide an accurate summary:

> For several reasons the campaign of 1884 will long be counted among the most memorable in American history. It is the only campaign in which the head of a great party has gone down to defeat because of charges impugning his integrity . . . [Blaine's]

nomination [on June 6] was the signal for a revolt which took the most experienced observers by surprise, for in volume and intensity it surpassed the hopes of the Democrats and the fears of the Republicans . . . . [Before Cleveland's nomination on July 11] The campaign had already taken on the quality of a great moral crusade. The uprising of the independent voters to vindicate the principle that the presidency must forever be barred to any man of doubtful integrity had gained tremendous momentum, arousing a fervor such as tens of thousands had not felt since the Civil War. . . . The hour was ripe for precisely such a movement. The health of a nation requires, from time to time, a far-reaching moral movement to awaken men from old lethargies and fix their eyes upon some new city in the heavens. Ever since Appomattox the government had in great part been subject to the selfish materialism of the worst wing of the Republican party . . . [details of corruption] men were in revolt against the entire system of government by special favor of which Blaine was simply the emblem. They knew that he would not take bribes in the White House. But they also knew that by virtue of his record, his associates, and his coarseness of fibre, his election would give new encouragement to the crew of lobbyists, spoilsmen, and seekers after privilege. They wanted an honest man who stood in hostility to the whole discreditable and dangerous tradition.

At the Republican Convention the rebels had mustered but a corporal's guard. Before the week was over, it was a brigade; before June ended, an army . . . . It was impossible to conduct such a campaign except upon an emotional plane. Men who were intent upon a change in the very spirit of government could not be bound down to prosaic issues like the tariff and currency. Seldom has so little account been taken of platform or pledges, for as George W. Curtis truly said, "the platforms of the two parties are practically the same." . . . It was evident that the real issue was the public integrity and capacity of the two candidates, and that old questions of private conduct [Cleveland's social indiscretions] were essentially irrelevant.[7]

What has been done here so far is to state in general terms the relative weight assigned to the causal factor, its widespread operation, and its considerable effect in changing voters' party support. It occasioned a revolt which "in volume and intensity . . . surpassed the hopes of the Democrats and the fears of the Republicans"; before June ended the rebels had mustered "an army," etc. But we have not

---

7. *Ibid.*, pp. 145-146, 156-157, 159, 166.

identified *any particular groups* who were affected by Blaine's candidacy, nor *any particular conditions* which could distinguish voters in areas affected by the issue from voters in areas not affected by the issue. ("Independent voters" obviously does not provide such identification.) Though the relevant chapters give no clue in this regard, since the hypothesis is assumed to be verifiable, it becomes necessary to devise a procedure yielding some specific statement concerning voting behavior subject to systematic demonstration.

Precisely because statements of the following kind seem to be obvious and are therefore frequently overlooked, one of the things we must demonstrate is that considerable *change* actually took place in voting behavior adverse to the Republicans. Men could not have been ripe for a political revolt precipitated by Blaine's nomination if, for example, the 1884 election returns showed little variation in the normal relative strength of the Republican and Democratic parties throughout the nation in general, and each state in particular. Thus, a logical way to begin to evaluate the hypothesis is to tackle the task of specifying *whom* the issue affected, and why, by employing systematic methods to learn what actually happened in the election of 1884, i.e., what spatial voting patterns can be distinguished in 1884, *in contrast to previous elections.*

The Importance of Constructing Time Series.   The two chapters discussing the 1884 campaign made little comparison between it and previous elections but did present statistics indicating that Cleveland won a very narrow victory over Blaine:

> His [Cleveland's] margin in New York was of less than 1200 votes, but it was decisive. He had carried every Southern state, together with Indiana, New Jersey, and Connecticut, and though his popular majority over Blaine was less than 25,000 in a total vote of more than ten million, he had 219 electoral votes to Blaine's 182.[8]

Because the 1884 election was extremely close, *for a marked change to have taken place, the Republican vote in previous elections must have provided that party with a comfortable margin of victory.* If we could

---

8. *Ibid.,* p. 187.

identify in geographic terms, i.e., states, counties, townships, etc., the areas where its vote declined perceptibly, we would be in a better position to identify the groups among whom vote-switching took place, and then attempt to demonstrate that Blaine's candidacy explained the switching. *But, conversely, if in fact no general pattern existed of marked Republican decline, the hypothesis would rest on an erroneous factual assumption.* In other words, attention is directed here to the necessity of demonstrating the accuracy and inclusiveness of the factual elements in the hypothesis before attempting to demonstrate the validity of its interpretative elements. And that it is possible for erroneous assumptions to be accorded status as accepted facts relative to the 1884 campaign is readily indicated.

Has the common assumption really been established that even in New York accidental features of the campaign "all counted" against Blaine? Though one can cite numerous *assertions* to this effect, to my knowledge no one has demonstrated that the much discussed "accidents" actually swung any votes from him. In fact, given the prevalence of anti-Catholic sentiments, it becomes a difficult problem even to think of how one would go about attempting to show that the Burchard incident *hurt or helped* Blaine. But perhaps the possible usefulness of systematic research methods for political history can be illustrated by examining another assertion concerning the impact of accidental factors upon voting behavior in 1884.

In the book from which the hypothesis is drawn, stress was given the idea that the 1884 Prohibition party vote was a consequence of actions taken at the Republican nominating convention; there "the Republicans painfully humiliated the temperance forces." This humiliation was said to have been a definite factor in the events which led to the decision to run a erstwhile Republican, John P. St. John, on the Prohibition ticket; "The Republicans were to rue their indifference to him."[9] Because in 1884 the Prohibition vote was about 150,000 for the nation and 25,000 in closely contested New York, it might appear that Republican arrogance did swing enough votes from Blaine to have been of some significance, given the central hypothesis that Blaine was "morally suspect."

---

9. *Ibid.*, pp. 174-175.

But when one constructs *a time series for voting behavior*, the candidacy of St. John and the vote given him are both seen in a considerably different perspective. The temperance forces had been running presidential candidates since 1872 and continued to do so after 1884. *Even more important, though the 1884 Prohibition vote in New York was much larger than in the previous presidential election, it was slightly smaller than the party had polled in 1882 for Governor. That is, the Prohibition candidate for Governor received 25,783 votes in 1882. Two years later the party's presidential candidate received only 25,006 votes, although the total was 200,000 more than in 1882.* Further, in 1882, the Democratic gubernatorial candidate, Grover Cleveland, was given a majority of unprecedented proportions. In 1884, Grover Cleveland, the Democratic presidential candidate, carried New York by a scant 1,149 votes out of 1,167,189 cast.

That the Prohibition vote in the state had been growing after 1880 is shown in the table below.[10] But in broad terms, the table also indicates that the Prohibition vote was relatively stable between 1882 and 1888, inclusive, whether it was cast in a state or national election.

Table I—NEW YORK STATE VOTE FOR PRESIDENT OR HIGHEST STATE OFFICER, 1880-1888

	Republican	Democratic	Prohibition	Prohibition %
1880	555,544	534,511	1,517	0.13
1881	416,915	403,893	4,445	0.53
1882	342,464	535,318	25,783	2.81
1883	446,108	427,525	18,816	2.08
1884	562,005	563,154	25,006	2.16
1885	490,331	501,465	30,867	2.98
1886	461,018	468,815	36,437	3.75
1887	452,811	469,888	41,850	4.00
1888	650,338	635,965	30,231	2.28

10. The table is based upon the voting statistics given in the *Tribune Almanac* (New York) for the years 1881-1889, inclusive; the index in each edition lists the pages on which the New York election returns are found. As in all the election statistics cited below probably there are minor inaccuracies in the data, but cross-checking has failed to turn up any error of significant proportions. Besides the Prohibitionists, other minor parties received votes; the Prohibition percentages are of the total vote.

When the New York Prohibition vote is viewed in historical perspective, i.e., over time, it obviously cannot be taken as an accidental product of the 1884 campaign. In assigning weight to Republican defections to the Prohibitionists, it must be recognized that these defections, if they were *Republican* defections, on balance, occurred before Blaine's candidacy. In New York, and elsewhere, compared with 1882, sharp losses were suffered *not by the Republicans with Blaine but by the Democrats with Cleveland.* For in 1882 the Democrats had achieved a "political revolution" throughout the country which may be said to have marked the first major post-Civil War switch to them from Republicans. And since the Prohibition vote in New York was practically constant in 1882 and 1884, an assessment of its impact upon Blaine's defeat focuses attention instead upon the sharp Democratic retrogression from 1882, and the extent to which the Republicans had recovered.[11] Thus, the conclusion appears warranted that the hypothesis concerning the 1884 election which assumes that the Republican party underwent a general, marked decline, runs counter to the fact that with Blaine as a candidate the Republicans *gained ground* compared to the major election contests immediately preceding. One index of their recovery is the close vote in New York (and elsewhere) compared to the 1882 Democratic sweep; another is the Republican gain in Congress. The party composition of the House of Representatives demonstrates the shift.[12]

Table II—CONGRESSIONAL ELECTION CONTESTS, 1876-1886

	1876	1878	1880	1882	1884	1886
Republican	140	130	147	118	140	152
Democratic	153	149	135	197	183	169
Other	0	14	11	10	2	4

---

11. The discussion of Cleveland's election is based upon material in Lee Benson, *Merchants—Farmers—and Railroads* (Cambridge, Mass.: Harvard University Press, 1955), pp. 174-203.

12. Compiled from data in U.S. Bureau of the Census, *Historical Statistics of the United States, 1789-1945* (Washington, D.C., 1949), p. 293.

Republican Performance in 1884.   Republican gains in 1884 with Blaine as a candidate do not in themselves indicate that he failed to hurt the party. Conceivably, certain events after 1882 could have improved the Republicans' position to such an extent that another candidate might have won. If this were the case, however, the historian would have to identify those events and demonstrate their political impact. For example, the argument might be advanced that a situation had developed analogous to the Republican recovery in 1880, which, the claim could be made, resulted from the end of depression in 1879 and the great burst of prosperity preceding the election. Just a reverse situation obtained, however, in 1884. After four years of high prosperity a recession did set in shortly before the 1882 elections, but it was not until the spring of 1884 that the depression of the mid-eighties really developed. Since a Republican administration was in office, if it had any political effect at all, economic depression worked against, not in favor of Blaine. Under these circumstances, a "great moral crusade" which by June had enlisted "an army" against Blaine should not have resulted in a Republican political resurgence. Other events would have to be subjected to similar analysis if it were argued that they explained Republican recovery.

Even if the significant political developments of the four years between elections are ignored, the 1884 voting record shows little evidence of a nation-wide revolt against Blaine's candidacy. Despite the fact that in 1880 the Republican percentage of the total vote was higher than in any election between 1876 and 1892, inclusive, *Blaine had only 00.09% less of the total vote than James Garfield, the victorious Republican candidate of 1880*, and the Democratic increased share was only 00.28%![13]

---

13. The table below is compiled from data in the *Tribune Almanac for 1885, 1889, 1893*.

Table III—PRESIDENTIAL ELECTIONS, 1876-1892, PERCENT OF POPULAR
VOTE CAST FOR REPUBLICAN AND DEMOCRATIC CANDIDATES

	Republican	Democratic
1876	47.87	50.86
1880	48.31	48.20
1884	48.22	48.48
1888	47.83	48.63
1892	42.96	45.90

Possibly the most remarkable feature of the election of 1884 was that in terms of net shift, compared to its predecessor, it showed *less* arithmetic percentage change than any other in American history.[14] Actually, Blaine received about 400,000 more votes than Garfield. An additional 9,000 votes would have enabled him to match the latter's percentage exactly because the total vote was larger in 1884. It cannot therefore be demonstrated, as our hypothesis requires that it must, that Blaine's candidacy cut into the popular vote attained by the Republican party at preceding elections. His vote actually represented *increased* Republican strength as compared to 1876, and greater strength than in 1888 and 1892. An unchanged popular vote means that if the Republicans suffered losses in certain states due to Blaine's candidacy, these losses *were counterbalanced* by Republican gains. At best, a hypothesis which can only be applicable to Republican losses must be considered partial. But this line of reasoning can be carried further. If Republican gains and losses were of equal magnitude, and if in certain states no change occurred, the hypothesis making Blaine's candidacy the "great central explanation of the [Republican] defeat" must be *capable of explaining all three sets of voting data if, without explicit restricting conditions, its general explanation of any one set is to be considered potentially verifiable.*

14. See the tables in Stuart A. Rice, *Farmers and Workers in American Politics* (New York, 1924), 26, and Louis H. Bean, *How to Predict Elections* (New York, 1948), 181. For elections prior to 1852, I inspected the returns in Edward Stanwood, *A History of Presidential Elections* (Boston, 1892 ed.).

In view of the remarkably small net shift in 1884 party strength as compared to 1880, no more justification exists for regarding Republican gains and constancy as deviant cases from a hypothesis based upon Blaine's *weakness* as a candidate than for regarding Republican losses as deviations from a hypothesis postulating Blaine *as a strong candidate*. Though numerous types of causal factors might have differential effects upon voting behavior among different groups or in different areas, the hypothesis under consideration does not offer one of that nature. Particularly since it makes no attempt to identify groups or areas more susceptible to charges against Blaine's integrity, the hypothesis in fact offers no explanation for the different types of voting behavior revealed in 1884 when the voting data is arranged systematically. For example, if sectional conflict were designated as the "real issue" of the 1884 campaign, and if each party were identified with a particular section, then in comparison with 1880 one would expect to find differential effects upon party strength consistent with the parties' sectional identification.

But if Blaine's nomination precipitated a widespread and considerable revolt against the Republican party in 1884, why should voting performance in 1884 have shown no net change in the parties' relative strength, as well as a markedly irregular pattern throughout the country when analyzed over time on a state level? Yet systematic analysis yields voting patterns of such irregularity as to prevent one from specifying the groups of voters, i.e., "Yankee stock," "voters in rural-agricultural or urban-industrial states," etc., *who* voted against the Republicans because of Blaine, and then attempting to explain *why* they did so. Because the hypothesis postulates that Blaine's nomination led both to widespread and considerable decline in Republican percentage strength, it is regarded here as demonstrably unverifiable. As shown below, it cannot satisfy the systematic voting data obtained when the time, space, and rate dimensions are employed.

Time, Space, and Rate of Change. Though even a crude index such as net change over time is of considerable utility in testing a hypothesis concerning voting behavior, more intensive examination of the voting data suggests a standard procedure for handling the problem in terms of the three dimensions available to historians, i.e., time, space, and rate of change. The popular national vote showed less net change in 1884 than in any election before or since, but it would be inaccurate to conclude that only an insignificant proportion of voters changed allegiances. Gains and losses might have been so closely balanced that a *gross turnover* of significant proportions could have occurred yet not be reflected in the *net turnover*. To study the extent to which voters switched allegiances, it is necessary to combine the time and space dimensions, i.e., break down the net turnover in the total *national vote* to the net turnover in the *individual state's vote*. If more precise data were desired concerning the gross turnover, the state totals would have to be broken down further and the units of analysis arranged in descending order, counties, towns, wards, election districts, or variations thereof. But for our purposes changes in the state totals are all that is necessary.

As indicated above, comparison of the Republican vote in 1880 and 1884 permits classification of state voting behavior in three distinct categories: states where the Republican party increased its percentage of the popular vote; states where its percentage decreased; states where its percentage remained constant. Constant is defined here as ±.99, an increase is +1.00 and over, a decrease is at least −1.00. Like all definitions of categories, the criteria are arbitrary. But only under unusual circumstances would they significantly distort the patterns of voting behavior because they operate identically in both directions, and there is room for movement in both directions. A larger number of categories would cut down the possibility and extent of distortions due to cluster around the criterion points, ±1.00, but would be less convenient to handle. Actually, the 1884 results are such that the amount of distortion due to specific criterion points is insignificant and can be ignored. (Slightly different results would be yielded if the criteria were ±.50 or ±2.00, but the basic picture would not be altered.) The table below is arranged in descending order of Republican

improvement in 1884 compared to 1880; the second set of columns
gives the improvement in 1888 compared to 1884.[15]

Table IV—REPUBLICAN IMPROVEMENT, 1880-1884, AND 1884-1888;
ARITHMETIC PERCENTAGE CHANGE IN POPULAR VOTE BY
STATES

	1	2	3	4
State	Rank	% Change 1880-1884	Rank	% Change 1884-1888
Virginia	1	+9.4	15	+0.6
Nevada	2	+8.7	8	+1.5
Missouri	3	+8.3	22	−0.7
West Virginia	4	+6.7	6	+1.7
Mississippi	5	+6.5	37	−10.2
Louisiana	6	+5.4	38	−16.0
Texas	7	+4.7	30	−3.9
Maine	8	+3.9	5	+2.2
Tennessee	9	+3.5	25	−2.0
Colorado	10.5	+3.0	11	+1.2
Kentucky	10.5	+3.0	4	+2.2
Pennsylvania	12.5	+2.1	19	−0.2
California	12.5	+2.1	26	−2.4
Alabama	14	+1.5	34	−6.0
Florida	15	+1.2	36	−7.0
Oregon	17	+0.4	3	+3.7
Maryland	17	+0.4	9	+1.4
Arkansas	17	+0.4	27	−3.2
Georgia	19.5	−0.7	33	−5.5
Ohio	19.5	−0.7	24	−1.5
New Hampshire	21	−0.8	23	−0.8
Illinois	22	−0.9	21	−0.6
Indiana	23	−1.2	13	+0.9
New Jersey	24.5	−1.7	10	+1.2
North Carolina	24.5	−1.7	14	+0.8
New York	26	−2.1	12	+1.0
Kansas	27	−2.3	28	−3.4
Connecticut	28	−2.5	16	+0.4
Vermont	29	−3.4	2	+4.8
Wisconsin	30	−3.7	20	−0.6
Rhode Island	31.5	−4.2	31	−4.2
Michigan	31.5	−4.2	7	+1.6

15. The data from which the table below is compiled are found in the *Tribune
Almanac* for 1881, 1885, 1889.

Minnesota	33	−4.4	32	−4.7
Delaware	34	−4.5	17	+0.2
Iowa	35	−4.5	18	−0.1
Nebraska	36	−5.6	29	−3.8
Massachusetts	37	−10.1	1	+5.0
South Carolina	38	−10.6	35	−6.2

The table shows that if only two categories are used, i.e., gains or losses, then in 1884 the Republicans gained in 18 states compared to *all parties* and lost in 20 states. Gains ranged from +9.4 (Virginia) to +0.4 (Arkansas); losses from −0.7 (Georgia) to −10.6 (South Carolina). Rather than a uniform trend below 1880, an arithmetic range of 20.0 existed between Republican performance in Virginia and South Carolina. The fact that a relatively smooth curve results when the improvement (positive and negative) in each state is plotted in graph form confirms the impression gained from the table that the 20.0 range does not simply reflect changes in Virginia and South Carolina. But dividing the data into two categories tends to obscure the fact that at least three basic patterns of voting behavior can be observed in the 1884 election. (A more precise analysis would distinguish at least five categories; the ±1.00 criterion, and a ±5.00 criterion to subdivide further, gains and losses.)

Any hypothesis concerning the 1884 election must be consonant with the fact that 15 states recorded gains for the Republicans, 7 were constant, and in 16 states the GOP lost support either to Democrats, minor parties, or both. More than that, the hypothesis has to be consonant with the *group characteristics* and *operative conditions* of the individual states within each category, the magnitude of the shift in each case, and the *rate* of shift. The magnitude can be calculated from the state totals for 1880 and 1884 but the *rate* of shift requires at least one more datum point, the vote in 1888.

If statistics are available only for one election the historian's analysis is restricted to the space dimension; if two elections are known he can use both the time and space dimensions to indicate party gains and losses in different states; three elections enable him, in addition, to make some limited statement concerning the *rate* of change between

1880 and 1884 in different states. That is, one must have two sets of successive elections in order to have the basis of comparison necessary to establish a rate. An arithmetic increase of 10.0 from 1884 to 1888 might be steep if the increase from 1880 to 1884 were 1.0, it would be shallow if the increase had been 30.0 instead of 1.0. If we introduce the rate dimension, therefore, instead of three categories reflecting a direct comparison between 1880 and 1884, it is possible to classify voting behavior in at least eight distinct categories. Before describing these categories it might be well to discuss their utility for evaluations of a hypothesis such as the one under consideration.

The contention might reasonably be made that systematic demonstration of three different categories of irregular state voting behavior (gains, losses, constancy) definitely requires restatement of the hypothesis but does not invalidate it entirely, nor limit its potential verifiability to a certain number of states. Conceivably, Blaine's candidacy checked a sharply rising *long-term trend* of Republican strength in the 22 states which showed increases or were constant in 1884, and accelerated a trend away from the party in the 16 states where losses were recorded. If we could determine the trend in each state, and the rate of change in 1880-1884 compared to 1884-1888, a more precise and meaningful statement would be available concerning voting behavior. We could then judge Republican performance in 1884 in short-run historical perspective and better identify those states which could have been affected adversely by Blaine's candidacy.

For example, there would be little likelihood that a Republican *down-trend* state showing a steep Republican *increase* in 1884 reacted unfavorably to Blaine; a steep *decrease* in a Republican *up-trend* state might have been due to him. The most significant states, therefore, are those which display counter-trend movements in 1884, and the rate dimension enables us to identify them. Less significant are those states which display uniform trends (up or down) from 1880 to 1888. Nonetheless, even where the trend is uniform, the rate dimension enables us to distinguish further between Republican performance in 1884 and 1888.

Categories of Voting Behavior.   The table above contains all the information necessary to form eight categories of voting behavior. A state such as Virginia, represented by a plus sign in both the second and fourth columns, is one in which the Republican trend was upwards from 1880 to 1888. Kansas has minus signs in both columns and exemplifies a continual Republican down-trend. Mississippi has first a plus sign and then a minus sign indicating that the Republican vote in 1884 was *higher* than in both 1880 and 1888. Not only did the Republican 1884 performance improve over 1880, it was clearly *above* the trend for the three elections. Contrariwise, Massachusetts has first a minus sign and then a plus sign. The Republican vote was *less* than in both 1880 and 1888 and clearly *below* the trend.

So far a method has been described to establish four categories of states to evaluate Republican performance. Category I comprises states such as Virginia in which the Republican trend was continually upward. Category II, states such as Kansas where the Republican trend was continually down. Category III, with Mississippi the prototype, states where Republican performance was better than trend. Category IV, Massachusetts, where Republican performance was worse than trend. Applying this method to the table above the 38 states participating in the three elections fall into these categories:

I (8 states)	II (11 states)	III (10 states)	IV (9 states)
Virginia	Kansas	Mississippi	Massachusetts
Colorado	Georgia	Alabama	Connecticut
Kentucky	Illinois	Arkansas	Delaware
Maine	Iowa	California	Indiana
Maryland	Minnesota	Florida	Michigan
Nevada	New Hampshire	Louisiana	New Jersey
Oregon	Nebraska	Missouri	New York
West Virginia	Ohio	Pennsylvania	North Carolina
	Rhode Island	Tennessee	Vermont
	South Carolina	Texas	
	Wisconsin		

Simply in terms of gain and loss, without the constancy criterion, these categories show that in 1884, Republican strength increased in 18 states (I and III), continued a down-trend in 11 more (II), and in 9 states declined counter to trend (IV). Thus, before the rate dimension is introduced, the trend data indicate *that only the 9 states in Category IV displayed adverse Republican voting patterns which might be attributed primarily to Blaine's candidacy.* For example, it would be illogical to offer this explanation in the case of a category II state such as Kansas where Republican strength declined *at every election after 1864 until 1896.*[16]

Table V—REPUBLICAN PERCENTAGE OF POPULAR VOTE, KANSAS, 1864-1900

Year	Percentage	Arithmetic Change
1860	—	—
1864	81.7	—
1868	68.8	−12.9
1872	67.0	−1.8
1876	63.2	−3.9
1880	60.4	−2.8
1884	58.1	−2.3
1888	54.8	−3.4
1892	46.7	−8.0
1896	47.5	+0.8
1900	52.6	+5.1

Not every state in category II shows a similar pattern of unbroken decline but with rare exceptions the Republican percentage in 1884 was *below* that recorded in all previous elections and *above* that recorded in all subsequent ones until 1896. And when the rate dimension is employed, as can be seen from the Kansas table, even more precise statements can be made. Though the Republican party continued to

16. Table V is based upon data found in appropriate editions of the *Tribune Almanac*, 1865-1901. In 1864 no Republican Party existed as such in Kansas and the vote in that election was for the National Union Party; it is not directly comparable with 1868 but it provides a crude basis for comparison. Although the same situation obtained throughout the nation, in some states, such as New York, the voting data for 1860-1868 indicates that the National Union and Republican parties received virtually the same support.

give ground in 1884 in Kansas, its rate of decline was *less* than in the two elections before and after.

The rate dimension now enables us to subdivide further the four categories and describe eight patterns of voting behavior in 1884. For example, the Republican gain in Virginia (Category I) from 1880 to 1884 was +9.4, much steeper than the +.6 recorded for 1884-1888. Had the Republicans continued to increase their strength at the same rate, the latter figure should also have been +9.4. Had their rate of increase in 1888 bettered that of 1884 it should have been at least +9.41. In Oregon, another Category I state, the Republican rate of increase did pick up in 1888, +.4 was followed by +3.7.

Similarly, it is possible to compare the rates of increase or decrease for the three other categories, and subdivide them accordingly. Diagrams A and B below represent a steep and shallow rate, respectively, in an uptrend state; C and D represent a steep and shallow rate in a favorable counter-trend state. Actually, D represents steeper than short-run trend gains in 1884 rather than what might be termed a true counter-trend movement. That is, the Republican percentage in 1888 is also higher than in 1880, although it is below that of 1884. In contrast, C represents an 1884 reversal of a short-run down-trend for 1888 is lower than 1880. Of these four patterns of voting behavior, only Diagram B could be offered as an example of a state in which the voting statistics show Republican improvement was possibly retarded by Blaine's candidacy. The other three represent more favorable than trend Republican voting in various degrees of *improvement*.

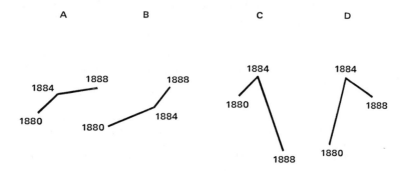

The four diagrams below represent the same patterns in down-trend states. Here G is the true counter-trend type, and F is a state such as Kansas where Blaine's candidacy might have slowed down the rate of Republican *decline.*

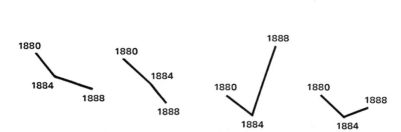

E   F   G   H

Evaluating Republican Performance in 1884. The information which can be obtained from analyzing the 1884 vote would increase with the number of datum points utilized to establish trends and rates. If the diagrams above were extended to include elections from 1860 to 1900 the short-run movements from 1880 to 1888 could be seen in terms of a long-run perspective, and interpretations of the 1884 election might be expected to fit not only the immediate events of the campaign but more fundamental patterns of American politics in the post-Civil War decades. According to the degree of precision desired, we could use more than three datum points, set up more than eight categories for all parties, and thereby obtain a clearer description of American voting patterns. Particularly if the analysis were carried down to the county level, where in the states the number of units occasionally runs in the hundreds and for the country at large, in the thousands, an increased number of categories would facilitate accurate thinking about the results of any one election. We would then know what we are attempting to explain, and, presumably, be in a better position to do so.

A uniform distribution of units in the various categories would indicate one pattern of national voting behavior; a sharply skewed distribution would have another meaning entirely. For our purposes such detailed diagrams are unnecessary and their results can be summed up in this fashion: With few exceptions the Republican party's state percentages declined perceptibly after 1872 in comparison with the average percentage of elections from 1860 to 1872 inclusive, and the process was not reversed until 1896. The exceptions are states in which recovery began one or two elections before 1896. In every state the party more or less declined after 1872.

Seen in long-run perspective and broken down into meaningful categories, Republican performance in 1884 obviously takes on a different aspect than the one usually given it. But even the information gained from analyzing the three elections, 1880-1888, is of considerable aid in evaluating the hypothesis under consideration. *It demonstrates that no factual basis exists for a possible assumption that Blaine's candidacy checked the rate of Republican increase and accelerated the rate of decline throughout the country.* Had this assumption been true the number of states in category G, unfavorable counter-trend, should have been large, and the number in C, favorable counter-trend, should have been small. The reverse pattern is found; there were six states in category C, and only one in G. Moreover, there were three times as many states in category A (steeper increase) than in category B (shallower increase), but categories E and F were equal in number. The 38 states break down as follows:

A	B	C	D
Virginia	Maryland	Mississippi	Missouri
Colorado	Oregon	Alabama	Pennsylvania
Kentucky		Arkansas	Tennessee
Maine		California	Texas
Nevada		Florida	
West Virginia		Louisiana	

E	F	G	H
Illinois	Kansas	Vermont	Connecticut
Iowa	Georgia		Delaware
Nebraska	Minnesota		Indiana
South Carolina	Ohio		Massachusetts
Wisconsin	Rhode Island		Michigan
			New Jersey
			New York
			North Carolina

New Hampshire (−.79 and −.79)

What emerges from a systematic analysis of the statistical data available on state voting behavior, therefore, does not support the hypothesis that Blaine's candidacy was "the great central explanation" of the Republican party's defeat in 1884. (Affirmative results which emerge from this analysis will be discussed in another section.) *Its arithmetic net loss in the national total vote was only 00.09 percent. The party had been declining since 1872. In a considerable number of states its performance was better than the short-time trend and in six states it clearly reversed an unfavorable trend.* At best, only in certain states (G and H) could the party be said to have done worse than might have been expected from the trend of presidential elections. *And this takes no account of the stunning defeats suffered by the Republicans in 1882 and other adverse political developments after 1880 for which Blaine cannot be held responsible,* nor the fact that both major parties were under increasing attack after 1872. Thus, in both New York and New Jersey where the Republican party declined slightly from 1880 and recovered slightly in 1888, Democratic strength also diminished in 1884. Moreover, if one examines in detail the political situation in the other seven states in categories G and H, additional possible explanations for Republican losses suggest themselves.

In Massachusetts, for example, where the party's percentage of the popular vote was 10.1 below its 1880 percentage, the decline might be explained by the vote polled for ex-Governor Ben Butler on a combined Anti-monopoly and Greenback ticket. Examination of the Massachusetts annual voting statistics from 1876 to 1884 indicates that when Butler ran for state office on a Greenback fusion ticket with the Democrats, as he did in 1878, 1879, 1882, and 1883, significant inroads were made into Republican strength. Thus, in 1880 he was not a candidate and the Republican presidential percentage was 58.5. Nor was he a gubernatorial candidate in 1881, and the GOP vote increased to 61.3 percent. But in 1882 Butler won the race for governor on a fusion ticket and Republican strength plummeted to 46.8 percent. He lost his bid for reelection in 1883 to a Republican but only by a small margin, and in 1884 his presidential campaign gave him 8.1 percent of the Massachusetts vote. Though Blaine's percentage was 10.1 lower than that attained by Garfield in 1880 and 9.1 lower than Hayes' in 1876, the Democratic party with Cleveland as its candidate only registered an increase of 0.7 over 1880 and was 1.7 less than the vote given Tilden in 1876. In other words, the marked decrease in Republican strength was not accompanied by anything like a corresponding increase in Democratic strength.[17]

Table VI—MASSACHUSETTS POPULAR VOTE; PARTY PERCENTAGES FOR PRESIDENT OR GOVERNOR, 1876-1884

Year	Office	Republican	Democratic	Greenback
1876	Pres.	58.0	42.0	—
1877	Gov.	58.5	39.7	1.9
1878	Gov.	52.6	4.0*	42.7*
1879	Gov.	50.4	4.1*	44.8*
1880	Pres.	58.5	39.6	1.6
1881	Gov.	61.3	34.6	3.1
1882	Gov.	46.8	52.2**	**
1883	Gov.	51.3	48.1**	**
1884	Pres.	48.4	40.3	8.1

*Democratic party offered candidates but bulk of party fused with Nationals (Greenbackers) to support Ben Butler.
**Fusion of Democrats and Greenbackers to support Butler.

The statistics above are not offered to "prove" that Butler's candidacy explains the Republican decline in Massachusetts. They are cited to indicate that even in a category H state such as Massachusetts little basis exists for the *automatic* assumption that Blaine was solely responsible for the decline. In similar fashion, having once indentified the states in categories G and H, it is possible to show that other explanations than the one given by our hypothesis may account for Republican losses.

Surely the fact that in 1882 Cleveland had scored the greatest victory

17. The data from which the table below is compiled are found in the *Tribune Almanac* from 1877 to 1885. Comparison of the 1884 Massachusetts Republican vote for President and Governor indicates that Blaine's percentage was 4.0 less than the state ticket. No doubt Butler's candidacy was not the only possible reason for the Republican 10.1 decline from 1880 in the presidential vote. As usual, the analysis here is illustrative rather than substantive. To indicate that a really intensive analysis is necessary to arrive at an explanation for the Republican presidential decline in Massachusetts; Blaine only ran 0.08 behind the Republican state ticket in Connecticut, like Massachusetts, a category H state.

in New York Democratic annals is worth consideration in explaining the slight Republican decline in that state during a political era when native sons were expected to attract votes. (Actually, the Democrats also declined slightly in Cleveland's home state, New York; their arithmetic percentage decrease was 0.1. Contrariwise, in Maine, the home state of Blaine, the Republican arithmetic increase was 3.9, the Democratic decrease was 6.0, and minor party increases made up the difference. If the real issue had been the public integrity of the two candidates, among people who presumably knew them best, Blaine had been given a vote of increased confidence, Cleveland had not.)

Even if other possible explanations are ignored, however, the procedures carried out above of reformulating our hypothesis and analyzing the pertinent voting data systematically have demonstrated that it is at best applicable to a small number of states. Logically, therefore, the hypothesis also must be required to state, and shown to be consistent with, the conditions which produced the different voting patterns described in the eight categories, A to H; a requirement which it cannot satisfy. Of more importance, however, is the logical requirement that it also state the conditions which made the personal characteristics of the Republican and Democratic presidential candidates the "real issue" of the campaign!

Just as Nevins acutely observed that accidental factors such as "Rum, Romanism, and Rebellion" were only significant under specific circumstances (assuming now that they were), analysis of the 1884 campaign indicates that the candidates became *the "real issue" only because certain conditions then prevailed in the country*. Again the 1896 election can be used as a reference point. After several years of deep depression and growing social conflict it is almost inconceivable that hypothetical indiscretions by Bryan and dubious transactions by McKinley could have replaced "free silver" and sectional antagonism as the primary issues in 1896. A comprehensive hypothesis concerning the 1884 campaign, or any other, must not only identify the causal factors which explain the systematic data, it must also answer the more fundamental question of why those specific causal factors were operative. If this contention is accepted, then the need becomes obvious to develop at least a crude body of theory concerning American presidential elections—a task, however, to which this study

will only call attention but prudently will not attempt to undertake.
The 1884 Election Reconsidered.   Having been employed above to
evaluate Nevins' hypothesis as unverifiable, the systematic data presented can also be employed to designate another impressionistic
explanation of the 1884 election as *potentially verifiable.* This
explanation also puts the fortuitous interpretation into proper perspective by answering the significant question posed by the campaign.
The question: Is it possible to identify the basic conditions which
explain why the candidates' personal characteristics dominated the
1884 campaign? Historians, it is contended here, would answer that
question with impressive unanimity. There simply were no significant
issues which distinguished the national Republican and Democratic
parties in 1884, nor indeed, at a minimum, between 1877 and the early
1890's. Nevins clearly should subscribe at least to the first part of that
proposition, for he quoted George W. Curtis approvingly, "the
platforms of the two parties [in 1884] are practically the same," and
himself affirmed that "Seldom has so little account been taken of
platform or pledges . . . ."[18] His explanation was that Blaine's candidacy
precipitated such a state of affairs. But after all, with virtually identical
platforms, with both parties animated by the same philosophy and
controlled by essentially the same groups, what else could Democrats
and Republicans stage an election "contest" around other than
Cleveland's private, and Blaine's public, indiscretions?

To borrow Harry Carman's and Harold Syrett's neat phrase, the
period between the end of Reconstruction and the emergence of
Populism can be described as "the politics of dead center." [19] Under
such circumstances the election of Cleveland or Blaine simply was
fraught with insignificance, except, of course, to the politicians
involved, their entourages, and the "special interests" which expected
to benefit if "their" candidate won. It was hardly an accident that
Republican gains and losses were nearly equal, that no new patterns
emerged and that a Republican net decline of 00.09 from 1880 in the
percentage of the popular vote was barely overbalanced by a Democratic increase of 0.28. Reinforcing this point is the fact that the net

---

18. Nevins, *op. cit.,* p. 159.
19. Harry J. Carman and Harold C. Syrett, *A History of the American People*
(New York: Alfred A. Knopf, 1952), II, 248.

turnover from 1884 to 1888 was the second smallest in American history. Republicans won the election although they recorded a −0.39 arithmetic percentage change, and Democrats lost though they improved their showing with a +0.15. (Gross turnover was even more restricted than in 1880-1884.)

Obviously, the voting data cited above do not prove the "politics of dead center" explanation. But they do indicate how systematic methods can be used to evaluate conflicting hypotheses derived from impressionistic research. Moreover, it seems reasonable to assert, by demonstrating the factual error in the "moral crusade" interpretation the systematic voting data have pointed up the methodological dangers of judging history from the documents, records, and publications of contemporary elite groups. (Here the term "elite group" embraces the political, economic, social, and cultural leaders of a given period in a broad sense; it does not refer to "social position" in the conventional usage.)

Impressionistic research is particularly vulnerable to the dangers of unintentional distortion and one-sidedness because, to a striking degree, source materials reflecting elite groups' views and experiences are the ones most frequently preserved and readily accessible to later scholars.[20] Perhaps the "Mugwumps" who led the "moral crusade" genuinely believed that Cleveland's election was imperative if American political institutions were to be preserved. (The genuineness of their moral crusade is debatable.) Perhaps they also were convinced that they embodied and reflected the nation's will and wisdom. (This point is more easily conceded—that is, their conviction as distinct from the fact.) But in the 1884 election, the voting returns appear to demonstrate that they can hardly be said to have represented anyone but themselves.

In New York County, for example, where the "crusade" attained its greatest publicity and commanded its most powerful press support, the Republican party percentage was almost identical in 1880, 1884, and 1888. The Democratic party percentage in 1884 was actually 1.4 *less* than in 1880, and 1.6 *less* than in 1888. (See the table on p. 64 below.)

---

20. cf. Thomas Cochran, SSRC Bulletin #64, 1954, 158-164.

Less intriguing than cryptic entries in carefully preserved private journals, less colorful than professional politicians' speeches or the public rhetoric of articulate leaders, *systematic voting statistics are more reliable indicators of popular attitudes and beliefs.* This is not to argue that impressionistic source materials such as the records and writings of elite groups in a given period are valueless. On the contrary, they are indispensable and can provide the historian with valuable insights into the whole range of contemporary politics. Nonetheless, the records of elite groups which happen to be preserved and accessible do not constitute an adequate basis for the description and interpretation of an American election's outcome. Their representative quality and accurate depiction of reality can best be evaluated when they are employed in conjunction with systematic data. Another key proposition of this study holds that such data give the historian a solid foundation upon which to stand in working through those documents fortunate enough to withstand the hazards of time, and the whims of mice and men.

III. Generalized Interpretation Analyzed in Terms of the Historian's Space Dimension

The space dimension becomes particularly valuable to a historian whenever a substantially new phenomenon occurs, or when the available data preceding or following the phenomenon under study is too fragmentary for adequate comparison. In those situations, though it can be put to limited uses, historians are largely deprived of their basic methodological tool, the recording and analysis of phenomena as they occurred over time. If the requisite data are available, it is possible to analyze phenomena in terms of subsequent developments or of other phenomena which preceded it, no matter how fragmentary the data. But the value of the time dimension is considerably diminished as a result. To paraphrase artillery gunners, when the "target" is not bracketed between "before" and "after," its significance is difficult to gauge. More than ever, it becomes necessary to utilize the space dimension fully in attempting to understand and explain the phenomenon at issue.

The space dimension is not only valuable in dealing with "new" developments; as the case study in Section II was designed to demonstrate, it is far more effective when combined with the other historical dimensions. But whether used alone or in conjunction with time and rate, spatial recording and analysis of data have two essential characteristics of particular interest to political historians; above all to American historians who must deal with a federal system placing a high premium on geography.

Plotted in spatial terms, a party's voting support, for example, can be recognized and described as widespread or restricted, random or regular in pattern, concentrated or spotty. Such determinations are extremely useful in describing *what happened*, and they are also good ways to begin the difficult task of learning *who voted for it to happen*. Once voting data are plotted spatially in units such as wards, townships, counties, states, etc., all other data which might help to answer the question, and capable of representation in the same form, can be similarly plotted. In effect, data pertaining to various kinds of designated voting groups are superimposed on voting performance data arranged in ecological unit order.

Consciously or otherwise, the two characteristics of the space dimension sketched above are almost invariably used by political historians, indeed, by political pundits of any kind or lack of qualification. For example, if the present farm price support issue becomes a topic of conversation, one "instinctively" thinks of particular geographic areas where it might be a significant voting determinant, and of particular voting groups in those areas who might be affected (corn-hog farmers, wheat farmers, dairy farmers, and the like).

Precisely because it is so conveniently and casually used, the space dimension lends itself to marked confusion and error in impressionistic research. A phenomenon which appears to be common and widespread may actually be rigidly restricted or erratically spotty. And voting performance apparently associated with a particular occupational group in a given area may actually cut across class lines and be far more accurately associated with religious affiliation. No claim is made here which even implies that systematic research methods and data eliminate all error and solve all problems connected with the space dimension's use. It is contended, however, that they can substantially increase its effectiveness and reliability when employed in political historiography. The case study in Section III is designed to illustrate these claims in practice, as well as amplify the points made above.

The Election of 1824.   The election of 1824 is of considerable interest to historians because it marked the break-up of the one-party rule developing after Jefferson's victory in 1800, because it was the first in which a country-wide popular vote was cast, and because Andrew Jackson, though unsuccessful in his bid for the presidency, was thereby established in national politics on a firm footing. Placing stress upon the latter point, Arthur Schlesinger, Jr. stated in his Pulitzer Prize work: "His immense popular vote in 1824 came from his military fame and from the widespread conviction of his integrity."[21] The sentence clearly offers an explicit explanation of voting behavior throughout the country in 1824 and will be analyzed in those terms.

At first sight, Schlesinger's explanation might appear to be of the type which cannot be verified but only argued about. The causal factors, i.e., Jackson's military fame and widespread conviction of his integrity, are of such a highly generalized nature as to make it difficult to measure their impact and separate them out from other possible determinants of voting behavior. Stated in terms of the original formulation, the explanation would force historians to rely upon impressionistic data, and scholars of equal competence might reasonably be expected to offer contradictory albeit plausible estimates of its validity. How, for example, could one even begin to attempt to determine whether an *undifferentiated* number of men voted for Jackson because they were impressed with his heroism and integrity or because he was, as an alternative hypothesis has it, a representative of the frontier? Without fairly precise delineation of the *kind* of men who voted *both for and against Jackson,* explanations of why a certain number of men voted for him are not subject to systematic tests of their potential verifiability.

But it is possible to reformulate Schlesinger's original statement and thereby render the hypothesis more susceptible to verification. The

21. Arthur M. Schlesinger, Jr., *The Age of Jackson* (Boston: Houghton Mifflin Company, 1946 printing), 36. The quotation below is from p. 38.

factual elements in the hypothesis are that a widespread conviction existed of Jackson's integrity, that his military fame was at least equally widespread (by implication), and that his popular vote was "immense." Thus, the common denominator in the factual elements of the formulation is their "widespread" incidence. Neither the size of the vote for Jackson nor the influence of his fame and integrity upon voting behavior is described in local or sectional terms but in terms of the nation as a whole. The relationship between fact and interpretation is clear when the implications are made more explicit. Stated in other words, Schlesinger's hypothesis is that a large if unspecified proportion of the "masses" throughout the country were impressed by Jackson's military fame, were convinced of his integrity, and primarily for those reasons, voted for him in the 1824 election. That such formulation does not distort his position is evident, it would seem, from this quotation:

> In the republic's early years, martial reputation had counted little for future political success. But the broadening of the suffrage, the thrill of surging nationalism and the declining glamour of the old ruling class created a favorable atmosphere for new idols, and the War of 1812 promptly produced the military hero. The old aristocracy resented such vulgar and *parvenu* prestige, and a man with Jackson's credentials was almost forced into the opposition. Moreover, while the newly enfranchised and chauvinistic masses regarded the military hero with wild enthusiasm, to the old aristocracy, raised on classical analogies, no figure could seem more dangerous to the republic.

Particularly when put in those terms, the assertion seems warranted that Schlesinger's thesis has to satisfy at least two stipulations: Jackson obtained *a large proportion of the "masses' " vote; his support was not restricted to specific states and sections but was national in scope.* When the thesis is restated, it is more subject to verification and calls for analytical emphasis to be placed upon the historian's space dimension. The presidential contest in 1824 was the first in which the American people directly participated to a measureable extent, or as H. J. Ford has put it, the first to mark "the beginning of a concentration of popular interest on the presidential election."[22] No comparable

---

22. Henry Jones Ford, *The Rise and Growth of American Politics* (New York, 1898), p. 191.

statistics of the popular vote are available before 1824 and in that election the national vote stood:[23] Jackson 153, 544; Adams 108, 740; Clay 47, 136; Crawford, 46, 618.

These statistics make it possible to translate the vague factual description, "immense vote," with its connotation of extremely widespread support, into an explicit statement that Jackson received approximately 43 percent of the popular vote, his nearest rival 31 percent, and his two other rivals, 13 percent each. (No statistics were presented by Schlesinger for either the popular or the electoral vote on a state or national basis.) Once the verbal description is translated even into such gross quantitative terms as the national totals and percentages, once the problem is not to explain why an "immense," or "overwhelming," or "very large" proportion of the American people wanted Jackson to be president, but why 43 percent of the "small" (defined below) number of people who actually cast ballots voted for him, the problem becomes easier to handle.

Who Voted for Jackson?   Because Jackson received less than 50 percent of the vote, the statistics appear to rule out the likelihood that all throughout the country the majority of the "chauvinistic masses" who voted cast ballots for Jackson, unless it can actually be demonstrated that his support was more or less uniformly distributed along tight class lines. This follows since the "masses" must logically be expected to outnumber the other classes or the term "masses" is not relevant to the election of 1824. If Jackson's support was very heavy in some areas and very light in others, in some places both the masses and the other classes voted preponderantly for him, and in other places both groups voted preponderantly against him. This conclusion would have to follow unless two conditions obtained; a different proportion of voters are to be designated as belonging to the "masses" and "other classes" in different areas, and both groups displayed uniform voting behavior throughout the country.

To my knowledge, no evidence has ever been offered that in 1824 significantly different proportions of the masses voted in the different states where popular suffrage obtained; moreover, breaking down the returns by states demonstrates anything but a uniform distribution. It

23. Stanwood, *A History of Presidential Elections*, p. 88.

suggests that if Jackson's widespread military fame and reputed integrity actually do explain his lead in the popular vote, then these generalized factors operated in a remarkably selective manner which demand both explicit statement and further specification. For he carried but eight of the eighteen states in which popular votes were cast, only in six did he get 50 percent or better, and as the table below shows, Jackson's margin over his nearest rival was two to one or better only in Alabama, Tennessee, and Pennsylvania.

The approximately 50,000 *plurality* given him in the last two states more than accounts for his lead over John Q. Adams in the nation-wide vote, a fact which should be central to any interpretation of the 1824 election results and of Jackson's popular lead. That is, roughly 42 percent of Jackson's entire vote came from three states which cast only 23 percent of the national vote. In these three states he got about 80 percent of the vote, whereas he had only 43 percent of the national total, and 32 percent in the other 15 states.[24]

Table VII—POPULAR VOTE, 1824—STATES CARRIED BY JACKSON

State	Jackson	%	Adams	%	Craw-ford	%	Clay	%	Total
Tennessee	20,197	97.5	216	1.0	312	1.5	—		20,725
Pennsylvania	36,100	76.2	5,440	11.5	4,206	8.9	1,609	3.4	47,355
Alabama	9,443	69.4	2,416	17.8	1,680	12.3	67	0.5	13,606
Mississippi	3,234	64.1	1,694	33.6	119	2.4	—		5,047
North Carolina	20,415*	56.7	—		15,621	43.3	—		36.036
New Jersey	10,985	51.6	9,110	42.8	1,196	5.6	—		21,291
Indiana	7,343	46.6	3,095	19.6	—		5,315	33.7	15,753
Illinois	1,901	40.4	1,542	32.7	219	4.7	1,047	22.2	4,709

*"Peoples Ticket," or anti-"Caucus" vote

24. These statements, and the table above, are based on the data found in *ibid.*, 88.

Several pertinent facts concerning the election in general, and the strong Jackson states in particular, further indicate the partial nature at best of an explanation which attributes his support primarily, if not exclusively, to "his military fame and . . . the widespread conviction of his integrity." That approximately 350,000 votes in all were cast, out of a population of nearly 11,000,000, indicates how small a percentage of the "chauvinistic masses" actually voted. (The comparable figures for 1828 were 1,150,000 votes, 12,250,000 people.)[25] And to quote Stanwood's standard work on American presidential elections, the figures given above credit to Jackson:

> . . . a great many votes which, like the 20,000 in North Carolina, were cast for no candidate in particular, but in opposition to the caucus ticket generally [opposition to nomination by a Congressional party caucus of Crawford as the "regular," albeit unofficial, candidate], and of which it was estimated at the time that 5,000 were given by friends of Adams; and other votes which, in some Northern states, were cast against Adams generally, without being for any particular candidate.[26]

A major source of distortion relative to the popular vote is that the statistics do not include six states where the legislatures made the choice. In three of the states Jackson received none of the electoral votes; in New York, the most populous state in the Union, he received one out of 36; he took 3 out of 5 in Louisiana, and all 11 in South Carolina. Hence as Jackson received but 15 of the 71 electoral votes of these states, pending a detailed study, the presumption seems reasonable that their popular vote would have substantially decreased his percentage of the national total. Such reasoning is speculative, yet to indicate how little is really known about the popular sentiment in 1824, Stanwood observed that: "there were real contests in very few of the States, so that the partisans of neither [sic] candidate were fully

---

25. Population and voting statistics for 1824 and 1828 are found in U.S. Bureau of the Census, *Historical Statistics*, 26, 289-290.

26. Stanwood, *op. cit.*, p. 87. A later study claims that the North Carolina vote *was* primarily for Jackson. The point is, however, that the confused nature of the 1824 campaign makes it difficult to comprehend the real significance of the vote given in the name of a particular candidate. The Electoral College vote, cited below, is given in *ibid.*, p. 93.

represented at the polls."[27] Thus, Massachusetts, home state of John
Q. Adams, where Jackson did not get a single vote, cast more than
66,000 ballots for governor in 1823 and only 37,000 in the presidential
election a year later.

Viewed in light of the above considerations, the conclusion seems
warranted that Schlesinger's hypothesis regarding the extent and
reasons for Jackson's vote in 1824 is not consonant with the election
statistics. *The factors denoted by him as voting determinants through-*
out the country could have been operative only in certain localities,
states, and sections; they could not have had the unrestricted
nation-wide impact demanded by his hypothesis.

Conditions Favorable to Jackson.   When attention is turned to the
three states in which Jackson was strongest, the historian's obligation to
specify the conditions under which causal factors actually function
becomes more obvious. In states where Jackson secured few votes, or
only a minor percentage of the total vote, either his fame and integrity
were unknown and unpublicized (subject to investigation if deemed
important), or far more likely, they were ineffective as determinants of
voting behavior. On the other hand, it is possible that those alleged
causal factors were operative in Tennessee, Alabama, and Pennsylvania.
Schlesinger's hypothesis then could be restated to set forth the
conditions under which Jackson's military fame and integrity determined voting behavior and those which yielded opposite results. By
way of illustration, among other conditions which it might be necessary
to take into account: Tennessee was Jackson's home when such a factor
was extremely important, particularly in a western state seeking
national influence (he ran about 40 to 1 in Tennessee). Neighboring
Alabama was a frontier area strongly responsive to the victor of the
Creek War of 1813-1814 which opened it to settlement. Jackson was of
Scotch-Irish descent when marked conflict existed between the New
England "Yankee" element, strongly based on the seaboard, and the

---

27. *Ibid.*, 87. The same page gives the information for the Massachusetts vote
cited below and indicates that the situation in the Bay State was not unusual.

Scotch-Irish and German elements west of the Alleghenies. Probably associated with those ethnic loyalties and conflicts as a determinant political behavior—here research using manuscript sources would be indispensable to verify the assumption—is the fact that as early as 1821 the leading politicians of Pennsylvania had decided to run Jackson as a candidate.[28] Local, sectional, and ethnic influences aided his rivals as well, but this only underscores the point that *the significance of the voting statistics is not apparent if only the national totals are considered in isolation and the basic conditions affecting voting patterns in various areas are left unspecified.*

The main point of the discussion has been that the greater the precision achieved in breaking down voting statistics over space, the greater the possibility of fixing the conditions under which a given explanation can be valid. Hypotheses take on more precision, and a greater possibility of verification, if the factual stipulations which they must logically be expected to satisfy are carefully thought out and then demonstrated rather than assumed.

In frontier Tennessee, the vote for Jackson was "immense"; in neighboring Kentucky, the home of Henry Clay, Jackson was badly beaten (roughly 17,000 to 6,000). Obviously, in Kentucky, military fame and reputed integrity were not key determinants of voting behavior. But it is possible, and, for purposes of illustration, it will be assumed here as fact, that in a number of Kentucky counties, Jackson did run ahead of Clay. A comprehensive explanation of the 1824 election would have to explain such phenomena, or at least it should state explicitly that it does not satisfy certain systematic findings.

If the deviant cases not satisfied by the explanation were of the magnitude indicated above—a number of Jackson counties in a strong Clay state—then it would be logical to expect the historian to deal explicitly with questions of this nature: What conditions, if any, differentiated the Jackson counties from those voting for the native son, Henry Clay? Was Jackson's fame greater, and belief in his integrity more firm, in certain counties than in others? If opposite voting patterns occurred in counties where detailed investigation leads one to

28. The information concerning Pennsylvania politicians is found in a letter from Samuel R. Overton to Andrew Jackson, Aug. 1, 1821, in John S. Bassett, ed., *Correspondence of Andrew Jackson* (Washington, 1928), III, 105-106.

conclude that his fame and integrity were uniform, what other conditions were different? Given Schlesinger's primary causal factors, why should those different conditions have operated to bring about different patterns of voting behavior?

The last question, the "why" question, would be the interpretative element in formulating that part of the hypothesis covering the deviant cases; the previous "what" questions are in the category of factual description. Factual questions yield information analogous to the natural scientist's statement of the conditions under which water boils at a certain temperature, but they fail to explain why the phenomenon occurs under those conditions. To take a hypothetical case: We might factually demonstrate that in all counties where over 50 percent of the entire population was Scotch-Irish, over 50 percent of the popular vote went to Jackson. To explain why this result occurs in such counties is a job of another order and explicit recognition of the distinction between fact and interpretation favors progress towards its solution.

The following possibility is suggested to bring out the potential dangers of generalized explanations which do not attempt to specify the conditions necessary for them to be verifiable. A careful analysis of the areas of Jacksonian strength and weakness, in order to state the conditions under which his military fame and reputed integrity operated as determining factors, might lead to the unanticipated conclusion that they were of relatively minor importance everywhere. It might be observed that Jackson was strong only in areas having certain characteristics: frontier areas not settled by New England migrants and no "native son" candidate; areas dominated by Scotch-Irish and German voters; agrarian areas dependent upon certain staple crops; and so forth. It might also be observed that in a number of areas where detailed investigation demonstrated little or no perceptible differences in awareness of Jackson's heroism or stress upon his integrity, his proportion of the vote *varied widely* depending upon the extent to which the area possessed the characteristics specified above.

If Schlesinger's explanation could be valid only in areas having specific characteristics in common, and does not hold true when these characteristics are absent, it would be more logical to try to explain the vote for Jackson in terms of those specific characteristics rather than general causes which did not in fact operate generally. No implication is intended that any of these developments took place in fact. The point is that the procedure of attempting to specify the conditions under which a given set of causal factors operate might yield systematic findings not consonant with the hypothesis. These findings might then lead to reformulation of the hypothesis, or to construction of a series of new hypotheses more consonant with the data. In turn these hypotheses would be subject to additional testing through the re-analysis of existing data and the collection of additional data necessary to their verification.

Because the amount of data bearing upon voting behavior in 1824 is circumscribed by the nature of that particular election, and because the time dimension cannot be adequately utilized, a more elaborate example follows of how the potential verifiability of a generalized explanation can be evaluated. The time period covered will be somewhat longer than in Section II, and the spatial units much more delimited than in either Sections II or III.

IV. Generalized Interpretation Analyzed in Terms of the Historian's Time Dimension

As suggested above the historian's time dimension is a complex construction; it is simultaneously a methodological tool and a subtle concept. Although this study confines itself to the methodological aspects of the time dimension, they are pointed up by discussing briefly the time dimension's conceptual role.

To convey more vividly the idea that "a historical phenomenon can never be understood apart from its moment in time," Marc Bloch quoted a nicely turned old Arab proverb: "Men resemble their times more than they do their fathers."[29] Though this idea of historical context is easily accepted and freely talked of, it is terribly difficult to apply in practice. Among other things, it calls for a creative, disciplined imagination, as well as an impressive store of substantive knowledge.

---

29. Marc Bloch, *The Historian's Craft* (New York, 1953), p. 35.

The concept associated with the time dimension, therefore, is much less easily handled than the method of recording and analyzing phenomena chronologically. Notwithstanding the consideration that a really thorough historical analysis must employ both the concept and method inherent in the time dimension—their separateness has been exaggerated here to clarify the point—the mere chronological recording of data is extremely useful in beginning an inquiry into voting behavior during a particular campaign. Just as one thinks in terms of the spatial distribution of voting performance, one "instinctively" thinks in terms of time. Members of some group voted as they "normally" did; others were "more Republican than usual"; still others "sharply broke with tradition," etc. To refer back to the example given in Section III: We would use the space dimension to locate the farm price support issue as a voting determinant for Iowa corn-hog farmers because they have been thought to be strongly Republican over time, and because essentially we want to know whether they cast a higher or lower than "normal" Republican vote.

But as in the case of the space dimension, it is dangerous to use the time dimension impressionistically. And perhaps because chronology is more subject to blurring than geography, the dangers are actually much greater. For unless we really know what normalcy [sic] is, we are easily liable to come a historical cropper. Down is up, up is down, climaxes beginnings, beginnings climaxes, unless we have some accurate objective historical standards to measure from and contrast with, and systematically do so.

The Election of 1896. Apart from its intrinsic importance, the election of 1896 is of particular interest to students of methodology in political history. It is particularly interesting because the Populist campaign of the nineties coming to a climax (of sorts) in 1896 has long been taken as proof of the Turner frontier thesis covering all phases of American history. Without going into the complicated material involved, the alleged closing of the frontier in 1890 was said to have been directly responsible for the emergence of Populism as a major current in American politics. And Turner and his followers claimed that the emergence of Populism after 1890 proved the broad thesis that the presence or absence of "free land" was the key factor in American history. Again, without going into details, a vital sub-proposition of the frontier thesis held that the dominant conflict form in the United States was sectional, i.e., conflict between the inhabitants of different geographic areas rather than conflict between groups or classes. Though Turnerians recognize the existence of socio-economic group and class conflicts, they essentially regard them as subordinate. In fact, "Un-American," in the best sense of the phrase, describes the view taken by Turnerians of group and class conflicts in the United States (particularly the latter); "Un-American" because their relative insignificance was viewed as stemming from the uniqueness of American society. Class conflict was looked upon as a foreign importation, untrue to the American genius and spirit.[30]

Because the Populist demands of the 1890's were held to be new departures in that they advocated collective action by government to benefit individual entrepreneurs or citizens *directly*, because the voting patterns show distinct sectional differences, because in 1896 the Populists fused with the Democrats, the election of 1896 was taken by Turner to prove his frontier thesis and its sectional subproposition. Note the logical consistency: after 1890 demands were made for collective action, "proof" that the alleged traditional individualism allegedly caused by the presence of alleged free land no longer had a basis in material conditions; the political conflict over the question of collective action found effective *sectional,* not *group or class, expression.*

During the 1930s, the Turner thesis came under increasing attack and alternative theses were proposed to explain American history. One alternative thesis, of which Arthur Schlesinger, Sr., was probably the chief proponent, attempted to substitute the rise of the city and the urban movement in America for the significance of the frontier and the westward movement. In place of sectional conflict as the dominant form, Schlesinger postulated the "clash between two cultures—one

---

30. See in this connection the series of essays brought together in Frederick J. Turner, *The Significance of Sections in American History* (New York, 1932). The importance assigned to the election of 1896 for the frontier thesis is perhaps made most explicit in "The Problem of the West," in Frederick J. Turner, *The Frontier in American History* (New York, 1950 ed.), pp. 205-221.

static, individualistic, agricultural, the other dynamic, collectivistic, urban."[31] The "urban thesis" attracted wide attention in the 1930s, and, in turn, was subjected to criticism. Probably the most elaborate and penetrating attack upon the thesis was made by William Diamond at the close of the decade. The quotation below suggests his main line of criticism:

> though urban-rural conflict may be as important as sectionalism, the significance of either one as the basis of an American history is open to serious question. It is certainly legitimate to ask whether emphasis on the existence and importance of the antagonism of city and country does not frequently obscure the further facts (true of sections as well) that "city" is a collective term and that in it lives a heterogeneous population made up of many interest groups and classes leading more or less different ways of life. The question of the meaning of urbanization requires further examination, for if the determining forces in human behavior are to be found in economic and social distinctions rather than in geographical or political groupings, then such a judgment as the one suggested [i.e., increasing urban-rural conflict] becomes not only of little value as a clue to the study of American political history but invalid as well. Nevertheless the flow of people into cities has changed the face of the nation, as once the westward movement did. The conflict of urban and rural populations must, therefore, be given its place as a factor in American history—a factor which has been perhaps as important as the frontier and the westward movement.[32]

In place of sectional or urban-rural conflicts, Diamond was suggesting that the *basic* determinants of American history were conflicts between interest groups and classes. As he saw it, whether in the form of sectionalism or urban-ruralism, political conflicts in the United States really stemmed from socioeconomic entities because, dependent upon their socioeconomic composition and functions, fundamental differences existed *between* cities, e.g., industrial, commercial, financial

---

31. Arthur M. Schlesinger, Sr., *The Rise of the City* (New York, 1933), p. 302.

32. William Diamond, "Urban and Rural Voting in 1896," *American Historical Review*, XLVI (January, 1941), 305. For Diamond's critical analysis of the "urban thesis" see his article "On the Dangers of an Urban Interpretation of History," in Eric F. Goldman, ed., *Historiography and Urbanization* (Baltimore: Johns Hopkins Press, 1941), 67-108.

cities, metropolises, seaports, inland centers, etc.[33] But though the cities differed from each other, Diamond accepted the view that they had at least one common feature, they all had significant conflicts with their surrounding rural areas. Whatever the *real basis* for the antagonism, therefore, urban-rural conflicts were characteristic of American life. In his words, as applied to the election of 1896:

> But whatever the basis of urban-rural antagonism, whatever the forces that accentuate or soften the clash of city and countryside, the fact remains that in the election of 1896 there was a high urban-rural tension.[34]

That sentence was stated as a proven proposition at the end of a factual demonstration rather than as a hypothesis to be tested. Quoted out of context here, the hypothesis is not clear. But before attempting to remedy the deficiency it is desirable to discuss briefly the challenging and important task Diamond set himself. Though his own approach differed from the urban thesis, it differed even more sharply from the frontier-section thesis. Since he was working at a time when the latter was dominant, and since the urban thesis was consonant with his own in form, if not content, his study concentrated upon establishing that:

> The urban-rural conflict has been of some importance in American history. Little, however, has been done to measure that importance. It is the purpose of this article to take a step in that direction by making a study of the conflict at one fixed point in American history, the first Bryan-McKinley campaign: to establish the existence of that conflict in the nation as a whole and to see whether or not it followed *a recognizable pattern* [italics added].[35]

The Real Significance of Urban-Rural Conflicts.   Diamond conceived his first task to be the demonstration of significant urban-rural conflicts throughout the nation. But stated in such terms, the demonstration would support the urban thesis against which his study was directed perhaps as much as against the frontier-section thesis. However, if instead of a general pattern of urban-rural conflict, there

---

33. Diamond, *op. cit.,* pp. 303-304.
34. *Ibid.,* p. 304.
35. *Ibid.,* p. 281.

was "a recognizable pattern" then, Diamond contended in effect, the urban thesis really would be specious. That is, if voting behavior in 1896 (and elections generally) could be shown to take different patterns according to the different socioeconomic structures of given urban-rural areas (Eastern industrial-dairy agricultural, Western commercial-staple agricultural, seaport-perishable agricultural, etc.), Diamond believed his broad thesis of group and class conflicts as the determinants of American history would be supported. Urban-rural tensions affected voting behavior all throughout the country, he maintained, but some cities voted more heavily for McKinley than their hinterland while other cities voted more for Bryan. According to him, these differences were not random but could be shown to follow "a recognizable pattern," i.e., they were associated with a definite socioeconomic pattern.

Diamond's article contains so many suggestive ideas that it is difficult to summarize his views without distorting them, but the quotations below provide us with a specific hypothesis subject to systematic analysis:

> It has become a commonplace that Bryan directed his entire campaign in 1896 to both farmer and laborer, to the inarticulate but potentially powerful workers and the vast lower middle classes that make up the bulk of the population of cities as well as to the farmers of the West and South. Yet because "a solid East and Middle West," the most highly urbanized sections of the nation, overwhelmed and defeated Bryan, it has gone almost unnoticed that he occasionally scored heavily in Eastern cities, the foci of the "toiling masses" to whom he addressed himself. John Giffin Thompson has pointed out—though without statistical evidence—that the "fact that Bryan carried a number of the agricultural states of the West, in 1896, while the East voted against him has obscured the further fact that he received strong support in many of the eastern urban centers while heavy majorities against him were in many cases rolled up in the rural sections of the East." This, if accurate, would be a highly significant comment on the factors which determined the election of 1896, and it would at the same time bear witness to the political cleavage between urban and rural populations.[36]

36. *Ibid.*, pp. 281-282.

The hypothesis still has not been made clear but another quotation facilitates doing so. (It is clear in context, the difficulty lies in making it clear in abbreviated form.)

> The cities of the East, with the highest *urban-rural tension* [italics added], were the oldest cities in the nation. In the northeast many of the cities were the products of the factory, sometimes the centers of finance. There the large laboring and immigrant populations were set off against a rural background of conservative landowners. There the cities were more radical than the countryside. Most of the cities between the Alleghenies and the Rockies were the offspring of the railroad; they were trading posts and transportation centers. In them frequently were centered the influences against which the farmer of the West rose in protest. They were often the centers on which they [sic] depended for the marketing of their products. Those cities, it has been shown, were more conservative than their surrounding rural populations.[37]

The 1896 Campaign as Catalyst.   Put in other words, Diamond's hypothesis really was that the Bryan campaign of 1896 *increased the intensity of urban-rural political conflicts throughout the entire country.* In given urban-rural political entities (cities within a state) possessing different socioeconomic structures, the intensified conflicts expressed themselves in different political forms. Northeastern cities were "more radical" than usual; the surrounding rural areas were "more conservative" than usual. The reverse was true in the West; there the rural areas were "more radical," the cities "more conservative." Whether in particular areas the city or its hinterland was "more radical," the same pattern held throughout the country; the Bryan campaign acted as a catalyst to intensify urban-rural political conflicts having their roots in persistent socioeconomic antagonisms.

Before discussing the meaning of "radical" or "conservative," it is necessary to indicate what Diamond meant by "urban-rural tension." He constructed an ingenious index to measure the differences in voting

---

37. *Ibid.,* p. 304. Certain voting groups were designated by Diamond in general terms, but the conflicts between them and the reason for their intensification by the Bryan campaign were only implied in a highly generalized fashion.

behavior between a city and its hinterland. The relationship was expressed in a "percentage ratio":

> The percentage ratio of a city is the ratio of Bryan's percentage of the votes in that city to the percentage of votes he received in the nonurban sections of the state. The percentage ratio of a state is the ratio of Bryan's total urban percentage to his rural percentage. The result in either case is a number which may be either greater or less than one. If greater, it means that the percentage of urban votes given to Bryan was greater than his percentage of the rural vote of the state. If less, then Bryan did better among the rural population.... Ratios from .9 to 1.1, while they show a clear-cut difference in urban and rural votes, will be called the range of low urban-rural tension. Ratios below .9 and above 1.1 will be regarded as representing a high degree of tension between city and country.[38]

Though his definition of urban-rural tension is exceedingly useful, his definition of "radical" is much less so. That the problem is more than semantic is evident to scholars familiar with the difficulties "radical" and "conservative" have caused for political historians. What "radical" means at a given time in American history has never been agreed upon, and Diamond's arbitrary definition, unfortunately, led him into serious trouble. Since Bryan was the nominee of more than one party—though the other parties were really insignificant in 1896—the statistical comparison was made between the returns for Bryan and McKinley, not for the Democratic and Republican parties:

> The Bryan vote, from no matter what source, was basically a radical vote. Given that definition of radicalism, the urban-rural percentage ratio of Bryan votes represents the degree to which cities were more or less radical than rural sections of the states in which those particular cities were located.[39]

Such a definition of radicalism is open to at least two kinds of objection, "substantive" and "methodological." Without attempting to do so here, a good case can be made out for the proposition that the majority of Bryan votes cannot in any meaningful sense be regarded as radical; indeed, in my opinion, it is better characterized as "reaction-

---

38. *Ibid.*, pp. 282-283.
39. *Ibid.*, p. 283.

ary." That proposition is certainly debatable but the "methodological" objection is not. The campaign of 1896 was not *tabula rasa.* Deeply felt, persistent traditions and party loyalties are basic to American political history and, in the short run at least, changes in voting behavior are confined to relatively narrow limits. *Within reasonable limits, no matter who ran on the Democratic ticket in 1896, or what kind of campaign the party waged, its nominee would have received a substantial percentage of the total vote.* As in the case of the 1884 election, the table below emphasizes the remarkably broad continuities in American voting behavior during the late nineteenth century despite basic socioeconomic changes.[40]

Table VIII—PRESIDENTIAL ELECTIONS, 1868-1900
            PERCENT OF POPULAR VOTE CAST
            FOR REPUBLICAN AND DEMOCRATIC CANDIDATES

	Republican	Democratic
1868	52.7	47.3
1872	55.6	43.9
1876	47.9	50.9
1880	48.3	48.2
1884	48.2	48.5
1888	47.8	48.6
1892	43.0	45.9
1896	50.9	46.8
1900	51.7	45.5

The "net turnover" in Democratic strength from 1892 to 1896 was only an insignificant +0.9, a figure which certainly indicates that a substantial number of people who voted for "conservative" Grover Cleveland in 1892 on the Democratic ticket voted for Bryan in 1896 on the Democratic ticket. The inference is undeniable that any political

----

40. The table has been compiled from material in the *Tribune Almanac* for the years included in the time span covered. The 1892-96 comparison is slightly distorted because of the erratic fusion of Democrats and Populists in several states; however, the basic point is not affected. The national percentages, of course, exaggerate the degree of stability because they obscure the impact of counter-balancing changes on the state and local level.

John Doe would also have attracted a considerable number of votes if he had been the Democratic standard bearer. A definition of "radicalism," therefore, which holds that it can be applied to *every vote for Bryan* "from no matter what source" is meaningless at best, and in this instance, positively harmful to Diamond's own intelligently conceived broad study. For had he attempted to find out *which votes* could reasonably be termed "radical," he would have been forced to examine both *the net turnover and the gross turnover in voting behavior.* And had he done so, unlike the 1884 election, he would have found that the *gross turnover* was not only considerable, but that it followed a definite *sectional pattern which invalidated his generalized hypothesis concerning the 1896 election.* Rather than follow the same procedure employed in the 1884 and 1824 analyses, attention here will be focused upon only one state. Such restricted scope enables us to demonstrate that the procedure applied broadly throughout the nation for those years can yield much more precise and definite results when the requisite data is available.

It must be emphasized that the concern here is not with the inappropriateness of "radical" as a description of all Bryan votes in 1896. In reality, the terms "radical" and "conservative" were irrelevant to the hypothesis under examination, and only served to confuse its conception and attempted verification. When reformulated, the hypothesis actually claimed that the dominant determining factors in the 1896 election were certain socioeconomic antagonisms taking the shape of urban-rural political conflicts, and that these antagonisms and political conflicts were *intensified* in 1896. Whether the result was increased or diminished "radicalism" really did not matter. The point at issue was that "the determining forces in human behavior are to be found in economic and social distinctions rather than in geographical or political groupings."

The claim that political conflicts were *intensified* in 1896 was not made explicit in Diamond's article but his hypothesis is meaningless if it does not include that claim. Clearly, if "urban-rural tension" in all Northeastern states, for example, was identical from 1880 to 1900 it would make no sense to maintain that Bryan "occasionally scored heavily in Eastern cities, the foci of the 'toiling masses' to whom he addressed himself." Similarly, the designation of certain cities as "more radical" than their hinterland in 1896 requires not only comparison between given urban and rural entities in 1896, but comparison of their "percentage-ratio" *over time.* Possibly the confused definition of "radicalism," a definition which ignored the time dimension, contributed to the more serious confusion in the hypothesis. For the evidence supporting the claim that voting behavior in 1896 was primarily determined by certain socioeconomic antagonisms not covered by the frontier-section and urban theses consisted of a statistical index interpreted as proof that "in the election of 1896 there was a high urban-rural tension."

But *high* in relation to what? Clearly, higher than the urban-rural tension in the previous election, or more meaningfully, higher than the *normal* urban-rural tension. But what was *normalcy* in this case? To find out, one must compile the data over space, as Diamond painstakingly and systematically compiled it for 1896, *for a number of elections and then demonstrate that the tension was higher than normal.* If the tension for a given urban-rural entity were the same in 1896 as in 1892 and 1900 one would hardly conclude that Bryan "scored heavily" in the city as contrasted to the countryside, or *vice versa.* If both the *urban-rural tension and the urban Democratic party percentage were considerably lower,* then there would be solid support for a hypothesis that either certain socioeconomic antagonisms, and the political conflicts stemming from them, between the city and its countryside were *diminished* in 1896, or that they became *less* weighty determinants of voting behavior.

An Alternative Hypothesis and Its Implications.   Had Diamond been able to carry out his systematic statistical analysis of urban-rural tension *over time* as well as over space, and introduced the rate dimension, in my opinion, he would have rejected the hypothesis holding that Bryan occasionally "scored heavily" in Northeastern cities because of vaguely defined, increased socioeconomic antagonisms between "laboring and immigrant populations" and rural "conservative landowners." On the contrary, the hypothesis might then have been postulated that the traditional antagonisms of these groups or classes were diminished, or were overshadowed, in 1896 *by shared antagonisms directed against other groups or classes.* That is, some other form of "tension" such as "sectionalism" might have assumed more importance as a voting determinant than the persistent socioeconomic antagonisms reflected in "urban-rural tensions," as Diamond defined them. And once this conclusion had been arrived at, one might well have gone on to make a higher level generalization for all American history—political and nonpolitical—which subsumes several essential features of all three theses, i.e., the "frontier-section," "urban," and "interest groups and classes" theses. For, again in my opinion, all three are partially correct, although, as they are usually stated, even their verifiable elements need considerable modification and reformulation.

If the reader anticipates an attempt to demonstrate the validity of that sweeping judgment, what follows will come as anticlimactic. The analysis is confined to demonstrating that in New York State, the systematic statistics of voting behavior indicate that intersectional antagonisms modified the determining impact of intrastate, or intrasection urban-rural antagonisms, and that the Bryan campaign raised issues which tended to narrow rather than widen the area of political conflict between the urban and rural populations. *That is, the issues raised by the Bryan campaign were such as to cut across group or class lines, and, in relative terms, united voters normally antagonistic to each other against voters in another section, also normally mutually antagonistic.*

Thus, whatever the political weight assigned to factors associated with the "frontier-section," "urban," "interest groups and classes" theses for longer periods of American history, *in 1896 more weight* should be given to the "frontier-section" factors and *less weight* to those associated with the other two. Actually, this formulation implies that *some* weight should be given to all three types of factors, and that estimates of the relative amount of weight could only be made after an exceedingly thorough, systematic, and complicated analysis. Moreover, the formulation implies that similar results would be found if the same procedure were followed in states other than New York. It does not imply, however, that the pattern would be the same everywhere.

The Bryan Vote Compared with the "Normal" Democratic Vote. Perhaps the discussion has wandered far enough afield to justify repetition in the interests of greater clarity. In the study under analysis, apart from other methodological objections, the failure to compare the 1896 election with those preceding and following it makes the real significance of the results impossible to comprehend. Though the space dimension was systematically employed to analyze voting behavior, the analysis was fundamentally ahistorical. Compilation of data over time, the basic tool of the historian, was ignored.

It is a major proposition of this monograph that quantitative data are meaningless when isolated from either their spatial or chronological contexts. Presented in ahistorical fashion such data might seem to have one meaning; in historical context they may have entirely opposite meanings. Were urban-rural conflicts a constant factor in American politics, were they in 1896 the start or culmination of a long-time trend, was the 1896 election a deviant?

Similar questions need to be asked in regard to sectional, as well as group and class, conflicts. Comparison with other elections was even more necessary than usual since the hypothesis claimed that intensified socioeconomic antagonisms resulted in Bryan occasionally "scoring heavily" among the "toiling masses" of Northeastern cities. Yet, in chronological isolation, the 1896 election returns cannot be taken to prove any proposition other than the relative strength in that year of the Republican and Democratic parties in given localities. Certainly they provide little factual basis for a hypothesis which assumes that workers in a number of Northeastern cities responded favorably to the Bryan campaign. (Actually the claim was made that this situation obtained in all five New England states having at least one city of 45,000 population, and in New York.) Reformulated, the hypothesis must demonstrate factually that *the Democratic vote among the working classes in those cities was heavier than usual, and that the increase can be definitely attributed to Bryan's campaign.* Only a factual demonstration of this kind would provide a systematic basis for the hypothesis under examination, i.e., that intensified socioeconomic antagonisms between the urban and rural populations in the Northeast were the major determinants of voting behavior in 1896.

In point of fact, when comparison is made with preceding elections, support appears to be lent to a hypothesis—advanced here solely for illustrative purposes—that the Bryan vote in New York and other Northeastern states, far from reflecting intensified "urban-rural tension" in 1896, *was a sharply diminished remnant of the normal Democratic vote.* Just the reverse appears to be true of the assumptions that Bryan occasionally scored heavily in the Eastern cities, and that acute urban-rural tension, intensified by his campaign, was responsible for the Democratic vote in that section. So far as can be determined readily from the *Tribune Almanac*, *every* major urban area in the Northeast gave Bryan a considerably lower vote than it had usually cast for Democratic candidates in previous elections. The decreased Democratic urban strength in 1896, and to a lesser extent in succeeding campaigns, is consonant with our hypothetical thesis; it is in flat contradiction to the hypothesis which claims that intensified socio-economic antagonisms taking the form of "urban-rural tensions" were the major determinants of voting behavior in the Northeast. One is even tempted to go so far as to speculate that the Bryan campaign *in 1896 perceptibly weakened the Democratic party for a number of elections thereafter in the Northeastern cities.*

Though the real concern here is not with the question of what "radical" and "conservative" means, or whether it is correct to characterize the Bryan vote as "radical," a reference to the latter question throws light on the hypothesis' basic weakness. The inappropriateness of denoting all votes in 1896 for Bryan as "radical" without examination of previous voting patterns perhaps is best seen in this paradoxical situation: If all votes for Bryan be taken as "radical," then New York and Kings counties, for example, were more "radical" than most rural counties but they were much more "conservative" in depression-ridden 1896 when Bryan vigorously denounced Wall Street than in relatively prosperous 1892 and 1888! (Brooklyn is Kings County.) Table IX below[41] appears to demonstrate convincingly that the urban-rural conflict in presidential elections needs to be considered in historical perspective.

Possibly it is belaboring the point but preparing such a table on a

41. The table is based upon unpublished data compiled by myself and various assistants in connection with a long term statistical analysis of New York voting patterns. The *Tribune Almanac* was the primary source of the raw data. The two urban counties selected were actually cities and contained an insignificant farm or rural population; all other urban counties show the same trend in 1896. Beginning in 1876, minor parties were on the ballot and hence the percentages above do not add up to 100%.

national scale would have presented enormous difficulties and it is easy
to appreciate why the author of the 1896 study confined his statistical
compilation to a single election. However, it seems obvious that the
value of his study would have been greatly enhanced had he not only
suggested an interesting approach to the Bryan campaign but been able
to carry his work to its necessary conclusion. Of course, it is easy
enough to write that the work should have been carried through to its
"necessary conclusion." The fact that numerous historical studies have
made statistical analyses based solely on a single set of election returns
indicates that the procedure cannot be attributed to personal failings
but has its roots in the nature of the material. At the same time it is
necessary to recognize that there has been a basic conceptual weakness
in American political historiography. Studies in political history which
make anything like a systematic analysis of voting behavior over time
and space are the exception rather than the rule.

Table IX—PRESIDENTIAL VOTE, 1860-1900, IN URBAN COUNTIES, THE
STRONGEST DEMOCRATIC RURAL COUNTIES, AND NEW YORK
STATE, IN PERCENTAGES

Year	NEW YORK COUNTY (Urban) Dem.	Rep.	KINGS COUNTY (Urban) Dem.	Rep.	SCHOHARIE COUNTY (Rural) Dem.	Rep.	SENECA COUNTY (Rural) Dem.	Rep.	NEW YORK STATE Dem.	Rep.
1860	65.2	34.8	56.4	43.6	56.2	43.8	49.7	50.3	46.3	53.7
1864	66.8	33.2	55.3	44.8	62.6	37.4	54.9	45.1	49.5	50.5
1868	69.4	30.6	59.0	41.0	59.1	40.9	53.9	46.1	50.6	49.4
1872	58.7	41.3	53.3	46.7	56.1	43.9	49.7	50.3	46.8	53.2
1876	65.7	34.2	59.5	40.4	59.9	39.9	46.8	47.8	51.4	48.2
1880	59.9	39.8	53.9	45.7	58.7	40.7	52.5	46.9	48.4	50.3
1884	58.5	39.5	54.8	42.4	59.2	38.5	51.6	46.5	48.2	48.2
1888	60.1	39.9	53.7	45.6	56.1	41.4	49.8	48.1	48.0	49.1
1892	61.5	34.7	56.8	40.0	55.3	39.5	47.7	46.4	47.9	44.6
1896	44.0	50.8	39.7	56.3	51.0	46.6	44.6	53.5	38.7	57.6
1900	52.2	43.9	48.3	49.6	51.6	46.2	46.8	51.2	43.8	53.1

Studying the table one can observe that the decline in normal
Democratic strength was *much sharper in the cities of New York and
Brooklyn than in the rural Democratic counties, and considerably more
than in the state as a whole.* Thus, in 1896 compared to 1892, the

Democratic percentage of the total vote was 17.5 less in New York County, 17.1 less in Kings (Brooklyn), only 4.3 and 3.1 less in Schoharie and Seneca respectively, and 9.2 in the entire state. In fact, Schoharie became the banner Democratic county in the state, and even Seneca, for the first time since at least 1860, cast a heavier Democratic vote than either New York or Kings counties. The Bryan campaign for monetary inflation, it might therefore be speculated, in relative terms was more favorably received in rural farming areas suffering from commodity price declines than in urban areas consuming farm commodities. And the inappropriateness of applying the term "radical" to groups waging such a campaign perhaps in underscored by the recognition that "tinkering with the currency" required no structural changes in American institutions or principles. Here again the time dimension is indispensable to historical analysis, for such "tinkering" had long been a part of the American political tradition.

Did Urban or Rural Voters Respond More Favorably to the Bryan Campaign? If urban-rural tension in New York is calculated from the ratio of the urban vote percentage to the rural vote percentage for the Democratic party—the index used by Diamond—then Bryan's campaign had the effect of reducing urban-rural tension in the state to a lower point than in any election from 1860 to 1900! This can be seen most readily by comparing the Democratic percentage in the most urbanized counties, New York and Kings, with the party's percentage in the state from 1860 to 1900. The extent to which the Democratic campaign in 1896 alienated the party's urban followers can also be gauged by comparing its sharp decline in New York and Kings with the relatively small decline in Schoharie and Seneca.

Contrasting urban and rural Democratic response in New York to Bryan's campaign illustrates the inaccuracy of what Diamond accepted as a valid "commonplace," i.e., "that Bryan directed his entire campaign in 1896 to both farmer and laborer, to the inarticulate but potentially powerful workers and the vast lower middle classes that make up the bulk of the population of cities as well as the farmers of the West and South." More precisely, if the group which controlled the Democratic party in 1896 actually believed that a program to raise commodity prices and the cost of living for urban dwellers, couched in terms of sectional conflict, was destined to win votes in that depression year, then the urban election returns in the Northeast must have come as a rude shock. (Whatever Bryan may have said in specifically addressing himself to Eastern audiences, a dominant theme in the free silver "crusade" was the conflict between the allied South and West against the Northeast—and the "goldbugs" made certain that this fact was brought home to Eastern voters.)

The objection might be raised that the statistics cited above showing sharp decreases in Democratic strength in New York and Kings counties do not necessarily indicate that Democratic "workers" or members of the "lower middle classes" deserted the party in 1896. Conceivably, nonworking and non-lower middle class Democratic support in New York County, for example, could have fallen off to such an extent as to account for the party's descreased percentage. *Probably this was the case to some extent, but it also appears clear that this was far from the whole story.* Unfortunately, the Assembly Districts were reapportioned between the 1892 and 1896 elections so direct comparison is difficult. But that Democratic support fell off in working class as well as in nonworking class areas is seen in the much smaller Democratic pluralities *in every Assembly District.* (Not even the most intricate pattern of gerrymandering could have eliminated a substantial number of "lower-class" districts in New York in the 1890's, and the larger number of Assembly Districts probably resulted in more homogeneous units.) Whereas in 1892 the Democrats carried every one of the thirty Assembly Districts, for the most part by extremely wide margins, in 1896 they only took eighteen of the thirty-six Districts by more than 100 votes, the Republicans carried fourteen, and of the remaining four, the Democratic plurality was less than 100 in two, and the Republicans also took two districts by a few votes.[42]

In an attempt to achieve greater precision a convenient device was employed to identify the working class districts without exhaustive research. The assumption was made that they were likely to be those in which the Socialist Labor party was strongest. Party percentages were calculated for the two "most Socialist" districts in 1896 and are shown in the table below.[43]

---

42. Based on data in the *Tribune Almanac* for 1893 and 1897.
43. Calculated from the *Tribune Almanac for 1897,* p. 226.

Table X—PARTY PERCENTAGES, 1896, IN THE MOST SOCIALIST
ASSEMBLY DISTRICTS

	12th A.D.	16th A.D.
Republican	39.6	43.3
Democratic	45.1	43.0
Socialist Labor	14.0	12.6

In 1892 the Socialist Labor party did not achieve anything like these percentages in any district; almost certainly, this indicates that its strength was augmented in 1896 by defections from the Democrats. *But the extent to which the Republicans also must have made inroads into the working class vote is suggested by the fact that even in the two "most Socialist" districts the combined Democratic (including the Populists) and Socialist Labor vote was less than the Democratic vote alone for the entire county in 1892.* The county Democratic vote in 1892 was 61.5 percent; in 1896 and 12th A.D. combined vote was 59.1 percent, the 16th A.D., 55.6 percent. If the 1892 county vote is combined for the Democratic, Populist, and Socialist Labor parties, the contrast is even greater, for it came to 64.6 percent. And in 1892 there were a number of Assembly Districts in which the Democratic vote alone was well above 70 percent, whereas in 1896 no district approached that figure.

That conclusions concerning voting behavior require painstaking analysis is illustrated by the paradox seemingly involved in the following statement. Both these propositions might well have been true in 1896: workers made up a *higher proportion* of New York County Democratic voters in 1896 than in any previous election; a *smaller proportion* of workers voted Democratic in 1896 than in any previous election. Given a much sharper decline in Democratic support among nonworkers than among workers, both propositions would be accurate and consistent with each other. But if considered alone, the first proposition lends itself to the erroneous conclusion that Bryan scored heavily among the New York masses to whom he allegedly addressed himself.

Table XI—COMPARISON OF DEMOCRATIC PERCENTAGES, 1892 AND 1896, IN NEW YORK COUNTY AND IN "MOST SOCIALIST" ASSEMBLY DISTRICTS

Year	Dem.	New York County Combined (D., Pop., S.L.)	12th A.D. Combined	16th A.D. Combined	12th A.D. Dem.	16th A.D. Dem.
1892	61.5	64.6	—	—	—	—
1896	44.0	47.2	59.1	55.6	45.1	43.0

The statistics cited above appear to invalidate the hypothesis which rests on the assumption that the Bryan campaign attracted greater than usual Democratic support in New York lower class districts; instead, they indicate a marked shift to the Republican party. Inspection of election returns in numerous cities, as printed in the *Tribune Almanac for 1897*, reveals that the pattern was uniform in the Northeast. The conclusion seems warranted, therefore, that both the space and time dimensions need to be utilized systematically by historians if accurate *descriptions* of voting behavior are to be achieved, let alone if verifiable *interpretations* are to be advanced for voting behavior.

V. Analyzing a Hypothesis for a Specific Causal Factor

Until this point hypotheses have been examined which did not differentiate between voting groups, or offered only generalized causal factors, or both. Section V deals with a hypothesis which is explicit in its identification of the group it claims to have been affected by a specific set of causal factors. Unlike the 1884 election, for example, the problem is not to find a way to learn which group's voting behavior could have been determined by a generalized causal factor. The problem tackled here is to establish that a specific causal factor, or set of factors, actually operated in accordance with a hypothesis' claims.

Necessarily, all explanations of voting behavior couched in group terms depend upon characteristics common to most, if not all, members of that group. Those characteristics may not be actually shared by every member of the group, nor are they rigidly confined to its members. But the logic underlying any claim that a certain group is responsive to a specific causal factor is that its members are more likely than nonmembers to possess the characteristics making voters responsive to that causal factor. Since few individuals other than hermits belong only to one group, explanations of group voting behavior have another logical premise which is best stated in connection with a concrete example.

Suppose a hypothesis to be offered claiming that Irish-Americans voted "strongly Democratic" because that party favored easier immigration and naturalization laws. In effect, this type of explanation connotes that one set of characteristics, i.e., those associated with Irish descent, is assigned greater weight in determining the voting behavior of individuals possessing them in common than unspecified characteristics of those same individuals which place them in other group classifications (class, education, etc.).

Our hypothesis gives primary emphasis to a specific causal factor but it does not rule out the possibility that other factors and characteristics associated with membership in other groups affected the voting decisions of Irish-Americans. It means only that their common ethnic characteristics or loyalties resulted in a common voting pattern cutting across the lines of class, education, etc. However, although other possible determinants of Irish-American voting behavior are not ruled out, at best our hypothesis assigns them a subordinate role. The main point might be stated in this form: For a hypothesis based upon group characteristics to be considered potentially verifiable, it must increase our predictive ability. Other things being equal, according to our hypothetical explanation, Irish-American workers should vote more Democratic than non-Irish workers; and so on for all economic classes, or other nonethnic group categories. *But it would be entirely consistent with the hypothesis if Irish workers were more Democratic than Irish employers.*

Taking leave of the balmy realm of logical abstraction, an attempt now will be made to test the line of reasoning sketched above on the rockier terrain of reality.

The Election of 1860.   A considerable number of explanations have
been offered for the outcome of the 1860 election and two foremost
American historians, Samuel Eliot Morison and Henry Steele Commager, synthesized the material in this fashion:

> Apart from the Democratic split, northern labor was the
> decisive force in the election. The German-Americans for the
> most part had joined the Democratic party as soon as they
> became naturalized; but they had suffered too much from
> tyranny in the fatherland to support it in any new shape. The
> personality of Lincoln swept them into a new party allegiance,
> and in conjunction with the New England element they carried
> the northwestern states . . . . And in some obscure way northern
> labor had come to look upon slavery as an ally of the northern
> capitalism that exploited him [sic].[44]

Of the various hypotheses which this paragraph holds to be valid,
analysis is given here to the one explaining why German-Americans
switched to the Republicans in 1860. For purposes of illustration the
assumption will be accepted that such a switch took place.

It is important to note that the hypothesis holds that voters of
German descent *all over the country* were more or less influenced by
the combined impact of the same two causal factors; experience with
tyranny in Germany led them to support the party (Republican)
opposed to tyranny (slavery) in the United States, and the personality
of Lincoln swept them from erstwhile political moorings. Precisely
because the causal factors were ascribed to *group characteristics* of
German-Americans, the hypothesis may reasonably be interpreted to
mean that throughout the country members of that group "for the
most part" cast Republican ballots essentially for the same reasons. The
phrase was used to describe their former allegiance and, while not
precise, "for the most part" conveys the idea that considerably more
than 50 percent of the German-Americans voted Republican in 1860.
Their voting behavior was described as a decisive factor in the
Northwestern states not as a result of sectionalism, or of any particular
conditions obtaining there, but because they constituted a sizeable
voting group only in that section. (In other areas their numerical

---

44. Samuel E. Morison and Henry S. Commager, *The Growth of the American
Republic* (New York: Oxford University Press, 1947 printing), I, 637.

strength was so limited as to be of only local significance in the popular or electoral vote.)

Though the hypothesis does not necessarily imply a rigid, uniform voting pattern among German-Americans the country over, it must mean that their votes were cast in somewhat the same proportion in most areas. Of course, variations are to be expected; other factors may have influenced German-Americans of different classes, sections, religious persuasion, etc. The hypothesis, therefore, is consonant with some variation in the group's voting percentage for the Republican party. For example, if good grounds existed for the belief that Northern capitalism was allied to slavery, other things being equal, German-American workers in the North might have cast a heavier Republican percentage than their compatriots who were capitalists.

Perhaps it is useful to translate the verbal formulation into statistical terms in order to develop the logical implications of the hypothesis more clearly, as well as to indicate the kind of systematic voting data which would make it potentially verifiable. As noted above, one cannot be expected to support a hypothesis based upon ethnic characteristics by demonstrating that members of all possible subdivisions within the group (class, section, religion, etc.) voted in the same proportion for a political party. What must be demonstrated, however, is that in *comparison* with voters in similar categories outside the group, German-Americans consistently voted higher. That is, the hypothesis in effect predicts that if the Republican percentage in 1860 among all workers were 60 percent, among all Northern employers 40 percent, among all voters in the Northwestern states 65 percent, among all Catholics 30 percent, etc., the Republican percentage among *German-American* workers, employers, Northwesterners, Catholics, etc., would be *higher* than 60 percent, 40 percent, 65 percent, 30 percent respectively. (To achieve greater clarity the important problems will be ignored of whether the German-American vote has to be consistently higher in *every* significant category, and how much above the average it has to be.)

Obtaining the Systematic Data.   Having indicated the kind of systematic voting data required, the task now is to find real-life data to support our hypothesis. That is, we must demonstrate that in 1860 voters of German descent "for the most part" switched over to the Republicans because of the combined impact of two causal factors: Experience with tyranny in Germany led them to oppose the party of tyranny in the United States, i.e., the Democratic party now dominated by slaveholders; Lincoln's personality appealed to voters of German descent. In reality, the hypothesis makes a considerable number of factual assumptions apart from its causal inferences, but attention here is only focused upon its assumptions concerning actual voting behavior.

For the hypothesis to be potentially verifiable, it is necessary to demonstrate that a common pattern exists for German-American voting behavior in 1860. In other words, within "reasonable" limits of variation, German-Americans grouped in subdivisions of one broad category such as economic class, geographic location, religious persuasion, etc., must be found to have made similar voting decisions. If, when classified in terms of a meaningful criterion which divides them systematically into subdivisions also containing non-Germans, the voting patterns of German-Americans do not vary greatly from subdivision to subdivision, and consistently tend to be more Republican than the average for their subdivision, then the systematic data would support the hypothesis. But the heavy weight given by the hypothesis to its claimed causal factors as determinants of German-American voting behavior does not permit a great deal of variation because of other factors.

Fortunately, long historical interest in the question of whether the "German vote" in the Northwest decisively affected the 1860 election outcome provides us with some systematic, albeit imprecise, group data in terms of geographic location. That is, we cannot classify German-Americans throughout the country according to economic class, social status, religion, etc., but we can roughly ascertain their voting patterns in terms of geographic entities such as wards, townships, counties, states, sections.

For reasons perhaps reiterated too frequently, while no rigidly uniform pattern is necessary, given the nature of the hypothesis, German-American voting percentages in the separate geographic entities must be expected to show some degree of consistency. To take an extreme case, suppose it were found that the patterns were completely random within states and between states. If that were true, German-Americans clearly were not generally affected by the causal factors the hypothesis holds to be the most weighty determinants affecting them *as a group*.

A random pattern means that German-American voters were no more likely to cast Republican ballots than the average voter in the different geographic entities. Yet if we cannot show that our causal factors had sufficient impact upon *enough* members of the group to make them *more likely* to have cast Republican ballots than the average of all voters in the different geographic entities, what warrant would there be for assuming that those causal factors influenced *any* member *because of his ancestry?* That is, some voters who happened to be of German descent may have decided to vote for the party of Lincoln because they believed it opposed tyranny, and because his personality appealed to them. But the same proportion of members of all other ethnic groups also might have voted Republican for the *same reasons*. If this were so, the hypothesis based upon German characteristics would be specious. Under those circumstances the problem would be why certain German-Americans voted Republican, not why members of that group in general voted Republican. Perhaps those individuals could be placed in another group but its criteria would not be characteristics associated with German descent.

Since the hypothesis is couched in terms applicable to German-Americans throughout the country, and our data is classified in geographic units, it is not enough to show that *German*-Americans in several localities or states voted preponderantly Republican. Even a factually correct statement that in the Northwest members of the group preponderantly voted Republican would not in itself lend support to our hypothesis. Such a statement in no way provides the requisite systematic data to demonstrate that German-Americans in the Northwest, let alone throughout the country, were *more likely* to vote Republican than non-German-Americans. If it could be shown historically that *as a group the German-Americans had never displayed any homogeneous voting pattern in the nation but tended to conform to the dominant pattern of the area in which they resided, if it could be shown that this pattern obtained in the 1860 election*, then clearly a different explanation would be called for than the one given in our hypothesis.

The Spatial Incidence of German Voting Patterns Over Time.   Various historians have commented upon German voting behavior in 1860 but probably the most comprehensive study, based largely on quantitative data, offers a hypothesis which is consonant with the systematic voting data pertinent to it. Moreover, it differs markedly from the one based on opposition to tyranny and the personality of Lincoln as distinctive factors affecting the decisions of German-American voters. According to Andreas Dorpalen:

> From the earliest colonial times the German element in this country had shown itself particularly susceptible to environmental pressure. It accepted, and adopted, conditions as it found them.[45]

Though his study hardly provides sufficient evidence to support this arresting thesis adequately, it is at least suggestive. Of more importance for our purposes, he analyzed in some detail the 1860 voting behavior of German-Americans throughout the country in terms of response to sectional environmental pressures. Rather than the German-American vote exhibiting the uniform national pattern demanded by our hypothesis, in percentage terms, it varied according to sectional, state, and even local patterns. Though the dominant patterns differed widely throughout the nation, to the extent that the German-American vote could be identified it *generally* tended to *conform* to the vote pattern of the section, state, and locality. It must be emphasized that the identification of the German vote necessarily was crude because of the study's national scope, but Dorpalen's work suggests that more intensive research and more precise methods might support the following formulation:

In different geographic subdivisions (sections, states, etc.), German-American voting percentages *tended to conform to the average of all voters* within each subdivision. But compared to members of their own ethnic group, German-American voters' behavior in one subdivision *varied widely* from German-American voters' behavior in other subdivisions. Stated in other words, German-American *group variations* in the different subdivisions tended to parallel the *average variations* in the

---

45. Andreas Dorpalen, "The German Element and the Issues of the Civil War," *Mississippi Valley Historical Review,* XXIX (June, 1942), 55.

different subdivisions. Thus, the systematic data Dorpalen marshalled supported his hypothesis of German-American conformity to environmental pressures.

Probably because the German influence in the Northwest had long been cited as *the* cause, or *a* cause, of the Republican victory in 1860, Dorpalen's most intensive analysis was given to that section. He employed a variety of quantitative techniques to determine the degree of Republican strength among Germans in the Northwestern states. The size of the area covered, and the difficulties in identifying the German vote apparently caused him to use fairly crude quantitative tests. But in the absence of more refined analyses yielding contrary results, Dorpalen's statistical findings appear to be convincing, and are reinforced by impressionistic evidence. Perhaps a seeming digression here really is pertinent.

Although this study is designed to suggest the contributions systematic research methods might make to historical studies, it hardly means to imply that impressionistic methods and data are valueless. On the contrary, as historians are painfully aware, there are valuable kinds of evidence which it is difficult, if not impossible, to convert to quantitative form. No doubt it is far harder to devise and *consistently apply* methods or rules which evaluate impressionistic evidence and enable scholars to arrive at some consensus (factual or interpretive) than it is to do the same thing for quantitative data. Yet efforts toward that end are more likely to be rewarded if the historian adds another set of tools to his intellectual equipment. That is, if historians explore the possibilities of simultaneously employing traditional impressionistic methodology and systematic quantitative techniques in attacking the complex problems involved in understanding man's past, they are likely to come closer to their goals and improve both types of methodology to boot.

To resume the discussion of Dorpalen's use of both quantitative and impressionistic evidence to support his hypothesis: Once he reformulated the long-debated problem to take into account the time and space dimensions of German voting patterns, Dorpalen, in effect, neatly delineated the systematic voting data which must be considered by any hypothesis treating any segment of those patterns in 1860. Whether his hypothesis is verifiable or not, the quantitative and impressionistic evidence cited by him demonstrates the factual inaccuracy of the interpretation which assumed that the "German vote" in the Northwest (or other sections or areas) was determined by causal factors which did not similarly influence non-German voters.

For example, Dorpalen showed that in the ten Indiana counties where Germans had mainly settled, Lincoln only carried three. Of more importance is the fact that though the Republicans scored considerable gains over 1856 in all ten counties, *the increases were not disproportionate to their gains* in other Indiana counties where few German-Americans lived! And in the nine Wisconsin counties with the strongest German-American concentration, Lincoln only carried five to Douglas' four. Again, as in Indiana, Republican gains in counties of German concentration were not disproportionate to those in non-German counties.[46] If in areas where the dominant voting pattern was not Republican the German-American vote also was not Republican, if in areas where German-Americans apparently gave strong support to Lincoln other groups also gave him strong support, if in certain states or sections Lincoln ran strongly both in non-German and German areas, then the thesis of German-American conformity to environmental pressures is given considerable credence.

The heart of Dorpalen's analysis was a comparison of statistics for German settlement and the vote in 1860 throughout the Northwest;[47] it affords little justification for a hypothesis requiring disproportionate German-American support for the party opposed to tyranny and offering a candidate with the personality of Lincoln. *That the interpretation of a fact depends on whether the fact is treated in haphazard isolation or seen as part of a body of systematic data* is nicely illustrated in Dorpalen's summary of his findings:

> ... while it is correct to say that Lincoln's victory in the northwest would have been impossible without German support, it is wrong to conclude that his German vote was out of proportion to the size of the German element in the northwestern states. In reality the Germans did no more to assure Lincoln's victory than did their American-born neighbors. Nor did they do so in any other section or in the nation as a whole.[48]

---

46. *Ibid.*, pp. 73-74.
47. *Ibid.*, p. 75.

If more intensive and comprehensive research than has been undertaken to-date confirms Dorpalen's description of the German-American voting pattern in 1860 and previous elections—that is, it closely conformed to dominant sectional or other spatial patterns—an excellent example would exist of the utility of stating a hypothesis in terms of the systematic voting data necessary to satisfy it. The hypothesis offered at the outset of Section V rested upon the assumption that German-American voters possessed characteristics which made them more likely to vote Republican than the average of all voters in the Northwest. *Although the hypothesis might appear to be consonant with the "facts" if attention were confined to the German-American vote in the Northwest, it does not hold true when the German and non-German vote in the Northwest, and throughout the country, is examined.*

Which Hypothesis to Test? Since our concern with this material is essentially illustrative rather than substantive, let us assume that Dorpalen's description of German and non-German voting patterns is accurate, and his thesis of German voting conformity to environmental pressures is verifiable. Now if we are interested in finding out why the Germans in the Northwest preponderantly switched to the Republicans, we must *first* determine what caused a significant proportion of the Northwestern population as a whole to switch over to the Republicans. (It is easily demonstrated that such a switch did take place when the Northwestern population is considered as a whole.) *Precise, comprehensive, and systematic statements of the facts of voting behavior are necessary to evaluate a hypothesis, but they are also necessary to arrive at a logical priority for which hypothesis to test out of a multitude of possibilities.* It seems logical to claim that even if data for German-American and non-German-American voting patterns were available only for the Northwest, any historian blessed with a normal amount of insight would give higher priority to the hypothesis of German-

48. *Ibid.*, pp. 75-76. I am aware of the considerable number of secondary studies concerning the German vote in 1860 but there seems little need to discuss them since the point here is illustrative rather than substantive. of all the approaches taken to the question, Dorpalen seems to me to have adopted the most interesting and logical; it is the kind of approach applicable to studies of ethnic groups in all elections.

American conformity than the hypothesis resting upon German-American characteristics making them peculiarly responsive to the Republican party. Such a priority would be especially logical because recent studies emphasize the conformist tendencies of immigrants in general.

When the problem of German voting behavior in the Northwest is stated in terms of why the section went over to the Republicans, a persuasive answer is given by Paul W. Gates's recent study.[49] Gates's work in the field of land history entitles his views to attention and his hypothesis can be stated in this oversimplified fashion: The position taken by the Buchanan administration on the public land question after the Panic of 1857 was favorable to Southern proslavery interests, certain land-speculator-politicians, and other interested parties identified with the South, and unfavorable to actual squatter-settlers, settler-speculators and "antislavery" land monopolists from the East and Middle West. The administration's policy was so unfavorably received in the Northwest that large numbers of voters in the public land states swung over to the Republican party which promised to enact a genuine homestead measure. Hence, Republican victory in the Northwest resulted from its campaign promises on the land question, and from the actual performance of Buchanan's administration which ran counter to the desires and needs of a majority of the section's residents.

Clearly, if Dorpalen's description of the German-American voting pattern in the nation is accurate, then Gates's hypothesis is consistent with it and is a logical one to explore in examining the Republican victory in the Northwest. Whether the hypothesis is more than potentially verifiable is immaterial here. The crux of the discussion has been to underscore the importance of recognizing the logical implications of a hypothesis based upon group voting behavior. Once such recognition is attained, it is possible to marshal the requisite systematic voting data and determine whether the hypothesis is potentially verifiable. If this procedure is not followed, however, the danger exists that specious causal factors may appear to be so plausible as to gain wide acceptance and thereby divert attention from the real determinants of voting behavior.

---

49. Paul W. Gates, *Fifty Million Acres* (Ithaca, N.Y.: Cornell University Press, 1954), pp. 72-105.

VI. Epilogue

Until this point the study has essentially dealt with the problems of learning what happened, where and when it happened, and who did it. In a sense, although filled with technical difficulties and demanding arduous research, those phases of inquiry are relatively the easiest in terms of satisfactory resolution. They call for a high order of intellectual clarity and articulation but the major difficulties they present might really be viewed as mechanical and administrative, requiring efficient organization and adequate forces rather than highly skilled, intelligent, imaginative historical research.

When attempts are made to answer questions involving the why and how of American political behavior, a considerably more complex field is entered. Granted that we were able to describe what happened accurately, and who voted for it to happen, we still would not know why they voted as they did, and how their beliefs came to be formed. In other words, what are the opinion-making and opinion-manipulating devices and institutions utilized at various times to persuade various groups that they should vote for a particular party or individual, for particular reasons? How effective are these several instrumentalities in achieving such persuasion, and under what conditions? To what extent does tradition condition voter beliefs; to what extent are voter beliefs the specific result of purposive action by specific individuals, groups or institutions; to what extent are these beliefs by-products of ostensibly nonpolitical groups, activities, social processes, and institutional patterns; to what extent are these beliefs consciously or unconsciously acquired or inculcated?

Obviously, questions involving the why and how of political behavior are extremely difficult to answer for so heterogeneous and dynamic a country as the United States. It cannot be overstressed that establishing the objective correlations indicated above does not automatically solve these questions. On the contrary, *they merely allow these questions to be put forth in meaningful form.* That is, questions can then be derived from known facts, not erroneous or metaphysical impressions, and the answers to the questions can be tested to conform with all known facts. Moreover, attempts to answer these questions may reveal that insufficient correlations have been established and lead to efforts to establish additional correlations.

But if one essays beyond simple description, correlations can only point the way for historical research, they cannot take its place. One may be able to establish beyond reasonable doubt, for example, that for given time periods German-Americans tend to conform to the dominant patterns of their community without knowing why they do so, how they came to be persuaded, and under what persuasion they ceased to do so. Correlations thus can be thought of on two levels, descriptive and interpretative; they are adequate for the first but merely suggestive for the second.

This study is not designed to deal with the complicated problems involved in the attainment of genuinely objective historical interpretations of systematic, well-described, known data; that is, interpretations which can be described accurately as consistent with scientific procedures. Yet it seems reasonable to maintain that before we can have such interpretations, or even argue logically whether they are possible under any circumstances, *we must have known data in manageable form.* Lacking sufficient data of this character, statements on the subject, both *pro* and *con*, really are incapable of resolution. No implication of mechanical separation is intended here. Obviously, the processes do not take place independently of each other, nor would it be desirable that they do so. Nonetheless, at the present stage of controversy and development, known data of the type called for above and techniques to handle them would seem to be a prerequisite if historiographic advances are to be made, and if arguments relative to "scientific history" are not to remain at the mercy of the rapid changes of intellectual climate so characteristic of the twentieth century.

2 CAUSATION and the AMERICAN CIVIL WAR

"AND then . . . and then . . ."

In his *Aspects of the Novel*, E. M. Forster observes that "what the story does is to narrate the life in time." Beginning with primitive man, storytellers have held their audiences by making them want to know what happens next. Something happens. "And then?" Something else happens. "And then?" So it goes until they end the story.[1]

Although historians also use the narrative device, "and then," to tell what happened to men over time, they aim to do more than tell a story or present a chronicle of events. For a history and a chronicle differ in essentially the same manner that a plot and a story differ in the novel. To quote Forster:

> Let us define a plot. We have defined a story as a narrative of events arranged in their time-sequence. A plot is also a narrative of events, the emphasis falling on causality. "The king died and then the queen died" is a story. "The king died, and then the queen died of grief" is a plot. The time-sequence is preserved, but the sense of causality overshadows it. . . Consider the death of the queen. If it is in a story we say "and then?" If it is in a plot we ask "why?" That is the fundamental difference between these two aspects of the novel.[2]

---

1. E. M. Forster, *Aspects of the Novel* (New York, 1954), 25-42.
2. *Ibid.*, 86.

Using Forster's criterion, we can define a historian as a plot-teller. Unlike the chronicler, the historian tries to solve the mystery of *why* human events occurred in a particular time-sequence. His ultimate goal is to uncover and illuminate the motives of human beings acting in particular situations, and, thus, help men to understand themselves. A historical account, therefore, necessarily takes this form: "Something happened and then something else happened *because* . . . ." Put another way, the historian's job is to explain human behavior over time.

I. General Laws of Causal Dependence

To do his job successfully, the historian has to assume the existence of general laws of causal dependence. That is, he has to adhere to certain logical principles (or laws) which, I suggest, govern any explanation of human behavior, whether the attempt finds expression in a poem, a novel, or a historical monograph. Suppose we were to concede that Aristotle is right and that poetry is more philosophic and of graver import than history. Nevertheless, the proposition asserted here holds that poets, novelists, and historians must adhere to essentially the same principles to achieve plausibility—although they may not know that they are doing it. Perhaps this point is best made by analyzing Forster's plot: "The king died, and then the queen died of grief."

If we read a novel built around that plot, what logical principles would we invoke before we accepted its causal inference?

The first logical principle that governs causal explanations is associated with the time-sequence of events. The alleged causal event must actually occur and it must precede the effect; in Forster's plot, the king must die before the queen. An elementary principle, of course. So elementary, in fact, that to cite it is to invite the charge of stating the obvious. And yet, despite its elementary character, perhaps because of it, that principle is sometimes ignored in historical explanations.

The second explanatory principle is an extension of the first. For us to accept Forster's plot, the king must not only die before the queen, the queen must know of the king's death. If the queen could not have known, or did not actually know, we would reject the "grief-stricken" explanation, even though it satisfied the time-sequence requirement.

Stated more generally, the second principle asserts that human beings must be aware—consciously or unconsciously—of antecedent events that allegedly produce certain effects upon them. True, if the queen were killed instantaneously by a falling gargoyle while she was walking around the castle walls, we might accept an explanation that "she did not know what hit her." But, obviously, that is not the kind of cause-effect sequence Forster was describing.

It is equally obvious that this principle does not require us to assume that men are aware of all the "historical forces" that affect them, directly and indirectly. Suppose the king had died in the Crusades. We might regard Forster's plot as plausible if he showed that the queen knew the king had died; he would not have to show, for example, that the event could be traced to the Moslems' loss of control of the Western Mediterranean. Suppose, however, that the plot centered on the idea that changes in control of the Mediterranean were ultimately responsible for the queen's death. To achieve even minimal plausibility, Forster would still have to show that the queen knew, or believed, that the king had died while on Crusade. If he failed to do so, his plot would be incredible, even if his historical scholarship were impeccable. I am suggesting here that we cannot treat so-called historical forces as though they were things in themselves, in some metaphysical way, independent of men's awareness. Men may not control their destinies, but "historical forces" can only operate through men who act on the *belief* that certain events have occurred, or will occur, or are more or less likely to occur. (For our present purposes, it is immaterial whether men's beliefs correspond to reality.)

Granted that Forster's explanation of death from grief passes the first two tests, we would then test it further by invoking general laws of human behavior. Despite its scientific ring, the term "general laws of human behavior" should not raise the tempers of humanistically-oriented scholars, nor raise the ghost of Henry Adams, who was convinced that the second law of thermodynamics could function as the first law of history. Aristotle, it will be recalled, ranked poetry above history on the ground that poetry is concerned with universal and pervasive phenomena; in other words, the art of poetry expresses, and bases itself upon, general laws of human behavior. Similarly, when Forster devised a plot based on the queen's dying of grief, it was predicated on the assumption that men believe human beings can die of grief. In short, when authors create plots that ring true, they are satisfying what we regard as general laws of human behavior.

The fourth and final explanatory principle is an extension of the third. To be convincing, a novel built around Forster's plot must not only pass the tests associated with time sequence, actors' awareness of antecedent events, and *general* laws of human behavior, it must satisfy us in respect to the *uniqueness* of the characters, relationships, and circumstances it has depicted. From all that the author has told us, we must feel that the plot, characters, relationships, and circumstances, are not only generally credible, but that they ring true in this particular novel.[3]

Since my discussion of the complex problems involved in the analysis of historical inquiry is designed to be suggestive rather than exhaustive, this essay makes no attempt to identify all relevant explanatory principles, nor to discuss any one in detail. But a concrete illustration may help to support the contention that historical, like literary, work must conform to the principles cited above.

Fortunately for our purposes, the most celebrated hypothesis in American historiography affords direct parallels with the plot Forster sketched. Forster said: "The king died, and then the queen died of grief." Frederick Jackson Turner said: "The frontier ended in 1890, and then American society experienced a series of fundamental shocks and changes". To quote, not paraphrase, what Turner wrote in 1893: "And now, four centuries from the discovery of America, at the end of a hundred years of life under the Constitution, the frontier has gone, and with its going has closed the first period of American history".[4]

3. In effect, Forster invoked the fourth principle while hailing George Meredith as "the finest contriver" ever produced by English fiction. "A Meredithian plot is not a temple to the tragic or even to the comic Muse, but rather resembles a series of kiosks most artfully placed among wooded slopes, which his people reach by their own impetus, and from which they emerge with altered aspect. Incident springs out of character, and having occurred, it alters that character. People and events are closely connected, and he does it by means of these contrivances. They are often delightful, sometimes touching, always unexpected. This shock, followed by the feeling, 'Oh, that's all right', is a sign that all is well with the plot. . ." *Ibid.*, 90-91.

4. Frederick Jackson Turner, *The Frontier in American History* (New York, 1950), p. 38.

And, in 1896—by then prepared to state his hypothesis more explicitly—he wrote that the rise of the Populist movement was due to the death of the frontier and the end of "free land":

> In the remoter West, the restless, rushing wave of settlement has broken with a shock against the arid plains. The free lands are gone, the continent is crossed, and all this push and energy is turning into channels of agitation . . . now the frontier opportunities are gone. Discontent is demanding an extension of governmental activity in its behalf.[5]

I need not belabor the point that the Turner hypothesis has powerfully shaped American historiography. The hypothesis breaks down, however, when we invoke the first, elementary explanatory principle. Just as the king had to die if the queen was subsequently to die of grief, "free lands" had to disappear if the Turner hypothesis was to be credible. Failure to invoke that elementary principle, I suggest, has burdened American historiography with a hypothesis based on a demonstrable error. It is not necessary here to assemble the data which show that "free land" had not disappeared by 1890, 1896, or 1900. An authoritative recent study, whose dedication paid homage to "the traditions of Frederick Jackson Turner", acknowledged that the "economic impact of the passing of the frontier was comparatively slight, largely because the westward movement continued after 1890 as before. Good land still waited newcomers in the West, for despite the pronouncement of the Census Bureau ['that there can hardly be said to be a frontier line' in 1890], only a thin film of population covered that vast territory".[6]

---

5. *Ibid.*, 219-220.
6. Ray A. Billington, *Westward Expansion* (New York, 1950), 749. Conceivably, one might rescue the frontier hypothesis by invoking the principle that truth in history is not only what actually happened, but what people believe to have happened. In this case, however, the rescue operation cannot succeed. In a study that has not yet been published, I have shown that, during the 1890's no significant segment of the American people were even aware that the frontier was supposed to have passed into history. Actually, the Populist Revolt came and went before Turner's erroneous assertions trickled down to the public by way of historians who did not subject them to adequate logical and empirical tests. [Subsequently, I published that study. See pp. 175-189 below.]

The example of the frontier hypothesis has been cited to illustrate the general proposition that the same logical principles govern causal explanations of human behavior, whether they are advanced by historians or by novelists. Having sketched some of these principles, I shall now be concerned with discussing one major difficulty that arises when historians attempt to put them into practice.

Though historians and novelists must adhere to the same logical principles, a crucial difference exists between the kinds of explanations they are likely to offer. Since novelists frequently build their plots around an individual, or around a relatively small number of individuals, they may conceivably present single-factor explanations of behavior. But historians deal with the complex interactions of relatively large numbers of individuals and groups, and, therefore, always face the difficult task of assessing the relative importance of more than one factor. In short, historians can neither resort to monistic explanations of specific events, nor substitute eclecticism for monism.

Because it contradicts our experience, an eclectic, unweighted list of "causes" fails to satisfy our need to know why an event followed some prior event. Ignoring the philosophical question of free will, we cannot deny that man has greater capacity than other forms of matter to choose between alternative goals and between alternative ways of attaining specific goals. Life plainly demonstrates to us, however, that men are subject to many influences and that, on occasion, some determine their choices or actions more than others. Everyday speech reflects our intuitive attempts to rank causes in some order of significance. We freely talk of "the most important cause," "the major factor," "a significant reason," "an unimportant consideration." Thus, even if impelled by no other consideration than personal experience, historians who try to reconstruct and explain the real-life complexity of human affairs must try to give relative weight to causal factors. An excellent example is provided by one of the classics of historiography, Thucydides' *History of the Peloponnesian War.*

II. *The Example of Thucydides*

Like his predecessor, Herodotus, Thucydides wrote about a great war.

But, according to Francis Godolphin, they differed radically in their conception of historiography:

> For Thucydides, above all, causes exist inside the human sphere, and it is the historian's business to find them and relate them to events. He rejects absolutely the external causation of Herodotus. He clearly objects to Herodotus' use of the single principle and the general hypothesis to explain particular events. The naiveté of the myths in Herodotus is likewise unworthy of history. For Thucydides a plurality of causes related to problems of economic wants and political power must replace the Herodotean Nemesis . . . . The irrational does exist for Thucydides . . . and he shows the profound effect it may have on established patterns, but it is chance only in the sense of the contingent or accidental, never the abstract power, Fortune or Providence, later deified by the Romans.[7]

As Thucydides' introduction demonstrates, however, he did not regard a plurality of causes as synonymous with an unweighted list of causes.

> War began when the Athenians and the Peloponnesians broke the Thirty Years Truce which had been made after the capture of Euboea. As to the reasons why they broke the truce, I propose first to give an account of the causes of complaint which they had against each other and of the specific instances where their interests clashed; this is in order that there should be no doubt in anyone's mind about what led to this great war falling upon the Hellenes. But *the real reason for the war* [italics added] is, in my opinion, most likely to be disguised by such an argument. What made war inevitable was the growth of Athenian power and the fear which this caused in Sparta. As for the reasons for breaking the truce and declaring war which were openly expressed by each side, they are as follows.[8]

And then he traced in detail the sequence of events that culminated in the declaration of war by Sparta and her allies against Athens and her allies.

Thucydides took the end of the Persian War as the starting point of his narrative. Structurally, Book One is built around three closely

---

7. Francis R. B. Godolphin, *The Greek Historians* (New York: Modern Library 1942), pp. xxiii-xxiv.

8. I, 25. The translation used here is that by Rex Warner (Penguin Book ed., Great Britain, 1956).

related themes: the state of public opinion over time and in different places; the processes whereby public opinion was formed; and the impact of public opinion upon events.[9] With skill and economy, he traced the increasing tensions between the Athenian and Spartan coalitions; and, in building his narrative to its war climax, he distinguished between the "real" causes of conflict and superficial "pretexts." He differentiated between immediate and underlying causes, and made unequivocal judgments about the "chief reasons," or "chief reason," for specific decisions and actions.

Thucydides' practice of assigning relative weight to causal factors shows up most clearly in passage describing the climactic meeting of the Spartan Assembly. At this meeting, leading Spartans, as well as delegates from Sparta's allies and from Athens, presented arguments for and against a declaration of war. Finally, the question was put to the Assembly by a Spartan leader: "'Spartans, those of you who think that the treaty has been broken and that the Athenians are aggressors, get up and stand on one side. Those who do not think so, stand on the other side', and he pointed out to them where they were to stand. They then rose to their feet and separated into two divisions. The great majority were of the opinion that the treaty had been broken."[I, 61].

But a number of different arguments had been presented to the Assembly in favor of a declaration of war. Appeals had been made to the Spartans to honor their treaty obligations, to redress their allies' wrongs, to rebuke the arrogant Athenians, and to protect their own interests. Which arguments controlled the action of the "great majority," and to what degree? What accounted for the persuasive force of those arguments? Here is Thucydides' summary statement of the considerations determining public opinion in Sparta on the issue of war or peace.

> The Spartans voted that the treaty had been broken and that war should be declared, not so much because they were influenced by the speeches of their allies as because they were afraid of the further growth of Athenian power, seeing, as they did, that already the greater part of Hellas was under the control of Athens. [I, 62]

9. My discussion refers only to the account in Book I, 13-96. Not being a specialist in the field, I do not presume to offer an account of Thucydides' concept of causation as such. His work is drawn on solely for illustrative purposes.

As the quotation suggests, Thucydides' treatment of causation rejects both the oversimplifications of monism and the indecisions of eclecticism. In essential respects, his book is written much as men talk in daily discourse and think in real life. And, like men in real life, he concluded that decisions were made and actions were taken "partly" because of one reason but "chiefly" for another. (The validity of his particular interpretation, of course, is irrelevant to my argument.)

Thucydides has been cited here as a classic representative of historians whose work rests upon three propositions: 1) causation is present in human affairs; 2) it therefore cannot be avoided in accounts which purport to tell what human beings did; 3) like other students of men in society, historians who attempt to explain the occurrence of events must make judgments concerning the relevance and significance of different causal factors.

Though these propositions have been acted upon since Thucydides' time, they involve difficulties which, in my opinion, historians have scarcely begun to attack systematically, much less resolve.[10] It is true that in everyday speech we do not hesitate to make the claims conveyed by expressions such as, "the chief reasons", "partly because", "mostly because." When we use them, we undoubtedly have some more or less definite idea in mind, and, succeed in communicating that idea to others. But it is extremely difficult to employ such terms in connection with specific historical events. When historians attempt to appraise the relative significance of causal factors, at least four questions arise:

What do historians intend to convey when they assert that one factor was the "main" or "principal" cause of an event such as the Peloponnesian War or the American Civil War, and another factor was of "minor" or "limited" significance? What data do they offer to support their assignment of relative weight? What procedures do they use to obtain the data? On what grounds can estimates be made of the degree in which data support a conclusion *when judgments conflict* about the relative importance of different factors?

---

10. "When as students of history we approach the subject of 'causation', we find ourselves in difficulties, for the problem is not one that has received sustained consideration. In accounting for historical events, every historian has been a law to himself." Frederick J. Teggart, "Causation in Historical Events", *Journal of the History of Ideas*, III (1942), 3-11.

These questions bring us to the core of historical inquiry, and the difficulties they involve may explain the sparseness of the theoretical literature which attempts to answer them concretely.[11] Confronted by this problem, and unable to wait for a theory, historians have had to proceed as though they already knew the answers to the questions. Such a practical approach seems both defensible and desirable. Yet it also seems desirable that historians attempt to advance beyond the practical by attacking some general problems of historical causation while dealing with specific events.

III. Causes of the American Civil War

A substantive example may again serve to focus the discussion. In this case, it is provided by the historical literature relevant to the coming of a war, rather than one historian's explanation of a war.

The number of studies touching upon the causes of the American Civil War has already reached awesome proportions. The number of different explanations advanced is not as large but is almost as awesome.[12] Yet a reasonably comprehensive survey of the literature[13] indicated that the structure of these explanations is strikingly similar to that found in Thucydides. Like him, historians of the Civil War build

---

11. See the penetrating essay by Ernest Nagel, "The Logic of Historical Analysis", *The Scientific Monthly*, LXXIV (1952), 162-69, reprinted in several anthologies. As recently as 1957, Professor Nagel expressed the view that, although "philosophic students of historical method have written much on problems of historical causation, in my opinion, the extant literature is on such a high level of generality that the conclusions reached do not effectively illuminate the logic of historical inquiry". Letter from Ernest Nagel to Charles Y. Glock, March 26, 1957, cited with the writer's permission.

12. See the excellent analyses by Howard K. Beale, "What Historians Have Said About the Causes of the Civil War", in Social Science Research Council, *Theory and Practice in Historical Study: A Report of the Committee on Historiography* (New York, 1946), pp. 55-102; and Thomas J. Pressly, *Americans Interpret Their Civil War* (Princeton: Princeton University Press, 1954).

13. This survey was partially reported in Lee Benson and Thomas J. Pressly, *Can Differences in Interpretations of the Causes of the American Civil War be Resolved Objectively?* (Bureau of Applied Social Research, Columbia University, 1956, mimeographed.)

their narratives around three themes: the state of public opinion over time and in different places; the processes whereby public opinion was formed; and the impact of public opinion upon events. Again, like him, they trace the rising tension between rival coalitions and the interaction between public opinion and events. In most accounts, the rivals are grouped into two major coalitions, North and South; but in a few, the West (or Northwest) is designated as a third.

Each historian whose work was examined employed some variant of the "and then" formula. Each selected some more or less specific date when tensions were low as the chronological starting point. Either the account was given in straight chronological order, i.e., beginning with the starting point and marching to the war climax; or a version of the "flashback" was used, i.e., beginning with the war, back to the starting point, and once again arriving at the war climax. The starting points differed widely but the narrative framework was essentially the same.[14]

According to some historians, different and clashing economic systems constituted the major source of conflict between the rival coalitions. Other historians found conflicts between different "cultures" to be the chief cause of tension. Still others stressed antagonisms stemming from divergent political theories and moral codes. In short, historians disagree about which groups were responsible for the rising tension, or about the issues over which groups fought, or about both. But in each account the outcome is the same. Opinions crystallize and significant segments of the population living in the rival areas become increasingly antagonistic until the war climax is reached. With rough accuracy, this is the structure of the works examined which touched upon causation in the Civil War.

A crucial difference exists, however, between Thucydides' explanation of the Peloponnesian War and those offered by historians of the Civil War. Possibly because he was concerned with small homogeneous city-states, some of them governed by direct democracy, Thucydides drew little distinction between elite groups and masses in tracing the events leading to war. Though he indicated that leaders influenced the

---

14. Of course, works focused entirely on the secession crisis did not follow this pattern. Nevertheless, even those works make implicit assumptions about the factors bringing tension to a high point from some prior date when relative calm prevailed.

masses, he ascribed their influence to the force or clarity of their arguments in public debate and to their record of accomplishment, not to their authority of office, disproportionate command of material resources, or conspiratorial skill. Discussing the Athenian answer to the Spartan ultimatum, for example, he noted that Pericles had suggested the answer in this speech to the Assembly. "The Athenians considered that his advice was best and voted as he had asked them to vote." [I, 96]. Thucydides did not argue that, prior to the outbreak of the war, members of the public on either side were lashed into frenzy by trusted leaders or skilled agitators who induced them to act irrationally. The Spartan decision for war was presented as the rational, inevitable reaction of thinking citizens to the developments affecting their collective interests. Neither the formation of public opinion, nor its impact upon decisions or events, was described as controlled by small elite groups seeking private or concealed objectives. In his account, the masses were not only theoretically sovereign, they appear to have effectively exercised their sovereignty.

Unlike Thucydides, historians of the Civil War deal with large political units whose form of government was *representative*, rather than *direct*, democracy. It is understandable, therefore, that with few exceptions, the historians whose works were examined tended to emphasize the disproportionate ability of certain men (or groups) to influence and control governmental decisions and actions. Some accounts made only rough distinctions between leaders and followers; other accounts established more precise categories. Whatever the system of classification, significant distinctions were made between men, both in respect to their decision-making power and in respect to their ability to shape public opinion. Thus in all works examined, public opinion was held to be a significant cause of events. But it was not viewed as the only determinant of governmental legislation or policy, not even by historians most inclined to invest the masses with sovereign power; it was recognized that certain men possessed disproportionate power to shape public opinion along lines most favorable to their convictions, interests, or prejudices.

Compared to Thucydides, Civil War historians clearly face a more complicated task when they try to determine the relative importance of causal factors. They must assess the relative power of "elite groups" and masses in the decision-making process. (Here the term "elite groups" refers to political, economic, and cultural leaders on all social levels.) And they must assess the role played by members of elite groups in the formation of public opinion prior to the acts of secession in the Southern states; they cannot assume that the evolution of public opinion was the rational, inevitable, reaction of informed citizens to developments affecting their collective interests.

But the task of Civil War historians is identical with Thucydides' in respect to one aspect of the causation problem. Just as he had to determine the proportion of Spartans who favored declaring war on Athens, Civil War historians must determine, for example, the proportion of Northerners who favored legislation to halt further geographic expansion of slavery. And just as Thucydides had to determine the extent to which the Spartans' decision for war was influenced either by fear of growing Athenian power or by pressure from their allies, Civil War historians must estimate the extent to which Northerners' opinions on the expansion of slavery were influenced by economic, political, moral, or other objectives. In more general terms, Civil War historians, like Thucydides, must make judgments concerning the state of public opinion on specific issues at a given time and place, and they must assign relative importance to the different "reasons" (motives, considerations) that led men to arrive at certain opinions. In my view, an attack upon this aspect of the public-opinion problem is not only the most effective way to *begin* an attack upon the overall problem of Civil War causation, but it may help us eventually to attack some general problems of historical causation. A summary and expansion of the discussion may justify these conclusions.

IV. Public Opinion as a Cause of the Civil War

The survey of Civil War studies offering causal explanations found that all treated certain factors as more important than others, explicitly or implicitly. Though every historian treated public opinion as a significant determinant of events ultimately resulting in the war, there was considerable difference in the emphasis placed upon it. Moreover, historians presented widely different estimates of public interest in certain issues, and they presented widely different—sometimes directly contradictory—descriptions of the state of public opinion on the *same* issue.

For example, historians made different or contradictory assertions about the extent, intensity, and motivation of popular support for, or opposition to, adoption of such policies as the abolition of slavery, limitation of the territory legally open to it, reopening of the African slave trade. Depending upon the specific assertions made, public opinion on certain issues was held to be a more or less significant determinant of decisions or actions taken by individuals, organized groups, and government agencies. In turn, those events (decisions and actions) were said to have brought about changes in the state of public opinion, which then led to still other events that ultimately resulted in the Civil War. Thus, although all historians viewed the interaction between public opinion and events as occurring in a specific, causally related sequence whose terminal point was the outbreak of war, the specific sequences they described differed widely.

If the analysis is correct, the following conclusion seem justified: Verifying claims concerning popular support for, or opposition to, certain government actions is a crucial, preliminary step in the verification of historical explanations that emphasize the impact of public opinion upon events. No causal relationship *necessarily* exists between the state of public opinion and the occurrence of a particular event, or set of events. If a historian asserts that such a relationship exists, it seems reasonable, therefore, to ask him to justify his description of public opinion before appraising his argument about its impact upon events. In other words, it would be logical to appraise the data and procedures used to *ascertain* public opinion on given issues before appraising the data and procedures used to *assess* its effect. To paraphrase Mrs. Glasse's celebrated advice on how to cook a hare, the recipe suggested here for assessing the role of public opinion as a cause of the Civil War begins, "First, catch your public opinion".

Thus, we come back to the first explanatory principle discussed in connection with Forster's plot and Turner's hypothesis. Brought to bear upon the Civil War, that principle requires historians to demonstrate the state of public opinion on specified issues before they

assert that public opinion produced specified effects ultimately
resulting in war and assign it relative weight as a causal factor.
Unfortunately, at present, historians are poorly equipped to
demonstrate the state of public opinion on any issue; adequate rules do
not exist to help them to ascertain it.

As I see it, a critical weakness in American historiography becomes
apparent when we recognize that the traditional rules of historical
method were not devised by scholars dealing with mass behavior, and
that these have not been amended in any systematic form by later
scholars concerned with such phenomena. As a result, historians have
few guide lines when they set out to assess the role of public opinion in
a mass society. Lacking such guide lines, but forced to cope with the
problem, historians have employed procedures of dubious validity to
arrive at equally dubious conclusions.

For example, spurred on in recent decades by the popularity
intellectual history has enjoyed, American scholars have relied heavily
upon the assumption that writers serve as the antennae of the race.
More specifically, they have assumed that the values, attitudes, and
opinions they find expressed in certain books, or other works of art,
accurately reflect the climate of opinion dominating a given time and
place. This assumption rests on a still more basic one; namely, that the
writer, or intellectual, accurately reflects public opinion because he
powerfully shapes it. Are those assumptions warranted? At present,
how do we know that specified writers serve as sensitive antennae at a
particular time and place? Granted that poetic insights reveal truths
obscure to less prescient men; when poets disagree, which poet (or
poets) are we to select as our guide? How do we know that specified
books had specified effects? How do we know which books changed
which people's minds in what ways, where, how, and why? In my
opinion, at present we do not really know the answers to any one of
those questions, but we have acted on the assumption that we know the
answers to all of them. The result is that explanations of the Civil War
rest upon extremely shaky foundations. One example, perhaps, makes
the point.

No matter what else they disagree upon, Civil War historians agree
that one book, Harriet Beecher Stowe's *Uncle Tom's Cabin*, reflected
and shaped American public opinion and significantly influenced the

course of events. True, Abraham Lincoln was disposed to speak of the Civil War as "Mrs. Stowe's War." I suggest, however, that despite such authority, no credible evidence now exists to substantiate the alleged influence of *Uncle Tom's Cabin*. Actually, scattered, impressionistic evidence indicates that historians have tended to exaggerate greatly the book's role as a reflection of, or influence upon, public opinion. More to the point, and more significantly, I do not know of any *systematic* attempt to study the book's influence. Ringing assertion has substituted for credible demonstration.

Stated in more general terms, my argument holds that no set of systematic propositions have yet been developed to define the relationships between literature and life, and that historians, therefore, cannot now use literature as a valid and reliable indicator of public opinion.

This view does not imply a nihilistic position on the relationships between literature and life. To say that historians have not yet systematically attempted to define those relationships, is not to say that they do not exist or that no possibility exists of establishing them. Further, the example of *Uncle Tom's Cabin* has not been used as a blunt instrument to attack intellectual history. Quite the contrary. I think we need more, but better, intellectual history—and I think that we may get it, if we try to adapt to historical materials and problems certain theories, concepts, and methods developed in other disciplines (e.g., the theory of "reference group," the concept of "social role," the method of "content analysis").

My main point, however, is that causal explanations require observance of certain logical principles. Even the most elementary principle, I have suggested, has been overlooked in explanations of the Civil War. That is, certain phenomena are alleged to have produced certain effects, but insufficient effort has been made to demonstrate that the phenomena actually occurred in the proper time sequence. We would not place credence in an explanation of the Civil War whose description of the state of public opinion was demonstrably erroneous; but, we would believe that, at least, a possibility existed of verifying an explanation whose description was accurate.

Whether historians will ever be able to verify estimates of the relative importance of public opinion (or any other factor) as a cause of an event can only be regarded as an open question at present. Conceivably, however, progress in historiography may eventually narrow the range of disagreement. That happy day would come about if certain explanations offered for an event could be eliminated on the ground that they made erroneous claims concerning the state of public opinion, and, therefore, violated the principle of causal dependence that holds that a causal factor alleged to exist must have preceded the alleged effect. In similar fashion, the other three general principles (actor's awareness, laws of human behavior, intrinsic plausibility) sketched at the outset could be invoked to narrow the range of potentially verifiable explanations of the American Civil War (or of any other "major event"). And narrowing the range of potentially verifiable explanations for the Civil War, I assume, would put us in a better position to assign relative weight to causal factors than the one we are in now.[15] It seems reasonable, therefore, to conclude with this observation: Historians of the Civil War might progress most directly and rapidly if they applied the general logic of historical inquiry to the systematic, explicit, and precise study of concrete events, and, in the process, deliberately attempted to develop more powerful conceptual and methodological tools with which to reconstruct the behavior of men in society over time.

---

15. It is worth emphasizing that the ultimate verification of any particular explanation of the Civil War will imply the elimination of all other explanations. *Cf.:* "... verification involves not only confirmation but the exclusion or disproof of alternative hypotheses". Morris R. Cohen, "Causation and Its Application to History", *Journal of the History of Ideas,* III (1942), 12-29.

3 QUANTIFICATION, SCIENTIFIC HISTORY, and SCHOLARLY INNOVATION

THE current state of historiography is deplorable, lamented Henry Buckle in 1857, in the "General Introduction" to his *History of Civilization in England:*

> In all the other great fields of inquiry, the necessity of generalization is universally admitted, and noble efforts are being made to rise from particular facts in order to discover the laws by which those facts are governed. So far, however, is this from being the usual course of historians, that among them a strange idea prevails, that their business is merely to relate events, which they may occasionally enliven by such moral and political reflections as seem likely to be useful.[1]

Distressed by the course historians usually took, Buckle demanded radical changes in direction. His lengthy "General Introduction," in effect, constituted a revolutionary manifesto proclaiming the coming triumph of the new science of history. Certain that scientific historians

---

1. Henry T. Buckle, *History of Civilization in England* (New York: D. Appleton and Company, 1892), from the second London edition), I, 3.

would discover "the principles which govern the character and destiny of nations," Buckle predicted that:

... before another century has elapsed, the chain of evidence will be complete, and it will be as rare to find an historian who denies the undeviating regularity of the moral world [i.e., human events], as it now is to find a philosopher who denies the regularity of the material [i.e., physical] world.[2]

Another century has elapsed. Buckle's prediction has not been fulfilled. Far from accepting his dictum, the great majority of Western historians today would undoubtedly deny that their business is to discover or develop general laws of human behavior. Thus we clearly should regard the scientific revolution so triumphantly proclaimed by Buckle as abortive—an unsuccessful rebellion inspired by illogical positivist delusions of historiographic grandeur. Or should we? Are the returns all in? Was Buckle more premature than deluded?

Buckle *was* more premature than deluded in my judgment. If we dispense with his non-essential, nineteenth-century notions of science (e.g., mechanical inductionism, undeviating regularities), the prediction does not seem absurd that two decades from now, say by 1984 [*sic*], a significant proportion of American historians will have accepted Buckle's two basic propositions: 1) past human behavior can be studied scientifically; 2) the main business of historians is to participate in the overall scholarly enterprise of discovering and developing general laws of human behavior.

Apart from naive and perversely wilful optimism untutored by experience, does any reasoned basis exist for this prediction about American historiography in 1984? I think so and propose to support the argument by examining Buckle's explanation for the low state of historiography in the 1850s:

... whoever now attempts to generalize historical phenomena, must collect the facts, as well as conduct the generalization. He finds nothing ready to his hand. He must be the mason as well as the architect; he must not only scheme the edifice, but likewise excavate the quarry. *The necessity of performing this double labour* [emphasis added] entails upon the philosopher such enormous drudgery, that the limits of an entire life are unequal to

2. *Ibid.*, 1, pp. 4, 24.

the task; and history, instead of being ripe, as it ought to be, for complete and exhaustive generalizations, is still in so crude and informal a state, that not the most determined and protracted industry will enable any one to comprehend the really important actions of mankind during even so short a period as two successive centuries.[3]

Buckle's predicted triumph of scientific history derived from his assumption that the "double labour" barrier to generalization would soon be demolished. Inspired by similar and successful work in other disciplines, historians, he anticipated, would undertake *systematic and cumulative* studies which, collectively, would produce the data necessary "to comprehend the really important actions of mankind." Moreover, given the requisite data ready to hand, historians would rapidly adopt statistical methods calculated to make most effective use of those data.[4] As a result, philosophically-minded historians would have greatly increased power to discover and demonstrate general laws of human behavior, and "before another century has elapsed, the chain of evidence will be complete. . . ."

My argument, woefully oversimplified and sketchy in deference to space limitations, claims that Buckle perceptively identified some conditions necessary for a genuinely scientific historiography. Writing in the 1850s, a "solitary student" strongly shaped by Victorian Radical individualism,[5] he understandably failed to recognize that for those conditions to obtain, major organizational and technological innovations had first to be made. The argument can most economically proceed by restricting attention to American political historiography and advancing this admittedly partial hypothesis: Given the hard job assigned American political historians (reconstruction and explanation of the highly complex behavior of great numbers and varieties of human beings unavailable for direct interview, observation, or experiment), their relative lack of scientific achievement to-date stems largely from

---

3. *Ibid.*, 1, pp. 166-167.

4. See *ibid.*, 1:24-25, for Buckle's eulogy to "statistics; a branch of knowledge which, though still in its infancy, has already thrown more light on the study of human nature than all the sciences put together."

5. See Giles St. Aubyn, *A Victorian Eminence: The Life and Works of Henry Thomas Buckle* (London: Barrie, 1958), *passim.*

the combined effects of two factors: 1) the primitive social institutions which, until very recently, have governed their social relations; 2) the primitive technology which, until very recently, has restricted their research operations.

By primitive social institutions and relationships, I mean that although political historians in theory comprise a "company of scholars" banded together to advance knowledge, in practice they operate in something like a Hobbesian state of nature, a war of "every man, against every man," each distrusting the other and all desiring power. Atomistic institutions and relationships have created conditions highly unfavorable to developing the advanced professional culture needed to generate and nurture talented individuals. Is the metaphor overdrawn? Somewhat. Universities, historical associations, councils of learned societies such as the SSRC and the ACLS, research libraries and depositories, *et al.* have long existed and long provided useful services and some kind of socialization. But when we calculate the extent to which these institutions have satisfied the requisites for an advanced professional culture, we can reasonably say that they have not yet enabled American political historians to move much beyond the primitive stage of every researcher his own raw-data gatherer. And as Buckle emphasized so eloquently, research at that primitive level of social existence proves either so exhausting to individual researchers that it limits their capacity to perform the hard intellectual work required to develop powerful concepts, theories, and methods, or so dull that it tends strongly to lead gifted scholars to flee from systematic, empirical research to impressionistic, non-empirical speculation, informed no doubt by intelligence and intuition, but characterized by merely haphazard scatterings of imprecise data. In short, when we identify the requisites of a good scholarly social system for American researchers dealing with past political behavior, we recognize the fairly primitive, present state of our institutions.

By primitive technology, I mean tools, not methodology. If our methodology is primitive, that fact derives from the combined effects of our unsophisticated institutions and technology. With regard to the latter, historians have shown an inability to *command effective use* of computers and other modern data processing and photocopying equipment essential to efficient collection, storage, and analysis of the large masses of diverse data required for systematic substantive research. For certain purposes, pens, typewriters, printing presses, adding machines, and the like do represent advanced tools; they are relatively primitive tools when used to collect, order, and analyze the data actually required by American political historians. Emphasis on data collection does not derive, of course, from the caricature of inductionist method which holds that researchers need do little more than amass mountains of vaguely related "facts" and then, somehow, the mountains themselves will move and reveal the "truth." Quite the contrary. Significant historiographic progress will not be made, I believe, until powerful concepts, theories, and methods are first developed. But we are highly unlikely to get to that advanced stage—even slowly and painfully—unless three conditions are satisfied.

First, basic data, both numerical and non-numerical in original form, must be systematically collected and logically ordered. These materials, indispensable to fruitful research on past and present American political behavior, would include election statistics, demographic data, legislative roll calls, party platforms, standard collective biographies of public officials and party leaders, and so forth. While we have long identified and gathered these items, we have too often been guided by crude methods and theories in doing so. Second, researchers need not individually collect the basic data required for systematic research. Instead, data must be readily available to all professional researchers at no financial cost to individuals, in a form permitting manipulation and analysis in any way researchers believe might prove profitable. Third, historians must effectively command the technology and techniques needed to test their theories.

Have the conditions sketched above been satisfied in the past? The answer obviously is no. Do grounds now exist to believe that they can be satisfied in the future? The answer, I think, is yes—partly because the American Historical Association has created an *ad hoc* Committee to Collect the Basic Quantitative Data of American Political History, a committee whose lengthy title accurately denotes its main function. But the present likelihood that the committee will fulfill its tasks in the future stems largely from its effective collaboration with a recently created, and basically new type of scholarly organization, the Inter-University Consortium for Political Research. Organized in 1962 with

eighteen charter members, the Consortium has its executive headquarters at the University of Michigan.[6] It is today perhaps best
described as a working confederation of political researchers at more
than seventy universities, banded together in a formal organization
designed to generate and foster the social relationships postulated by
academic ideology and hitherto mocked by academic practice.

Cordially collaborating with the AHA committee, and aided by
generous grants from the National Science Foundation and the Social
Science Research Council, the Consortium is now developing the
cumulative data archives which, in effect, Buckle postulated as
necessary to the achievement of "behavioral science." In addition, the
Consortium is constructing mechanisms designed to provide individual
researchers with ready access to the modern technology and technical
services needed to make productive use of central data archives.
Moreover, the organizational structure of the Consortium, its sponsor-
ship of coordinated conferences and research seminars, and its rapidly
expanding summer training programs aided by a substantial grant from
IBM to support historians and staffed by combinations of specialists
unavailable at any single university, all enable it to serve as an
unprecendentedly effective communication network linking individuals and groups engaged in similar or complementary research. In
short, the Consortium, by developing and servicing a computer-oriented
central archive for data required by political researchers, and by
constructing and utilizing mechanisms for the rapid dissemination and

---

6. Inquiries about the operations and plans of the Consortium should be
addressed to its executive director, Professor Warren Miller, P.O. Box 1248, Ann
Arbor, Michigan. [a. To support the optimistic predictions I made in 1966, it
seems useful to update this note. The Consortium has flourished and its
membership and functions continue to grow. As of May 1, 1971, its membership
consisted of 150 institutions on three continents—North America, Europe, and
Australia. Its address remains unchanged, but Richard Hofferbert has succeeded
Warren Miller as executive director. b. The present title of the AHA Committee is
the "Committee on Quantitative Data," a change in title that reflects the vast
expansion in the scope of its activities, as well as the growing number of historians
interested in the development of genuinely scientific historiography. To speed
that development along, the AHA Committee and the Consortium plan to hold a
conference in the summer of 1972 on "Theory in Historical Research," a
conference, it seems reasonable to predict, that will give major impetus in the
1970s to the movement that got underway in the 1960s.]

exchange of ideas, skills, and information, has begun to provide the conditions under which political researchers are most likely to engage in fruitful scientific work.

One point cannot be overemphasized. The Consortium is designed to aid researchers who may share widely different approaches to the study of political phenomena, not to centralize research or direct or manipulate individuals into specified types of research for predesigned goals. To revert to my Hobbesian metaphor, the Consortium is best viewed as a prototype of those genuinely *liberal* social inventions which, in the future, will aid scholars both to advance beyond the state of near-natural anarchy lamented by Buckle and simultaneously remain free from the pressures of Leviathan (or his Big Brother). Instead of centralizing power to control individuals, the Consortium centralizes resources, converts them into public goods freely available to all, and thus helps researchers to achieve genuine freedom for creative thought and work. Its organization and rapid growth seem, therefore, to support the claim that the conditions will exist in the not distant future for American political historians to achieve the scientific estate predicted by Buckle, or, more precisely, the claim that such conditions will exist for those individuals able and willing to pay the psychological costs required to break free from old routines. By 1984, I have argued, a significant proportion of American political historians will have proven themselves both able and willing. Henry Buckle will then stand vindicated as a premature prophet rather than a deluded Utopian.

AN APPROACH to the
4 SCIENTIFIC STUDY of PAST
PUBLIC OPINION

LACKING relevant opinion surveys or polls, can contemporary researchers study past public opinion scientifically? Yes. Has past public opinion been studied scientifically? No. If I answer "No" to the second question, how can I responsibly answer "Yes" to the first? That is *the* question this essay tries to answer. A final question-answer set completes our agenda: Should social scientists other than historians seriously concern themselves with the study of past public opinion? Yes.[1]

I. Defining Concepts

Some definitions may help to minimize communication difficulties.

---

1. During the 1950s, Paul Lazarsfeld stimulated my interest in the problems considered in this essay. He bears no responsibility, of course, for the particular solutions proposed here. I am glad to have this opportunity, however, to acknowledge my intellectual indebtedness to him.

They are presented here, it cannot be overemphasized, as working "specifications of meaning," not as definitive statements.[2]

A. Public Opinion.   "Vox Populi may be Vox Dei, but very little attention shows that there has never been agreement as to what Vox means or as to what Populus means." Coined many years ago by Henry Maine,[3] that epigram wittily suggests the confusion still beclouding the concept of public opinion. The confusion stems partly from the concept's moral implications. Particularly in societies boasting democratic forms of government, it seems mandatory that the will of the people prevail. The claim that public opinion supports one side has considerable potency, and the question of "who" constitutes the public represents, therefore, more than a scholastic exercise in concept clarification. Not surprisingly, political theorists, statesmen, and assorted pundits have displayed marked ingenuity in answering it according to different predispositions and interests.[4]

In similar fashion, the concept's moral connotations have provoked other difficult questions: What is meant by "opinion"? When is "opinion" simply the product of habit rather than thought? When is it a "real opinion" instead of a "mere prejudice or meaningless impression"? About what subjects is the "public" capable of having opinions

---

2. In this connection, see Abraham Kaplan, *The Conduct of Inquiry* (San Francisco: Chandler Publishing Company, 1964), pp. 71-78.

3. As quoted in A. Lawrence Lowell, *Public Opinion and Popular Government* (New York: Longmans, 1914), p. 3.

4. Excellent historical reviews of the public opinion concept that deal with this question, and with other questions posed below, are presented in Paul A. Palmer, "The Concept of Public Opinion in Political Theory," in Bernard Berelson and Morris Janowitz, eds., *Reader in Public Opinion and Communication* (Glencoe, Ill.: Free Press, 1953 ed), pp. 3-13; Hans Speier, "Historical Development of Public Opinion," *American Journal of Sociology*, LV (January, 1950), 376-388; Paul F. Lazarsfeld, "Public Opinion and the Classical Tradition," *Public Opinion Quarterly*, XXI (1957), 39-53; Harwood L. Childs, *Public Opinion: Nature, Formation, and Role* (Princeton, N.J.: D. Van Nostrand Company, 1965), pp. 12-41. See also George Carslake Thompson "The Evaluation of Public Opinion," in Berelson and Janowitz, eds., *op. cit.*, pp. 14-20; A. V. Dicey, *Lectures on the Relation Between Law and Public Opinion in England During the Nineteenth Century*, (2nd ed.; London, 1914), pp. 1-47; Lowell, *op. cit.*, pp. 3-54; James Bryce, *Modern Democracies* (New York, 1921), 151-162.

worth consideration by public officials? What degree of coercion by government, or by other agencies or agents, makes it invalid to speak of the existence of public opinion? Under what conditions, and in respect to what type of issue, should a minority submit to majority opinion?

The last question suggests another possible source of conceptual confusion. "Public opinion" sometimes is equated with concensus. Does "public opinion" imply unanimity, near-unanimity, or numerical majority? Does it refer to the "effective" rather than the numerical majority? Differences on these and similar questions have confused the concept and provoked heated but unilluminating controversies.

The final source of confusion considered here illustrates the validity of Gresham's Law, whether applied to the minting of currency or of concepts. Pollsters have become so ubiquitous, man-in-the-street interviews so commonplace, that the concept of "public opinion" has lost its original meaning. Instead of referring only to political issues of consequence to governments, "public opinion" now connotes views on questions of such different mettle as: Do Europeans make better lovers than Americans? Should teenagers "go steady"? Should the United States halt the bombing of North Vietnam?

As Harwood L. Childs persuasively argues, despite numerous attempts, no *intrinsic* reasons can be found to restrict the term "public opinion" to opinions of a certain type held by individuals of a certain type.[5] But scientific disciplines, and fields of specialization within a discipline, seem to progress most rapidly when, at any given time, they abstract from "total reality" a limited range of phenomena for intensive study. As noted in more detail below, historians have not yet generally even *begun* to try to develop scientific procedures to study past public opinion. It seems good strategy, therefore, to begin that job by sharply restricting attention to one type of opinion—and one that historians are likely to find *relatively* easy and congenial to study systematically. At any rate, that is the strategy advocated by, and adopted in, this essay. For our purposes, "public opinion" is *arbitrarily* defined to refer only to opinions on "political issues." It has neither moral, majoritarian, nor effective connotations, and does not imply legitimate, correct, or informed opinion, which should prevail.

---

5. Childs, *op. cit.*, pp. 14-26.

In the sense of "who," the "public" is defined as referring to all inhabitants of a specified political entity having the right, *or claiming the right*, explicitly or implicitly, to influence government actions, directly or indirectly. (The famous "strong-minded" women of the pre-Civil War period had no right to vote, but few American historians would deny that they exercised more influence than many men legally entitled to participate in the decision-making process.) In the sense of "what," "public" refers to government "actions" of concern to members of the political entity and about which they hold opinions—including no opinions. "Actions" are broadly defined to encompass the laws, policies, rulings, personnel, and structure of government. "Opinion" is taken to mean the *position* or *stand*—favorable, unfavorable, undecided, and variations thereof—held by individuals (or groups) on proposed, future, present, or past government actions. It refers either to action on a specific issue or to some over-all course of action on related issues. Clearly, therefore, as defined here, government action forms the core of the public opinion concept.[6] But conceptual clarification also requires us to distinguish explicitly between "opinions" and "attitudes."

As defined here, an opinion always connotes a *position* on some specific government action or general course of action; an attitude represents a persistent, general *orientation* toward some individuals, groups, institutions, or processes, but it does not necessarily result in a specific position on specified public issues.[7] A substantive example may highlight the distinction. Americans' positions during the 1840's relevant to government actions to abolish, restrict, or foster slavery are, according to our definition, viewed as their *opinions* on issues relating to the institution. Their evaluations of slavery as "good or bad," "moral or immoral," are viewed as their *attitudes* toward the institution. (At the boundary line between opinions and attitudes, blurring occurs, of course, but that familiar classification problem need not detain us.)

---

6. I have freely adapted the definition of public opinion suggested by Speier, *op. cit.*, p. 376.

7. Once again, I have freely adapted a definition offered elsewhere. See Theodore M. Newcomb, Ralph H. Turner, Philip E. Converse, *Social Psychology*, (New York: Holt, Rinehart and Winston, 1965), pp. 47-114.

Distinguishing between opinions and attitudes is more than a semantic exercise. The claim that a large majority of Northerners had antislavery attitudes during the 1840's, for example, may well be credible. But it may also provide little credible information about the distribution of Northern opinion on specific public issues related to slavery and may, in fact, encourage a highly distorted description. It is easily conceivable that men had similar *attitudes* toward slavery and directly contradictory opinions on, for example, the annexation of Texas. They may have disagreed on the consequences of that action, they may have differed in their views on the powers of the Federal government or the importance of national unity, they may have differed in their political or economic interests, and so on. Equating an antislavery or proslavery attitude with an opinion for or against annexation, therefore, confuses very different things. To say that is not to deny that attitudes may *help* to shape opinions and that both may be used as indicators of each other. The argument is that the complex interrelationships between opinions and attitudes can perhaps be uncovered and disentangled after painstaking investigation; they cannot be automatically assumed, a priori, to take a particular form. This problem will be further discussed below. But it seems worth emphasizing at the outset that, in my judgment, failure to distinguish sharply between opinions and attitudes hampers public opinion research in general and research on past public opinion in particular.

B. Historical Study of Public Opinion.   As defined here, "historical" study of public opinion connotes more than the study of past phenomena, it connotes research carried out by procedures that secure data by means other than personal interviews, mail questionnaires, or direct observation. Put another way, the concept, "the historical study of public opinion," for our purposes, means the use of procedures to secure data from *documents* (broadly defined) that the researcher *locates and selects but does not create, directly or indirectly.* By selecting documents and, so to speak, "interrogating" their authors, historical researchers *generate* data designed to answer questions about past public opinion.

Contemporary opinion researchers also generate data, but they do so by conducting more or less structured interviews with respondents selected according to some specified sampling criteria. When they use documents not created by researchers for that purpose as data sources, they are, according to our definition, engaged in the historical study of public opinion. In short, it is not the "distance" from the present that determines if a study is historical in character, it is the procedures used to generate data about some dimension of public opinion. Can historical procedures be scientific, however, or must that term be restricted to procedures that, to quote Daniel Lerner, yield "largely quantified data accumulated by structured observation in empirical situations approximating (with specified deviations) the model of controlled experiment"?[8]

C. Scientific Historical Study of Public Opinion   Is history art or science? An old question, much chewed over, never resolved—never to be resolved because it is a badly formulated old question. A better question, I think, is: Can past human behavior, e.g. past public opinion, be described and explained "scientifically," as well as "artistically"? That question poses a prior one: What is science? More precisely: What do we mean by "science"?

In my judgment, Ernest Nagel's definition of science can help us develop a fruitful approach to the study of past public opinion. According to his liberal definition, the enterprise has two main dimensions, goals and means. The main goal, or "the distinctive aim of the scientific enterprise is to provide systematic and responsibly supported explanations [of phenomena]." The main means to achieve that goal is the practice of scientific method: more specifically, "the persistent critique of arguments, in the light of tried canons for judging the reliability of the procedures by which evidential data are obtained, and for assessing the probative force of the evidence on which conclusions are based."[9]

As Joseph Strayer has noted, historians have "been talking about the importance of public opinion for several generations, longer perhaps

8. As quoted in Allen H. Barton and Paul F. Lazarsfeld, "Some Functions of Qualitative Analysis in Social Research," *Frankfurter Bertrage Zur Soziologie*, Band 1, 1955, p. 321. This important methodological essay is particularly relevant to historical research and is conveniently reprinted as "S-336," in the Bobbs-Merrill Reprint Series in the Social Sciences.

9. Ernest Nagel, *The Structure of Science* (New York: Harcourt, Brace and World, 1961), pp. 1-15.

than any other professional group."[10] It seems indisputable, however, that they have not yet developed "tried canons for judging the reliability of the procedures by which evidential data [relevant to public opinion] are obtained," nor "tried canons . . . for assessing the probative force of the evidence on which conclusions are based."[11] Why not?

One answer may be that such canons or principles cannot be developed, given the nature of public opinion and the kinds of documents available for historical research. That may turn out to be the right answer. At present, however, no warrant exists for it other than as a hypothesis that, ultimately, may or may not be confirmed. A more optimistic, and in my judgment a more compelling, answer is that "tried canons" for research on historical public opinion have not been developed because historians have not systematically tried to develop them.[12] Instead, historians studying public opinion have strongly tended to rely upon "historical method" to perform tasks for which it was not designed and for which, as it now stands, it is grossly inadequate.

My basic assumptions are that historical method, as developed to date, cannot satisfy the demands made upon it by researchers interested

10. Joseph Strayer, "The Historian's Concept of Public Opinion," in Mirra Komarovsky, ed., *Common Frontiers of the Social Sciences* (Glencoe, Ill.: Free Press, 1957), p. 263.

11. *Ibid.*

12. See the stimulating critiques in Ernest R. May, "An American Tradition in Foreign Policy: The Role of Public Opinion," in William H. Nelson, ed., *Theory and Practice in American Politics* (Chicago: University of Chicago Press, 1964), pp. 101-122; Robert A. Kann, "Public Opinion Research: A Contribution to Historical Method," *Political Science Quarterly*, LXXIII (September, 1958), 374-396. Though focused on foreign policy, May's essay provides an excellent overview of the American literature relevant to the study of public opinion. For a comprehensive bibliographic guide to the literature, see the chapter notes and supplementary reading suggestions in Childs, *op. cit.*

May has carried further his study of the impact of public opinion upon American foreign policy in his "American Imperialism: A Reinterpretation," in Donald Fleming and Bernard Bailyn, eds., *Perspectives in American History*, (Cambridge, Mass.: Harvard University Press, 1967), I, 123-286. It appeared too late for consideration in this essay. Another essay in the same volume, Donald Fleming, "Attitude: The History of a Concept," *ibid.*, pp. 287-365, also appears to warrant intensive study.

in mass behavior, and that a serious methodological gap therefore exists in historiography that will require large-scale, sustained efforts to close. Widespread recognition of the gap, I further assume, must precede its eventual elimination—an assumption consonant with my fond hope that this paper will be viewed as an essay in constructive criticism.

As is well known, modern historical method was founded in Germany during the early nineteenth century. Trained in philology, Barthold Niebuhr, Leopold von Ranke, and others then brilliantly applied that discipline's critical method to ancient, medieval, and early modern documents. As a result, "scientific history" came into being—a term that primarily meant the critical study of primary sources, not science in Nagel's sense. Essentially, the rules laid down by the founding fathers of the discipline focused attention upon the authentication of documents and the evaluation of testimony that credibly could be extracted from different kinds of authentic documents. A quotation from the preface of one of Ranke's major works illustrates the point:

> The basis of the present work, the sources of its material, are memoirs, diaries, letters, diplomatic reports, and original narratives of eyewitnesses; other writings were used only if they were immediately derived from the above mentioned or seemed to equal them because of some original information.[13]

Later scholars added important refinements to the rules laid down by Niebuhr, von Ranke, and other pioneers but did not greatly extend the boundaries originally mapped out for the "new science." And it is equally well known that historical method in the United States today differs little from that taught in European universities during the late nineteenth century.

Though the *methods* taught today in seminars and described in manuals essentially remain unaltered, historians' *interests* have shifted radically. Since Western historians no longer focus primarily upon ancient, medieval, and early modern events, research necessarily is not confined to the activities of relatively homogeneous, small, elite groups in a highly stratified society. In particular, American historians largely

---

13. As quoted in Fritz Stern, ed., *The Varieties of History* (New York: Meridian, 1956), p. 57.

concern themselves with mass behavior in a dynamic, pluralistic, mass society. Thus a serious gap between historiographic theory and practice has resulted; the traditional rules of historical method were not devised by scholars dealing with mass behavior and have not been amended in any systematic form by later scholars concerned with such phenomena. It follows, therefore, that historical method, as developed to date, can have only limited value as a guide to researchers trying to study public opinion in a mass society.

Instead of directing criticism against the general principles of historical method, the purpose here is to call attention to the necessity of extending them. For example, one will search in vain through the manuals of historical method for observations that offer anything but elementary guidance to researchers engaged in studying public opinion. Moreover, the task of prying out useful procedures from specialized studies is greatly complicated by the tendency of historians to avoid making them explicit. In sum, good ground is believed to exist for the assumption that historical method, as now codified, is inadequate to the demands made upon it by scholars interested in an aspect of mass behavior such as public opinion. A recent statement on the advantages of codifying the research procedures employed in different disciplines is put so cogently as only to require repetition.

> The advancement of research procedure in social science as elsewhere depends on making explicit what researchers actually do, and systematically analyzing it in the light of logic and of substantive knowledge. Such a 'codification' of procedures points out dangers, indicates neglected possibilities, and suggests improvements. It makes possible the generalization of methodological knowledge—its transfer from one specific project or subject matter to others, from one researcher to the scientific community. Finally, it makes possible a more systematic training of students, in place of simply exposing them to concrete cases of research in the hope that they will somehow absorb the right lessons.[14]

As discussed in Section V below, an implicit pattern can be seen in the procedures American historians have spontaneously and intuitively

---

14. Barton and Lazarsfeld, *op. cit.,* in Bobbs-Merrill Reprint "S-336," p. 321.

developed to study past public opinion. Those procedures, used painstakingly and imaginatively, as the three articles in this issue by Helbich, Lancaster, and Maxwell on public opinion and the Versailles Treaty concretely suggest, can yield data that significantly improve our understanding of the role public opinion played in past governmental decisions. In my judgment, however, if we hope to make major advances in the historical study of public opinion, we must sharply reverse our priorities and concentrate primarily upon methodological rather than substantive problems.

Codification of *existing* procedures, although helpful, will not get us very far. Until we consciously try to develop a general analytic model, or system of analysis, and seriously engage in theory construction and concept and index formation, we are not likely to develop a genuinely scientific study of past public opinion. Bluntly stated, we historians need to move beyond that "brute empiricism" which relies upon "saturation" in primary sources unguided by canons for generating data and for making inferences from the data generated. Before sketching an approach that at least points in that direction, it seems useful to suggest that non-historians also have a vital stake, and should therefore participate vitally, in the enterprise.

II. Social Scientists and the Historical Study of Public Opinion

Bernard Berelson and Morris Janowitz, in the second edition (1965) of their *Reader in Public Opinion and Communication*, optimistically observed that significant progress had been made in developing a "generally accepted theory of public opinion" since the first edition appeared fifteen years earlier. "It is still true," they conceded, however, "that there is no generally accepted theory of public opinion, nor does it appear likely that one will emerge in the immediate future." Lack of long-term trend data, they suggested, seriously retards theoretical progress:

> The main contribution of opinion polling to the understanding of opinion formation is through the accumulation of trend data over time. After public opinion polling had provided a body of

answers to standardized opinion questions, it became possible to chart trends in the gross development of opinions and relate them to external political and military events. Unfortunately, the number of such long-term bodies of data is limited because survey organizations have generally not accepted responsibility for this task.[15]

Almost a decade earlier, in the twentieth-anniversary issue of this journal, Herbert Hyman had similarly pointed to the "deficiencies of discontinuous data" as:

perhaps the most crucial deficiency for the growth of a theory. The absence of data which provides a sound description of even the *lack* of public opinion on a problem, at a time when it is not under discussion, means that there is no basis for developing adequate theory as to the formation of public opinion. Similarly, the waning of an issue has generally meant the neglect of it by survey research. Thus, no theory can really be built as to either the formation or decline of public opinion. . . . Obviously, what would be desirable would be to extend public opinion research from the *ad hoc* description of whatever part of the current social world is hot to the systematic description of both the hot and the cold. With such an extension, theory could develop in a number of fruitful directions. Taking any point in time, the *structure* of public thinking, the *mental organization* of public attitudes, would be better understood by seeing the connections between different bodies of opinion. And if these same areas were dealt with over long spans of time, providing trend data, a theory of public opinion formation and opinion change would be well on its way to formulation. As a result of the rise of panels, part of that theory is now available, but only that part which deals with the flux of opinion over short ranges of time in relation to very specific stimuli or psychological factors. By contrast, long term trends in the systematic description of public opinion would enable us to relate opinion processes to much more macroscopic determinants: for example, law, social change, demographic processes, and the like. And such trend data in juxtaposition with political analysis would lead not merely to theories of opinion formation, but also to theories about the *consequences* of popular opinion for political actions.[16]

15. Berelson and Janowitz, *op. cit.* (2nd ed., New York: Free Press of Glencoe, 1965), I, 65-66.

16. Herbert H. Hyman, "Toward a Theory of Public Opinion," *Public Opinion Quarterly*, XXI (1957), 56-57.

Paul Lazarsfeld, probably more than any other individual, has focused attention on the value of long-term trend studies for opinion research. Beginning at least as early as his 1950 presidential address to the American Association for Public Opinion Research, he repeatedly called for such studies, and urged establishment of a " 'commission for the utilization of polls in the service of future historiography,' whose specific task it would be to furnish us [pollsters] with appropriate ideas [on significant questions to ask]."[17] But, as the recent observation by Berelson and Janowitz suggests, the programatic statements of Lazarsfeld and Hyman have had relatively little effect. Historians certainly have not joined with pollsters in the service of future historiography and survey organizations have generally not accepted responsibility for the task of developing long-term bodies of data.

The situation may change to some extent, of course. But it seems reasonable to believe that the Lazarsfeld-Hyman-Berelson-Janowitz statements, by restricting attention to public opinion research carried out by survey methods, do not go far enough. That is, serious deficiencies in long-term trend data, in my judgment, must continue to exist and handicap theory construction if public opinion research continues to depend exclusively, or primarily, upon *non-historical sources of data.*

For one thing, macroscopic social and cultural changes tend to take a very long time indeed to develop and make their consequences felt. Only extraordinarily long-lived and patient pollsters or survey organizations, therefore, might be expected to devote the resources needed to measure continuously the impact of macroscopic changes on opinion formation, and, in turn, the impact of opinion change over time on government policies. For another, lacking the perspective gained by "20-20 hindsight," it is doubtful that any group could identify in advance most of the issues that, in time, would come to be recognized as important. And it is even more doubtful that significant opinion-forming events (broadly defined) could be recognized, as it were, on the spot, and surveys quickly organized and conducted to secure *valid* retrospective before-and-after data. Moreover, even under the best

17. See Lazarsfeld's essay in the "Debate" on history and public opinion research, "The Historian and the Pollster," in Komarovsky, ed., *op. cit.,* pp. 242-268.

circumstances, contemporary researchers surely find it difficult to secure valid data about the impact of public opinion on government action. Not only are contemporary researchers unlikely to have continuous access to decision makers and get truthful answers to probing questions, but government officials and political influentials are highly unlikely, *retrospectively*, to provide comprehensive, candid, accurate answers—even if they really tried hard to do so. In respect to this dimension of public opinion research, non-historians could profit from the emphasis historians place upon the painstaking procedures needed to extract reliable and valid data from primary sources.

Other difficulties could be sketched but would only belabor the main argument: If we need many "long-term bodies of data" to develop a powerful general theory of public opinion, heavy, although certainly not exclusive, reliance will have to be placed upon historical studies. The argument should not be caricatured as maintaining that historical procedures can be developed to secure all the types of data that can be secured by contemporary opinion research. Under the best of foreseeable circumstances, serious gaps will remain, e.g. historical data about the influence of primary groups and personality traits upon opinion formation. But historical study of public opinion can be significantly improved and its improvement would contribute significantly to the general study of public opinion. If that argument has merit, it follows that all social scientists interested in public opinion have a vital stake in developing the scientific character of its historical study.

III. The Concept Of Public Opinion: Main Dimensions And Subcategories

Non-historians may find it surprising, but the three main dimensions of the concept of public opinion were clearly identified by a historian over two thousand years ago. Thucydides, in his classic *History of the Peloponnesian War*, organized his book around three closely related but different themes, the *distribution* of public opinion, the processes of opinion *formation*, and the *impact* of opinion upon government decisions.[18] Unfortunately, historians did not exploit the lead Thucydides provided and did not go on to develop a classification system for the different phenomena subsumed under the over-all concept, "public opinion." As a result, the historical study of public opinion has been seriously handicapped by lack of a good classification system to (1) distinguish among different types of phenomena; (2) provide a logical framework for ordering data; (3) suggest the need to devise different procedures to study different phenomena; (4) help bring complex relationships into focus; and (5) illuminate uniformities and differences. On the assumption that a good classification system is indispensable to fruitful research dealing with complex phenomena, it seems useful to try to develop one based upon Thucydides' dimensions as, in effect, elaborated by modern opinion researchers.[19]

A. Distribution of Opinion.

> "Spartans, those of you who think that the treaty [with Athens] has been broken and that the Athenians are aggressors, get up and stand on one side. Those who do not think so, stand on the other side," and he pointed out to them where they were to stand. They then rose to their feet and separated into two divisions. The great majority were of the opinion that the treaty had been broken.[20]

That is how Thucydides described the decision taken at the climactic meeting of the Spartan Assembly that declared war on Athens in 431 B.C. As the quotation indicates, he provided some explicit information about what we can call the "direction of opinion" but none about the "quality of opinion." Those two categories constitute the main subdivisions of the proposed classification system's first dimension, "distribution of opinion." In turn, each can usefully be subdivided to

---

18. See the discussion of Thucydides in Lee Benson, "Causation and the American Civil War," *History and Theory,* Vol. 1, No. 2 (1961), 167-168. (Reprinted in this volume pp. 90-93 above.)

19. They differ somewhat in emphasis, but see the classification systems in, V. O. Key, *Public Opinion and American Democracy* (New York: Knopf, 1961); Robert E. Lane and David O. Sears, *Public Opinion* (Englewood Cliffs, N. J.: Prentice-Hall, 1964); Childs, *op. cit.*

20. Thucydides, *History of the Peloponnesian War,* Rex Warner translation (Harmondsworth: Penguin Books, 1956), Book I, p. 61.

permit more precise categories for differentiating, ordering, and relating phenomena.

1. Direction of opinion. What do we want to know about the direction of public opinion on an issue over time and place? At least two very different things: (a) the quantitative *divisions* of opinion among the public; (b) the *attributes,* or *characteristics,* of the individuals who held different positions on the issue. We can combine them, of course, to make statements about the distribution of opinions among members of specified groups, or the group characteristics of the individuals holding a specified position. But the two categories are significantly different, a simple observation that forcefully points up the limitations of the information Thucydides provided, as well as the desirability of developing a good classification system for research on public opinion, past or present.

We know from Thucydides—assuming his account to be accurate— that "the great majority [of the Spartans] were of the opinion that the treaty had been broken." But we know nothing else about them. For example, we do not know how, if in any way other than their different positions on the issue, they differed from the small minority of Spartans who believed that the treaty had *not* been broken. As a result, although this essay is not the appropriate place to do so, I think it could be shown that Thucydides' explanation of the Peloponnesian War can neither be confirmed not disconfirmed. The relevant point is to observe that systematic research requires us to get data about both the quantitative divisions of opinion *and* the attributes of the members of a public who hold different positions. This observation gives us two categories, "Positions" and "Attributes," under the more general heading, "Direction of opinion."

a. Positions. For each of the different possible positions on a specific issue, we want to know the distribution of opinion of the members of the groups we designate as constituting "the public." Such information would permit us to identify who held what position, to state the distribution of opinion *within* a specified group, and to compare the distributions *between* different groups. Giving the "Ayes and Nays," as, in effect, Thucydides did, is the simplest form of stating divisions of opinion. Though numerous positions might be created, the range of useful variations on the "aye-nay" formula is narrow; it is hard to go much beyond some variant of "Favorable, Neutral, Undecided, No Opinion, Unfavorable." In short, when the qualitative content of opinion is ignored and each head is counted as an equal unit, there are not many ways to count heads on an issue.

b. Attributes. We can identify only a limited number of different positions on an issue, but, at least in theory, no limit exists to the number of attributes or characteristics we can use to stratify (or divide) a public into different groups. In practice, particularly in historical research, the range of choice tends to be much more restricted. For example, we might wish to group individuals according to personality type because we believe that significant relationships exist between personality type and opinion formation. Obviously, we cannot do so "historically," except perhaps with individual members of elite groups for whom we happen to have the requisite personal documents. Such limitations upon some aspects of historical opinion research need only induce caution, however, not paralysis.

It seems unlikely that personality characteristics are the only, or even the most significant, attributes relevant to opinion formation. Moreover, it seems reasonable to assume that significant relationships exist between some types of group membership (i.e. "interacting" rather than "categorical" groups) and personality characteristics. As John J. Honigman, a specialist on culture and personality, observes, "the members of any enduring group tend to manifest certain relatively common personality characteristics." That proposition, by enabling historians to treat personality, in effect, as only *one* "intervening variable" between group membership and opinion formation, puts our inability to secure data about individual personalities in much less alarming perspective—particularly if we sensibly restrict our claims about public opinion to those dimensions for which we can secure empirical data, do not pretend to offer exhaustive reconstructions and explanations, and do not feel compelled to imply perfect confidence in our claims. Nevertheless, given the past tendency of historians to ignore personality characteristics in opinion research, it seems useful to emphasize that we do not exhaust the range of possible determinants when we group men according to "external" attributes.[21]

To help overcome the "deficiencies of discontinuous data" pointed to by Hyman, it clearly would be highly desirable for studies of past (and present) opinion to use *comparable* (not necessarily identical) attributes to stratify the publics studied. But the choice of attributes inevitably is influenced by the specific issue(s) involved, the source materials available, the degree of precision desired, and the hypotheses being tested. Only a specialist in Greek history, therefore, could identify the attributes that Thucydides, ideally, would have used to study the relationships between public opinion and the coming of the Peloponnesian War. It is possible, nevertheless, to identify four *types* of attributes generally relevant to opinion studies. Because the papers in this issue that deal with public opinion and ratification of the Versailles Treaty provide concrete examples of how they are used in substantive research, the attributes will be identified in American terms. With appropriate changes in terms, however, the typology seems widely applicable.

Place is the type of attribute perhaps most commonly used to divide "a public" into "publics." That is, researchers can try to ascertain the quantitative divisions of opinion on specified issues at specified times among Americans as a group, or among the inhabitants of different sections, states, localities, and the like.

"Political role" identifies another type of attribute. "Formal political roles" permit researchers to distinguish members of the electorate, voters from eligible nonvoters, *et al.* "Informal roles" in principle—that is, if the requisite data can be obtained—permit researchers to distinguish the members of a political system according to party or faction, "liberal" or "conservative" attitudes, differential power to influence decisions (e.g. "elites" and "masses"), or other attributes that seem theoretically relevant.

Demographic attributes can be used to stratify "the public" into a

---

21. For a somewhat less optimistic view of the problems personality variables pose for historical opinion research, see May, *loc. cit.* On the relationships between personality and culture, see John J. Honigmann, *Culture and Personality* (New York: Harper and Row, 1956), pp. 195-225; and, a particularly relevant essay for historians, Anthony F.C. Wallace, "The Psychic Unity of Human Groups," in Bert Kaplan, ed., *Studying Personality Cross-culturally* (New York: Harper and Row, 1961), pp. 128-163.

very large number of smaller "publics." Relevant demographic attributes vary according to time, place, issue, *and theory*, but the standard divisions are some variant and combination of economic, ethnic, religious, urban-rural, educational, age, and sex differences.

Formal voluntary association is the last type of attribute identified in the typology sketched here. To some extent, these attributes overlap with demographic ones, but the difference is that they connote "voluntary" membership (or nonmembership)) in formal *organizations* (e.g. Chambers of Commerce, trade-unions, farmers' organizations, veterans' organizations, religious organizations, ethnic societies) rather than "categorical" membership in some group identified by a demographic attribute.

In principle, of course, the four types of attributes can be combined into an extraordinarily large number of subdivisions among "the American public." In practice, limitations of resources and data sharply restrict the ability of researchers to deal with all publics that might be theoretically relevant. This observation again need induce only caution, not paralysis. To know what theoretically ought to be done, even if historians cannot do it, is useful—and chastening. But inability to do *everything* worth doing is not equivalent to inability to do *anything*.

 2. *Quality of opinion.*   Attention thus far has been restricted to *quantitative divisions* of opinion among the members of different groups. Two assumptions, however, seem reasonable: heads do not count equally in determining the impact of public opinion on government actions; the *qualities* of men's opinions form a significant component of their relative will and power to influence government actions. If we accept those assumptions, it seems useful to create subdivisions under the general category, "Quality of opinion."

a. State (or crystallization) of opinion. At any given time, have the members of a group crystallized their positions on a given issue or are opinions in a formative state? The two main states have been termed "latent" and "manifest." That historians feel both compelled and able to distinguish between these states is nicely illustrated in the paper by James L. Lancaster on "The Protestant Churches and the Fight for Ratification of the Versailles Treaty," in this issue. In effect, one of his basic themes is the transition of opinion from a latent to a manifest state. For example, he emphasizes that specified types of Protestant leaders, those of "liberal theological persuasion," were overwhelmingly sympathetic to the general idea of a league of nations but not necessarily favorable to "whatever specific plan emerged from Versailles." He then advances and supports the claim that three specific events helped to crystallize their latent support into manifest support: "the release of the text of the Covenant, the speeches made by ... President [Wilson] on its behalf, and the debate in Boston on March 19, 1919, between President A. Lawrence Lowell of Harvard University and Senator Henry Cabot Lodge."

b. Saliency of opinion. For the members of specified groups, how "salient" (important) is a given public issue *compared* either to other public issues or to other "issues" affecting their lives? That question points up the need to study opinion on an issue not in isolation from opinions on other issues, but as one strand of an interrelated web of opinion. Men may share the same position on an issue but vary enormously in the importance they attach to it. Historians, therefore, must grapple with the problem of ascertaining the relative saliency of an issue to different groups at the same time, or to the same group at different times.[22] That dictum can also be illustrated by Lancaster's paper.

In effect, Lancaster explains the tremendous *activity* certain Protestant leaders engaged in to secure ratification of Wilson's plan by noting its extraordinary *saliency* for them. For one minister, "the League [of Nations] was the practical application to the whole world of Christ's teachings concerning individuals"; for another, it was "cementing the nations of earth so that the Kingdom of God may come."

c. Intensity of opinion. How convinced are men that their position on an issue is the right position? That is, in addition to wanting to know something about the saliency of an issue to members of a group, we want to know something about the relative intensity (or strength) of their convictions concerning the positions they favor. Depending upon the data available and the precision desired, we can try to group men in

---

22. In this connection, see the chapter, "Texas Annexation and New York Public Opinion," in Lee Benson, *The Concept of Jacksonian Democracy: New York as a Test Case* (Princeton, N.J.: Princeton University Press, 1961), 254-269.

categories ranging from some variant of "strongly favorable" to "strongly unfavorable."

d. Duration of opinion. One determinant of the strength of an opinion, it seems reasonable to postulate, is how long an individual holds it. To treat "duration" separately from "strength," however, is not to engage in conspicuous creation of categories. Duration is by no means the only determinant of strength of conviction. Moreover, if we treat determinants separately, we improve our ability to measure and explain their relative contributions to the strength of opinion. Still another consideration is that when we deal with opinion formation, we particularly need to secure data about the durability of opinions.

e. Knowledgeability of opinion. As conceived here, no more legitimacy is attributed to "informed" than to "uniformed" opinion. But the assumption seems reasonable that informed opinions tend to be stronger and more durable than uniformed ones, and that government officials take those qualities into account when considering opinion distribution on an issue. The "Knowledgeability" category is therefore included in the classification system, although I cheerfully concede that it may be difficult to secure relevant historical data.

B. *Formation of Opinion.*   The papers in this issue focused on the Versailles Treaty provide answers to a wide variety of questions related to opinion formation. To order such questions systematically and comprehensively, the dimension can conveniently be subdivided into five categories: (1) formative agents, (2) agents' motives, (3) agents' actions, (4) impact of agents' actions, and (5) explanation of impact of agents' actions. Those categories, although interrelated, are analytically distinct. To secure historical data about the different types of phenomena assigned to them requires, therefore, different procedures and, in Nagel's terms, different "tried canons" for judging both the reliability of the procedures and "the probative force of the evidence on which conclusions are based."

I. *Formative agents.*   "Every factor that makes the individual what he is attitudinally enters into the formation of political opinion."[23] That all-encompassing proposition may be true, almost by definition, but it gives little guidance to researchers trying to develop an operational strategy for the study of opinion formation. Rather than

---

23. That sentence begins the section on "Formation," in Key, *op. cit.,* p. 291.

begin by trying to identify either the diverse environments in which members of the public form their opinions or their even more diverse predispositions, historians might better begin by trying to identify the relatively small number of individuals or groups actively working to form opinions on specific issues. The basic assumption here is that public opinion on an issue (broadly defined) does not evolve spontaneously but strongly tends to be "made" by the conscious actions of a relatively small number of "formative agents." Once we explicitly identify the issues that concern us in our research, it seems reasonable to assume—and the three papers support the assumption—that we can systematically identify the "leading agents" if we consciously try to do so and saturate ourselves in the historical situation. And once we systematically identify the leading agents, it can be further assumed, we place ourselves in a better position to try to reconstruct and explain the complex processes of opinion formation.

No implication is intended that formative agents either act with perfect knowledge and rationality or achieve the precise results they want or expect. On the contrary, I assume that all agents fall considerably short of perfection, that they display wide variations in knowledge and rationality, and that their actions frequently "boomerang." Moreover, I assume that the actual distribution of opinion on any given issue at any given time represents the outcome of conflicting actions whose impact could, at best, have been predicted only within wide limits—if for no other reason than the occurrence of uncontrollable changes in the general historical situation. But my operative assumption is that if we begin with *conscious agents acting purposively*, we stand on solid theoretical ground and can conduct research according to a workable design.

Granted that assumption, it seems useful to try to develop a standard typology of formative agents. Among other advantages, its development and adoption would tend to produce comparable, cumulative studies and thereby contribute to both theoretical and substantive progress. The typology sketched below obviously is neither elegant nor exhaustive. It represents a beginning rather than an end; its deficiencies, I trust, will stimulate other researchers to repair them rather than to dismiss the enterprise as hopeless.

a. Government officials. Of the different types of formative agents, government officials head the list. We can safely assume that, to some extent, they always consciously try to form public opinion on all "major" issues because we can safely assume that, to some extent, public opinion always affects their operations. Depending upon the subject, officials can be differentiated according to position, level, branch, unit of government, etc. A less obvious but significant differentiation is between "official role" and "nonofficial role." That is, in addition to opinion-making power derived from their government positions, officials may also have influence on various groups, organizations, or individuals, and they may use their influence to help shape public opinion. To cite only one possible reason for making the distinction: It may help us to understand why different men occupying the same position, or similar positions, differ markedly in their ability to influence the distribution of opinion.

b. Political leaders. In this context, "political leaders" connotes men who either do not hold public office or who function as officeholders in one type of nonofficial role. Like government officials, political leaders have a vital stake in the distribution of public opinion and can reasonably be assumed, therefore, to act constantly to shape it. Distinctions between government officials and political leaders may not be universally applicable, but the latter term is not restricted to the modern era. In any era, I assume, a relatively small group of men lead "parties," "factions," "cliques," "circles," and variants thereof.

c. Mass media directors. This term is restricted to the modern era. It designates men who own, operate, or significantly influence the mass media used to communicate information and views. Actually, sharp distinctions between "information" and "views" tend to be somewhat misleading. As George Gerbner suggests, the best proposition to adopt in studying opinion formation is, "all news are views."[24] But it is important to recognize that the opinion-forming power of any communication medium varies widely over time, place, and type of issue, an observation particularly relevant to the problem considered in Section V below of constructing *indicators* of opinion distribution.

d. Leaders of nonpolitical formal organizations. We might extend Gerbner's proposition to claim that, at least in the United States, all

---

24. George Gerbner, "Ideological Perspectives and Political Tendencies in News Reporting," *Journalism Quarterly*, XLI (Autumn, 1964), 495.

major formal organizations (e.g. National Council of Churches, National Association of Manufacturers, AFL-CIO) are political organizations. To do so, however, would be to engage in reductionism and obliterate the boundaries between a political system and its environment. A more reasonable position is to assume that the leaders of all major organizations *consciously* act to form public opinion at some times, on some issues. Depending upon the issue and situation, therefore, we could estimate the likelihood that the leaders of specified organizations acted to form opinion, and design our research operations accordingly. To illustrate the point concretely, Lancaster's paper can again be cited, although the other two papers, by Maxwell and Helbich, also provide striking examples.

Given the long history of participation by American Protestant organizations in the "crusade for peace," dating from 1815, and the specific work of the Federal Council of Churches of Christ in America during 1917-1918, Lancaster "naturally" (my term) focuses on that organization's efforts to gain support for the League of Nations. Accordingly, he finds:

> The Executive Committee of the Federal Council of Churches issued on December 12, 1918, a ringing endorsement of President Wilson's plan for a league of nations. Acting on the recommendation of its Commission on International Justice and Goodwill, the committee challenged its affiliates to strengthen the President's position in Paris and at home. ... The Federal Council asked local churches to provide suitable courses of study on the League of Nations and directed its Commission on Inter-Church Federations to secure expressions of approval of the League by public vote in local congregations. Sunday, January 12, 1919, was designated a day of prayer for the establishment of a league of nations.

In similar fashion, his paper, essentially a study of opinion formation, focuses on the activities of other religious organizations that, given their nature and history, might have been expected to support or oppose Wilson's plan.

e. Pressure-group leaders. To a considerable extent, the analytic distinction between "pressure-group leaders" and "leaders of nonpolitical formal organizations" is arbitrary and not easily applied in practice. The main criterion suggested for assigning organizations to different categories is neither their size nor power but the range of issues likely to concern their leaders and members. The National Council of Churches and the American Medical Association, for example, both function today as pressure groups. But the activities of the latter are far more circumscribed—if less circumspect—than those of the former. I would therefore classify the AMA leaders, in their opinion-making roles, as "pressure-group leaders," the leaders of the National Churches of Christ as "leaders of nonpolitical formal organizations." Since one aim of the classification system proposed here is to help provide operational guidelines for opinion researchers, it seems useful to create categories that distinguish between men who lead such different kinds of pressure groups.

f. Influentials. "Influentials" is the label for the final type of formative agent considered here. Following Robert Merton, they can be further subdivided into "cosmopolitan" and "local" influentials.[25] The characteristic that differentiates them from other opinion leaders (who, of course, can also be viewed as "influentials"), is that their power derives from their personal qualities rather than their control of governmental or organizational resources.

Walter Lippmann serves as a convenient example. Hundreds of other individuals also write columns designed to influence public opinion, and many of them are more widely syndicated. It seems safe to say, however, both that he is the most influential publicist in the United States today and that his influence derives from his reputation and persuasiveness rather than from his relationships to the media that present his views.

In short, the "influentials" assigned to this category influence public opinion through their control of personal rather than corporate resources.

2. *Agents' motives.*   As the three papers below by Helbich, Lancaster, and Maxwell concretely suggest, different agents, impelled by different motives, can try to move public opinion in the same direction. The "liberal" editors of the *Nation* and the "hyphenated" leaders of Irish-American groups, for example, both worked to defeat

25. Robert K. Merton, *Social Theory and Social Structure* (rev. and enlarged ed.; Glencoe, Ill.: Free Press, 1957), pp. 387-420.

ratification of the Versailles Treaty. But their motives differed significantly. To ignore this dimension would make any study of their activities seriously incomplete. Questions about *why* men wanted to form public opinion in specified ways force historians (and other researchers), of course, to explore motivational thickets abounding in thorns and pitfalls. Their exploration can be avoided, however, only by sharply reducing a study's explanatory power and theoretical interest.

3. Agents' actions. It is relatively easier to reconstruct the actions agents take to form opinion than to reconstruct their motives for wanting to do so. But some difficult questions need to be answered about phenomena assigned to this category: In addition to *overt* actions to form opinion, what *covert* actions did specified agents take? Which groups constituted the main targets for specified activities by specified agents? Which groups constituted the "real" targets as distinct from the "nominal" targets? (For example, in the current controversy over "open housing," do the groups opposed to "fair housing laws" *nominally* address themselves to "property owners" but *really* aim at "whites," irrespective of their propertied status?).

4. Impact of agents' actions on specified groups. Apart from other considerations, we need answers to the questions posed immediately above if we are to assess the relative success of different agents. The main question posed here is really a composite question: In relation to specified issues, which agents influenced which groups how much? The groups influenced can be characterized as "nominal target," "real target," "unintended target" ("boomerang" or "windfall" effects). "How much" refers to both the direction and the quality of opinion.

5. Explanation of impact of agents' activities. After we have answered the questions posed immediately above, *and only then*, we can tackle the hard job of explaining the differential success achieved by different agents. In other words, we need to secure data that permit us to say who took what actions, which had what impact, on what groups, in relation to what issue, *before* we can hope to develop systematic and responsible explanations of opinion formation. We may not be able to do so in any event, of course, but, if we first secure the specified types of data, our chances improve considerably.

Six types of determinants can be identified as helping to explain the impact of agents' actions upon public opinion. Again the typology is neither elegant nor exhaustive. But the brief notes below at least provide a beginning.

a. Group receptivity. It seems reasonable to assume that the predispositions of the members of a group are the most important determinants of their response to the actions taken by different agents.

b. Group attitudes toward agents. Contemporary studies support the proposition that "who" says something to someone significantly influences the response to what is said.[26] No reason exists to assume that the proposition applies uniquely to the present.

c. Agents' resources. One obvious determinant of the differential success agents enjoy is the differences in the financial and organizational resources available to them.

d. Arguments used. I assume that, except in unusual cases, the arguments used by agents have *some* significant weight in determining the opinions members of a group form on an issue. Another assumption: Persuasive arguments need not be "rational"—whatever we mean by "rational"—but researchers can hope to identify at least some of the reasons arguments *seem* rational and persuasive to the groups influenced by them. Put another way, I assume that, to respond favorably (or unfavorably) to arguments, most individuals need to perceive them as rational (or irrational). If that assumption is accepted, historians need only try to demonstrate that arguments *were* rational, they need only [*sic*] try to explain why specified arguments *seemed* rational to specified groups.[27]

e. Agents' skill in presenting arguments. Except to make explicit the assumption that skill is a significant determinant of success in opinion formation, no comment seems necessary.

---

26. See M. Brewster Smith, "Opinions, Personality, and Political Behavior," *American Political Science Review,* LII (March, 1958), 1-17. This article seems particularly useful for historians since it provides, in reasonably clear terms, a review of the "major foray[s] by psychologists into the personal determinants of opinion. . . ."

27. The perspective adopted here leads to a more optimistic and less relativistic position than the one suggested in May, *op. cit.,* pp. 103-108.

f. Historical situation. Here I refer to phenomena that occur independently of actions agents take to form public opinion. For example, Maxwell points to "events in Ireland" as one of three sets of factors helping "to provide the framework within which Irish-American opposition to the League of Nations was to emerge and grow." In effect, what might be called the "specific historical situation" relevant to a particular issue or group, and the "general historical situation" relevant to all issues and groups, strongly tend to *condition* responses to actions designed to form opinion.

C. Impact of Public Opinion on Government Decisions. That public opinion significantly influences public policy has long been assumed. In fact, that assumption probably serves as the main scholarly justification for opinion research in general and historical opinion research in particular. How much hard evidence exists to support it, however? Rather little, according to V. O. Key, Ernest May, and Harwood L. Childs. All three have specifically focused on that question and all three essentially agree.[28] To quote the most recent (1965) statement by Childs:

> ... notwithstanding the accumulation of much data regarding voting behavior in elections and referenda, mounting quantities of opinion survey data, and many specialized studies of pressure groups, the mass media, and other links between citizens and government, few of the many hypotheses and speculations on the influences of public opinion on government found *concrete, empirical verification*. Specifically, even though public opinion is expressed regarding a specific public policy, it is seldom known which officials or agencies were aware of this state of public opinion, and what, if anything, was done about this awareness. [Emphasis added.]

Agreeing with Key that "the sharp definition of the role of public opinion as it affects different kinds of policies under different types of situations presents an analytical problem of extraordinary difficulty," Childs observed that:

> For more than twenty-five years polling agencies have been

---

28. Key, *op. cit.*, pp. 409-431; May, *op. cit.*, pp. 102-103, 113-122; Childs, *op. cit.*, pp. 291-319.

making nationwide surveys of public opinion, and a wealth of opinion data has been collected regarding the views of the American people on issues of domestic and foreign policy. The question arises to what extent, if at all, public opinion actually influences public policy. There has been much theoretical speculation regarding the answer but very few hard facts.[29]

Historians might be tempted to adopt a superior tone to "pollsters" on the ground that historical method, applied to manuscript and other primary sources, has yielded the hard data so elusive to researchers lacking access to such sources. Any historian yielding to that temptation, however, would find it a chastening experience to read May's devastating critique.

Relationships between public opinion and American foreign policy have long concerned historians, May observed, but we still have little credible knowledge about them. That embarrassing state of affairs, he suggested, and my researches on the historiography of the annexation of Texas and other pre-Civil War issues lead me to agree strongly, in large measure derives from the fact that historians have "scarcely . . . raised, let alone answered," the key questions. His concluding paragraph is particularly pertinent for our purposes:

Our chief reason for believing that public opinion has influenced and does influence foreign policy is our knowledge that American statesmen have traditionally thought themselves responsible to, and supported or constrained by, some sort of general will. The national tradition is to accept as true the definition attributed to William of Malmesbury: *vox populi, vox Dei.* American political

---

29. *Ibid.,* pp. 291-292, 309-310. It should be noted, however, that Childs reports upon six case studies directed by him that were explicitly designed to secure some "hard facts" to answer the question "to what extent, if at all, public opinion actually influences public policy." As he summarizes those studies, they provide highly interesting and suggestive answers to the question. But it is not another incident in interdisciplinary warfare, I trust, to observe that historians would strongly tend to doubt that firm conclusions can be drawn from case studies not based on intensive examination of correspondence and other personal documents of the government officials involved. No implication is intended that Professor Childs presents the studies as conclusive; on the contrary, my point is to reinforce his observation about the difficulty of securing relevant and significant "hard facts."

leaders have hearkened to the voice of the people as their seventeenth-century forebears did to the voice of God. Perhaps scholars, instead of listening for these voices themselves, ought to begin by inquiring what it is that these men thought they heard.[30]

In effect, May observed that historians have strongly tended to assume that something like one-to-one relationships exist among the *distribution* of opinion, the *perception* of opinion by government officials, and the *decisions made* by government officials. But it is very difficult, he suggests, for anyone, contemporary official or later historian, to ascertain the actual distribution of public opinion at any specified time on any specified issue. Historians therefore would be better advised to begin research by focusing on decision makers' perception of public opinion rather than by "listening for these voices themselves. . . ."

As indicated in Section IV below, I incline toward a different research strategy from the one advocated by May. But he has made a significant contribution to historical opinion research, I believe, by forcefully directing attention to the problem of identifying the main categories of the dimension variously referred to by different authorities as "linkage," "influence," or "impact."

In the classification system suggested in the present essay, the "impact" dimension is subdivided into four main categories: (1) communication of opinion to officials; (2) impact of opinion on distribution of political power; (3) officials' perception of opinion; and (4) impact of perception on specified decisions.

1. Communication of opinion to officials.　Although the term "communication" has some misleading connotations when used to identify the phenomena assigned to this category, I have thus far been unable to find or devise a better one. To minimize misconceptions arising from the term's connotations, it is useful to emphasize that the category contains data designed to answer three questions: (a) Who *initiates* the processes by which government officials ultimately receive "information" about the distribution of opinion on issues? (b) What are the sequences of *"steps"* by which information about specified issues

---

30. May, *op. cit.,* p. 122.

reaches officials? (c) What *"media"* are used to convey information on specified issues to officials?

Data relevant to each of those questions, I believe, are best grouped in a separate subcategory. They are identified here only in broad terms because different studies will require different sets of more or less detailed subcategories.

a. Initiators of communication process. For reasons previously suggested, I assume that, generally speaking, government officials actively try to form public opinion. For the same reasons, I assume that officials actively seek information about the distribution of opinion on issues over time. It would severely distort reality, I believe, to depict public officials only, or even primarily, as passive recipients of information. On the contrary, American public officials have always used a wide variety of devices (e.g. consultation with "expert" observers, analysis of newspapers, commissioning of "surveys") in their hot pursuit of information about public opinion.

An astonishing variety of "nonofficials" also exercise initiative in communicating information about the distribution of opinion on an issue to relevant or potent officials. One main type of "initiator" can be characterized as "spokesman" (authorized or self-appointed) for specific groups; another main type can be labeled "middleman." The "middleman" category connotes some on-going institution such as, for example, newspapers which poll the "man on the street" and *publicly* report their "findings," organizations that purport to have studied the distribution of opinion on specific issues and *privately* report their "findings" to selected officials, and so forth.

What difference does it make who initiates the processes that culminate in officials having specific perceptions of opinion distribution on an issue? Hard data to answer that question are lacking, it must be confessed. But the assumption seems reasonable that official perceptions vary considerably depending upon who initiates the communication processes and who thereby helps to determine the selection of information communicated. Granted that assumption, it follows that researchers ought to try to identify "initiators" of information on specific issues.

b. Sequence of steps in communication process. In addition to variations in official perceptions depending upon variations in who initiates the process, I assume that perceptions will vary significantly, depending upon (1) which officials receive the information in what order, and (2) the number, kind, and sequence of steps in the communication process.[31] For example, spokesmen for a group may directly communicate their perception of its opinion to one official rather than another, they may communicate it to party leaders who in turn communicate their *perceptions* to one official rather than another, they may communicate it to specific mass media, and so forth.

No implication is intended that historians (or contemporary researchers) can reconstruct all the steps in any sequence of communication flows by which specific officials receive information about public opinion on a specific issue. But it seems axiomatic that historians ought to *try* to reconstruct such sequences if they hope to reconstruct official perceptions with any reasonable degree of precision and credibility, or hope to understand and explain how those perceptions came about. May's point, in effect, is that historians have not acted upon that axiom; my point is that, to do so effectively, they need to develop and use a classification system that explicitly indicates the kinds of data to secure relevant to officials' perception.

c. Media of communication. Marshall McLuhan's guru-like dictum about "the medium is the message" at best represents only a half-truth. But opinion researchers have long been aware that the type of media used to communicate information to officials does significantly influence their perceptions of the messages communicated. No need exists to present a long list of the different media that can be used in different sequences of steps in the communication process from public to official. Two points, however, seem worth making: (1) Not only the source of information about public opinion and the circumstances under which the information is received, but the form (or media) of communication must be taken into account when we try to reconstruct and explain how the voice of the people sounded to specified officials. (2) In addition to written and verbal forms of communication, various types of action, e.g. riots, demonstrations, meetings, serve the same

---

31. For a stimulating analysis of the way information flows influence opinions and decisions, see Elihu Katz, "The Two-step Flow of Communication: An Up-to-date Report on an Hypothesis," *Public Opinion Quarterly,* XXI (1957), 61-78. See also Key, *op. cit.,* pp. 411-431.

function—and frequently speak louder, and more persuasively, than words.

2. Impact of opinions on distribution of political power.   Voting can be regarded, of course, as simply another form of communication of information about public opinion to public officials. It is important and complex enough, however, to warrant separate treatment.

We need not assume perfect democracy in a political system to recognize that voting is a particularly potent form of communication. Its potency stems from its dual character. Voting may simultaneously function as a form of communication of opinion to public officials and an act which, in a formally democratic system, formally determines who the officials ultimately are to whom opinions are to be communicated. The problem, of course, is that opinions on any specified issue, or set of issues, do not *necessarily* play any significant role in determining voting behavior; they may, but then again they may not.

Put another way, we are entitled to assume that voting can function as a form of communication about public opinion. But how do we know when it actually does perform that function to any significant degree and how do we know what information it actually does convey? Those questions have long bedeviled politicians and researchers. Further discussion of them is best reserved for Section V, which deals with the general problem of constructing indicators and indexes of public opinion.

3. Officials' perception of public opinion.   Truth in history is not only what happened but what men believed to have happened. Public officials may—and frequently do—misperceive public opinion. For our present purposes, that does not matter. What does matter is that the *reality*, not the *accuracy*, of their perceptions influences their actions— to the extent that they consciously allow public opinion to influence their actions. "Reality" here means what they "really" think they perceive, not what they *say* they perceive.

Which officials? What is perceived? Those are the two main questions relevant to this category.

Different officials, it is obvious enough, may have radically different perceptions of the distribution of public opinion on an issue, or set of issues. Researchers, equally obviously, must therefore specifically identify the officials about whose perceptions they make claims; if they cannot do so with some reasonable degree of specificity, they are not entitled to make claims about the impact of public opinion on public policy.

The problem of identifying what is perceived by specified officials is more complex. As indicated previously, the dimension "Distribution of opinion" contains numerous and radically different components. It is not very useful, therefore, to describe the perceptions of specific officials in vague terms, e.g. "public opinion **favored** (or opposed) Texas Annexation." Since it seems reasonable to assume that officials are influenced by perceptions of both the "direction" and "quality" of opinion, data are needed relevant to the different subcategories of those broad headings. Again, no counsel of perfection is being urged here. Such data may be impossible to get, even if one really tries hard to get them. The point is, one really ought to try hard—and to recognize the implications for one's study if one does not succeed.

4. Impact of officials' perception of public opinion on specified decisions.   This category is the "pay-off" one for studies focused on the relationships between public opinion and public policy. In a sense, research carried out in respect to all other categories of the proposed classification system can be regarded as preliminary research to help answer two main types of questions:

a. *What kind* of impact did officials' perception of public opinion have on the *timing* (e.g. accelerate, delay) of specified decisions? On the *direction* (e.g. reinforce, or weaken, an official's adherence to his own perferred position)?

b. *How much* impact, i.e. how much "weight," did officials' perception of public opinion have on both the timing and direction of specified decisions?

Posing those questions gives rise to another: Can historians really be expected to answer them systematically with any reasonable degree of credibility? For reasons indicated previously, I do not think historians can *now* be expected to do so, but I do think that eventually they may be able to do so. Development and wide *use* of a classification system of the type sketched in this essay, I have tried to suggest, would contribute significantly to the coming of that happy day. But an even more important contribution, I suggest, would be development and wide use of a general research strategy and system of analysis for the historical study of public opinion. It is to that problem that attention can now be appropriately directed.

IV. A Research Strategy And Tentative System Of Analysis For The Historical Study Of Public Opinion.

A. A Research Strategy.   The strategy advocated here assumes that historians who undertake opinion research should schedule their operations according to the classification system sketched above.[32] That is, researchers should, *in sequence,* try to (1) reconstruct the distribution of opinion on specified issues over time, (2) reconstruct and explain the formation of opinion, (3) reconstruct and explain the impact of opinion upon policy.

Like all research strategies, the one advocated here derives from a particular theoretical orientation that should be stated explicitly. No implication is intended, of course, that I have developed anything resembling a general theory capable of stating the conditions under which public opinion has varying degrees of impact upon specified types of public policies. My "theoretical orientation," if the term does not seem overblown, simply assumes that public officials strongly tend to play the most important roles both in consciously forming public opinion and in determining its impact upon government decisions. Given that orientation, the research strategy advocated here seems to follow logically.

How can we hope to find out who played significant roles in forming public opinion, or to explain their ability and desire to do so, if we do not *first* reconstruct the distribution of opinion over time? Similarly,

---

32. I make a sharp distinction between the operations involved in *conducting* research and those involved in *reporting* the results of research; my comments refer only to the former set of operations.

how can we reconstruct and explain the impact of opinion on policy if we do not first reconstruct the distribution of opinion?

Granted that what "counts" in decision making is not the "real" distribution of opinion but officials' perception of the distribution of opinion. Surely, however, a systematic and responsible explanation requires us to make some estimate of the relationships between reality and officials' perception of reality. If officials misperceived the distribution of opinion and acted to some significant extent on their misperceptions, did those misperceptions derive from the officials' having already decided on the policies they wanted to follow, or from poor channels of communication, or both? And *before* we try to estimate the extent to which officials acted on what they thought they heard as "the voice of the people," shouldn't we try to find out whether they essentially were listening only to their own voices as echoed by people who, in effect, they had taught what to say?

Put another way, the research strategy advocated here derives from the following line of argument:

Verifying claims about popular support for, or opposition to, specified government actions is a crucial *preliminary* step in the verification of explanations that emphasize the impact of public opinion upon public decisions. No causal relationship *necessarily* exists between the distribution of public opinion and the occurrence of a particular decision, or set of decisions. If a researcher asserts that such a relationship exists, it therefore seems reasonable to ask him to justify his description of public opinion before evaluating his argument about its impact upon events. In short, it seems logical to evaluate the data and procedures used to *ascertain* public opinion on given issues before evaluating the data and procedures used to *assess* its effect. Paraphrasing Mrs. Glasse's celebrated advice to how to cook a hare, the recipe suggested here for assessing the causal role of public opinion begins, "First, catch your public opinion."[33]

---

33. It may be pedantic to note that the recipe was attributed to Mrs. Glasse erroneously; it actually appeared in a *Cook Book* published in 1747. See Kate Louise Roberts (reviser), *Hoyt's New Cyclopedia of Practical Quotation* (New York, 1922), p. 138. The recipe goes, "To make a ragoût, first catch your hare."

B. A Tentative System of Analysis for Historical Opinion Research.   How can historians—or anyone doing historical research—proceed to "catch" public opinion? To begin with, I suggest, by recognizing the implications of an obvious "fact": the distribution of opinion on an issue changes constantly. It may not change much, it may fluctuate wildly. Over time, it changes. Indeed, measured finely enough, we can assume that opinion distribution changes daily. But no researcher, of course, is likely to want to try to "catch" it on a daily basis, except for extremely limited periods of time.

1. Selection of periods for measurement.   From those elementary observations, a basic problem emerges for historical opinion researchers: Which "poll days" or "poll periods" should be chosen to measure trends in the distribution of opinion on an issue over time? Depending upon the general nature of the study and the specific claims made, the poll periods might vary in length from a single day, to a month, or, in unusual cases, to a year (if the study focused on long-lived, relatively unchanging issues such as "the tariff" prior to the Civil War). But, in systematic opinion research, some specific dates must be selected on which public opinion must be described as having had some specific distribution. Obviously, to perform the operations required to develop valid descriptions of opinion distribution over time, some principles of selection must be used to minimize distortions due to "accidental circumstances" affecting opinion at certain times. "Accidental circumstances," in this context, are those not covered by the principles of selection.

One solution to the problem of identifying valid poll periods, i.e. periods when a researcher can reasonably expect to measure what he says he is measuring, is to use a sampling formula designed to lessen the chances of "accidents" distorting opinion distribution. For example, beginning with a carefully selected date, "polls" might be taken every five or seven or eleven months, or any other interval that rotates the dates in different years. Such solutions undoubtedly tend to lessen distortion due to chance factors and increase reliability; i.e. different researchers using the same formula, and using the same procedures and sources with comparable skill, would get similar results. But to use such solutions we must pay a heavy price; we must sacrifice the flexibility that constitutes one of the great advantages historians enjoy over contemporary researchers.

As noted in the discussion of Hyman's incisive observations about the "deficiencies of discontinuous data" that retard theoretical development, contemporary researchers lack the "20-20 hindsight" enjoyed by historians. Unless they resort to retrospective interviews, of dubious validity even after short periods of time and ever more dubious thereafter, they are *"locked into"* the questions that happened to be asked about particular issues at particular times. In contrast, historical researchers, given the availability of relevant documents—a large "given," I concede—have unlimited flexibility to benefit from historical perspective and range over issues and events, as well as choose any poll periods they regard as best suited to test any theories or hypotheses they (or others) have formulated. (The "relevant document" problem is discussed in Section V below.)

By unlimited flexibility to choose dates, I mean, of course, unlimited flexibility to choose poll periods *controlled by some objective criteria.* Put another way, systematic opinion research requires historians to develop a "chronicle of events," or "narrative framework," for the issue(s) studied that specialists would strongly tend to agree was based on reasonable, unarbitrary criteria.

Once historians have developed an objective narrative framework appropriate to their particular studies, they can systematically proceed to identify the poll dates (or periods) on which to measure opinion distribution. Having done so, they can try to carry out, in sequence, research designed to secure the data called for by a classification system of the type sketched above. (The question of whether we have, or can develop, methods capable of securing those data is also postponed until Section V below.)

If the argument thus far is accepted, or merely granted for the sake of argument, it follows that development of an objective narrative framework is the indispensable first operation required by the proposed system of analysis for historical opinion research. Do we now know how to perform that operation?

2. *Constructing a narrative framework to catch public opinion.* My unpublished research on Texas Annexation has convinced me that it is

possible to construct an objective narrative framework for historical opinion research; alas, I cannot yet cite published work to support the claim. What I can do now, however, in addition to emphasizing the importance of the problem, is to identify three main types of events (broadly defined) that can be combined to construct a narrative framework for any historical opinion study: (a) sequence of relevant government *decisions*; (b) actions (other than government decisions) taken by agents to form opinion; and (c) events contributing to significant changes in the historical situation. For convenience and clarity, my illustrations are all drawn from the Texas Annexation issue, but the typology and operations seem generally applicable.

a. Government decisions. On December 29, 1845, President James K. Polk signed the congressional resolution that formally made Texas the thirtieth state in the Union. To what extent, and in what ways, did public opinion influence the sequence of events that culminated in that decision? The volume of historiographic literature touching on that problem is large—and shallow. Its shallowness, I suggest, stems from the general lack of recognition among historians that to solve the problem we must begin by trying to construct a narrative framework. Failure to recognize the importance of that operation, I maintain, is primarily responsible for the failure to perform it. Put another way, the argument here is that if historians doing research on the Texas Annexation issue made a concerted and systematic attempt to construct such a framework, they would be able to achieve substantial agreement on its main parts and basic shape.

If we begin by explicitly designating Polk's action on December 29, 1845, as the decision that we ultimately have to explain, we can reasonably regard it as the terminal decision in a series of government decisions that began on February 22, 1819, with the signing of the "Transcontinental Treaty" between the United States and Spain. That treaty dealt with the southwestern boundaries of the United States, including its claims to Texas as far south as the Rio Grande. Just as it is reasonable and unarbitrary to designate the Transcontinental Treaty as the initial decision, it is possible to designate other actions, on various governmental levels, as constituting the sequence of "main decisions" between the initial and terminal decisions.

The argument can be summarized and extended as follows: Using reasonable criteria, we can identify a sequence of governmental decisions from February 22, 1819, to December 29, 1845, as "the decision to annex Texas." We can then go on to designate those decisions as major parts of an objective narrative framework for studies dealing with some aspect of public opinion and Texas Annexation. Their major role stems from their dual character; they are the decisions upon which public opinion may have had some impact and, once made, we can assume, they had some impact upon the formation of public opinion.

b. Agents' actions. Government decisions do not constitute the only parts of a narrative framework for historical opinion studies; actions taken by agents consciously trying to form opinion on an issue must also be included. We need not expect specialists unanimously to agree on all actions to be included. It seems reasonable, however, to expect that substantial agreement would be reached if an explicit, systematic, sustained attempt were made to identify the "main actions" agents took to form opinion on an issue.

Based upon a survey of the relevant secondary literature, I am confident that specialists on Texas Annexation would unanimously agree that its narrative framework should include, for example, the following actions: Senator Robert J. Walker's "immediate annexation" letter, published on February 3, 1844; Henry Clay's "anti-immediate annexation" letter, published on April 27, 1844; Martin Van Buren's "anti-immediate annexation" letter, also published on April 27, 1844; the Democratic national convention's nomination of Polk for President on an "immediate annexation" platform, May 29, 1844. In similar fashion, it seems reasonable to suggest, agreement could be reached to include many other "main actions" between 1819 and 1845.

Given the proverbially disputatious temperament of historians and the nature of the problem, some disagreements undoubtedly would persist on whether specific actions should be included in the narrative framework for a specific issue. But no need exists to belabor the point that such disagreements do not alter the basic argument made here, and that a variety of means could be used to handle the problem of what might be called "marginal actions." In general, if disagreement continued after direct and conscious confrontation of specialists, I would favor including "marginal" actions on the ground that an overly inclusive framework is preferable to an overly restrictive framework.

c. Events that change the historical situation. In relative terms, specialists trying to construct a common narrative framework for a specific issue would probably find it most difficult to agree on the type of event included in this category. Again it seems reasonable, however, to expect substantial agreement if attention is explicitly focused on the problem of deciding which events should be included and the grounds for inclusion (or exclusion) are made explicit.

For example, in respect to Texas Annexation, I think agreement could be secured among specialists that the narrative framework for the issue ought to include the 1835-1836 Congressional conflict over antislavery petitions and President Tyler's break with the Whig Party in August 1841. Neither set of events originated as conscious actions taken to influence public opinion on Texas Annexation. But those events significantly contributed to changes in the historical situation that made it both necessary and possible for agents favorable to, and opposed to, Texas Annexation to take certain actions consciously designed to influence public opinion—actions that probably would *not* have been taken if the events specified had not occurred. Moreover, without now attempting to support the claim, I think it could be shown that the distribution of public opinion on Texas Annexation differed significantly before and after each set of events cited above.

In short, the argument here is that a narrative framework designed to facilitate systematic reconstruction and explanation of opinion distribution and formation should not be restricted to government decisions and agents' conscious actions. It should also include events that, in effect, conditioned "the climate of opinion" by producing changes in the historical situation relevant to specific issues.

V. *Operations To Measure The Distribution Of Opinion*

According to the research strategy advocated here, after constructing a narrative framework relevant to some specified issue(s), researchers proceed to perform operations designed to secure, in sequence, the data called for by the three main categories of the classification system.

Although my own work has not progressed to the point where I can try to deal systematically with all three categories, it seems useful to make a start on the operational problems they pose by restricting attention to the first category and trying to codify, on a fairly primitive level, the procedures historians have used to find out the distribution of opinion. The discussion that follows is based on an analysis of the historical literature specifically dealing with the Civil War but it holds, I believe, for American historiography in general.[34]

A definite pattern can be detected in the procedures historians have intuitively and implicitly developed to study the distribution of opinion relevant to the coming of the Civil War. In general terms, they have acted on the assumption that information about the distribution of opinion *can reasonably be inferred* from data found in contemporary documents not originally designed for that purpose. Put another way, historians have extracted related "facts" from a wide variety of sources and grouped them together to form *indicators* of public opinion.

For example, newspaper editorials dealing with a proposed law are frequently taken to reflect some aspect of public opinion regarding it, and historians use those editorials to buttress or justify their claims about public opinion. Instead of relying on a single indicator, however, historians have tended to combine several of them to form an index. Thus, if editorials are used as one indicator, the public speeches or private views of influential or "representative" men might be a second, mass meetings on the issue a third, and so on. Many different indicators have been devised and an even larger number of different indexes constructed. But the pattern invariably has been the same: (1) attempts are made to establish certain facts from source materials; (2) certain *inferences* are then drawn from those facts about the distribution of public opinion.

If some contemporary researchers believe that personal interviews are the only means by which reliable and valid information can be secured about public opinion, they would be impressed, perhaps appalled, by the astonishing variety of sources historians have ransacked

---

34. Part of this study was reported in Lee Benson and Thomas J. Pressly, "Can Differences in Interpretations of the Causes of the American Civil War Be Resolved Objectively?" (New York, Columbia University, Bureau of Applied Social Research, 1956), pp. 43-63, mimeographed.

in their search for opinion indicators. Unfortunately, the ingenuity displayed by historians in creating such indicators is matched by their casualness and reticence concerning their procedures. Only rarely does one find an explicit statement of the logical considerations dictating the choice of sources or justifying the inferences drawn from the factual data.

Such an individualistic, spontaneous approach to the creation and use of indicators might suggest that historians follow no rules in trying to reconstruct the distribution of public opinion on an issue. At first sight, the motto appears to be "anyone can play." Closer examination reveals that "historical opinion indicators" can be arranged into three distinct types and that some unarticulated, but loosely understood, rules govern their creation and use. The incomplete, tentative, and compressed classification system sketched below is designed to be suggestive, not exhaustive. Its purpose is simply to identify the main types of indicators created by American historians; no attempt will be made to discuss the considerations governing their formation and use. But one general point can be stressed. *Indicators are made, not found.* That is, a fact (or set of facts) extracted from historical documents does not constitute an indicator of public opinion. *It becomes an indicator only when an inference is drawn from it.* Granted this point, it will be unnecessary to distinguish hereafter between an indicator and the documents from which it is created.[35]

---

35. In the classification scheme presented here, an effort has been made to demonstrate that distinctions can be drawn not only between types of indicators, but between the same indicators when different kinds of sources are used. As a result, the compressed classification scheme is not presented uniformly. In dealing with the problem of devising historical opinion indicators, I have benefited heavily from two articles by Paul F. Lazarsfeld and Allen H. Barton: "Qualitative Measurement in the Social Sciences: Classification, Typologies, and Indices," in Daniel Lerner and Harold D. Lasswell, eds. *The Policy Sciences* (Stanford, Calif.: Stanford University Press, 1951), pp. 155-192, and Barton and Lazarsfeld, *op. cit.*, pp. 321-361.

A. *Types of Historical Opinion Indicators and Rules to Use Them*
  I. Actions or events
    A. Official government actions
      1. Legislative
        a. Laws
        b. Resolutions
        c. Etc.
      2. Executive
        a. Actions on legislation
        b. Recommendations in prescribed or customary addresses
        c. Etc.
      3. Judicial
        a. Formal decisions
        b. Charges to juries
        c. Etc.
      4. Etc.
    B. Official actions, nongovernmental institutions
      1. Resolutions or platforms adopted
      2. Literature published
      3. Etc.
    C. Individual, customary, or prescribed actions
      1. Voting at elections for public office
      2. Voting at elections for private office
      3. Etc.
    D. Individual, spontaneous, nonprescribed actions
      1. Demonstrations or riots not planned by existing organizations
      2. Acts of violence against officials
      3. Etc.
    E. Etc.
  II. Expert estimates of the distribution of public opinion
    A. Official estimates made in performance of duty
      1. Government officials in reports
      2. Nongovernment officials in reports to their organizations
      3. Etc.
    B. Estimates made for, or published in, mass media
      1. Newspaper surveys (as distinct from editorial expressions of opinion)

      2. Expert estimates reported in mass media
      3. Etc.
  C. Private estimates of knowledgeable individuals
      1. Politicians or "unbiased" ovservers
      2. Foreign travelers or visiting experts
      3. Etc.
  D. Etc.
III. Expressions of opinion (oral or written in origin)
  A. Influential men
      1. Private opinions (letters, diaries, etc.)
      2. Public opinions (speeches, publications, etc.)
  B. Representative men (merchants, farmers, workers, etc.)
      1. Private opinions (letters, diaries, etc.)
      2. Public opinions (petitions, letters to editors, etc.)
  C. Sensitive men (writers, artists, intellectuals, etc.)
      1. Private opinions (letters, diaries, etc.)
      2. Public opinions ("works of art," books, articles, etc.)
  D. Mass media
      1. Influential media (prestige papers, large circulation papers, etc.)
         a. Newspaper editorials
         b. Magazine editorials
         c. Etc.
      2. Representative media (class, section, ethnic group, etc.)
         a. Newspaper editorials
         b. Magazine editorials
         c. Etc.
  E. Etc.

One example may be enough to support the assertion that some informal rules govern historians engaged in studying the distribution of public opinion. Suppose the issue is repeal of the Fugitive Slave Act after 1850. Suppose the assumption is granted that newspaper editorials can be analyzed in such a way as to form a "good" indicator of opinion, i.e. that the opinions expressed in specific newspaper editorials varied as the opinions of specific groups varied. Let us further suppose that a historian relied heavily on newspaper editorials as an indicator of the distribution of "Northern" public opinion. Finally, let us suppose that the newspapers used consisted exclusively of the *New York Tribune* ("rabidly antislavery"), the *Liberator* (William Lloyd

Garrison's abolitionist paper), and several semi-official organs of the Free Soil Party. Clearly, the indicator created could not be a *valid* one. At best, it did not measure "Northern" public opinion but only an extremely unrepresentative segment of it.

Though no explicit standard operating procedures have been agreed upon by historians, it is *taken for granted* that a representative, weighted sample of extant newspaper files should be used in creating an indicator.[36] And it would be possible to cite other informal "rules" that historians are supposed to observe while using newspaper editorials to construct an opinion indicator. In fact, those "rules" are so much taken for granted that they are sometimes ignored and violated by historians who probably would subscribe to them in theory.

This last observation enables us to answer, in general terms, the basic question posed by this section of the essay. A logical way for historians to try to reconstruct and distribution of public opinion is to do systematically, explicitly, and precisely what has tended to be done impressionistically, implicitly, and vaguely. For there can be little doubt that even impressionistic methods have enabled historians to secure a great deal of information about the distribution of opinion over time and place.[37] The assumption seems logical, therefore, that an attack upon the problems that historians encounter in systematically creating and using opinion indicators is at least likely to yield modest returns. Couched in such general terms this answer does not get us very far, but it leads to consideration of other questions that may.

The methodological problems historians face in trying to reconstruct the distribution of public opinion can be identified broadly as follows: (1) What indicators are most appropriate for a particular study? (2) Given a number of appropriate indicators, how can they be combined in one index that maximizes their individual advantages and minimizes their disadvantages? (3) How does one actually go about creating and

---

36. Some interesting but general comments on newspaper editorials and public opinion are found in Lucy M. Salmon, *The Newspaper and the Historian* (New York, 1923), pp. 252-253, 270-286, 439-440, 470-471.

37. See the discussion in Henry David, "Opinion Research in the Service of the Historian," in Komarovsky, ed., *op. cit.*, pp. 270-271. But, in my opinion, that commentary exaggerates the methodological differences between historians and contemporary researchers engaged in studying public opinion. In this connection, see the two articles by Lazarsfeld and Barton cited in note 35.

using opinion indicators and indexes? (4) What sampling principles can be devised to govern the selection of documents from which data can be extracted to form an indicator? A few general observations relevant to the first problem will be offered below; the other three are best treated specifically in relation to substantive events and will be dealt with in a future book, tentatively titled "New York Public Opinion and American Civil War Causation."

B. *Choosing the "Best Indicator" for a Study.* Under ideal conditions, historians might use all the indicators in the classification system sketched in the preceding section. If the requisite source materials were available, and if enough time and effort could be given to the task, every indicator probably would yield *some* information about public opinion. But since conditions never are ideal, historians always must choose among possible indicators. In effect, they must decide upon a hierarchical rank order of "best indicators" for the particular aspects of public opinion that concern them. An example might make the point more clearly than an abstract definition.

His terminology was different but James Bryce was essentially dealing with the problem of "best indicator" when he posed the question, "How is the drift of Public Opinion to be ascertained?" After analyzing the advantages and disadvantages of several different indicators, Bryce concluded, in his famous chapter on "Public Opinion":

> The best way in which the tendencies at work in any community can be discovered and estimated is by moving freely about among all sorts and conditions of men and noting how they are affected by the news or the arguments brought from day to day to their knowledge. In every neighborhood there are unbiased persons with good opportunities for observing, and plenty of skill in "sizing up" the attitudes and proclivites of their fellow citizens. Such men are invaluable guides. Talk is the best way of reaching the truth, because in talk one gets directly at the facts, whereas reading gives not so much the facts as what the writer believes, or wishes to have others believe. Whoever, having himself a considerable experience of politics, takes the trouble to investigate in this way will seldom go astray. There is a *flair* which long practice and "sympathetic touch" bestow. The trained observer learns how to profit by small indications, as an old

seaman discerns, sooner than the landsman, the signs of coming storm.[38]

Translated into our terms, Bryce designates as the best indicator of opinion distribution some version of "private estimates of knowledgeable individuals." And examination of the literature dealing with causes of the Civil War demonstrates that historians have viewed private estimates of knowledgeable individuals as a good indicator of opinion. But the literature also demonstrates that historians have relied much more heavily upon an indicator that Bryce and other theorists tend to deprecate—voting for public office.[39] The literature in fact, demonstrates that historians have depended much more heavily on voting than upon any other indicator for evidence to "prove" their claims about the distribution of public opinion in the pre-war period. To anyone familiar with the ruggedly individualistic traditions of American historiography, this similarity in research design appears highly suggestive. Together with other considerations, it tends to support the following conclusion: Given the American political system and the actual course of events, *as a general rule*, voting for public office provides the single best indicator of public opinion.

1. Advantages of voting behavior as an observable indicator of opinion distribution. An objection to this line of reasoning is immediately apparent. Because historians have taken voting to be the best indicator of opinion, it does not necessarily follow that they are correct. Consensus is not the only criterion of validity and reliability. But in this case consensus has resulted from the independent and continuous efforts of historians to reconstruct the distribution of opinion rather than from routine adherence to standard procedures. Unless convincing arguments to the contrary are presented, their collective experience supports the proposition that voting is the historian's best indicator of American opinion distribution.

---

38. Bryce, *op. cit.,* I, pp. 155-160. The quotation is from p. 156.

39. The reader can test the statement's accuracy by picking up at random works dealing with the coming of the Civil War and examining them in the light of this analysis. In addition to Bryce's criticisms of voting as an opinion indicator, see Lowell, *op. cit.,* pp. 24-25, 70-128; Walter Lippmann, *Public Opinion* (New York, 1922), pp. 193-197.

"But," critics may immediately reply, "haven't leading theorists—Bryce, Lowell, Lippmann—presented just such convincing arguments, and don't they apply to the pre-Civil War period in the United States, as well as to other times and places?"[40]

Without analyzing the arguments of these men in detail, four points can be made in rebuttal. In the first place, they were not writing about historical studies and their judgments cannot be applied mechanically to historical source materials. Second, some of their criticisms demonstrate only that voting is not a perfect indicator, not that other indicators are relatively better. Third, to some extent their criticisms derive from moral judgments as to *what public opinion should be and how it should be formed;* such judgments are not applicable to the study of public opinion as defined here. Finally, their most telling points are directed against faulty and impressionistic use of election results as an opinion indicator, not against the potential value of voting records studied systematically.

That American voting behavior has been imperfectly studied as an indicator of opinion is readily conceded, and the present essay partially stems from a long-range, continuing research project which attempts to document that conclusion in detail. But the project has also led to the conclusion that systematic procedures can be devised to increase the value of voting records as an opinion indicator. In works already published, I have tried to support the conclusion in practice; here the aim is to suggest some general advantages they offer compared to other opinion indicators.[41]

Voting records have at least one unique advantage; they are the only documents left by the American public from which inferences can *directly* be drawn about mass opinions concerning public policies. All

40. *Op. cit.*
41. The project was partially reported in Benson, "Research Problems," in Komarovsky, ed., *op. cit.,* pp. 113-181. A substantive demonstration of how voting behavior can be systematically used to reconstruct opinion distribution on an issue is presented in Benson, *Concept of Jacksonian Democracy,* pp. 254-269. But the major "demonstration" belongs to that familiar category of scholarship known as "research in progress." According to present plans, it will be reported in a book jointly written with Professor Joel Silbey, tentatively titled, "New York Public Opinion and American Civil War Causation: An Essay in the Logic and Practice of Historical Explanation."

other documents from which indicators can be created require making two different types of inferences. Like voting records, other historical documents require drawing an inference from them about the distribution of opinion. But other documents require the additional inference that they actually reflect the views of the public *en masse*, not merely the views of the men responsible for the particular documents *selected* by historians as sources of opinion data.[42]

For example, when used as an indicator, newspaper editorials are assumed to reflect the opinions of "publics" that actually had no part in their composition or publication. The serious problems that arise in connection with that type of inference need little comment except to note that the problems would exist even if all relevant newspaper files were extant, equally accessible, and good sampling methods were used. But the hard job of finding out whose opinions are reflected in editorials—the publisher, the editor, the readers, the public in general— is complicated by the fact that extant files frequently are not a representative or adequate sample of the newspapers published at a given time and place. It seems to be a law of history that the party which ultimately dominates a particular area gets its papers preserved more frequently, and in more accessible places, than the losing party. In contrast, both the winners and the losers—even the very minor parties—secure immortality [*sic*] in the voting records. The argument here is that voting records usually are more complete, detailed, and precise, and *comparatively* more easily worked, than the materials from which any other indicator can be formed—and that those advantages will increase enormously when a major project now well under way is completed.[43]

---

42. In a somewhat different context and formulation, the same point has been strongly emphasized by the Social Science Research Council's Committee on Historiography. See Thomas C. Cochran, "Methods: Theory and Practice," in *Bulletin 64, The Social Sciences in Historical Study,* (New York: Social Science Research Council, 1954), pp. 158-164.

43. Thanks to the joint efforts of the Inter-university Consortium for Political Research and the American Historical Association's Committee to Collect the Quantitative Data of History, the county voting and relevant demographic statistics from 1824 to date will be available in machine-readable form in the near future. When that day arrives, and when historians have acquired the methodological training needed to make good use of those data, I predict that major advances will be made in the use of voting behavior as an opinion indicator.

An analogy may suggest the serious disadvantages of other historical opinion indicators compared with those based upon voting for public office. Suppose contemporary researchers wish to reconstruct the distribution of public opinion on given issues. They first have to draw up a representative sample of the public. Failure to meet that requirement would open the study to serious criticism and probably invalidate it. Having drawn up their sample, they try to interview all its members. Some *reasonable* degree of incompleteness is not fatal; the operative word is "reasonable." But if the sample design was poorly drawn, or if the design was poorly executed, the study's findings would be given little credence.

Now let us suppose that contemporary researchers were forced to draw their sample of people to be interviewed from the same "elite" groups whose records constitute the historian's sources. (On any social level, the records of unusual or atypical individuals are the only ones available to historians.) And let us further suppose that interviews could be secured only with a small, unrepresentative fraction of the original sample. Under those conditions, historians undoubtedly would view contemporary findings about public opinion with even greater skepticism than they do at present. Yet those are the conditions under which historians ordinarily work when they use opinion indicators other than voting behavior. That historians have been able to obtain useful information by using such indicators testifies only to their ingenuity in overcoming difficulties and to the insights gained from "saturation" in source materials.

The difficulties suggested above apply most strongly to the type of indicator classified as "Expressions of opinion," but they are also encountered in using "Expert estimates." Bryce claimed that a talk with experts was the "best way" to learn the drift of opinion, but he was careful to emphasize the necessity of "moving freely about among all sorts and conditions of men. . . ." Historians do not have that freedom. Except in rare cases, the highly unrepresentative nature of "surviving" historical documents prevents historians from following Bryce's research design.[44]

For any period, the expert estimates available to historians were made by men who cannot be viewed as representative of all groups comprising the "American public." Historians have learned enough about their own "frames of reference," and other scholars enough about the "sociology of knowledge," to recognize that the truly "unbiased observer" is an extremely rare bird. When expert estimates are contradictory, as they frequently are, the differences tend to be closely associated with the different group characteristics of the men making the estimates.

Unless logical or factual flaws can be demonstrated in one set of conflicting estimates, the only way to decide between them is to check them all against other opinion indicators. But if those indicators also simply represent expressions of opinion, we run into the same problem of establishing their representative quality. In practice, historians implicitly try to find some act or event against which conflicting expert estimates can be checked. But this is a circular procedure, for it first must be established that the acts or events really do indicate something specific about public opinion. Carefully staged and costly "spontaneous demonstrations," for example, have been known to occur in places other than opera houses. Thus, *whenever possible*, it seems more logical to start with acts or events as indicators of public opinion, and to use "expert estimates" and "expressions of opinion" to supplement them. Additional arguments can be offered to support this line of reasoning.

2. *Action the best test of opinion.* Attention has been directed thus far to the advantages voting data have in respect to the representative quality of documents from which inferences can be drawn about past opinion. But such data also have advantages in respect to the validity of the inferences about public opinion that can reasonably be drawn from any document.

In the classification scheme outlined above in section V.A., it will be recalled, voting for public office is designated as an "Action or events" type of indicator. Simply on the face of it, the claim seems reasonable that, other things being equal, men's actions are better *tests* of their opinions than verbal or written expressions and better *measures* of

---

44. Historians may occasionally unearth a fairly complete file of documents written by government officials charged with the responsibility of reporting the distribution of public opinion. That excellent public opinion indicators can be created from such documents is demonstrated in Lynn M. Case, *French Opinion on War and Diplomacy during the Second Empire* (Philadelphia: University of Pennsylvania Press, 1954).

opinion than expert estimates.[45] The key phrase is, of course, "other things being equal."

Things never are exactly equal. Judgments must always be made about the degree of inequality that permits meaningful comparisons, and borderline cases inevitably produce differences in judgment. But substantial agreement is not always difficult to achieve. If life, fortune, or liberty had to be risked to "express" an opinion through a public act such as voting or signing a petition, and a "private" written or verbal expression of opinion posed no such risk, hardly anyone would dispute the claim that things were not equal. When such dangers are not attached to public acts, however, things frequently are equal *enough* to warrant the claim that action is a better test of opinion than written or verbal expression. Moreover, if acts do entail much heavier risks *and men do act,* more valid inferences can be drawn about the *saliency* and *intensity* of their opinions from their acts than from their verbal or written expressions.

Recognizing that many exceptions to the rule exist, and that it can never be automatically assumed to hold, the claim seems warranted that in American history the act of voting is the best single *test* of opinion. Under the American political system, even with nonsecret ballots, voting *ordinarily* does not entail a heavy risk, nor are extremely heavy external pressures (governmental or social) brought to bear upon men to vote a given ticket. Some social pressures undoubtedly are brought to bear upon voters almost everywhere and at all times; but those pressures usually do not prevent some reasonable degree of "free choice." Moreover, the fact that Americans are not completely free agents in their political behavior increases rather than decreases the value of voting as a test of opinion.

To change allegiance after long attachment to one party usually forces a voter to overcome considerable social pressures. Such pressures are especially heavy when voters change to a new party, or to a minor party challenging the *status quo* (however defined). Pronounced changes in an area's voting patterns, therefore, usually are excellent clues to the saliency and intensity of opinion and indicate that

---

45. See, in this connection, Strayer, *op. cit.,* pp. 264-265. But I have somewhat changed Strayer's emphasis upon action as a test of opinion and tried to suggest the conditions under which the assumption is likely to hold.

"something is up." But long periods of stability are also revealing, for they suggest the absence of intense discontent.

Skeptics may not be convinced that the American people exercise their theoretical power to control government actions; only uninformed cynics fail to recognize that they attach great importance to it. In theory, at least, the American political system is dominated by the voting process. The political realities may not strongly resemble the theory, but being a "good citizen" to an American means that *he is supposed to make his opinion count.* That supposition is so basic to the democratic ideology that not having the right to vote condemns one to inferior social status.

For the vast majority of Americans, it can be assumed, voting has been the only direct means used to make opinions count. Whether their opinions were worth counting, or whether they made them count for much, are irrelevant for our present purposes. What is relevant is that the record of American history convincingly demonstrates that the masses occasionally have exercised considerable control over government actions. Even the Supreme Court, the irreverent Mr. Dooley observed, follows the election returns.

Unlike verbal or written expressions of opinions or expert estimates, voting produces some direct consequences that can be credibly reconstructed, even if the consequences are only to continue the same administration in power by the same majority. Government officials may not want to heed public opinion. They are acutely aware, however, that it *can* make itself felt through the voting process. Failure to win newspaper approval, for example, need not affect an administration's actions; failure to win voters' approval on election day inevitably affects the administration's power to act. The direct link between voting and government action is summed up in the aphorism, "Before you can be a statesman, you gotta get elected—and re-elected."

Because voting for public office directly indicates the opinions of the masses, and because it has direct consequences that can be traced, we can say that American historians have acted reasonably in implicitly treating it as the single best indicator of public opinion in the pre-Civil War period. But the discussion cannot end here. In effect, historians have agreed that the act of voting is the best *test* of opinion but they have sharply disagreed about the opinions *indicated* by the election returns. This observation might lead to the paradoxical conclusion that although voting is the best test of opinion, Bryce and others are right that it is not a good indicator of opinion. That conclusion, however, does not necessarily follow.

Like all sensitive instruments, to produce accurate results, opinion indicators formed from voting records must be carefully constructed and skillfully used. Disagreement among historians and contemporaries over the "meaning" of an election outcome only underscores the central propositions of this section: (1) opinion indicators are made, not found; (2) systematic procedures have to be developed to obtain reasonably accurate results from them. In short, voting records cannot be studied casually and impressionistically, for they do not automatically yield correct inferences about the distribution of opinion on specific issues. But a marked difference exists between using the results of one election as the basis of inferences about public opinion and using the entire range of voting behavior displayed in a number of successive elections. In other words, contradictory answers can be given to two questions which frequently are treated as the same but which are essentially different. What can be learned about the distribution of opinion on given issues from an election outcome? Frequently, very little or nothing. What can be learned from *the entire range of voting behavior in a number of elections?* If the data are studied systematically, almost invariably a good deal can be learned about the distribution of opinion and, under certain conditions, a great deal.[46]

It would only belabor the point to show in detail that similar

46. I have tried to demonstrate that argument concretely in my *Concept of Jacksonian Democracy*, pp. 254-269, and *passim*. The tendency of historians to focus attention upon election results rather than upon voting behavior patterns is cogently treated in Robert T. Bower, "Opinion Research and Historical Interpretation of Elections," *Public Opinion Quarterly*, XII (1948), 457-458. In this connection, see the incisive critique of historians' use of congressional voting as an indicator of public opinion in Joel Silbey, "The Civil War Synthesis in American Political History," *Civil War History*, X (June, 1964), 130-140. And for an incisive critique of historians' use of legislative resolutions, as well as a demonstration of how they can systematically be used as an indicator of public opinion, see an unpublished masters' thesis written under my direction by Madeleine S. Shapiro, "Michigan Public Opinion, the Mexican War, and the Wilmot Proviso: A Study of Legislative Resolutions as Opinion Indicators," Detroit, Wayne State University, 1964.

observations can be made about all other types of documents used as sources of data to construct indicators of opinion distribution. The point is that they yield remarkably different results depending upon whether systematic or impressionistic procedures are used.

The basic argument can now be stated: To practice scientific method and develop good indicators of opinion distribution, historians must consciously and systematically tackle the hard job of developing valid and reliable procedures to "generate" specific types of data from specific types of documents. In similar fashion, historians must tackle the even harder job of developing principles, in Nagel's words, "tried canons," that permit them reasonably to judge the validity of inferences drawn from the data generated.

This essay can appropriately end with a restatement of its basic argument: Historians have not yet scientifically studied past public opinion, not because it is impossible to do so, but because they have not yet tried to do so. The approach sketched here, I trust, at least focuses attention upon the problem and suggests a specific course of action that might ultimately lead to its solution or, more precisely, might stimulate other researchers to propose courses of action that might ultimately lead to its solution.

THE EMPIRICAL and STATISTICAL BASIS for COMPARATIVE ANALYSES of HISTORICAL CHANGE

5

The unfortunate peculiarity of the history of Man is, that although its separate parts have been examined with considerable ability, hardly anyone has attempted to combine them into a whole, and ascertain the way in which they are connected with each other. In all the other great fields of inquiry the necessity of generalization is universally admitted, and noble efforts are being made to rise from particular facts in order to discover the laws by which those facts are governed. So far, however, is this from being the usual course of historians that among them a strange idea prevails, that their business is merely to relate events, which they may occasionally enliven by such moral and political reflections as seem likely to be useful....history has been written by men so inadequate to the great task they have undertaken, that few of the necessary materials have yet been brought together. Instead of telling us those things which alone have any value... the vast majority of historians fill their works with the most trifling and miserable details.... This is the real impediment which now stops our advance. It is this want of judgment, and this ignorance of what is most worthy of selection, which deprives us of materials that ought long since to have been *accumulated, arranged and stored up for future use* [emphasis added]. In other great branches of knowledge, observation has preceded discovery; first the facts have been registered, and then their laws have been found. But in the study of the history of Man, the important facts have been neglected, and the unimportant ones preserved. The consequence is, that *whoever now attempts to generalize historical phenomena, must collect the facts, as well as conduct the generalization* [emphasis added]. He finds nothing ready to his hand. He must be the mason as well as the architect; he must not only scheme the edifice, but likewise excavate the quarry. The necessity of performing this double labour entails upon the philosopher such enormous drudgery, that the limits of an entire life are unequal to the task; and history, instead of being ripe as it ought to be, for complete and exhaustive generalizations, is still in so crude and informal a state, that not the most determined and protracted industry will enable anyone to comprehend the really important actions of mankind, during even so short a period as two successive centuries.[1]

THAT *cri du coeur* came from Henry Buckle in 1857 when he wrote the introduction to his great study, *History of Civilization in England*. It both expressed his conviction that the comparative study of human behavior over time and space was the best way to develop the science of social inquiry and explained why he had been forced to abandon his "original scheme" to reconstruct the history of "general civilization."

We need not take Buckle's observations literally to recognize the contemporary relevance and force of his basic argument. Although comprehensive theories of human behavior are perhaps best generated by individuals, they ultimately derive from, and depend upon, coordinated, rational division of scholarly labor. Unless we achieve such division, we are unlikely to get the *comparable* cross-temporal and cross-cultural studies needed to test and refine comprehensive theories of human behavior—particularly when they require vast quantities of varied data not previously "accumulated, arranged, and stored-up for

1. Henry Thomas Buckle, *History of Civilization in England* (from the Second London Edition, New York, 1903, originally published 1857), I, 3, 166-167. The quotations are spliced together from different pages but are in context and accurately reflect Buckle's position. His book might reasonably be described as the first systematic, cross-cultural, cross-temporal comparative study of the processes of nation-building and national integration. See in particular Vol. 1, Chapters 9 and 10.

future use. " Specifically, the following proposition seems reasonable: If we hope to develop comprehensive theories concerning the "processes of nation-building and national integration," we must achieve some significant degree of coordinated, rational division of labor.

That proposition emphatically does not imply creating an organization to coerce scholars working on nation-state problems to divide their labor according to some master-plan, even if we had some master among us convinced that he had "*the* plan." UNESCO, the ISSC, the ICSSD, however, might appropriately sponsor an organization to facilitate some degree of *voluntary* coordination and division of labor. That proposition probably finds widest agreement when it remains most abstract. Disagreements multiply, no doubt, when we get down to specifics. What is to be done? Who should do what? What organizational innovations can most effectively aid specialists to determine: 1. what to do; 2. who does what; 3. how can specified work be done and in what order?

To those questions, alas, I can only give elementary and general answers. This paper primarily is designed to serve as a springboard for more elevated discussion of questions relevant to Theme II of the Conference,* "the comparative analysis of historical change." (Getting jumped on is, of course, a time-honored, main function of springboards.) Since the questions posed above essentially represent variants of the three sets of questions posed by the organizers of the Conference, the paper is organized according to the standard format they suggested.

I. Which Lines of Comparative Research Appear to Have Been the Most Promising So Far, and Why?

To answer that question comprehensively requires far greater mastery of the relevant literature than I possess. Apart from other considerations, my answer necessarily is fragmentary and tentative because I can

*An International Conference on Comparative Social Science Research under the auspices of the International Social Science Council held at UNESCO House in Paris, April 22-24, 1965.

claim acquaintance with only a small fraction of the large number of studies presently available in *English* on "nationalism," "national growth," "nation-building," "emerging nations," "political moderniza-tion," "political cultures," "political development," "comparative politics," and the like. It seems reasonable to think, however, that the bewildering proliferation of terms used to designate more or less related phenomena reflects, and perhaps partially explains, the underdeveloped status of research on "comparative politics," particularly the branch dealing with "historical" nation-state building, and political develop-ment, i.e., change over relatively long periods. Concepts apparently are cloudy, researchers revel in semantic free play, and cumulative research suffers.

Lucian Pye, at a "Conference on Political Development," recently [1965] sponsored by the University of Pennsylvania, cited ten different definitions now extant in the scholarly literature (they by no means exhausted the list). After identifying three characteristics common to most definitions (equality of participation, capacity of government, differentiation and specialization of political institutions and struc-tures), he suggested that systematic research might permit us:

> to distinguish different *patterns of development according to the sequential order in which different societies have dealt with the different aspects of the development syndrome* [emphasis added]. In this sense development is clearly not unilinear, nor is it governed by *sharp and distinct* stages [emphasis added], but rather by a range of problems that may *arise separately or concurrently* [emphasis added].[2]

If I correctly understand Mr. Pye's noteworthy attempt to bring order out of confusion, it differs significantly in at least two respects from the solution proposed by Karl Deutsch—if I correctly understand Mr. Deutsch.[3]

---

2. Pye's paper on "The Concept of Political Development" was published in the *Annals of the American Academy of Political and Social Science* (March, 1965), pp. 1-14. The entire issue is devoted to "political development," and I am grateful to its special editor, Professor Karl von Vorys, for providing me with the advance set of galley proofs from which I quote. I am also indebted to him, and to Professor Henry Teune, both of the University of Pennsylvania, for helping me to clarify some of the ideas presented in this paper—to the extent, at any rate, that they have been clarified.

3. Karl W. Deutsch, in the introductory chapter to K. W. Deutsch and William J. Foltz, eds., *Nation-Building* (New York: Atherton Press, 1963), pp. 1-16.

1. Pye delineates a general system of analysis applicable to the development of any type of political community—empire, city-state, tribe, nation-state, and the like. Deutsch focuses on a single type, the nation-state.

2. Pye's system, if used in research on historical political development, *eventually* might permit us to establish categories to which we could assign different nation-states. These categories would emerge, however, only retrospectively—after the "facts" were in, so to speak. That is, unless I have badly misunderstood him, we could establish categories to assign specified societies only after we had integrated the results of a great many studies of the particular historical development of individual societies. Moreover, even if societies had developed similar solutions to specified political problems, they would *not* be grouped together unless they had also dealt *in the same "sequential order"* with a wide range of problems "that may rise separately or concurrently."

In sharp contrast, Deutsch's scheme postulates a *predetermined* set of relatively few categories, identified by a relatively small set of (presumably) strategic variables common to all nation-states. Moreover, it explicitly is based upon the "stages" concept explicitly discarded by Pye.

Pye's discussion of the concept of political development is illuminating. I doubt, however, that his system of analysis can provide an economical or manageable framework for coordinating research on historical change in "the processes of nation-building and national integration." It does not identify strategic variables relevant to those processes and, in effect, *precludes* establishment of a standard classification system until the entire history of a number of nation-states has been reconstructed. It does not seem to provide a general framework, therefore, for scholars interested in designing their research to facilitate comparisons of different nation-states over time. In contrast, a system based on stages of national political development, identified by specified variables, might serve as a framework within which we could advance a number of promising lines of comparative research.

The political stages in Deutsch's system of analysis seem to be conceived hierarchically; in other respects, they differ from those used in evolutionary, organic theories of social change. Societies need not pass through a fixed, unilinear sequence of stages, he postulates, and they can make both forward and backward "leaps" (my term). His key assumptions seem to be: 1. a specified society at a specified time can be accurately identified as being at a specified stage of political development; 2. it is useful to do so. Granting his assumptions, we could assign different societies existing at the same time (or period of time) to different stages, and different societies existing at different times to the same stage. Clearly, if this procedure could be applied, it would give us a far larger number of case studies of political development than if attention were confined to contemporary nation-states, or to the history of each nation-state treated as a single case.

Like Marx, Rostow, and others whose analyses are based on the concept of stages, Deutsch uses a few variables which can be combined to designate stages of political development. Summarizing his summary observations on the processes of nation-building and national development, Deutsch noted:

> Open or latent resistance (by some proportion of the population living in the national territory) to political amalgamation into a common national state; minimal integration to the point of passive compliance with the orders of such an amalgamated government; deeper political integration to the point of active support for such a common state but with continuing ethnic or cultural group cohesion and diversity; and, finally, the coincidence of political amalgamation and integration with the assimilation of all groups to a common language and culture - these could be the [four] main stages on the way from tribes to nation.[4]

In effect, Deutsch delineated four stages identified by an index combining three variables: 1. demands by government on population (e.g., taxes, regulation, military service); 2. compliance with governmental demands by public (population); 3. cultural integration of population. These four stages, however, all follow establishment of a nation-state, an impersonal, autonomous political entity with more or less distinct territorial boundaries. Should they be described as stages of "nation-building," or stages of "national political development," or do the terms make any difference? If we called them stages of "national political development" and restricted the term "nation-building" to

---

4. *Ibid.*, pp. 7-8.

phenomena and processes occurring during the period which terminates with establishment of a nation-state, we would, I believe, reduce semantic confusion and might increase conceptual clarity.

For example, prior to July 4, 1776, we might say that "American nation-building" occurred in some British colonies on the North American mainland; after that date, "American national political development" occurred. Apart from semantic considerations, I suggest that the two terms be differentiated because I assume that establishment of a nation-state structure is the great central dividing line in the political evolution of any society which eventually "adopts" that form. Even an abortive attempt at independence can have long range consequences, e.g., the Confederate States of America. What analysts may perceive as the same phenomena, I suggest, actually appear as qualitatively different to participants when they occur in the different contexts of the *non-existence* of a national political structure and the "visible" existence of such a structure. Why then blur these differences by using "nation-building" and "national political development" as synonymous terms?[5]

If the semantic distinctions proposed above are accepted (or merely granted for the sake of argument), Deutsch's sequence should logically be extended to include "stages of nation-building." For example, although my terms are clumsy and the concepts primitive, we might say that the sequence begins with "consolidation of core territory," followed by "transition to nation-state form." In one case, consolidation might occur as a complex set of "centralizing" processes mainly directed by dynastic kings over the centuries; in another, as a relatively simple set of "colonizing" processes directed mainly by agents of European imperial powers over a few decades. The "details" [sic] could differ widely but the outcomes would be essentially the same, territorial consolidation in a single political system. Whether that

---

5. A recent newspaper article dramatically illustrates the point. The headline read, "Macedonians Hunt Own Identity in Complex of Balkan Peoples," and the account begins, "The young hitchhiker said his father was Bulgarian and his mother Greek, but 'I am a Macedonian.' " That sense of national identity, the account makes clear, was crystallized by the creation of "the Republic of Macedonia, a constituent member of the Yugoslav Communist State". David Binder, *New York Times*, February 15, 1965.

particular category is defensible does not matter; the point is that it (or a substitute) would permit us to assign different societies at different time periods to the same stage of nation-building. But the most promising lines of comparative research can now best be pursued, I believe, within the context of "national political development," and it therefore seems useful to examine more closely the index suggested by Deutsch's observations.

Both methodological and operational considerations militate against including "cultural integration" in an index designed to identify *political* stages. "Governmental demands" and "public compliance" can reasonably be used to measure political development, cultural integration cannot. Depending upon our objectives, we might treat levels of cultural integration as either dependent or independent variables in relation to levels of political development. But nations which score the same on a "demand-compliance" index may, if they happen to differ widely in the heterogeneity of their populations, differ widely in their levels of cultural integration.

Let us assume, for example what we know is empirically not true but theoretically could be true: France, India, and the Soviet Union now score exactly the same on a demand-compliance index and differ widely in their level of cultural integration. (That assumption could be disputed only if we made the *a priori* claim that cultural integration bears a one-to-one relationship to demand-compliance.) Couldn't we nevertheless reasonably predict that by 2065 the populations of those societies would *continue* to differ widely in their levels of cultural integration? Why then use cultural integration to measure *political* development?

Even if methodological objections were waived, operational objections remain against inclusion of cultural integration in an index to identify political stages. Unless we confine research to the very recent past, valid and reliable indices of cultural integration are extremely difficult to devise. And even if they could be devised, the data needed *responsibly* to use them—or other "attitudinal" indicators of "nationalism"—in historical research could be obtained only at a very high cost and over considerable time. Thus, rather than helping us now to *begin* to make systematic comparisons of the processes of national political development, including cultural integration in an index of political stages would seriously delay us.

"Governmental demands" and "public compliance" are, of course, complex concepts. Particularly when used 'to construct an index of political stages for nations which vary widely in "vertical power distribution" (degree of federalism), they pose conceptual and methodological difficulties. These difficulties could be overcome, I believe, by "teams of specialists," i.e., intellectually compatible historians and non-historians, working together on the political development of a specified nation. Such teams could, in the relatively near future and with relatively modest resources, develop a reasonably good demand-compliance index for a specified nation and identify its stages of political development.

In developing an index of political stages, I think it justifiable at present to relax strict methodological standards and not insist that precisely the same indicators of "demand" and "compliance" be used for all nations, or for any one nation over its entire history. The immediate task is to develop a common framework within which researchers can systematically begin to make "cross-temporal cross-cultural" comparisons. We can best do this, I believe, if we establish a standard classification system of political stages; we would bog down badly if we first try to specify a standard set of indicators for researchers to use in applying that system.

II. Classification System for Political Stages

Because a concrete proposal may at least stimulate counter-proposals, I propose establishment of a standard classification system having six categories (stages) of national political development. It uses a three point scale to measure "demands:" "low," "moderate," "high;" a two point scale to measure "compliance": "low to moderate," "moderate to high." Combining the two components, we have the following six stages of national political development:

Table I—POLITICAL STAGES

Stage	Government Demand—Public Compliance Index
1.	Low demand, low to moderate compliance
2.	Low demand, moderate to high compliance
3.	Moderate demand, low to moderate compliance
4.	Moderate demand, moderate to high compliance
5.	High demand, low to moderate compliance
6.	High demand, moderate to high compliance

Researchers, I assume, could responsibly use that classification system to identify empirically the sequence of political evolution (broadly conceived) of all (or most) nations. Crudely put, the question remains: So what? Not quite so crudely: How would this help us to generate, test, and refine fruitful theories about the processes of national political development? It would do so, I suggest, by giving us a systematic *political* basis for grouping and differentiating nations other than comparing their specified characteristics at a given time, e.g., in 1960 some nations had a "competitive electoral system," others had various types of "non-competitive" systems.

To compare nations on a strict chronological scale only permits statements about the distribution of phenomena at specified times, or periods; it neither really permits us to ask nor answer interesting questions about the *processes* of national political development. In contrast, the proposed system of stages might help us to deal with such questions as: Can general patterns of "movement" from one stage to another be found? Do causal relationships exist among a range of political and non-political data? Can the history of "politically developed" nations be responsibly used to make predictions about the outcomes if specified courses of action are adopted in "politically underdeveloped" nations with specified characteristics?

To be concrete: Does history "show" the different patterns of political participation and stability indicated in Table II below?

Table II—POLITICAL STAGES, PARTICIPATION AND STABILITY

Stage	Demand	Compliance	Popular Participation	Political Stability
1	Low	Low	Low	High
1	Low	Low	High	Low
5	High	Low	High	Low
6	High	High	High	High

Whether such patterns have actually occurred is, for our present purposes, irrelevant. Again the relevant point is that the proposed classification system provides a framework for collecting, ordering, and analyzing the data needed to determine whether such patterns have existed and whether the indicated relationships are causal or spurious. (No implication is intended, of course, that the hypothetical table contains all the requisite data to test relationships.)

III. Historical archives of national political Data

Among other things, Table II indicates how the proposed system of stages might provide a framework for advancing the line of research which, in my opinion, holds out the greatest promise for the comparative analysis of national political development. I refer here to a solution which has recently been found to the problem posed a century ago by Henry Buckle: How can scholars effectively generalize from historical phenomena if they "must (simultaneously) collect the facts, as well as conduct the generalization... scheme the edifice... [and] excavate the quarry"? The solution has been to free individuals from the crushing burden of collecting "the facts" of national political development by recognizing that it is a social task which must be socially performed and paid for. In other words, the solution has been to establish what might be called "Historical Archives of National Political Data."

Stein Rokkan has thus far, to my knowledge, made the most comprehensive and effective use of historical data in *theoretically-oriented* studies of national political development. In his essay on "Electoral Mobilization, Party Competition and National Integration," he persuasively presents the case for establishing historical archives for political data which, in Buckle's words, "ought long since to have been accumulated, arranged, and stored up for future use. . . ." Describing the archive he and his associates established to permit them to study systematically Norwegian political development, Rokkan observes:

We are currently at work on the development of an *historical archive of ecological data* on Norwegian politics and hope in this way to be able to pursue much more detailed analyses of variations between localities in the rates and directions of change. This punched-card archive was originally built up to allow multi-variate analyses of local variations in turnout and party strength for the elections from 1945 onwards, but efforts are now under way to extend the time series for each local unit. We are also making efforts to extend the *range* of data for each unit: we have so far punched on decks for each *commune* not only data from local and national elections but also data from censuses, from educational, agricultural, industrial and fiscal statistics, data from a church attendance count, data on local party organizations and memberships as well as on nominees to party lists for parliament. We have found such data archiving an essential tool in our cooperative research work and we hope in the years to come to expand the scope of our archive both backwards to the earliest partisan contests and forwards to the oncoming local and national elections. *We think our experiences justify us in recommending that similarly conceived archives be set up in other countries of the West and we are convinced that the greater control of the data masses achieved through such archiving will facilitate systematic comparisons of rates of development in different countries* [emphasis added] .[6]

_____

6. Stein Rokkan, "Electoral Mobilization, Party Competition and National Integration," in Joseph LaPalombara and Myron Weiner, eds., *Political Parties and Political Development* (Princeton: Princeton University Press, 1966).

I strongly endorse Rokkan's recommendation. His experiences in Norway correspond to those we have encountered in the United States in establishing an historical archive for American political data. Aided by "seed money" grants from the Social Science Research Council and subsequent development grants from the National Science Foundation, the archive is a joint project of the Inter-University Consortium for Political Research and a committee of the American Historical Association. It is located in the headquarters of the Consortium at the University of Michigan, Ann Arbor, Michigan.

Apart from direct benefits to researchers, the project to establish the archive has brought about a significant degree of enthusiastic cooperation among a large number of American political scientists and political historians. By developing organizational innovations—the Inter-University Consortium for Political Research and the American Historical Association Committee—to centralize resources, American political researchers have begun to coordinate and rationally divide their labor. Our highly rewarding experiences thus far suggest that social organization makes it possible to avoid the frustrations of Henry Buckle, a "Renaissance Man," who nobly but futilely, tried single-handedly to study the processes of nation-building and national political development.

In addition to organizational innovations, modern data processing technology and techniques give contemporary researchers interested in cross-cultural cross-temporal comparisons enormous advantages over their nineteenth century precursor, Henry Buckle. Thus, the American historical archive now underway is designed for maximum computer use in all phases of operations and data are being stored in machine-readable form suitable for computer retrieval, ordering, and analysis.

At present, the American archive has two main foci, electoral behavior and legislative behavior. In other words, to use now familiar concepts and terms, data is being collected relevant to both the "input" and "output" components of the American political system from 1789 to date;[7] eventually the archive will be extended to include data prior to 1776. More specifically, in addition to data relevant to changes over time and space in the composition of the electorate, turnout of eligibles, social and territorial bases of partisan support, all Congressional roll call votes from 1789 to-date are being recorded on IBM cards. Moreover, computer programs are being developed to aid analyses of electoral behavior and legislative behavior, as well as the interrelationships between electoral and legislative behavior. This paper has grown much too long and, in any event, it probably is unnecessary to describe in greater detail the American data now scheduled for collection. In some respects, they probably are directly comparable to historical data Rokkan and his associates have collected for Norway. But the schedule of collection reflected particular interests of American researchers and was *not* drawn up to facilitate cross-cultural comparisons. This observation dramatically highlights both the great opportunities and dangers presented by current activities in a number of Western countries to create historical archives of national political data.

Given modern data-processing technology and techniques, we now have the *potential capacity* to create the historical data archives required for systematic cross-cultural and cross-temporal studies. To translate potential capacity into actual capacity, however, requires a high degree of international cooperation and coordination. Unless we immediately achieve such cooperation and coordination, we can safely predict that different national archives will fail to collect comparable types of data, will collect them out of phase, will use different standards of evaluation, and different—probably incompatible—storage and retrieval systems. It seems imperative, therefore, immediately to establish an organization effectively linking researchers in different countries now in the process of creating historical archives. To that problem I now turn.

II and III. What can be done to accelerate the accumulation, standardization and evaluation of information and data for comparative analysis of historical political change? What can UNESCO, the ISSC and the ICSSD most profitably do to advance that type of comparative research and what concrete steps should be taken over the next 10-year period?

---

7. David Easton, *A Framework for Political Analysis* (Englewood Cliffs, N.J.: Prentice-Hall, 1965); Gabriel Almond and G. Bingham Powell, Jr., *Comparative Politics: a Developmental Approach* (Boston: Little, Brown and Co., 1966). The approaches taken by Easton and Almond differ, but I have profitted heavily from both their pioneering attempts to develop a general theoretical framework.

At this early stage of development, the simplest and best answer to those complex questions seems to me to propose that an appropriate international agency take responsibility for organizing a "Committee on Historical Archives of National Political Data." To permit immediate attention to be given to problems which will become far more difficult if delays are experienced in working out solutions, I suggest that, to begin with, the Committee consist of men representing national archives now in existence. The suggestion derives from our experience in creating an American historical archive.

We began operations by organizing a communication network *formally* linking individuals and institutions engaged in similar activity. This procedure gave us detailed, comprehensive information on what actually was being done in a variety of places. We then found ourselves in a better position to decide what should be done when, as well as how best to do it. Moreover, we found that in the process we had developed the relationships and the organizational forms which helped us to implement our decisions, and to stimulate increasing numbers of researchers and institutions to participate in the work and extend the range of activities and resources.

Put another way, my suggestion is to bring together, as quickly as possible, representatives of institutions which already have experience in coping with the complex problems inherent in collecting and using historical data to study the processes of national political development. In the absence of such an organized group, detailed answers to questions II and III probably will derive from particular experiences and interests, and thus highly likely to be crude, fragmentary, and shortrun. At any rate, my answers would now have that character. To avoid the fallacy of misplaced (or mistimed) concreteness, therefore, I think it best to restrict myself to proposing that the first step be taken of what must be a long-range program, namely, rapid formation of an international "Committee on Historical Archives of National Political Data."[8]

---

8. As this volume goes to press [1967], two conferences are being held by the AHA Committee to help establish such a Committee (among other purposes).

THE HISTORIAN as
6 MYTHMAKER:
TURNER and the
CLOSED FRONTIER

HISTORIES make history. More precisely, historians significantly influence men's conceptions of the past, and men's conceptions of the past significantly influence their present behavior. If we accept those assumptions, the making of histories is responsible work that historians should perform responsibly. A truism? Of course. But a truism that historians would do well to dust off constantly, particularly when they report their findings and present their conclusions.

Ideally, historians reconstruct the past accurately; they "tell it like it was," to restate Ranke's nineteenth-century credo in contemporary idiom. Sometimes, however, historians unwittingly function as mythmakers; i.e., they invent legends or myths that gain credence and influence behavior. Frederick Jackson Turner, this essay contends, functioned as a mythmaker when he popularized Achille Loria's "free land" theory of history and applied it to America in the form of the "frontier thesis."[1]

---

1. I showed, at least to my own satisfaction, that Turner took over the Lorian system in an article, first published in 1950, "Achille Loria's Influence on American Economic Thought: Including His Contributions to the Frontier Hypothesis." It is reprinted in my *Turner and Beard: American Historical Writing Reconsidered* (New York: Free Press of Glencoe, 1960), pp. 1-40. All citations below are to this edition. Additional information, particularly a letter to Turner from Loria cited below, and more reflection, have strengthened my conviction that the

Why label Turner a mythmaker? Why not simply write that the frontier thesis is wrong, or unfounded, or invalid? I do not claim that Turner consciously helped to invent a myth. I do claim that we can better understand Turner's influence on American historiography if we recognize that the remarkably uncritical acceptance of the frontier thesis for several decades and its uncanny ability to survive logical and empirical refutation neatly fit the "sociological" definition of "myth": "a collective belief that is built up in response to the wishes of the group rather than an analysis of the basis of the wishes."[2]

Briefly summarized, the Loria-Turner thesis assumed that, as Turner paraphrased Loria in 1893, "The existence of an area of free land, its continuous recession, and the advance of American settlement westward explain American development." In 1892, he had expressed the same basic proposition in slightly different form: "In a sense, American history up to our own day has been colonial history, the colonization of the Great West. This ever retreating frontier of free land is the key to American development."[3] Commenting upon those sentences, Fulmer

---

"Turner frontier thesis" is better characterized as the "Loria-Turner free-land thesis." American historians may resist the idea that the "frontier thesis" essentially is Turner's version of Loria's version of Karl Marx's theory of historical development. But it now seems clear to me—contrary to my 1950 observation that "Loria was a Lorian; he was *sui generis*"—that Loria served as the major medium for the transmission of Marx's ideas, although in distorted form, to American historiography. That claim, which I hope to develop at length in a book analyzing economic determinism in American historiography, is strengthened by a letter (in my possession) received in 1951 from Walter Prescott Webb. Webb's letter explicitly acknowledges that his ideas came directly from Lindley M. Keasbey, the American translator of Loria's *Economic Foundations of Society*. (See my article on Loria.)

2. As defined in C. J. Barnhart, ed., *The American College Dictionary* (New York, 1959), 805.

3. Fulmer Mood, ed., *The Early Writings of Frederick Jackson Turner* (Madison: University of Wisconsin Press, 1938), pp. 72, 186. The first quotation, of course, comes from Turner's famous essay, "The Significance of the Frontier in American History," which was first read as a paper in 1893 and published in 1894. This edition, in my judgment, is by far the most useful one extant, since it contains an appendix that compares differing versions of the essay as Turner changed it in various reprintings.

Mood significantly observed, "In this reference to free land, Turner for *the first time in print* [italics added] put his finger upon the material cause, the fundamental economic factor, that he was to stress in his interpretation of our history."[4]

Because the young provincial professor had simply extended in greater detail Loria's own application of his "Landed System of Social Economy" to American history, upon publication of "The Significance of the Frontier in American History," he naturally sent a copy to the world-famous Italian theorist whose books had been extravagantly praised by leading American scholars and whose theory had been summarized at length in the June 1892 issue of the *Political Science Quarterly*.[5] Just as naturally, Loria delightedly responded in February 1894 that he had read Turner's lecture with "the very greatest interest" and found in it "many documents important in support of *my* [italics added] economic theses."[6] Had the title of the lecture literally conveyed the essence of Loria's "economic theses," however, we would know it as "The Significance in American History of Unoccupied Land Which Can Be Cultivated and Possessed without Capital." As both Loria and Turner made clear and contemporaries recognized, that is what free land meant, not simply unoccupied land.[7]

Turner, in his *text*, explicitly emphasized that the "most significant thing about it [the American frontier] is that it lies at the hither edge of free land."[8] In his *title*, however, he focused attention on the census concept of a "frontier line" of population density rather than on Loria's concept of free land. As a result, as Turner popularized the application of Loria's "economic theses" to American history, they came to be known as the "frontier thesis." Thus their economic determinist character was blurred by association with the romantic

---

4. *Ibid.*, 37-38.
5. Historians who resist recognizing that Turner took over the Lorian system also seem to resist reading Loria's writings and the reviews of, and articles about, his work in the leading American scholarly journals, beginning in December 1890. See my discussion in *Turner and Beard*, pp. 10-20; better yet, read the items cited in those pages.
6. Loria to Turner, Feb. 17, 1894, in Turner Papers, Henry E. Huntington Library, San Marino, Calif. (quoted by permission of The Huntington Library). Loria wrote in French, and I have tried to keep the original tone.

myths of "noble savages" and primitive unspoiled "virginal nature" that seem to have been so powerful in the American imagination after the eighteenth century.[9]

Loria had emphasized that the experience of seventeenth-century Britons transported to a "virgin region" like Pennsylvania or Virginia, where land was available to everyone without capital, demonstrated that a "rebirth of mankind" takes place under those conditions. But as free land disappeared in the erstwhile virgin region, society proceeded "to pass through the stages of economic evolution." The entire historical process, he argued, could be discovered by using the

---

7. Ray Billington unfortunately has misread Loria and defined "free land" as meaning only "unoccupied land." He has also failed to recognize that Loria's theory about "the economic foundations of society" explicitly claimed that the presence or absence of free land determined a nation's culture and society. Instead, Billington asserts that Turner "learned" this concept from Henry George. He seems to dismiss the statement he quotes from a letter Turner wrote in 1931: "I never saw his [George's] earlier essays and think that I never read his *Progress and Poverty* before writing the 'Frontier.' " Wilbur R. Jacobs, in my judgment, also tends to overestimate George's influence on Turner. After observing that the "notes which Turner made on Loria refer frequently to the importance of 'free land' in American history," Jacobs wrote, "Henry George, as well as Loria, provided basic ideas for Turner's frontier hypothesis. Upon discovering in Loria's *Analisi* a quotation from *Progress and Poverty* translated into Italian, Turner jotted down the reminder: 'Be sure to get this quotation from George.' " Surely this shows that George influenced Turner by way of the former's incorporation into Loria's system. See Wilbur R. Jacobs, ed., *Frederick Jackson Turner's Legacy: Unpublished Writings in American History* (San Marino, Calif.: Huntington Library, 1965), p. 15. Systematic comparison of Loria's writings and the "Frontier" essay demonstrates that the basic ideas in the latter work, with one exception, are all integral parts of the Lorian system that had been summarized in the June 1892 issue of the *Political Science Quarterly*. My article on Loria showed that Turner's ideas prior to 1892 radically differed from those presented in the "Frontier" essay. As Loria's 1894 reply to Turner shows, he regarded the latter's work as merely documenting Loria's "economic theses." Compare the discussion of "Frederick Jackson Turner's Debt to Loria," in my *Turner and Beard*, pp. 21-35, and Ray Billington, *America's Frontier Heritage* (New York: Holt, Rinehart and Winston, 1966), pp. 10-11, and 239-240, n. 29.

8. *Early Writings*, p. 187.

9. The growth of Romanticism and the celebration of the "natural man" are commented upon in Merle Curti, *The Growth of American Thought* (3d ed.; New York: Harper and Row, 1964), pp. 230-233, 362-363.

comparative method to observe its repetition in a land such as America. There we can "read in the book of the present, pages torn from social history." The East exhibited a society which had evolved into the advanced stage characterized by "the New York factories," while the West simultaneously exhibited a society in the primitive stage characterized by "the Dakota fields."[10]

Turner, echoing Loria, affirmed:

> American development has exhibited not merely advance along a single line [of social evolution] but a return to primitive conditions on a continually advancing frontier line, and a new development for that area. American social development has been continually beginning over again on the frontier. This perennial rebirth, this fluidity of American life, this expansion westward with its *new opportunities* [italics added], its continuous touch with the simplicity of primitive society, furnish the forces dominating American character.[11]

"Perennial rebirth" could only occur, however, if "virgin land" were cost-free land freely available to anyone dissatisfied with conditions in settled regions. Given this premise, from the observation that "never again will such gifts of free land offer themselves" to Americans now that "the frontier has gone," Turner logically deduced that with its going "has closed the first period of American history." Clearly, the Loria-Turner thesis was economic determinist in character, despite the romantic metaphors and symbols used to state and support its propositions.[12]

---

10. See the translation of Loria's chapter "The Historical Revelation of the Colonies," in my *Turner and Beard,* 35-36, 39-40.

11. *Early Writings,* p. 187.

12. *Ibid.,* 228-229. Ray Billington has recently presented a "frontier hypothesis" about the development of American society and culture that avoids economic determinism and is likely, in my judgment, to prove more fruitful than the Loria-Turner thesis, although I do not agree with all its propositions. His book presents and defends what is most accurately called the "Billington frontier hypothesis." My discussion in the present essay is restricted to the Loria-Turner thesis. See Billington, *America's Frontier Heritage,* pp. 3, 23-46, 219-235, and *passim.* Subsequent research and greater maturity led Turner later to say that he had merely presented "an hypothesis." If one reads them as originally published, however, his early essays of 1892, 1893, and 1896 do not have this tentative character. They make such sweeping and self-assured claims that I cannot read them as merely presenting a tentative hypothesis for systematic exploration.

If the thesis were valid, so long as free land existed, American society and culture would differ radically from contemporary European societies and cultures. Once men who lacked capital could no longer move west to take up and possess unoccupied land, America's uniqueness must disappear. When that stage was reached, Loria claimed, America would have recapitulated all the stages of European history, including the present "era of capitalist production relations."[13] It is crucial to recognize that Turner explicitly and unequivocally endorsed Loria's "recapitulationist concept" (my term). "America has the key to the historical enigma which Europe has sought for centuries in vain," Loria asserted, "and the land which has no history reveals luminously the course of universal history." Commenting upon this sentence, Turner just as flatly asserted: "He is right. The United States lies like a huge page in the history of society."[14]

Suppose, however, that despite the continued existence of free land, basic changes occurred in American society and culture, changes that made contemporary America increasingly resemble contemporary Europe. The Loria-Turner thesis then would be demonstrably invalid, for its postulates required that so long as free land existed, America must experience "perennial rebirth" and remain basically different from Europe.

If we brush aside the romantic metaphors and symbols beclouding the frontier thesis and perceive its rigid economic determinism, we can better understand why Turner found it necessary in 1896 to claim that the rise of Populism was due to the end of free land. Basic changes were occuring in American society and culture—Populism was only one expression of them, according to Turner—because America no longer possessed the *material* basis for continued social and cultural rebirth.

> In the remoter West, the restless, rushing wave of settlement has broken with a shock against the arid plains. The free lands are gone, the continent is crossed, and all this push and energy is turning into channels of agitation. *Failures in one area can no*

---

13. Benson, *Turner and Beard*, pp. 5-9.
14. *Early Writings,* pp. 198. I have quoted Turner's translation of Loria's sentence; it differs slightly from the translation provided me. In 1895, Turner reaffirmed his belief in Loria's recapitulationist thesis in an unpublished lecture. See Jacobs, ed., *op. cit.,* pp. 155-156.

longer be made good by taking up land on a new frontier [italics added] ; the conditions of a settled society are being reached with suddenness and with confusion. . . . Now the frontier opportunities are gone. Discontent is demanding an extension of governmental activity in its behalf. In these demands, it finds itself in touch with the depressed agricultural classes and the workingmen of the South and East.[15]

Turner treated Populism as confirming Loria's proposition that the presence or absence of free land was the basic determinant of American society and culture. Contrary to his assumptions, however, "free land," as noted below, continued to exist for several decades after 1890. It follows, therefore, that the frontier thesis is demonstrably invalid, and that the Loria-Turner thesis should not have gained credence among historians, for it is based on antihistorical postulates and substitutes superficial assertions for systematic research on the complex interactions of economic and noneconomic phenomena.

To show that "free land" never actually operated in America as Loria and Turner claimed would require a lengthy paper.[16] For our purposes, rather than presenting such a paper or assembling the data to show that no essential differences existed in the availability of "free land" before 1890 and during at least three decades thereafter, it is only necessary to cite some relevant passages from Ray Billington's book, *Westward Expansion*.[17]

Turner opened his famous essay by quoting the observation from the *Census Bulletin* that there "can hardly be said to be a frontier line of settlement." He went on to describe this brief official statement as marking the "closing of a great historic movement."

---

15. Frederick Jackson Turner, *The Frontier in American History* (New York: Holt, Rinehart and Winston, 1962 printing), pp. 219-220.

16. In my judgment, apart from the fallacious assumption that "free land" was generally available in America, the most glaring error in the "free land thesis" is the assumption that raw land operated as a constant in world and American history. Even if we restrict attention to American experience, the assumption seems untenable. Not "free land" but "fee simple" has been the key characteristic of land in influencing the development of American economy and society. Unlike European societies, neither American law nor culture inhibited the treatment of land as a commodity to be bought and sold for profit.

17. (New York, 1949). Citations below are to the second edition, published in 1960.

Billington explicitly tried "to follow the pattern that Frederick Jackson Turner might have used had he ever compressed his voluminous researches on the American frontier within one volume."[18] But he knew that subsequent research had demolished Turner's claim that "free land" had ended around 1890. He conceded, therefore, that "the economic impact of the passing of the frontier was comparatively slight, largely because the westward movement continued after 1890 as before. Good land still waited newcomers in the West, for despite the pronouncement of the Census Bureau, only a thin film of population covered that vast territory."[19]

How could Billington make so sweeping a concession and not go on to the necessary conclusion that the frontier thesis was demonstrably invalid? He invoked the concept that truth in history is not only what actually happened but also what men *believed* had happened.

> The great mass of the people in the 1880's still looked to a rosy future of continuous expansion. To them the announcement of the Superintendent of the Census in 1890 that the country's "unsettled area has been so broken into by isolated bodies of settlement that there can hardly be said to be a frontier line" remaining, came as a distinct shock. Since that time they have been adjusting themselves—economically, psychologically, and politically—to life in a nonexpanding land. ... Continued expansion into the Canadian Northwest and the submarginal lands of the American Far West softened the impact of the frontier's closing on the nation's economy but had little influence on the popular mind. The *psychological effects* [italics added] of the dramatic Census Bureau announcement of 1890 far out-weighed the material. Suddenly, unexpectedly, the nation realized that its age of expansion was over, its age of adjustment to closed boundaries at hand. To thousands of thinking citizens the implications seemed staggering. Overnight they must answer a dozen difficult questions. ... [Examples are given.] Little wonder that *the American people* [italics added] ... succumbed to a panicky fear that helped transform their rural economy, their foreign policy, and their theories of government.[20]

18. *United States Census, 1890: Distribution of Population According to Density, 1890, Extra Census Bulletin 2* (Washington, April 20, 1891), hereafter cited as *Census Bulletin:* Billington, *Westward Expansion*, p. vii.

19. Billington, *Westward Expansion*, p. 751.

20. *Ibid.*, pp. 751-753. I have spliced together statements on different pages but have kept them in sequence.

Given the "psychological" closed frontier hypothesized by Billington, both Turner's explanation of Populism and the general thesis from which it derived might be retained. The motivating force in American life after 1890 would no longer be the sudden disappearance of free land; it would be the sudden "panicky fear" created by "the dramatic Census Bureau announcement of 1890." To put it another way, while writing an epitaph for the myth Turner invented about the *material* closed frontier, Billington raised it from the dead to be reborn in the form of a myth of the *psychological* closed frontier.

Nothing indicates the power of the frontier myth in American historiography so well, in my judgment, as Billington's gallant attempt to prevent its demise. Though his long and distinguished scholarly career has been characterized from the start by excellent command of source materials and intensive research, in this instance he cited no evidence to support his claims about the remarkable impact of the *Census Bulletin* on American public opinion.[21] Like Turner in the 1890's, Billington acted as though it were unnecessary to test his claims before asserting them. Billington's hypothesis supports the proposition that once myths created by historians gain professional acceptance by satisfying some emotional deep-seated psychological need or ideological premise, they take on a life of their own.

What warrant do I have for so negative—and so confident—an assessment of the psychological closed-frontier hypothesis? For one thing, the *Census Bulletin* simply did not have the connotations attributed to it by Billington; it made no dramatic announcement of structural changes in American society. For another, it is extremely unlikely that more than a minuscule fraction of the American public ever saw the *Census Bulletin,* or even heard about it indirectly via Turner's essays, until late in 1896, when Populism had reached, or perhaps passed, its high point of popular appeal. It follows that American public opinion could not possibly have experienced the "distinct shock" hypothesized by Billington.

The *Census Bulletin* was not issued by the Superintendent of the Census in 1890; it was anonymously published in Washington and dated

21. Though critical of what I regard as Billington's misguided attempt to save the Loria-Turner thesis, I have high regard for, and have profited heavily from, his many and varied contributions to American historiography.

April 20, 1891. By that date, of course, Populism was well developed. Therefore, the *Bulletin* could not have caused the diverse movements conveniently grouped under the generic term "Populism." Moreover, far from making any dramatic announcement, that much cited and little-read publication consisted of four pages whose content were in all respects routine, except for the brief observation couched in matter-of-fact language that there "can hardly be said to be a frontier line of settlement."[22] Its anonymous author did not draw any implications about American development from that observation.

No evidence has ever been presented, and no reason exists to think, that the *Census Bulletin* was distributed to any individuals or institutions other than those on the mailing list for that class of census publication. As late as November 1892, when the Populist candidate received over one million votes, Turner could not be numbered among the select few who might have read it.

On November 4, 1892, Turner published an article in the student newspaper of the University of Wisconsin. He called it "Problems in American History" and later noted that it was "the foundation" of his 1893 essay.[23] He did not refer to the *Census Bulletin* or to the end of the frontier. On the contrary, as Rudolf Freund perceptively observed some time ago, internal evidence shows that he had not seen the *Bulletin* before he wrote the article; he explicitly referred to the "new frontier line" which would be shown on the population map for the 1890 census. Moreover, Turner sent a copy of the article to Woodrow Wilson, who followed its argument closely in a book review published in December 1893. Since the review assumed the continued existence of the frontier, we can reasonably infer that Turner made no marginal comment about the frontier's alleged demise on the copy he sent to Wilson.[24]

I do not have "hard" evidence to fix the date when Turner first saw the *Census Bulletin*. But a reasonable speculation is that it occurred after March 20, 1893. That date's issue of the National Geographic Society's magazine contained an article entitled "The Movements of

22. *Census Bulletin*, 4.

23. *Early Writings*, p. 185, n. 1.

24. The argument that Turner had not seen the *Census Bulletin* before writing "Problems in American History" is developed in my *Turner and Beard*, pp. 21-24.

Our Population." Written by Henry Gannett, the probable author of the *Census Bulletin*, the article reviewed the findings of the 1890 census on population density and specifically commented on the significance of the passing of the frontier line of settlement. Turner apparently did not belong to the Society and did not therefore automatically receive a copy of the issue. Professor Charles Van Hise, one of his colleagues, did, and he probably brought the article to the attention of his younger colleague.[25]

Internal evidence supports the conclusion that by 1893 neither the 1891 *Census Bulletin* nor Gannett's later article had significantly influenced Turner's thinking. Except for the "Frontier" essay's highly dramatic opening and closing paragraphs, it could have stood as written, whether or not free land had ended in 1890.[26] Moreover, in direct contradiction to the position Turner subsequently took in his 1896 essay, "The Problem of the West," in 1893 he explicitly attributed Populism to the *existence* of a frontier society, not to its *disappearance*. The inference seems reasonable that he had not become acquainted with the *Census Bulletin* in time to recast his thinking before he published "The Significance of the Frontier in American History." By 1896, however, Populism had taken on such a character and scope that Turner now apparently recognized that it could not be dismissed as simply another instance of the "paper-money agitation" recurrent in American history. As noted above, he then explicitly attributed Populism to the end of free land rather than, as he had in 1893, to the "lax financial integrity"

25. Henry Gannett, "The Movements of our Population," *National Geographic Magazine*, March 20, 1893, p. 26. Pages vi and lxiv of that volume of the *Geographic* provide the information that it was regularly sent to all members and that Van Hise was a member. His friendship with Turner is mentioned in a note printed under the title "Turner's Autobiographic Letter," in *Wisconsin Magazine of History*, XIX (September, 1935), 101. The speculation that Gannett probably was the author of the *Census Bulletin* is based on a comparison of it and his *Geographic* article, as well as on information supplied to me by Fulmer Mood. Mr. Mood, of course, should not be held responsible for any of my claims, but I happily take this opportunity to acknowledge my indebtedness to him for information about Gannett and the *Census Bulletin* in particular and Turner's activities in general.

26. One sentence is an exception to this statement, but its brevity and tone actually reinforce the point; *Early Writings*, pp. 185-186, 196, 228-229.

characteristic of the "primitive society" recreated on "successive frontiers."[27]

Once we become aware that Turner himself was unacquainted with the *Census Bulletin* until 1893, it surely becomes unlikely that its publication in 1891 produced sudden "panicky fear" among "the great mass of the American people." Contrary to the hypothesis advanced by Mr. Billington, the claim then becomes reasonable that, at least until August 1896, when Turner's essay "The Problem of the West" was in print,[28] the *Census Bulletin* had no significant effect upon either "mass" or "thinking" public opinion.

To test my hypothesis, I made a systematic content analysis of five periodicals widely read from 1890 through 1896, including the monthly *Review of Reviews*, which regularly abstracted articles from forty other magazines.[29] I went through the table of contents of every issue and then read every article that either from its author or title might be expected to refer to the *Census Bulletin* directly or indirectly. For the seven years I found a total of *three* references to the end of the frontier that can reasonably be attributed to knowledge of the *Census Bulletin*.[30] The first, in July 1895 by Woodrow Wilson, clearly derived from Turner's 1893 essay; the second, in September 1896, was by

---

27. *Ibid.*, p. 222. Internal evidence suggests that Turner's 1896 interpretation of Populism derived from his close study of the July 1894 issue of the *Review of Reviews*, pages 30-46. Compare his comments on Senator William V. Allen and Populism with Albert Shaw's sketch of Allen and Professor J. Willis Gleed's letter on Western discontent, printed under the title "Bundle of Western Letters."

28. The essay was published in the September issue of the *Atlantic Monthly*. A letter from its editor, Walter Hines Page, to Turner, August 22, 1896, Turner Papers, indicates that the issue was in print before that date. For information on the article's origins and reception that suggests the extent to which it reflected Turner's "present-mindedness," see my *Turner and Beard*, pp. 88-89.

29. The other magazines were *Arena, Atlantic Monthly, Forum,* and *North Atlantic Review.*

30. It is possible, of course, that the method used did not uncover every reference. It would have taken exhaustive research to find other references, however, and they certainly could not, therefore, have had a strong impact on public opinion over the period of six years from 1891 to 1896 inclusive. (The periodicals for 1890 were searched, since references to the census findings might have been made in advance of formal publication.)

Turner; the third, in October 1896, was an editorial based on Turner's article of the month before.[31] Thus he was the direct source or inspiration of all references to the end of the frontier found in five magazines that can be treated as good indicators of what the "thinking public" read. Hence Billington's assertions about the "psychological" closed frontier caused by a dramatic announcement about the census of 1890 have as little factual basis as Turner's assertions about the "material" closed frontier.

To my knowledge, no one has systematically studied the impact of the closed-frontier myth upon American opinion *after* August 1896. To the extent that it took hold of educated or popular opinion, it seems reasonable to say that Turner, not the author of the *Census Bulletin,* bears the prime responsibility.[32]

During the early 1890s a wide variety of special-interest groups did try to influence American opinion by using some variant of the argument that the arable public domain was "exhausted." Probably the most widely publicized version of the argument was advanced by C. Wood Davis, a self-taught disciple of Malthus. But he boasted no scholarly credentials, carried the stigma that was then attached to proponents of Malthusianism, and had the misfortune fatal to prophets of making a flat prediction subsequently discredited by events. Convinced that the public domain was virtually exhausted and that food shortages would therefore soon appear, in 1891 Davis confidently predicted two-dollar-per-bushel wheat and a price of "one hundred golden dollars" for an acre of good farm land "not later than 1895." Alas for prophecy: grain prices and land values continued to drop to disastrous lows. As a result, Davis was assailed by "an army of critics" who ridiculed his claims and ideas on grounds subsequently confirmed by the historical research summarized by Billington. For example, numerous invitations were extended to Davis to come and see for

31. "The Proper Perspective of American History," *Forum,* XIX (July 1895), 547; Frederick J. Turner, "The Problem of the West," *Atlantic Monthly,* LXXVIII (September, 1896), 296-297, and "The Political Menace of the Discontented," *ibid.,* LXXVIII (October, 1896), 450.

32. For a brief but informative survey of the reception given to the "frontier hypothesis," see Billington, *America's Frontier Heritage,* pp. 13-15, and notes for those pages.

himself that there was "plenty of land out West," and Canadians particularly ridiculed the "hoary nonsense" of his "Malthusian ideas," pointing to the immense Canadian prairies awaiting cultivation.[33]

Davis and other spokesmen for special-interest groups that emphasized "land exhaustion" used clumsy arguments and had transparent objectives that induced distrust and opened them to effective ridicule from men opposed to the policies they advocated. Unlike them, when Turner published the 1896 version of his "Frontier" essay in the *Atlantic Monthly*, he could and did invest himself with the aura and authority of a professional historian whose explanation of the present "problems of the west" derived from disinterested scholarly study. His magisterial survey of American history, though actually based on superficial, impressionistic, and limited research,[34] and his definitive pronouncement that the end of free land caused the contemporary political agitation and demands for governmental action apparently

---

33. See my essay "The Historical Background of Turner's Frontier Essay," published in *Agricultural History*, XXV (April, 1951), 50-82, and reprinted in my *Turner and Beard*, pp. 41-91, particularly 58-63.

34. That Turner's research had been extremely limited until then, and that he had not even yet done systematic research on the West, is evident from Turner's letter to Walter Hines Page, August 30, 1896 (Turner Collection, Harvard University). The letter reveals that, at best, Turner can be said to have done something like systematic research only on the Old Northwest. His 1892, 1893, and 1896 essays, nevertheless, purported to explain all American history. And in 1893, the young man who had not yet published even one article in a scholarly journal directed to professional historians, grandly confirmed Loria's intrinsically antihistorical "thesis" that American history recapitulated and thereby revealed "the course of universal history." Critically analyzed, the "Frontier" essay consists of a series of remarkably sweeping assertions supported by a hodgepodge of selective and sporadic quotations from scattered primary sources, travel accounts, and secondary works. Given the sketchiness of his research, the self-assured tone adopted by Turner in his early essays cannot be justified. It can be *explained*, perhaps, by recognizing that the basic ideas came from Loria, then receiving acclaim from leading scholars throughout the western world, and that Loria claimed to have derived his general theory especially from "researches in the economic development of the United States." In this connection, see my *Turner and Beard*, 10-17. My unflattering estimate of Turner's early research is supported by Stull Holt's assessment of the doctoral dissertation Turner had written, "The Character and Influence of the Indian Trade in Wisconsin," printed in 1891. See W. Stull Holt, review of *Early Writings*, in *Journal of Southern History*, V (August, 1939), 387-388.

were taken as the products of responsible and authoritative scholarship by men in positions to influence public opinion. Thus the editor of the *Atlantic Monthly* wrote to him from the East, "The newspapers here are at once taking up your article for discussion—very favorably." Turner quickly replied that he was sending the editor a copy of an editorial in the Chicago *Tribune* "giving a western version of my Atlantic paper." Numerous other contemporaries must have commented on it, for Turner later noted that he had collected copies of "reviews, letters, editorials on this article."[35]

Clearly, the frontier thesis has functioned as the most influential set of ideas yet presented in American historiography. By significantly influencing American thinking it has influenced American history. If my claim that it is best viewed as a myth rather than a thesis has merit, the observation seems warranted that historians ought constantly to remind themselves that making histories is responsible work.

---

35. Benson, *Turner and Beard,* pp. 88-89, n. 105. In that Note, I regretted my inability to locate the folder Turner referred to as containing the "copies." Ray Billington subsequently found it in the Turner Papers at the Huntington Library after they were opened to researchers in 1960. See his *America's Frontier Heritage,* p. 241, n. 41.

7 MIDDLE PERIOD HISTORIOGRAPHY: WHAT IS TO BE DONE?

JOHN W. Burgess prefaced the book that gave the "Middle Period" its name with this call to historiographic arms: "There is no more serious and delicate task in literature and morals than that of writing the history of the United States from 1816 to 1860."[1] Since 1897, when Burgess published his book, American historians have *acted* as though the validity of his manifesto were self-evident. In the first seven decades of the twentieth century, more scholarly man years probably have been devoted to "the history of the United States from 1816 to 1860" than to any other historiographic field of specialization, American or non-American.[2] How should we assess the results?

As the title suggests, the primary goal of this essay is to stimulate debate on general questions of what historians as a group should do in the future rather than on particular questions of what individual historians have done in the past. Wide variations exist in the quality of individual work, of course, and scholars such as Roy Nichols, Charles Sydnor and Paul Gates have made lasting contributions in their specialized fields. But this essay deals with what might be called the

---

1. John W. Burgess, *The Middle Period* (New York: Houghton Mifflin Company, 1897), p. vii.

"total scholarly product" and does not single out specific studies for praise or criticism. (A critique of two books is presented in Section V but only to illustrate the general argument.)

Has the value of the total scholarly product justified the social and intellectual resources expended upon Middle Period historiography? I do not think so. Why not? The latter question can mean two very different things: 1) How can I *justify* my evaluation? 2) How can I *explain* such low returns from so much hard work and thought?

The enormous number of historical studies that deal with the Middle Period have produced a great deal of varied information about what many Americans experienced, thought and felt from 1816 to 1860. But that information is best characterized as unsystematic and trivial, in my judgment, when viewed as the total product of a major field of scholarly specialization. By this I mean that: 1) the vast mass of information does not add up to *generalized knowledge;* 2) it has not significantly helped Americans (or any other people) to better enjoy and order either their lives or their societies. (No implication is intended that I believe that Middle Period historians as a group have produced uniquely unsystematic and trivial results; I speak only of the field that I know best.)

One example may be enough to support my unflattering assessment of Middle Period historiography. Just as more scholarly man years have probably been devoted to the Middle Period than to any other field of specialization, more scholarly man years have probably been devoted to "the coming of the Civil War" than to any other past event, American or non-American.[3] But specialists no more agree now on the "causes of

2. Five excellent bibliographical essays thoroughly cover the Middle Period. See George Dangerfield, *The Awakening of American Nationalism* (New York: Harper and Row, 1965), pp. 303-21; Edward Pessen, *Jacksonian America* (Homewood, Ill.: Dorsey Press, 1969), pp. 352-93; James G. Randall and David Donald, *Civil War and Reconstruction* (2nd ed.: Boston: D.C. Heath and Company, 1961), pp. 703-55; Charles E. Cauthen and Lewis P. Jones, "The Coming of the Civil War," in Arthur S. Link and Rembert W. Patrick, eds., *Writing Southern History* (Baton Rouge: Louisiana State University Press, 1965), pp. 224-48; David M. Potter, *The South and the Sectional Conflict* (Baton Rouge: Louisiana State University Press, 1968), pp. 87-150.

3. That estimate is impressionistic. Since it is not central to my argument, I have felt free to present it "without fear and without research."

the Civil War" than they did decades ago. Their explanations are no more credible now than they were then. Critically assessed, Civil War historiography exemplifies the model of the Buddhist wheel of fate: round and round it goes but it never gets anywhere.

To explain the relatively limited contributions of Middle Period historiography we might simply dismiss Middle Period historians as intellectual lightweights, hardworking but not terribly bright. But to do so would be to indulge in the "great man" theory of historiography and divert attention from basic weaknesses. In my judgment, it is not the men but the historiographic system within which they have had to work that is bad.

I. History-as-Actuality   and   History-as-Discipline

To begin a critique of the historiographic system, we need to distinguish sharply between the unity of history-as-actuality and the unity of history-as-discipline (to use Charles Beard's terms). As actuality, history can be regarded as "a seamless web." Undoubtedly, we distort reality when we abstract out of the total configuration of human behavior occurring in a reasonably delimited-time and place (for example, the Middle Period) some particular aspects of some particular phenomena for intensive study while deliberately ignoring other aspects and other phenomena. At some God-like level of observation, no doubt, history-as-actuality constitutes a unified set of phenomena. But it does not logically follow, however, that we can or should try to play God and study the human past as a single discipline.

Burgess set scholars an impossible task: "writing the history of the United States from 1816 go 1860," largely because he conceived of history as a single discipline—a misconception that, in my view, continues to plague us. My basic proposition is that if the diverse groups of scholars concerned with the human past continue to view history as a single discipline, they must seriously limit their capacity to achieve their different aims.

In my view, history-as-discipline is best conceived of as a *congeries of related disciplines* with radically different aims that require radically different methodologies, training programs and forms of scholarly organization and communication. Since the late nineteenth century, scholars have continuously debated the nature of the historical enterprise. But that debate has been conducted within the conceptual framework that views history as a single discipline and the usefulness of that framework has been taken for granted. Quotations from two works written two thousand years apart make the point. In Aristotle's *Poetics* we find this dictum:

> Poetry is more philosophical and weighty than history, for poetry speaks rather of the universal, history of the particular. By the universal I mean that such or such a kind of man will say or do such or such things from probability or necessity; that is the aim of poetry, adding proper names to characters. By the particular I mean what Alcibiades did, or what he suffered.[4]

In 1967, Professor Trygve Tholfsen in a thoughtful book on *Historical Thinking* reaffirmed Aristotle's dictum. Quoting with approval two statements distinguishing "history from the generalizing disciplines," Tholfsen asserted: "In emphasizing the historian's overriding interest in the particular, Huizinga and Bullock are echoing the convictions of the vast majority of their colleagues." Throughout his book he assumed that historians are united in their aims and used the definite article to refer to "the historian" as believing something or doing something, in effect, from "probability or necessity," as Aristotle would say.[5] Unless we bow down to definitional authoritarianism à la Aristotle, however, we need not assume that the study of the past must

---

4. As quoted in M. I. Finley, "Myth, Memory and History," *History and Theory*, IV (No. 3, 1965), 281.

5. Trygve R. Tholfsen, *Historical Thinking: An Introduction* (New York: Harper and Row, 1967), pp. 1-2 and *passim*. The same insistence that history must be a unitary discipline is seen in the following statement: "The historian usually consumes social science generalizations; he does not seek to produce such generalizations." See Robert Berkhofer, *A Behavioral Approach to Historical Analysis* (New York: Free Press, 1969), pp. 264-65. Mr. Berkhofer's book is highly illuminating and his erudition is impressive. But he offers neither logical nor empirical reasons to support the position that historians should not try to develop social science generalizations and function as social scientists. Some historians may not want to try to do that; others may. Who can deny either group the right to try to do what they want to do?

constitute a single, unified discipline restricted to the particularities of human existence. To challenge that assumption is the main aim of this essay. If we free ourselves from the intellectual tyranny it imposes upon us, we can better proceed to reorient and reorganize the historical *disciplines.*

One way to engage in productive discussions about the aims and functioning of the historical disciplines is to focus attention on four different questions:

1. What have historians in different countries (or societies) done in the *past?*
2. What are historians in different countries doing *now?*
3. What *can* historians do?
4. What *should* historians do?

The last two questions, of course, radically differ from each other. "What can historians do?" is a *descriptive* question. Scholars may argue about it. But their answers must essentially derive from empirical evidence about the types of questions they claim historians have been able to answer credibly. "What should historians do?" is a *prescriptive* question. Unlike answers to descriptive questions, answers to prescriptive questions must be based upon subjective preferences and must derive from value judgments; scientific procedures cannot resolve differences between competent specialists.

To my knowledge, no systematic attempt has ever been made to answer the four questions posed above.[6] Parts of one or another of them are discussed in a vast, ever-increasing literature. But nowhere are they effectively distinguished and disentangled from each other. As a result, they tend to be mixed up and answers to them tend to confuse different things. To try to answer the four questions systematically is beyond the scope of this essay; its more modest aim is to indicate that historiographic progress requires that we differentiate and disentangle them.

Aristotle claimed that *ancient poets* spoke of the universal while *ancient historians* spoke of the particular. Professor Tholfsen claimed tha the vast majority of *modern historians*, like their ancient predeces-

---

6. I have discussed those questions more fully in an essay, "On 'The Logic of Historical Narration,' " in Sidney Hook, ed., *Philosophy and History* (New York: New York University Press, 1963), pp. 32-42.

sors, speak of the particular. Suppose we grant their *descriptive* claims. Must we then also grant that, *by necessity rather than preference*, historians cannot and should not speak of the universal (i.e., develop general theories or propositions)? If we accept that conclusion, we must then conclude that Frederick Jackson Turner and Charles A. Beard, by common consent the two most influential American historians, were not historians.

In the 1899 version of Turner's celebrated "Frontier" essay, he emphasized that:

> By approaching American history from its Western side, as well as from its seaboard side, a fresh and stimulating view will be gained, and above all the sociological interpretation will be facilitated. The history of the United States finds its *chief claim to attention in its value as a field for the scientific study of social development* [emphasis added]. The spread of settled society into these continental wastes, and the free development of a democracy in relation to unoccupied lands constitute the peculiar features of our national life.

Henry Adams has well said:

> Should history ever become a true science, it must expect to establish its laws, not from the complicated story of European nationalities, but from the methodical evolution of a great democracy. North America was the most favorable field on the globe for the spread of a society so large, uniform, and isolated as to answer the purposes of science.[7]

Contrary to the dictum laid down by Aristotle and Tholfsen, Turner and Adams probably expressed the dominant view among leading American historians around the turn of the century, namely that historians not only *could* speak of the universal, their overriding aim *should* be to speak of it. In effect, they claimed that the American past provided the best possible conditions for viewing the human past as the raw material for a science of social development that used the method of *controlled investigation* to enable researchers to hold certain factors constant, vary other factors, observe the results, ascertain causal relationships, and generate credible theories of human behavior. For

7. *The Early Writings of Frederick Jackson Turner* (Madison: University of Wisconsin Press, 1938), p. 279.

example, Beard explicitly designed his study of the American Constitution to support an all-encompassing general theory of human behavior, "the theory of the economic interpretation of history [which] as stated by Professor Seligman seems as nearly as axiomatic as any proposition in social science can be."[8]

To be forced to conclude that Turner and Beard cannot be regarded as historians because history is not a generalizing discipline, illustrates the logical difficulties that stem from the illogical assumption that history must be a single discipline. History-as-discipline, I maintain, is best conceived of as a pluralistic set of related scholarly disciplines. We place ourselves in a better position to advance knowledge and the human condition when we focus attention on what should be done to advance the historical *disciplines* rather than on what should be done to advance *the* historical discipline.

II. Differentiating the Historical Disciplines

How can scholarly disciplines be differentiated to achieve some rational division of labor? Following Aristotle's lead, we can differentiate them according to 1) aims; 2) subject matter; 3) methodology. By aims (the most important criterion in this scheme), I mean the desired outcomes if a discipline achieves a high level of competence; by subject matter, the particular aspects of the empirical world subjected to inquiry; by methodology, "the study—the description, the evalua-

---

8. Charles A Beard, *An Economic Interpretation of the Constitution of the United States* (New York: Macmillan Company, 1913, paper ed. 1965), pp. 1-18, and 15 n. 1. The argument that controlled investigation represents the functional equivalent in the social sciences of the controlled experimentation characteristic of the physical sciences is effectively developed in Ernest Nagel, *The Structure of Science: Problems in the Logic of Scientific Explanation* (New York: Harcourt, Brace and World, 1961), pp. 447-59. In my judgment, Mr. Nagel's argument supports the conclusion that a genuinely scientific historiography is *indispensable* to the development of social science, a conclusion that social scientists used to accept and, I predict, increasingly will again come to accept in the not too distant future.

tion, and the justification of methods," as well as the methods themselves.[9]

What constitutes the subject matter of the historical disciplines? On this question, broad agreement exists. Their subject matter is the human past, i.e., the behavior (broadly defined) of human beings whom we cannot observe, experiment with, or question contemporaneously. (It seems unnecessary here to discuss such minor issues as the characterization of studies based primarily on retrospective interviews or past survey data.)

Not all past human behavior can be studied, nor are all studies of the human past necessarily "historical" in character. As M. I. Finley has cogently observed, simply to concern oneself with the human past does not mean that one is engaged in a historical enterprise. "The past is an intractable, incomprehensible mass of uncounted and uncountable data. It can be rendered intelligible only if some selection is made, around some focus or foci." Another useful criterion for the "historical" study of past human behavior is that it constitutes a chronological survey over "a long period of continuous time." To quote Finley again, "dates and a coherent dating scheme are as essential to history as exact measurement is to physics."[10]

If we accept those elementary criteria, we must develop some reasonable principles of selection to identify that miniscule proportion of past human behavior to which attention should be paid. As Aristotle emphasized, our principles of selection should logically be determined by our aims: 1) by what we want to know; 2) by what we want *to do* with what we know. Different aims, different principles of selection. Different principles of selection, different subject matters—and therefore different histories of the "same past," defined in broad terms of space and time. (The argument here is anti-relativist since the aims discussed are of the Aristotelian functional type rather than the Mannheimian subjective type.)

If scholars who concentrate on the Middle Period do so in order to achieve different aims, it follows that there cannot be one "true"

9. For an illuminating discussion of the concept of methodology, see Abraham Kaplan, *The Conduct of Inquiry* (San Francisco: Chandler Publishing Company, 1964), pp. 18-19, and *passim.*

10. Finley, in *History and Theory,* IV (No. 3, 1965), 283-85.

history of the period. To imagine as Burgess did under the spell of Hegelian metaphysics that such a thing could exist as the task of "writing *the* history [emphasis added] of the United States from 1816 to 1860" is to commit the logical sin of reification, that is, to convert the American past into a genuinely organic entity. In my judgment, it is a non-task to try to write its "political" or "economic" or "social" history. Such topical rubrics can help us to identify our subject matter only when we specify the kinds of questions we want to answer. And only when we have done that, can we then justify a decision to allocate the immense social and intellectual resources we need to study systematically and responsibly certain types of phenomena that we think occurred in the United States between 1816 and 1860, e.g., the disintegration of the political system, the democratization of the political system.

If the argument thus far is granted, we should be able to agree that there is not and cannot be any such thing as "the discipline of history." Instead, there are a congeries of related scholarly disciplines, all equally entitled to be described as historical in character. More precisely, there are a related set of disciplines whose practitioners primarily restrict their *research* to the human past and whose main sources of data are documents not written or compiled for the purposes to which they are put. But practitioners of the several historical disciplines have radically different aims. As a result, their studies will focus on different past phenomena, or different aspects of the same past phenomena, and will probably employ different methods to secure data and support claims.

All disciplines are man-made, of course, and are not found in nature. They are defined by what their practitioners want to do and have to do to achieve their aims. And no discipline is really a tight little island inhabited by a homogeneous tribe of researchers having few connections with members of other scholarly tribes. But the aims and subject matter and methods of economists are relatively similar, for example, compared to the aims and subject matter of historians. Except for their methods, which until recently have tended to be uniform, historians now constitute the most heterogeneous group of scholars organized in a single discipline. As a result, they suffer from the schizophrenia attendant upon trying to play radically different roles simultaneously and from the methodological deficiency of trying to use the same procedures to study radically different phenomena.[11] (The fallacious assumption that quotation from contemporary sources is a universally valid historical method is discussed in Section V below.)

If we differentiate the historical disciplines according to the aims of their practitioners, we can identify four main disciplines (or at least subdisciplines):

1. History as Literature or Entertainment ("entertainment" in Graham Greene's sense of the term, the human comedy). Everything that happens to human beings can be entertaining to other human beings. The human past, therefore, offers the widest and most fascinating variety of entertainment.

2. History as Identity. That is, history as the self-conscious study of selected aspects of the human past to answer the need of individuals to identify themselves with some enduring group whose existence defines and transcends their own.

3. History as Philosophy. The primary goal of this historical discipline is to help liberate men from parochial outlooks and give them the widest possible range of choice of "values to live by." In effect, it views the human past as a museum that displays the whole range of human conduct. It thereby aids men more freely and more consciously to develop a set of preferred social arrangements and value systems than they could if they were restricted to their own experience and social environment.

4. History as Social Science. In broad terms, this historical discipline focuses on past human behavior in order to contribute to the overall scientific study of human behavior, past and present. Its primary goal is not to provide specific advice for decision-makers in specific situations; instead, it is to help develop general laws of human behavior that can aid human beings to identify the alternative courses of action available to them in specified types of situations, as well as make rational choices among alternatives in order to best achieve desired outcomes.

Historians undoubtedly can play the roles demanded by the entertainment, identity, and philosophy functions, although I am

---

11. See my essay, "An Approach to the Scientific Study of Past Public Opinion," *Public Opinion Quarterly*, XXXIV (Winter, 1967), 526-29 [Reprinted in this volume, pp. 105-159.]

convinced that when those roles are separated, the general level of performance will be significantly raised. But can they function effectively as social scientists? That is, can scholars who specialize in historical studies significantly contribute to the development of general theories of human behavior useful to men trying to find solutions to the practical problems that confront them in their social existence?

Around the turn of the twentieth century, Burgess, Adams, Turner, Beard and the advocates of the "New History" tried to show that historians could effectively function as social scientists. They failed. But it does not logically follow, therefore, that attempts to develop social science history must always fail.

At present, the evidence permits only a Scots verdict: the case for social science history is neither proven nor disproven. Among other considerations that inhibit us from responsibly going beyond agnosticism, the four historical disciplines identified above have never been differentiated in practice; would-be social science historians, therefore, have never received the kind of specialized training needed to play that role successfully. One main proposition of this essay asserts that we cannot determine whether a genuinely scientific history is possible until we radically revise the undergraduate and graduate history curricula and train a "critical mass" of historians in the scientific style of analysis, i.e., explicit conceptualization, theory construction, model building, systematic comparison, standard criteria of measurement. Because such training is nowhere available (although winds of change can be detected in a few institutions), because the four roles have not been separated out effectively, the concept of *scientific history* has essentially been an honorific term devoid of real content. (Economic history has been changing rapidly and my observations are not intended to apply to that field of specialization.)

It may turn out that there indeed is some peculiar quality about the study of *past* human behavior that prevents scholars who specialize in it from functioning as social scientists (as that term is defined in this essay). But that proposition can only be established empirically, that is, after the appropriate conditions have been created to test its validity. For, as Ernest Nagel has brilliantly shown, "there appears to be no foundation for the contention that historical inquiry into the human past differs radically from the generalizing natural or social sciences, in respect to either the logical patterns of its explanations, or the logical structures of its concepts."[12]

This essay began with the observation that the value of the scholarly product of Middle Period historiography has failed to justify the social and intellectual resources expended upon it. My explanation of that failure is now clear, I trust, namely, that the study of past human behavior has been highly undifferentiated and poorly organized. Failure to differentiate and disentangle the different historical disciplines, failure to provide appropriate training and organization for each of them, have robbed historical studies of much of their potential contribution to human understanding and human welfare. Because non-historians increasingly have become convinced that history is too important to be left to historians, they increasingly have found themselves forced to try to do historical studies—a role for which *their* training is inadequate. In short, my argument is that the social sciences are now badly organized to maximize the contribution that the study of the human past might make to the development of general theories about human behavior.

What can be done to remedy the present situation? For one thing, we can recognize it. Having done so, we can then begin to debate ways of changing it. To stimulate such debates, it seems useful to show that important (identified below) phenomena that occurred during the Middle Period have been studied inadequately and that their study can be improved. Before trying to do so, however, some brief comments follow about the problem of historical periodization.

III. Was There Really a Middle Period?

Given the professionalization of scholarship in the late nineteenth century, specialization was natural. Given the nationalistic drives that strongly influenced the development of professional historical scholarship, given the nature and location of source materials, it was equally natural that the combined criteria of geography and chronology determined fields of specialization. Given the development of the

---

12. Nagel, *op. cit.,* p. 575.

nation-state as the unifying theme around which the study of the past was organized, it was also equally natural that political criteria determined historical periodization.

More than twenty years ago, Thomas C. Cochran devastatingly criticized the "presidential synthesis" that forced all studies of American history into the chronological framework of successive presidential administrations.[13] As he suggested, one way out of that intellectual straitjacket is to recognize that studies of different types of phenomena may require different systems of periodization (as regional scientists have recognized that different types of phenomena are most effectively studied by creating different systems of spatial differentiation). It then becomes clear that researchers, depending upon their aims and interests, need to *create* appropriate historical periods, rather than try to *discover* what might be called natural historical periods.

To observe that we need to free ourselves of the tyranny of fixed historical periods suitable for all studies is not to deny the utility of conceiving of a specified number of years in the history of a society (or societies) as possessing a certain unity. As Robert Berkhofer's illuminating discussion of the problem suggests, "Periodization [of the traditional kind] rests upon the belief that at a given duration of time a cluster of characteristics permeates many areas of life and supposedly relates diverse trends and events in a society."[14] That belief, of course, can be empirically tested, although no American historian (myself included) seems ever to have done so before bestowing a label upon a specified number of years (e.g., the Age of Jackson, the Age of Egalitarianism).

For Burgess, the unity of the years between 1816 and 1860 was determined by the growing hostility between Northerners and Southerners. In good Hegelian fashion, however, he viewed the Civil War as an inevitable event predictable from the general theory of progress that postulated material realization of man's spiritual right to personal liberty. Accordingly, his principles of selection were dictated by his general theory and he organized his book around the theme of the coming of the Civil War.[15] Turner shared some of Burgess'

---

13. Thomas C. Cochran, "The 'Presidential Synthesis' in American History," *American Historical Review*, LIII (July, 1948), 748-59.

14. Berkhofer, *op. cit.*, pp. 226-27.

15. For Burgess's "philosophy of history," see his *Middle Period*, pp. 242-46.

emphasis upon the growth of sectionalism after 1816 (although his thesis required a tripartite division of geographic consciousness). As suggested in the earlier quotation from his 1899 version of the "Frontier" essay, however, Turner mainly emphasized the democratization of American life that followed the "Rise of the New West." That emphasis, in turn, was largely derived from his uncritical acceptance of Achille Loria's antihistorical thesis that the American past provided a scientific laboratory to study the development of society because it recapitulated all human history.[16]

We need not accept Burgess's and Turner's theories and hypotheses to recognize the logic of their periodization schemes. In effect, they studied American history during the Middle Period (given Burgess's theory, a highly appropriate label) because they believed that it provided a particularly good test of their general theories of human behavior. Following their lead, relatively large numbers of historians have studied developments between 1816 and 1860 to explain the explosive disintegration of the American political system in 1861 and the democratization of American life. *For those purposes*, it does seem useful to treat the Middle Period as a chronological device that facilitates the fruitful study of important general phenomena, namely the violent disintegration of political systems and the democratization of societies. Despite the excellent raw material provided for such studies by American experience from 1816 to 1861, however, Middle Period historiography has made relatively little contribution to *generalized knowledge about those general phenomena.* That record can be improved if we develop a more sophisticated approach to social science history than Burgess and Turner had available to them, as I will now try to show concretely by turning to the problem of Civil War causation.

------

16. For Turner's views, see his *Rise of the New West* (New York: Collier Books, 1962), pp. 25-29; *The United States: 1830-1850* (New York, 1935, reprinted 1950), pp. 575-91. For Turner's dependence upon Loria, see my *Turner and Beard: American Historical Writing Reconsidered* (New York: Free Press, paper ed., 1965), pp. 21-35; and my essay, "The Historian as Mythmaker: Turner and the Closed Frontier," in David M. Ellis, ed., *The Frontier in American Development: Essays in Honor of Paul Wallace Gates* (Ithaca, N.Y.: Cornell University Press, 1969), pp. 3-19. [Reprinted in this volume, pp. 175-189.]

IV. A Scientific Approach to the Study of American Civil War Causation

The American Civil War is occasionally discussed as a particular instance of a general class of events, i.e., revolutions or internal wars. To my knowledge, however, it never has been *systematically studied* in that fashion. Critically examined, studies that focus on "the coming of the Civil War" essentially treat it as a unique and non-recurrent event; in Aristotle's terms, they speak of its particularity rather than its universality. Studied in that fashion, the Civil War cannot be credibly explained, any more than we can credibly explain the impact of "the frontier" on American development without making systematic comparative studies of "frontiers" in other societies. In my judgment, only when we conceive of the Civil War as one instance of a general class of events that have basic similarities, despite their "unique" characteristics—measured finely enough, of course, every human action is different from every other human action—only then will we systematically begin to develop a credible explanation of its occurrence. Put another way, to explain the Civil War credibly, we need to develop a credible general theory of separatist internal wars.

On a high level of generality and abstraction, the Civil War can be conceived of as one instance of sustained, large-scale collective violence or "war." On a somewhat lower level of generality, it can be conceived of as one instance of "internal war." In my judgment, however internal war ("attempts to change by violence, or threat of violence, a government's policies, rulers, or organization") is too inclusive a category to provide a useful theoretical and analytical framework for studies designed to develop a credible explanation of the Civil War.

In a widely acclaimed book, Barrington Moore has treated the American Civil War as belonging to the same class of events as the English and French Revolutions, i.e., as a social revolution. But to treat it in that fashion, I think, is to misclassify it and thereby seriously reduce the possibility of explaining it credibly. In contrast to Moore, I think it is best treated as a particular instance of separatist internal wars, a class of events significantly different from social revolutions, colonial-imperial revolutions, *coup d'etats*, etc.[17] By classifying the American Civil War as a separatist internal war, I view it as representing one instance of sustained, large-scale violent conflict between (or among) territorial culture groups (defined below) living in contiguous territory and bounded by a single political system.

To increase the number and widen the range of related cases, and thereby facilitate our developing a powerful general theory to help explain the Civil War, it is crucial to note that sustained territorial culture group conflicts do not invariably result in internal wars. Sometimes they endure for long periods of time and then diminsh without ever taking the form of large-scale violent conflict. Sometimes they continue unabated but internal war is avoided.

Once we view the Civil War as a large-scale instance of violent conflict between territorial culture groups, we can see, I think, that it has basic similarities to the separatist internal wars currently being fought, for example, in Nigeria and the Sudan. But we can then also see that it "belongs" to the same general class of events (or phenomena) now manifesting themselves in such diverse forms as French-Canadian separatism in Canada, Welsh and Scots nationalism in Great Britain, Fleming-Walloon tensions in Belgium, Russian-Ukrainian tensions in the Soviet Union, the multitude of territorial culture group conflicts in India, and great numbers of similar conflicts in past and present political systems. When we conceive of the Civil War in such terms, we take a long step towards achieving the historiographic goal of eventually explaining it credibly, as well as the policy goal of helping men to avoid or, if they prefer, bring about, separatist internal wars in particular and territorial culture group conflicts in general.

Studied by social scientists whose field of specialization is past human behavior, whose subfield is past political behavior, and whose research focuses on territorial culture conflicts, the American Civil War poses two broad types of question:

1. Under what conditions do territorial culture groups tend to engage in political conflicts that culminate in separatist internal wars? Put another way, what general theories or laws can be derived from systematic studies of past and present phenomena that can reasonably

17. The brief definition of "internal war" quoted in the text is from Harry Eckstein, ed., *Internal War* (New York: Free Press, 1964), p. 1. For Barrington Moore's treatment of the American Civil War, see his *Social Origins of Dictatorship and Democracy* (Boston: Beacon Press, 1966), pp. 111-55.

be assigned to the general category: conflicts between territorial culture groups (e.g., the 1861 American Civil War, the 1967 Nigerian civil war, the present French Canadian-British Canadian non-violent political and cultural conflicts).

2. In addition to helping us to pose and try to answer general theoretical questions, the American Civil War enables us to pose what can conveniently, if clumsily, be called a "direct policy question." How could the Civil War have been prevented, or its occurrence made less likely, by groups that wanted to prevent it, but who adopted policies that failed to achieve that goal? That is, prior to April 15, 1861, when Lincoln's proclamation calling the state militia into active service can be said to have begun the Civil War, which men and groups *could* have adopted policies that would have prevented its occurrence or significantly reduced the likelihood of its occurrence? To dismiss that contrary-to-fact conditional question on the ground that it is an "iffy" question seriously lessens the significance of our research. In real life, that is precisely the type of question men must answer, consciously or otherwise, when they choose one course of action rather than another. In effect, they must always calculate the net balance of the values they place upon certain outcomes, the resources available to them that can be used to satisfy their preferences, the costs incurred if they follow policy A rather than B, the likelihood that A rather than B will secure the outcome(s) they prefer at a price they are prepared to pay. Contrary-to-fact conditional questions about Civil War causation represent, therefore, essentially the same kind of questions that now confront, for example, Canadians, Indians, Britons, Belgians, Pakistanis, i.e., men now living in societies where separatist movements endanger the stability of the existing political system.

Because the way the historical disciplines have developed has prevented historians from effectively functioning as social scientists, because no comprehensive and systematic attempt has been made to study past instances of separatist internal wars and non-violent conflicts, no well-grounded body of theory now exists upon which decision-makers (broadly conceived) can draw to help them prevent (or speed) the secession of Quebec, reduce (or heighten) tensions between Walloons and Flemings, retard (or accelerate) the growth of Welsh and Scots nationalism, and the like. It can be argued, of course, that no such body of theory can ever be developed because 1) the task is beyond human competence; 2) human phenomena are too idiosyncratic to be explained by general laws applicable to Americans prior to 1861 and Nigerians prior to 1967. That argument can be made, but it cannot now be demonstrated. Until we try to do so, we will never know whether we can develop general theories to explain and thereby help to control the occurrence of separatist internal wars.

How can we go about trying to do so? A comprehensive programmatic statement, of course, is beyond the scope of this essay. Briefly, however, I think that priority must be given to problems of concept formation, theory building, and index construction.[18]

To test the possibility that we can develop a discipline or sub-discipline that might reasonably be called social science history, the concepts used in historical research must be explicitly identified and clearly defined. From the discussion above, it should be clear that the concept, *territorial culture group*, is central to my approach to Civil War causation. What does that term mean? To what empirical phenomena does it refer?

Three sets of characteristics can be said to identify territorial culture groups in a specified society (or country):

1. The members of a territorial culture group inhabit a common territory more or less clearly demarcated and made "visible" by some line (e.g. Mason-Dixon) or geographic feature that separates their "boundaries" from the "boundaries" of some other group(s).

2. In addition to geographic location, the members of a territorial culture group share some "visible" attribute(s) that differentiates them from members of other groups (e.g. linguistic, ethnic, religious, labor system, socioeconomic system).

3. The cultural patterns (as anthropologists define the term, the "ideational patterns") of a territorial culture group significantly differ

---

18. Historians interested in tackling those problems, and the problems of index construction emphasized in Section V below, will find it profitable to consult the section on "Concepts and Indices," in Paul F. Lazarsfeld and Morris Rosenberg, eds., *The Language of Social Research* (Glencoe, Ill.: Free Press, 1955), pp. 15-108; and Allan H. Barton and Paul F. Lazarsfeld, "Some Functions of Qualitative Analysis in Social Research," *Frankfurter Beiträge zur Soziologie,* BAND I (1955), 321-361, conveniently reprinted as "S-336," in the Bobbs-Merrill Reprint Series in the Social Sciences.

from those of other groups in some way(s) that its members strongly tend to value (e.g. beliefs about the morality and legitimacy of slavery as a labor and social system).

Concept clarification is a never-ending job. But the three sets of characteristics sketched above, I believe, suggest the main dimensions of the concept with sufficient clarity for researchers to begin to construct indicators and indices that validly measure the phenomena referred to by the concept of territorial culture group, i.e., measure the presence or absence of such groups, their strength, their cohesiveness, etc.

Having defined my key concept, it becomes possible to try to state a logically coherent general theory of separatist movements and internal wars. (The one offered below is best viewed as an attempt to focus attention on the problem rather than as a "definitive" solution to it.) The theory holds that:

The more strongly the members of different territorial culture groups value their own cultural patterns, the more strongly they perceive their group's cultural patterns to be competing for dominance with those of other groups, the greater the interaction between (or among) the members of different groups, the more centralized the political system and the more indivisible real and symbolic power within it (e.g. the strong American presidency created under Jackson), the greater the tendency for relatively weaker (e.g. economically, politically, ideologically) groups to develop separatist movements that propose secession from the existing political system (e.g. pre-1861 Southern secessionists, contemporary French Canadian and East Pakistani and Welsh nationalists.)

For our present purposes, it is immaterial whether that general theory of separatist internal wars is valid, or whether, if valid, it specifically applies to the American Civil War. The point is that we need to develop and test general theories of that type if we hope eventually to solve the problem of Civil War causation. In my judgment, that task now constitutes one of the main tasks of Middle Period historians. More precisely, developing and testing theories of that type now represents one of the *main opportunities provided* by the study of American experience from 1816 to 1861.

V. The Democratization of American Life

To further support the argument that historians can significantly improve the way they study important general phenomena and thereby contribute to generalized knowledge, I now turn to the other main theme of Middle Period historiography, the democratization of American life. As Edward Pessen has recently shown in a valuable review essay, that theme commands increasing attention.[19] And it seems safe to predict that Mr. Pessen's own stimulating book-length synthesis of life in what he resignedly calls "Jacksonian America" will heighten interest even further and inspire numerous studies.

Mr. Pessen recognizes that Arthur Schlesinger, Jr., did a disservice to historical scholarship when he reinforced belief in the cult of personality and labeled an era as "the Age of Jackson." But Mr. Pessen not only pays his disrespects to that anti-intellectual cult, he does the same to the view that the second quarter of the nineteenth century can usefully be regarded as the "Era of the Common Man" or the "Age of Egalitarianism" (my own contribution to the battle of the historiographic labels).[20]

"Whatever it might have been," Mr. Pessen observes, "the era named after Andrew Jackson was neither an age of egalitarianism nor of the common man."[21] As he reads the historical record, the American political system did not become more democratic during the period I labeled the "Age of Egalitarianism."[22] In effect, if not precisely in those words, he dismisses the impact of *legal* changes in suffrage and officeholding requirements and in the electoral and governmental systems, as well as the impact of *extralegal* changes responsible for unprecedentedly high rates of participation by eligible voters in elections and intense general interest in politics—changes emphasized by the historians with whose claims he disagrees. In one place, Mr. Pessen says he does not accept the contemporary charge made by "many of the nation's working men [who] believed American to be a class

19. Pessen, *op. cit.*, pp. 352-93.
20. *Ibid.*, pp. 57-58, 347-51, 384-86.
21. *Ibid.*, p. 58.
22. Lee Benson, *The Concept of Jacksonian Democracy: New York as a Test Case* (New York: Atheneum Publishers, 1964 paper ed.), p. 336.

society dominated by a powerful few."[23] Yet his own formulations add up to a position not markedly different from the "radical" labor leaders whose views he studied closely in his doctoral dissertation.

"While extant evidence proves nothing so extreme [as the working men's charges]," Mr. Pessen observes, "it does appear to show that wealthy men commanded an inordinate political influence over American society." What are we to understand, however, by the term "inordinate"? From his text, it appears that that term connotes a distribution of political power very similar to that described by the "working men." As he reads "many excellent" historiographic studies of the past 20 years, they

> . . . tell a tale of major parties during the Jacksonian era, which, for all the difference in their political rhetoric, were more like than unlike, not least in the extent to which their basic structures and policymaking apparatus were controlled by unusually wealthy men.

> How much power could the common man exercise when there was little real choice open to him by the parties that counted? In the states, small groups of insiders *had a tight control over nominations and policymaking* [emphasis added], with popular influence more nominal than real. . . . Wealth exerted power most directly on the local level.[24]

And when Mr. Pessen came to summarize his conclusions, he again emphasized that a relatively small socioeconomic ruling elite controlled the American political system:

> Political authority belonged not to . . . [the common man] but to the uncommon men who typically controlled the major parties at every level. It goes without saying that unusual men will emerge as leaders, even in the most democratic society conceivable. The era's political leaders were distinctive, however, not only in their ability but also in the possession of status and wealth that were unrepresentative of the mass of men. The seats of power in society and the economy were also filled by men whose origin and outlook were not plebeian.[25]

The last sentence quoted above reflects Mr. Pessen's conviction that

23. Pessen, *op. cit.*, pp. 55-56.
24. *Ibid.*, pp. 55-56.
25. *Ibid.*, p. 348.

we falsify history if we claim that any significant degree of democratization occurred after 1825 in the American political, economic, social, and cultural sub-systems. "The Jacksonian era witnessed no breakdown of a class society in America. *If anything, class lines hardened, distinctions widened, tensions increased* [emphasis added]."[26] A lengthy quotation from his "conclusions" underscores the unqualified character of his thesis:

> The era's egalitarianism seems also to have been more apparent than real. American farmers and working men *were* better off than their European counterparts. Their material condition was superior, as were their opportunities, their status, and their influence. Yet this remained a class society. The small circles that dominated the life [*sic*] in the great cities of the East as well as the new towns of the West, lived lives of relative opulence, while socially during the Jacksonian era they became, if anything, more insulated against intrusion by the lower orders. Social lines were drawn even tighter in the slave states. For all the era's egalitarian reputation, evidence is lacking that movement up the social ladder was any more commonplace than it was in subsequent periods of American life; eras whose reputations for social fluidity have been largely deflated by modern empirical studies that characteristically reveal that the race was to the well born.[27]

I trust that the quotations above are in context. If I have not misread him, Mr. Pessen is convinced that the available data entitled him to dismiss the now dominant historiographic view that American society (broadly conceived) became significantly *more democratic* during the Middle Period. If anything, according to him, it became less democratic—at least in some major respects.

Because I wish to discuss a general historiographic tendency rather than particular historical studies, it also seems useful to summarize the thesis Douglas T. Miller recently advanced in a monograph used by Mr. Pessen. Unlike Mr. Pessen who wrote a synthesis based primarily upon secondary works, Mr. Miller wrote a monograph whose title suggests its

---

26. *Ibid.*, p. 57.
27. *Ibid.*, pp. 348-49.

subject matter and thesis, *Jacksonian Aristocracy: Class and Democracy in New York: 1830-1860.*[28] The jacket of his book conveniently summarizes his thesis:

> The period from Andrew Jackson's presidency to the Civil War has traditionally been considered the age of democracy triumphant in the United States. This book sharply contradicts that assumption, contending that while democracy advanced substantially in the political sense, social and economic distinctions became, if anything, more marked. Powerful forces, especially in the economic field, were working toward the stratification of society. . . .
>
> This book is a significant commentary on the effects of economic transformation on American life, and shows that these changes began earlier than previously assumed. Although the work concentrates on New York [state and city] for its data and examples, the findings clearly have much broader implications. The study also holds lessons for today since many new nations are just now undergoing *the same kind of economic development and social dislocation* [emphasis added].

According to Mr. Miller's statement of his aims, his book should be assessed as "social science history." Described as a substantive case study designed to advance theoretical knowledge about the complex interrelationships of political, economic and social phenomena, it aims to help men learn "lessons for today." That is, it aims to contribute to generalized knowledge useful to men now grappling with difficult problems of social existence. An admirable goal. But did Mr. Miller achieve it? More significantly, given the present development of American historiography, could Mr. Miller achieve it? No. Why not? His personal qualifications aside, in my judgment, he could not have achieved his goal because his reach exceeded the present grasp of American historians.

In citing the works of Messrs. Pessen and Miller, my primary aim is not to focus attention on the question of whether their claims ultimately will be demonstrated to be valid or invalid, but is to stimulate historians to consider whether we now are in a position

---

28. The book was published in 1967 by Oxford University Press. The quotation below is from the book jacket; I assume Mr. Miller wrote the statement quoted.

responsibly either to accept or reject their claims. If it turns out that we are not, we then will confront the problem of what to do to change that situation.

In my judgment, the data and methodology now available do not permit us to assess, *with any significant degree of confidence*, the *types* of claims Pessen and Miller make about the democratization of life during the Middle Period. Their books illustrate two of the basic weaknesses of Middle Period historiography, namely, the longstanding failure of historians to devote attention to concept formation and index construction (or measurement procedures). More specifically, historians (myself included) have tried to determine whether American society became significantly more democratic between 1816 and 1860 without systematically defining such key concepts as *political power, political elites, social stratification, social mobility, class society,* and the like. In my judgment, it cannot be done. If we fail to define our concepts and do not explicitly identify the phenomena to which they refer, we cannot develop systematic procedures that validly and reliably measure the phenomena referred to in our claims. Specific examples best support that argument.

Mr. Miller challenges the dominant view that democracy "triumphed" in the early nineteenth century. But he concedes that it "advanced substantially in the political sense."[29] Mr. Pessen, a more radical revisionist, does not concede that much. Like their predecessors, however (alas, myself again included), neither recognized that their claims logically compelled them to define the concept *democratic political system.* If they did not, how could they find out whether the American political system was significantly less (or more) democratic in 1845 or 1860 than it had been, for example, in 1800 or 1816?

In more general terms, my argument takes this form: Until historians stop dodging the problem of explicit conceptualization and clearly specify what they mean by a democratic political system, they cannot recognize one when they see it, they cannot develop the procedures needed to determine whether a political system is becoming significantly more (or less) democratic, they cannot make any systematic and responsible comparisons over time, or place, or both.

---

29. Miller, *Jacksonian Aristocracy,* vii-viii, 11-13.

Given the present state of historiography, we can readily understand why Pessen and Miller essentially ignored the problems of concept formation and index construction. By criticizing their work, therefore, I mean nothing personal. On the contrary, my purpose in doing so is to convince historians of the Middle Period that we can no longer avoid tackling the conceptual and methodological problems inherent in any study of the democratic (or nondemocratic) character of the American political system. To speed that process—not least of all by provoking criticism—I sketch some of my own ideas about what the concept "democratic political system" should be taken to mean.

Before we can agree on a definition of a *democratic political system*—or if we cannot agree, at least know what we each mean by the term—we must agree on (or know) what we mean by a *political system.* The latter term, of course, has been defined in a variety of ways. Since all concepts are arbitrary, our present purposes can be served by a definition worked out in my graduate seminar.[30]

A political system is the relatively persistent set of patterned interactions that result in *authoritative decisions* for a specified body politic or society. A society consists of all the inhabitants of a specified territory. Authoritative decisions are made only by those organizations of a society that legitimately control the use of physical force (although they can delegate it to other organizations). Thus the American political system is the set of patterned interactions that result in governmental decisions on all levels (i.e., national, state, county, local) applicable to the inhabitants of the territory under the jurisdiction of specified governmental entities.

As I conceive it, *authoritative decisions* form the core of the concept, political system. Given that definition, political power can then be defined as follows:

Political power is the relative impact that political actors exert upon the quality of life of the members of a society during a specified time period, *to the extent that the quality of their lives is determined by the*

---

30. For the past few years, my graduate seminar has concentrated on the problem of identifying the American political elite during the Middle Period. The definitions presented in the text represent a joint effort and have benefitted from discussions involving, among other students, Richard Coronitis, Robert Cort, Gerald Ginsburg, James Hannan, and Robert Widdop.

authoritative decisions (positive and negative) made in that society.
Relative impact has two dimensions: 1) the relative importance of
specified decisions; 2) the relative importance of actors in specified
decisions. The relative power of actors is, therefore, some combination
of the two dimensions.

From the definitions sketched above, a democratic political system
consists of two dimensions: 1) the *distribution* of political power in a
society; 2) the *philosophy* (or ideology) governing the distribution of
political power in a society. (Strictly speaking, the second dimension is
redundant. I include it to emphasize my assumption that a democratic
political ideology is a necessary—but not sufficient—condition of a
democratic political system.)

In a perfectly democratic political system, all competent adults
(defined by universalistic criteria, e.g. age) are full citizens and have
equal power. That is, all adults "of sound mind" are legally entitled to
play all roles in the political system and actively participate in the
process of authoritative decisionmaking. At any particular time, citizens
vary in the roles they play and in the degree and type of political power
they can exercise. But during their lifetimes, on balance, all the
members of a generation group exercise an equal amount of power in
determining the authoritative decisions made in the society.

Given that definition, no *perfectly* democratic political system has
ever existed (or probably ever could exist in a large, complex society).
But the definition provides us with some standard against which we
can, in principle, develop methods to measure the *relatively* democratic
character of a specified political system over time, or compare the
political systems of different societies, or compare the political systems
of different states (e.g. New York, South Carolina) in the same society.
But such methods obviously are much harder to develop for federal
political systems (e.g. the United States) than for unitary political
systems (e.g. France).

Because the ideology governing participation can vary from state to
state (and even locality to locality), measuring the democratic character
of the American political ideology over time and place poses many
difficulties. But those difficulties are relatively slight compared with the
difficulties inherent in attempts to measure the distribution of political
power in the United States. Because jurisdiction is widely dispersed and

a tremendous number of governmental entities make authoritative decisions, because the relative importance of the decisions made by different governmental entities (and branches of the same entity, e.g., the President, Congress) can vary enormously, it is very difficult to develop systematic methods to measure the relative distribution of political power in the United States. Certainly no one has yet done so for the Middle Period. It follows, therefore, that neither Mr. Miller nor Mr. Pessen could make responsible claims about whether the American political system did or did not become significantly more democratic during the Middle Period.

Miller points to changes in suffrage and officeholding requirements after 1816, as well as the sharply increased participation of the masses in electoral politics, as clear evidence of a significant redistribution of political power. Pessen, in effect, dismisses those changes as valid indicators of democratization on the ground that the "common man" could actually exercise "little real choice" because the "basic structures and policymaking apparatus [of the parties that counted] were controlled by unusually wealthy men" and because "small groups of insiders had a tight control over [party] nominations and [governmental] policymaking. . . ."

Pessen's objections are well taken. But his own claims are not well grounded. I agree that neither the legal right to participate and hold office nor the increased participation of the masses in politics *necessarily* gave the "common men," in 1845, let us say, a significantly greater share of power than their counterparts had in 1800 or 1825. It is even *conceivable*, for example, that the development of highly organized parties and the development of intense party loyalties concentrated political power more tightly in a small elite in 1845 than in 1800. That development is conceivable. But it must be demonstrated; we cannot simply assert it.

Critically examined, no basis exists for Mr. Pessen's claim that the common men in 1845 *could not* have collectively possessed a greater share of the total political power available in the system than their counterparts in earlier decades because the Jacksonian era's political leaders "were unrepresentative of the mass of men" in their "possession of status and wealth." In making that claim, Mr. Pessen confused two different things, the *power* of political leaders and their *social attributes.*

Suppose we use the term *political elite* to designate those individuals in a society who possess relatively much greater political power than other individuals. (Preliminary work to date by my graduate students suggests that it is relatively easy to establish a cut-off point to separate the elite from the nonelite.) In that sense, a political elite has always existed in the United States. But in evaluating the relatively democratic character of the American political system over time and place, the critical questions do not concern the *social composition* of the political elite; they concern the proportion of power held by the political elite, compared to other political strata. In effect, Mr. Pessen assumed: 1) relatively little change occurred in the social composition of the occupants of important governmental and party offices between, 1825 and 1845, or 1825 and 1860 (to lengthen the time span); 2) *therefore*, relatively little change occurred in the proportion of power held by the political elite. A full discussion of the weaknesses inherent in those assumptions would require a lengthy essay. Some brief comments, however, make the main point.

To begin with, no one has yet made the studies needed to justify Pessen's implicit claim that the social composition of governmental and party officeholders did not significantly change during the Middle Period, particularly as compared with earlier periods. He may be right, he may be wrong. (I think he is wrong.) The available data do not permit us to make responsible claims. More significantly, however, it does not logically follow that even if the social attributes of officeholders had remained unchanged, then the proportion of political power they (and their "class") held must have remained essentially unchanged. Pessen *assumed* what he must *demonstrate*, namely, that legal and extralegal changes in the functioning of the American political system during the Middle Period did not significantly redistribute political power in the United States and result in its greater democratization. That assumption is incorrect, in my opinion.

When the necessary conceptual and methodological advances have been made and the necessary substantive studies have been completed, I think we will find that the political system did become significantly more democratic during the Middle Period. It is important to emphasize, however, that a more democratic political system does not necessarily function more effectively in the interests of the "common man." I think that Pessen underestimated the extent to which the masses, on balance, benefitted from the operations of government during the Middle Period (e.g., canals, public schools), particularly as compared to earlier periods. But that is not the point. Among other considerations, because the masses did not constitute a homogeneous class unified around a common program, we cannot reasonably estimate their power simply by estimating the benefits to them of government operations; disunity may have prevented them from aggregating their resources to bring about government actions favorable to them.

In my opinion, no one can now either confirm or disconfirm the hypothesis that the American political system became significantly more democratic during the Middle Period. Having avoided the relevant problems of concept formation and index construction, we have been unable to make the empirical studies needed to reconstruct the distribution of political power in the United States over time. But I think that we can lend some support to the hypothesis by applying some theoretical propositions about the relationships between ideology and behavior.

As noted previously, I define the concept "democratic political system" to include the ideology governing the distribution of political power in a society. Judged by rigorous standards, we cannot now make firm claims about whether American political ideology became significantly more democratic between 1825 and 1850 (or 1816 and 1860). But the available impressionistic evidence all seems to point in a direction that justifies characterizing the second quarter of the nineteenth century as the "Age of Egalitarianism".

As a caption for the period, the "Age of Egalitarianism" refers to its *central ideological tendency*. The caption did not connote and does not connote—at any rate, it *should not* connote—that by 1850 or 1860 a roughly equal distribution of political power existed among American adult white males (to say nothing of all adults). To quote myself, "In Karl Mannheim's phrase, the caption expresses 'the ideology of an age.' "[31] But I assume that significant reciprocal relationships tend to exist between the value system and the behavior patterns of a society. If that theoretical assumption is granted, it follows that the "triumph" of democratic ideology after 1816 should have both caused and reflected a significantly more democratic distribution of political

---

31. Benson, *Jacksonian Democracy*, p. 336.

power. That theoretical conclusion supports, but obviously cannot confirm, the post-1815 increased democratization hypothesis. The validity of the hypothesis remains to be tested. To test it, a series of empirical studies are needed and, in my opinion, they should be given high priority by historians interested in the opportunities the Middle Period provides for the advancement of generalized knowledge about political behavior.

The other claims Miller and Pessen made about the democratization of American life during the Middle Period also warrant a Scots verdict. Neither seem fully to have considered the implications for historical studies of the difficult conceptual and methodological problems identified by social scientists who have systematically studied "social stratification."[32] Had they done so, their claims might not have been stated so confidently.

Had Miller fully considered the implications of the problems discussed in the scholarly literature, for example, he might not have assumed—as he did—that claims about such multidimensional collective phenomena as the shape of the American stratification system over time and its rates of social mobility (up *and* down) can responsibly be supported by following historiographic tradition and presenting haphazard quotations from a haphazard sample of contemporary observers. As Pessen observed in one place, "Contemporaries, of course, thought a variety of things, their viewpoints about class running the gamut from denial of its existence to enthusiastic recognition of class division. A few would maintain, even try to widen, the existing cleaveage."[33]

According to Miller, "New York society [broadly conceived] was probably less democratic in Jackson's time than in Washington's."[34] We find that claim in the concluding paragraph of a chapter that took

---

32. For a comprehensive survey of the literature, see Reinhard Bendix and Seymour Martin Lipset, eds., *Class, Status, and Power: Social Stratification in Comparative Perspective* (2nd ed.; New York: Free Press, 1966). For a specific discussion of the problems that confront historians who study social stratification, see Bernard and Elinor Barber, eds., *European Social Class: Stability and Change* (New York: Macmillan Company, 1965), pp. 1-12, and *passim.*

33. Pessen, *op. cit.,* pp. 54.

34. Miller, *op. cit.,* pp. 80.

as its epigraph this quotation from an 1836 book on *The Laws of Etiquette:*

> [In America] There is perfect freedom of political privilege, all are the same upon hustings, or at a political meeting; but this equality does not extend to the drawing-room. None are excluded from the highest councils of the nation, but it does not follow that all can enter into the highest ranks of society. In point of fact, we think that there is more exclusiveness in the society of this country, than there is in that even of England—far more than there is in France.[35]

How much weight should those contemporary observations be given if we wish to compare the shape and rigidity of the American stratification system in 1790 and 1840? I think they deserve no weight at all and should not be used for the purposes to which Miller put them. Such differences can only be resolved when and if historians develop the methods needed to make the extraordinarily complex intersocietal and intrasocietal comparisons casually tossed off by the author of *The Laws of Etiquette.*

That generations of historians have resorted to what might be called "proof by haphazard quotation" does not make the procedure valid or reliable; it only makes it traditional. So much the worse for historiographic tradition. If we wish to have our research taken seriously, we will have to disabuse ourselves of the notion that we can confirm or disconfirm claims about complex social phenomena by haphazardly culling quotations from haphazard assortments of contemporary sources.

If we shift attention to conceptual problems, Pessen's book offers a convenient example of the problems created when similar words are used to refer to different phenomena. Historians who have claimed that American society became significantly more democratic between 1816 and 1860 have assumed that, among other things, the volume and rate of upward *social mobility*, on balance, significantly increased in that period, as compared with earlier periods. Pessen tends not to use the standard term, "social mobility," to refer to movement from one social stratum to another. Instead, he uses "social fluidity" and "movement up the social ladder." *But as he uses them, those terms mean something*

---

35. *Ibid.*, p. 56.

very different from what "social mobility" is generally understood to mean.

To Pessen, "social fluidity" means one-step upward movement from the lower classes of a society into the most favored class. The volume of social fluidity depends, therefore, solely upon "the relative ease of access [from the lower] to the most favored class." If we were to accept his definition, for a significant degree of social fluidity to have occurred during the Middle Period, we would have to show that in 1850 or 1860 a "substantial minority of the rich . . . [had been] born poor. . . ."[36]

When Pessen summarizes his conclusions, to repeat an earlier quotation, he observes that:

> . . . evidence is lacking that movement up the social ladder was any more commonplace than it was in subsequent periods of American life; eras whose reputations for social fluidity have been largely deflated by modern empirical studies that characteristically reveal that the race was to the well born.[37]

The studies referred to, it is critical to note, primarily focused on movement into the top elite; they did not try to measure the total amount and rate of *social mobility* in American society.[38]

If we are familiar with the relevant sociological literature, we can appreciate how significantly Pessen's conception of "social fluidity" differs from what is generally understood by "social mobility" and *how heavily his revisionist claims depend upon his particular definition.* For what he means by "social fluidity" is actually a special type of "movement up the social ladder," namely, one form of that rare type of social mobility that some sociologists refer to as "mobility of large degree."

As a result, Pessen's specialized terminology forfeits for him the right to have his claims considered by researchers who accept the standard definition that upward social mobility refers to the net balance of all movement between strata classified in occupational or income or wealth or status terms.

Pessen's specialized terminology, however, should not obscure his

---

36. Pessen, *op. cit.*, pp. 51-52.
37. *Ibid.*, pp. 348-49.
38. *Ibid.*, p. 359.

significant contribution to Middle Period historiography. His claims can easily be reformulated to assert *that we now lack evidence* that upward social mobility, on balance, significantly increased during the Middle Period and that the American economic and social and cultural systems then became significantly more "egalitarian." Reformulated in that fashion, I accept his claims—but only when they are reformulated.

I do not think it useful to conceive of the concept "egalitarian society" as unidimensional, nor do I think that most historians have thought of it in such terms. Instead, it seems useful to conceive of the concept as consisting of four different, although related, dimensions: 1) equality as a *legal* condition; 2) equality as a *value* governing the way men ought to regard other men; 3) equality as an *opportunity* to obtain the "impersonal" things valued in the society (i.e., wealth, status, power, culture, not personal beauty or artistic talent); 4) equality as a *distributional condition* (i.e., a roughly equal distribution among generational peers of the impersonal things valued in the society).

If we conceive of an egalitarian society in such multidimensional terms, I think that we will eventually find that American society did become significantly more egalitarian during the Middle Period than it had been in earlier periods. (That statement, of course, is couched in comparative terms; it should not be caricatured as denying that wide and intensely felt and experienced group differences continued to exist after 1816.) Apart from other considerations, my hypothesis again derives from theoretical assumptions about the reciprocal relationships between ideology and behavior. Although we badly need systematic studies before we are entitled to make confident claims, it seems reasonably clear that the shift towards a more egalitarian ideology after 1816 was not restricted to the political system. Pessen should agree with that hypothesis for, in discussing the American value system, he asserts:

> High on the American's scale of values was his egalitarian belief that one man—particularly an American—*was as good as any other, certainly that he should be treated like any other* [emphasis added].[39]

By 1860, I believe, the American *value system* had become relatively

---

39. *Ibid.,* p. 27.

far more egalitarian than it had been in the "deferential society" of 1790. Given that ideological "revolution," the tremendous expansion of the American economy after 1816, the great increase in the settled geographic area and the high rate of *physical mobility*, I hypothesize that by 1860 changes in the "opportunity structure"[40] had produced a relatively more egalitarian society than had existed in 1790 (or 1816). Pessen rejects that hypothesis.

"The Jacksonian era," he claims, "witnessed no breakdown of a class society in America. If anything, class lines hardened, distinctions widened, tensions increased." But claims about the *rigidity* of social class lines, the *distance* between social classes, the intensity of social class *tensions*, refer to different types of phenomena. In relative terms, I think that class lines "softened" and "narrowed" after 1816 but that class "tensions increased." And not unreasonably. Social researchers no longer are locked into the dogmatic assumption that tensions increase *only when conditions and opportunities decline;* we also assume that improved conditions and opportunities can (they need not invariably do so) bring "rising expectations" and increasing tensions. (To state the conditions under which "improvement" does, and does not, increase tension is a major theoretical job that falls into the "what is to be done" category.)

Conclusion

Having provided specific examples to clarify the basic argument of this essay, I can now summarize it as follows:

If we wish to make significant progress, we need to revolutionize our approach to Middle Period historiography. That is, instead of dispersing scarce scholarly resources on substantive studies only casually related to each other, we should undertake substantive studies primarily to solve basic conceptual and methodological problems of the kind suggested in the preceding section and theoretical problems of the kind suggested in the section on Civil War causation. We can best bring about that

---

40. For a succinct discussion of changes over time in social mobility and the "opportunity–structure" of societies, see Barber and Barber, *European Social Class,* pp. 4-7.

historiographic revolution, I believe, if we conceive of history as a congeries of related disciplines. When we do that, we can seriously begin the difficult job of reorganizing the historical disciplines so that their practitioners can better achieve their different aims. And having done that, I think that we will significantly increase the contributions to human knowledge and human welfare that we make when we study the human past.

EXPLANATIONS of AMERICAN CIVIL WAR CAUSATION: A CRITICAL ASSESSMENT and a MODEST PROPOSAL to REORIENT and REORGANIZE the SOCIAL SCIENCES

8

THE world now holds more promise and more threat than mankind has ever experienced.[1] To develop valid general theories that might help human beings solve the awesome problems of existence constitutes the primary goal of social scientists.[2] To achieve that goal, to respond

1. This essay represents a consolidation and drastic revision of papers presented at the 1968 convention of the Southern Historical Association and the 1971 convention of the Organization of American Historians. It has benefitted from severe and penetrating criticisms of those papers made by so many friends, and other critics, that space precludes listing them all. I wish to acknowledge, however, that the research upon which it is based has been supported by grants from the American Philosophical Society, the Social Science Research Council, and the American Council of Learned Societies.
2. "I think that the only real life justification of the study of politics is to help people go about the task of changing political systems a little more intelligently. In other words, if political science is to be applied, obviously it is to be applied in order to change things, make them in some way or other, according to some notion or other, better than they have been." Comments of Dankwart Rustow in Lewis J. Edinger, ed., "Conference on Theory and Method in Comparative Elite Analysis . . . 1969" (Columbia University: Mimeo, 1969), p. 13.

effectively to the most important intellectual challenge of the last third of the twentieth century, social scientists must radically reorient and reorganize their disciplines.

Contrary to self-styled radical intellectuals who decry reason and exalt passion (thereby revealing that they are neither radical nor intellectual), the *main* obstacles to further progress in the social sciences are not the pressures exerted by "The Establishment" nor the self-corruption of scholars grown fat and complacent. The main obstacles, in my judgment, are the increasingly dysfunctional effects that have accompanied and been produced by the unplanned, uncontrolled explosion of "Little Social Science" into "Big Social Science."[3]

Can those obstacles be overcome? I think they can. But I think that they can only *after* scholars generally—and clearly—recognize that the institutional development of social science since 1900 has produced an increasingly dysfunctional system for the production of scientific knowledge about human behavior. What men have done unwittingly, they can undo wittingly. To do so, however, they must not only recognize what needs to be done and how best to do it: they must recognize and be prepared to pay the psychological costs required to break free from habitual adherence to old institutions and routines— institutions and routines once progressive and liberating but now ritualistic and oppressive. Speeding that process—not least of all by stimulating debate and provoking criticism—is the primary goal of this essay.

Thus far, my basic proposition has been stated in general and abstract terms. To support that proposition specifically and empirically, I have adopted a two-fold strategy: 1) present a critical assessment of explanations of American Civil War causation; 2) then sketch a proposal designed to increase the chances that social scientists eventually will develop credible theories to explain the general class of phenomena of which the Civil War represents one instance.

Among other considerations, that strategy seems reasonable to me because I am convinced that:

1. Although no other event has probably had as many man—years

---

3. Here I apply the line of argument developed in Derek J. de Solla Price, *Little Science, Big Science* (New York: Columbia University Press, 1963).

devoted to its study as the Civil War, scholars have failed to make significant progress in their attempts to explain its occurrence.

2. Failure to make significant progress in studies of Civil War causation should not be attributed to the deficiencies of individuals but to the deficiencies of the established historiographic system in particular and the established social science system in general. (By the historiographic and social science systems, I mean the overall social and cultural enterprises that now recruit, train, socialize, organize, guide, support and reward scholars who study past or present human behavior.)

3. Especially since World War II, many social scientists trained in other disciplines than history have been intensely interested in developing good general theories of *internal war*, a term used to designate the general class of phenomena of which the Civil War is one instance. (That term will be defined in a later section.) Like the scholars who have studied Civil War causation, however, they have made relatively little progress.

4. The absence of a genuinely scientific historiography—as distinct from a nominally scientific historiography—constitutes a major obstacle to the further development of social science.[4] Stated positively rather than negatively, as many nonhistorians are again coming to recognize, the development of scientific historiography is indispensable to the development of fruitful general theories about social stability and social change.

5. The proposal sketched in the concluding section of this essay specifically focuses on the problem of reorienting and reorganizing the study of internal wars, past and present. But it derives from a

---

4. The argument here, as readers who have read the essays in sequence will recognize, has been stated earlier; see pp. 196-201 above. It seems useful to observe, however, that the historical evolution of the "discipline" of history helps us to understand why it consists of a curious hodgepodge of elements that are incongruous at best and antithetical at worst. In my judgment, one of the main obstacles to the development of a genuinely scientific historiography has been the widespread acceptance of the nineteenth-century notion that scientific method is what astronomers or physicists do. That conception seems to me to have inhibited historians from going beyond the elementary notion that "scientific history" essentially consists of the authentication of documents and the appraisal of eyewitness testimony, modelled along the lines of Biblical criticism and early nineteenth-century philology.

perspective generally applicable to the problem of reorienting and reorganizing the social sciences. Put another way, I believe that an economical, effective way to stimulate debate and action on that general problem is to advance a proposal designed to stimulate debate and action on the specific problem of reorienting and reorganizing the study of internal war.

Having indicated the basic proposition of this essay and the strategy adopted to support it, I can now proceed to implement that strategy. To do so, I shall: 1) try to demonstrate that extant explanations of Civil War causation are untenable; 2) offer some general observations on the failure of social scientists to develop good general theories of internal war; 3) sketch a tentative explanation of Civil War causation designed to suggest that, even within the framework of the established scholarly system, some progress might be made if scholars conduct sustained, intensive empirical research, focused on specific internal wars and informed by the scientific style of analysis; 4) sketch a proposal to reorganize and reorient the study of all forms of violence, not only that form designated by the term, internal war.

I. *Explanations of American Civil War Causation*

In a previous essay, I briefly observed that "specialists no more agree now on 'the causes of the Civil War' than they did decades ago. Their explanations are no more credible now than they were then. Critically assessed, Civil War historiography exemplifies the model of the Buddhist wheel of fate: round and round it goes but it never gets anywhere."[5] To support that assessment, I present in this essay, a detailed critique of explanations of Civil War causation advanced by Barrington Moore, Jr., Eugene Genovese, David Donald and Eric Foner.[6] Although contradictory, all four explanations are taken seriously by specialists. In relative terms, they are representative of the *best* work done to date on Civil War causation.

No reason exists to think that Civil War historiography is measurably inferior to research focused on other past events. The conclusion seems

5. See pp. 191-192 above.

logical, therefore, that if little progress has been made in developing credible explanations of Civil War causation, the established historiographic system cannot produce or sustain the critical mass of researchers required to develop credible explanations of large-scale, complex past human phenomena.

A. Barrington Moore's Explanation of American Civil War Causation. The American Civil War is only one of many major historical events treated in Mr. Moore's lengthy book, *Social Origins of Dictatorship and Democracy: Lord and Peasant in the Making of the Modern World.* As that title suggests, Mr. Moore set himself a truly heroic task, *singlehandedly (sans* collaborators or research assistants) to reconstruct and tell "the story of the transition from the preindustrial to the modern world."[7] Or to quote his later description of the problem he posed and tried to answer, *"Social Origins* is mainly about different forms of social structure, their varying origins and political consequences."[8] Highly praised on publication, the book gained something akin to the instant fame that greeted the first volume of Tocqueville's *Democracy in America.*[9]

---

6. That these explanations are taken seriously is evident from the fact that two of them (Moore's and Genovese's) are the two "conflicting interpretations" in the third edition of a widely used text. See Sidney Fine and Gerald Brown, eds., *The American Past* (New York: Macmillan Company, 1970), pp. 600-652.

7. Barrington Moore, Jr., *Social Origins of Dictatorship and Democracy: Lord and Peasant in the Making of the Modern World* (Boston: Beacon Press, 1967, paper). All my references are to this edition; the book was first published in 1966.

8. See his "Reply to Rothman," *American Political Science Review,* LXIV (March, 1970), 84. His reply claimed that his work had been badly misrepresented in Stanley Rothman, "Barrington Moore and the Dialectics of Revolution: An Essay Review," *ibid.,* LXIV (March, 1970), 61-82. I cannot be certain that I have correctly understood and summarized Mr. Moore's explanation of Civil War causation. If I have not, it is not because I haven't tried. He not only used reified terms, he explicitly invoked the right to be inconsistent and, if he chose, to mean different things by the same term.

9. Among others, J.H. Plumb hailed *Social Origins* as "a profoundly important book" and predicted that it would "influence a whole generation of young American historians..." *New York Times Book Review* (October 9, 1966). Even a review-essay that criticized the book severely in some major respects, hailed it as a "massive and impressive book" that deserves "the most serious study." David Lowenthal in *History and Theory,* VII (1968), 257-278.

1. Mr. Moore's explanation summarized.   My critique makes some observations about Mr. Moore's book as a whole but focuses on his explanation of Civil War causation. Unfortunately, he failed to state his explanation clearly—a condition that tends to produce heated arguments over the boring, trivial question, "What did the author really say or *mean* to say?", rather than potentially fruitful arguments over the interesting, significant question, "How credible are his claims or sets of claims?"

Asserting the right to "remain candidly and explicitly inconsistent in the use of terms,"[10] Mr. Moore also freely exercised the right to use the metaphysical language of reification. That is, he created abstract, vague concepts, then treated his own creations, e.g., "urban or bourgeois capitalist democracy," as though, somehow, they functioned as real-life human beings who had lived, felt, thought, and engaged in "revolutionary offensives." Despite his lack of clarity, however, we can be sure that he regarded the American Civil War, like the English and French revolutions, as a "bourgeois social revolution" that significantly contributed to the achievement of "competitive democratic capitalism" or, a different label for the same thing, "the Western form of democracy."[11]

Following two chapters on the English and French revolutions, Mr. Moore titled his third chapter, "The American Civil War: The Last Capitalist Revolution." Early in that chapter, he summarized his "conclusion" about its "causes and consequences":

> . . .the American Civil War was the last revolutionary offensive [in the sequence begun by the English Revolution] of what one may legitimately call urban or bourgeois capitalist democracy. Planta-

10. Moore, *Social Origins of Dictatorship and Democracy*, pp. 428-429. Candor here is used to justify Mr. Moore's confused and confusing practise of characterizing some revolutions by their "causes" and others by their "consequences." My discussion of his treatment of the Civil War is restricted to his claim about its causation, not its consequences. After secession occurred, a sequence of events occurred that did result in armed force being used to abolish black slavery. As Mr. Moore knows, the consequences of secession cannot be used to "prove" anything about Civil War causation. Otherwise we would have to say, for example, that a social revolution "caused" World War I because the Bolsheviks took power in Russia in 1917.

11. *Ibid.*, 111-112, 152-153, 413-414, 429.

tion slavery in the South, it is well to add right away, was not an economic fetter upon industrial capitalism. If anything, the reverse may have been true; it helped to promote American industrial growth in the early stages. But slavery was an obstacle to social and political democracy.[12]

To understand Mr. Moore's explanation, it cannot be overemphasized, we must recognize that he accepted the view presented decades earlier by Lewis C. Gray (among others), that Southern plantation owners functioned as capitalists who employed servile labor to maximize their profits. Mr. Moore noted, however, that urban growth in the South "remained far behind that in the rest of the country." The relatively low level of urbanization in the South, he claimed, significantly contributed to the coming of the Civil War.

The South had a capitalist civilization, then, but hardly a bourgeois one. Certainly it was not based on town life. And instead of challenging the notion of status based on birth, as did the European bourgeoisie when they challenged the right of aristocracies to rule, Southern planters took over the defense of hereditary privilege. Here was a real difference and a real issue [between Southern planter capitalists and Northern bourgeois capitalists].[13]

---

12. *Ibid.*, 112.
13. *Ibid.*, 121. If I correctly understand Mr. Moore, he claimed that the value system of the Southern slaveowning capitalists differed from that developed by the European bourgeoisie mainly because Southern capitalists were not town dwellers. Unless he meant to claim that only capitalists *who resided in towns would oppose hereditary privilege,* I cannot follow his reasoning or his sequence of sentences. In any event, his claim about Southern capitalists is misleading and inaccurate. To my knowledge, no one has yet made a systematic study, but the impressionistic evidence available in secondary studies suggests that a considerable proportion of the largest plantation owners lived in towns and cities, at least during a good part of the year. Were the town dwelling slaveowners less in favor of hereditary privilege than the backwoodsmen? If they were not, what happens to Mr. Moore's argument concerning the differences between Northern capitalists whose civilization was "based on town life" and Southern capitalists whose civilization was not? Moreover, in another passage quoted below in the text, Mr. Moore explicitly claimed that, as groups, Northern and Southern capitalists wanted "to suppress the issue of slavery rather than seek structural reforms...." Surely that claim contradicts the claim that the Southern non-urban capitalists' "defense of hereditary privilege" created a "real difference and a real issue"

Mr. Moore insisted that the "fundamental causes [of the Civil War] were . . . economic ones."[14] But he explicitly rejected the crudest form of economic determinist explanation of complex phenomena.

It is impossible to speak of purely economic factors as the main causes behind the war, just as it is impossible to speak of the war as mainly a consequence of moral differences over slavery. The moral issues arose from economic differences. Slavery was the moral issue that aroused much of the passion on both sides. Without the direct conflict of ideas over slavery, the events leading up to the war and the war itself are totally incomprehensible. At the same time, it is as plain as the light of the sun that economic factors created a slave economy in the South just as economic factors created social structures with contrasting ideals in other parts of the country.[15]

In effect, although not in so many words, Mr. Moore presented something like a Marxian analysis of the relationships between the different modes of production characteristic of Northerners and Southerners and their *different and conflicting ideologies.* He claimed that purely economic considerations motivated capitalist-minded men in the South to develop a mode of production predominantly based on slave labor, just as purely economic considerations motivated capitalist-minded men in the North to develop a mode of production based on free labor. But as a result of the different forms of economic relationships developed by Northern and Southern capitalists who sought the same objective, profits, different types of societies with different *and incompatible* ideals must have developed, and did actually develop, in the North and South.[16] Conflicts between northerners and southerners had to become increasingly intense, and therefore, increas-

_____

between them and Northern urban capitalists. I cite this contradiction to illustrate a general point: Mr. Moore's chapter contains many significantly contradictory claims that he apparently failed to recognize as contradictory. It seems difficult to believe that he felt entitled to make contradictory claims, as well as "remain candidly and explicitly inconsistent in the use of terms."

14. *Ibid.,* 134.

15. *Ibid.,* 123.

16. "To sum up with desperate brevity, the ultimate causes of the war are to be found in the growth of different economic systems leading to different (but still capitalist) civilizations with incompatible stands on slavery." *Ibid.,* 141.

ingly had to express themselves in political form.

> The fundamental issue became more and more whether the machinery of the federal government should be used to support one society or the other.... Political leaders knew that the admission of a slave state or a free one would tip the balance one way or another.[17]

One quotation perhaps best summarizes Mr. Moore's thesis and helps us understand why he characterized the Civil War as "The Last Capitalist Revolution," a "revolutionary victory for industrial capitalist democracy *and necessary* [emphasis added] to this victory." After citing, only to dismiss, arguments that might be used to contradict his thesis, he wrote:

> Once again the inquiry leads back toward political questions and incompatibilities between two different kinds of civilizations: in the South and in the North and West. Labor-repressive agricultural systems, and plantation slavery in particular, are political obstacles to a *particular kind* [original emphasis] of capitalism, at a specific historical stage: competitive democratic capitalism we must call it for lack of a more precise term. Slavery was a threat and an obstacle to a society that was indeed the heir of the Puritan, American, and French Revolutions. Southern society was based firmly on hereditary status as the basis of human worth. With the West, the North, though in the process of change, was still committed to notions of equal opportunity. In both, the ideals were reflections of economic arrangements that gave them much of their appeal and force. Within the same political unit [the United States] it was, I think, inherently impossible to establish political and social institutions that would satisfy both [i.e., satisfy both Northern and Southern "societies".][18]

Mr. Moore knows, of course, that "societies" do not engage in conflict, that "the North" was not an organic entity that unleashed a "revolutionary offensive" against "the South," and so on. Unfortunately, because his reified concepts and terms lack empirical meaning, they can neither describe nor explain "what really happened" to real-life human beings. It seems possible, however, to reformulate them into a set of claims capable of empirical confirmation or disconfirmation. To

---

17. *Ibid.,* 136.
18. *Ibid.,* 151-152.

do so, his statements must be translated into claims designed to answer the useful question, "Who caused the Civil War?", rather than claims somehow related to the traditional, but useless question, "What caused the Civil War?"; or in Mr. Moore's version, "What were the ultimate causes of the Civil War?"[19]

According to Mr. Moore, five sets of causally-related developments helped to make civil war inevitable between Northerners and Southerners:

1. After 1790, primarily as a result of the continued existence and geographical expansion of slavery in the South, the Northern and Southern economies became increasingly different.

2. Given the increasing differences in the Northern and Southern *economies,* the Northern and Southern *societies* became increasingly different in their dominant value systems or ideologies; not only increasingly different, but increasingly, irremediably incompatible and antagonistic.

3. Because they were members of two antagonistic societies governed by a single political system, Northerners and Southerners became consciously, irremediably antagonistic.

4. Increasing antagonisms between Northerners and Southerners inevitably expressed themselves politically; among other reasons, because the politically dominant members in each section inevitably tried to gain control of the national government in order to use its power to support their form of society and weaken their opponent's form of society and the ideology which it produced.

5. Because the political conflicts between Northerners and Southerners derived from their membership in irremediably antagonistic societies, by mid-nineteenth century their conflicts could neither be compromised nor long contained within the existing American political system. Put another way, by mid-nineteenth century, it was impossible for the members of two such antagonistic societies to continue to function as members of one body politic.

Those five sets of claims obviously derive from—or at least are compatible with—a traditional Marxian analysis of social conflicts that

19. For a fuller statement of this argument, see my *Concept of Jacksonian Democracy* (Princeton, N.J.· Princeton University Press, 1961), pp. 270-271, 288-290, 335-338.

result in civil wars. However, when Mr. Moore answered the key question that must be answered in any *empirically testable* explanation of Civil War causation, "Who caused it to occur?", he directly contradicted traditional Marxian propositions about the relationships between economic and political power.

From the Marxian-sounding claims summarized above and the Marxian-sounding passages I have quoted (and numerous other passages of the same character), we might reasonably infer that Mr. Moore claimed that Northern urban industrial capitalists and Southern nonurban planter capitalists constituted the main antagonists in the sequence of events that resulted in the Civil War. We would be badly mistaken to do so, however. Typical of the freewheeling eclecticism that pervades his book, he invoked an anti-Marxian theory of political power. A few individuals might have behaved differently, he claimed, but Northern and Southern capitalists generally "furnished the core of moderate opinion" in their respective sections and "wanted to suppress the issue of slavery rather than seek structural reforms. . . ."[20] That is, Mr. Moore's explanation asserts that the Civil War came about *in spite of,* rather than because of, the wishes and activities of Northern and Southern capitalists (as groups).

Unless words have no meaning, Mr. Moore asserted two basic claims: 1) Although they failed, Northern capitalists tried to suppress the slavery issue. But some *Northerners* consciously led at least a significant minority of the Northern population in a "revolutionary offensive." That offensive was consciously designed to abolish slavery in the South because its existence there constituted "a threat and an obstacle" to the existence and development in the United States of a formally democratic society, i.e., a society whose members were all *legally* free and equal. 2) To a significantly greater extent than any other set of actors, the Northern revolutionaries were responsible for the causally-related sequence of events that culminated in the Civil War.

Who were the Northerners who caused the Civil War? That question is the key one for Mr. Moore's explanation. But he answered it sketchily and ambiguously in only one paragraph (about a half page) of a fifty page chapter. And if I have correctly understood him and

---

20. Moore, *op. cit.,* pp. 136-141.

correctly traced his answer back to its source, he simply adopted *part* of the argument advanced by the "revisionist school" of Civil War historiography, particularly one of the numerous versions advanced by Avery Craven in his numerous books and articles. To quote Mr. Craven:

> Lincoln's attitude and actions were also the product of certain great changes that were gradually transforming his part of the nation. A new interdependent age was dawning there—an age in which national unity was essential to social-economic welfare and in which the enslavement of human beings *could not coexist with the labor requirements of free enterprise* [emphasis added] or the ethical standards of a competitive society. For the realization of the American democratic ideals, the Union had to be preserved, and slavery had to be put on the road to ultimate extinction. *There was no other choice* [emphasis added].[21]

Whether or not Mr. Moore consciously (or otherwise) adopted part of Mr. Craven's thesis, he clearly agreed with the claim that the "ethical standards of a competitive society" and the realization of "American democratic ideals" required the abolition of slavery. But he flatly disagreed with the claim that "the enslavement of human beings could not co-exist with the labor requirements of free enterprise [i.e., industrial capitalism]." As noted above, he explicitly asserted that plantation slavery "was not an economic fetter upon industrial capitalism" and dismissed the notion that, as an economic system, "it generated serious frictions with the North." Moreover, he also dismissed the notion that any freesoil, containment policy to put slavery "on the road to ultimate extinction" would actually have put it on that road. To quote Mr. Moore:

> One consideration we can dispose of rapidly. Slavery was almost certainly not on the point of dying out for internal reasons. The thesis is scarcely tenable that the war was unnecessary in the sense that the results would have come about sooner or later anyway by peaceful means and that therefore there was no real

---

21. Avery Craven, *Growth of Southern Nationalism* (Baton Rouge: Louisiana State University Press, n.p., 1953), 391-392, and the rest of the chapter titled "Some Generalizations." Mr. Craven, of course, cannot be held responsible for Mr. Moore's invention, namely the use of "revolutionary violence" to remove the obstacles to "democratic competitive capitalism."

conflict. If slavery were to disappear from American society, armed force would be necessary to make it disappear.[22]

Which Northerners not only wanted to use armed force to make slavery disappear but had the power to unleash and conduct a revolutionary offensive that actually made it disappear? To answer that question, Mr. Moore abandoned Marx and took over a revisionist thesis. He asserted that the men who controlled political power were politicians who were not controlled by, in fact, acted contrary to the wishes of the Northern capitalists who "furnished the core of moderate opinion" in their section (as Southern capitalists did in their section). "It was primarily a politician's war," he claimed, "perhaps even an agitator's war, if the terms are not taken to be merely abusive epithets." As the last clause demonstrates, the basic claim made by Mr. Moore asserted that Northern politicians (and journalists and clergymen to whom he ascribed lesser roles) functioned *neither* as irresponsible agitators (*à la* James Randall) nor as hysterical paranoids (*à la* Randall's student, David Donald). On the contrary.

Given the development of urban industrial capitalism in the North and plantation slave capitalism in the South, Mr. Moore claimed, the Civil War was an inevitable social revolution. But Northern capitalists were moderates who shied away from anything that might bring about radical change because they were "beneficiaries of the prevailing social order, and [were] mainly interested in making money. . . ." To bring about the necessary social revolution in American society, Northern society assigned that task to its politicians. (To convey the nature of Mr. Moore's claim and the functional theory of society from which it derives, I have used the language of reification here.) In effect, Mr. Moore relied upon a functional theory of social roles to account for the revolutionary activity of Northern politicians. Contrary to the standard revisionist thesis (except as I have noted, one version presented by Avery Craven), he claimed that Northern politicians properly played the "modern democratic politician's role" when they agitated and acted to bring about the Civil War.[23]

22. Moore, *op. cit.,* pp. 117-118, and pp. 118-121.

23. Paraphrase or brief quotation fails to convey the Hegelian-Parsonian reified quality of Mr. Moore's version of functionalism. One must read the original to appreciate its idealist—and antidemocratic, elitist—character. See, *ibid.,* 136-137.

My summary necessarily fails to convey the eclectic (and contradictory) nature of the variety of claims included in Mr. Moore's explanation of Civil War causation.[24] I believe that we best grasp the nature of his particular explanation of the Civil War, however, when we grasp the importance he attached to the general thesis advanced in *Social Origins,* namely, that "revolutionary violence" was indispensable to the removal of preindustrial or predemocratic obstacles blocking the Western route of bourgeois transition to "the modern world." To gain credence for that general thesis (and its far-reaching implications for basic changes in contemporary society), Mr. Moore *had* to show that the American Civil War satisfied its claims. He had to depict the Civil War, therefore, as "The Last Capitalist Revolution." It was a revolution primarily caused, by bold Northern politicians. They correctly recognized—as timorous Northern capitalists refused to recognize—that historical necessity (Hegel is alive and well in *Social Origins*) required them to unleash a revolutionary offensive designed to abolish Southern slavery in order to achieve the changes in the "structure of society" required to enable American society to become a modern industrial democracy.[25]

2. Mr. Moore's explanation assessed.   Mr. Moore's good intentions notwithstanding, in my judgment, both his book and his general

---

24. In addition to Marxian and revisionist elements, it throws together claims derived from Beard about the (alleged) bargain struck between Northern industrialists and Western farmers, claims derived from Nevins about the (alleged) Northern moral fervor aroused by the continued existence of black slavery in the South, and a *melange* of other claims from equally diverse sources—all described by Mr. Moore as "partial truths." For the purposes of my critique, I have only. tried to identify and assess what I take to be Mr. Moore's basic claims.

25. The key to Mr. Moore's book, I believe, is found in the concluding pages of his Epilogue, entitled "Reactionary and Revolutionary Imagery." There he defended the use of revolutionary violence as necessary to achieve "the ancient Western dream of a free and rational society. . . ." As I read those pages, he hinted, without explicitly asserting, that revolutionary violence is the *only* means by which that ancient dream can be achieved. Whatever one thinks of that thesis—I think it is terribly wrong and damaging to the noble cause it is designed to advance—it helps us to understand both the nature of Mr. Moore's explanation of Civil War causation and how he came to develop it. See, *ibid.,* pp. 484-508, especially 505-508.

orientation to the study of past human behavior are best characterized as *highly reactionary*. By *highly reactionary*, I mean that his book and orientation basically derive from an old dangerous myth that long ago should have been relegated to the dustbins of historiography, but which still, alas, continues to dominate and prop-up the established historiographic system.

The myth informing Mr. Moore's work derives from the fallacious analogy between the "memory" of an individual (or group of individuals) and the scientific study of past human behavior. That Everyman can function, indeed must function, as his own historian about his own life may be true. It does not follow, therefore, that every intelligent, educated man can responsibly, usefully function as a historian of any past human phenomena that happen to interest him. That is the myth that informs Mr. Moore's work; at bottom, it still serves as the "charter myth" of the established historiographic system.

Perhaps the classic, almost certainly the most direct and candid statement of that myth was proclaimed, appropriately enough, by Samuel Eliot Morison, in his 1950 presidential address to the American Historical Association, "Faith of a Historian." Contemptuously deriding methodology and methodologists, Mr. Morison urged young historians to ignore them. He insisted that the three main ingredients in the formula for doing good history are "common sense," a "sense of balance" about human affairs, and "an overriding urge to get at the truth." Asserting that his views were representative of "the great majority of practicing historians in the Western world," he laid down this general law:

> Courses on historical methodology are not worth the time that they take up. I shall never give one myself, and I have observed that many of my colleagues who do give such courses refrain from exemplifying their methods by writing anything. It is much more fun to pick to pieces the works of their contemporaries who do write. Historical methodology, as I see it, is a product of common sense applied to circumstances.[26]

If historical methodology requires nothing more than "common sense applied to circumstances," then, of course, every intelligent,

---

26. Samuel Eliot Morison, "Faith of a Historian," *American Historical Review,"* LVI (January, 1951), 263.

educated man, possessed by "an overriding urge to get at the truth" can function as a responsible, useful historian of any past phenomena that interest him.

In 1950, as Mr. Morison claimed, the great majority of practicing historians probably shared his contempt for what methodologists refer to as "the logic of social research." But "The times they are a'changin' " and winds are beginning to blow through the corridors of power in the historiographic system. Mr. Morison's orientation, however, still predominates among historians in general and the leading "Establishment Historians" in particular. (In this context, "Establishment Historians", of course, does not refer to social or political ideology. On the contrary, it refers strictly to historiographic ideology, a clumsy but convenient term. As the example of Mr. Moore suggests, no invariant relationship exists between social and historiographic ideology.)

As I suggested earlier, Mr. Moore's explanation of the Civil War forms a small, but vital, part of his remarkably wide-ranging book. In the mid-nineteenth century, it probably was useful, perhaps even progressive, for an individual, *singlehandedly*, to try to synthesize all extant knowledge about a vast range of complex historical phenomena (e.g., Henry Buckle's *History of Civilization in England*). In the mid-twentieth century, such attempts and such works are literally reactionary.[27] They look backward to when atomistic liberalism reigned and the "Leonardesque aspiration" drove men to try to function as "The Hero in Historiography."[28] That dream never was noble. It now represents a form of romantic individualism that, in my judgment, should be discouraged rather than rewarded by fame and

---

27. Mr. Moore will not appreciate the comparison but I think that he unwittingly identified the ethos that informed his book when he acidly described the "ideal of the amateur" and the disdain for "the technician" prevalent among the "reactionary" section of the English landed aristocracy (and other landed aristocracies). See his *Social Origins,* 484-496.

28. I have borrowed the "Leonardesque aspiration" concept from Donald Campbell's witty and important critique of the established social science system; he calls for radical changes to achieve the goal of a "comprehensive, integrated multiscience." See his essay, "Ethnocentrism of Disciplines and the Fish-Scale Model of Omniscience," in Muzafer and Carolyn W. Sherif, eds., *Interdisciplinary Relationships in the Social Sciences* (Chicago: Aldine Publishing Company, 1969), pp. 328-348.

prizes. One reason for criticizing Mr. Moore's explanation of the Civil War is to try to discourage others from following his example. In my judgment, it works against the development of scientific historiography and a good general theory of social change.

As I have emphasized in the preceding summary of his claims, Mr. Moore claimed that the Northerners chiefly responsible for the Civil War consciously acted to bring about a social revolution designed to remove the threat and obstacles slavery posed to the existence and establishment of "competitive democratic capitalism" in the United States. By the mid-1960s, when Mr. Moore wrote his book, the crude Beardian version of economic determinism had been discredited. Northern capitalists could no longer be credibly depicted (as the Beards had depicted them) as the leaders of a "revolutionary offensive" designed to abolish slavery in the South. Nor could that role be credibly assigned to the small group of Northern abolitionists who remained active in the 1850s. Forced either to identify some politically powerful Northerners who played that role, or abandon his general thesis about the Western democratic "route of bourgeois revolution," Mr. Moore had to assign that role to Northern politicians.

Given the remarkably amoral and opportunist nature of American politicians (particularly after Martin Van Buren had shown how "Old Hero" Andy Jackson could be elevated to the presidency in 1828), Mr. Moore's thesis required him to cast Northern politicians in an unlikely role. That role is startingly different from the one assigned them even by historians who reject the revisionist thesis and who believe that the "containment=ultimate extinction" equation neatly solves the problem of Civil War causation. Although some historians who themselves offer versions of the containment thesis think highly of Mr. Moore's work, they apparently fail to recognize that his explanation fundamentally, directly contradicts the containment thesis in any of its vague formulations. Unlike advocates of that thesis, Mr. Moore recognized that slavery would have long flourished in the South had the Civil War not occurred.

Not only was slavery highly profitable to the slave-owning capitalists, Mr. Moore noted (following Lewis Gray, Kenneth Stampp, Paul Gates *et al*), it was "no anachronistic excrescence on industrial capitalism. It was an integral part of industrial capitalism and one of its prime motors in the world at large." Given that accurate assessment of the Southern mode of production, Mr. Moore obviously could not cast Northern politicians in roles similar to those in which containment historians cast them. Instead, he resorted to a reified, functional theory (of the Hegel-Talcott Parsons type) that treats "societies" as organic entities that somehow consciously act to assign some of their members the task of overcoming internal contradictions when those contradictions become too severe to be tolerated.

Why should the dominant group of amoral, opportunistic Republican politicians consciously initiate and lead a social revolution requiring them to use revolutionary violence to abolish slavery in the South? They did what they did, Mr. Moore claimed, because they had to—that was their role. That is, when they functioned as agents of a Northern society *inevitably* driven to abolish slavery because it contradicted the ideological requirements of competitive democratic capitalism, they played the role assigned them by "a complex society with an advanced division of labor. . . ."

To criticize Mr. Moore's invocation of a metaphysical functional theory that treats a society as an organic entity would be to beat a long dead horse. To the extent that he made empirically testable claims about Civil War *causation* as distinct from claims about Civil War *consequences,* he can only be understood to have claimed that it occurred because the dominant group of Northern Republican politicians consciously agitated and acted to secure political power to abolish Southern slavery by the use of armed force. What evidence did he offer or could he offer to support that claim? None.

Closely examined, in those pages of his chapter that dealt with the "causes of the war," Mr. Moore made no attempt to show that Northern Republican leaders, *prior to the outbreak of secession,* even advocated a program designed to bring about the *abolition* of Southern slavery by any means, let along by the use of armed force. Only in the pages that deal with developments *after* the Civil War had broken out did Mr. Moore offer any evidence designed to show that:

> From abolitionist ideologues and Free Soil radicals, a small band
> of Republican politicians took over the conception of slavery as
> an anachronistic "remnant of a dying world of 'baron and
> serf—noble and slave.' " The Civil War itself they perceived as an

opportunity to root out and destroy this oppressive anachronism in order to rebuild the South in the image of the democratic and progressive North, based on "free speech, free toil, schoolhouses, and ballot boxes".[29]

Mr. Moore's economic determinist treatment of *post-secession* positions taken by some Radical Republicans distorts both their social bases of support and their motives. For example, he depicted Thaddeus Stevens as an agent-for-hire of the "infant iron and steel industry of Pennsylvania" and a "set of railroad interests," rather than as a dedicated leader of a small group of evangelical Yankee Protestants long and fiercely opposed to slavery for noneconomic reasons. My main point, however, is that positions taken after the outbreak of war cannot be used as evidence that, prior to 1861, politically powerful Republicans had done what Mr. Moore's thesis required then to have done, namely, consciously acted to unleash a revolutionary offensive against the existence of slavery in the South.

As a close reading of the passage quoted above shows, Mr. Moore admitted that it was only *after* the Civil War had broken out that a "small band of Republican politicians" came to perceive that development "as an opportunity to root out and destroy" slavery. Whatever their postsecession perceptions might have been, they cannot be credibly used as evidence of the inclination and power of the dominant group of prewar Republican politicians to bring about "The Last Capitalist Revolution." To argue in that fashion is equivalent to arguing that some Bolsheviks' post-1914 perceptions about the opportunities for overthrowing capitalism in Russia can be used as evidence of their inclination and power to bring about World War I.

At bottom, despite disclaimers and despite his reliance upon a Parsonian-like functional theory to explain the occurrence of the Civil War, Mr. Moore invoked an economic determinist theory of human behavior. For example, reading his account, we would never imagine that noneconomic attributes and institutions (e.g., religious groups, ethnocultural groups, voluntary associations, schools) operated as significant determinants of group consciousness and group conflict in

---

29. Moore, *Social Origins,* 142-143. Those same pages also contain the references to Thaddeus Stevens quoted in the text below.

antebellum America, or significantly affected the distribution of political power. According to him, social structure means *economic group structure* ("economic factors created social structures with contrasting ideals"), the classic "non-vulgar" economic determinist error that Karl Marx unfortunately took over from the "bourgeois economists" and St. Simonians and infused into modern social theory.[30]

Given Mr. Moore's economic determinism and his general thesis about the "transition from the preindustrial to the modern world," it is not difficult to understand why he used the wrong general model to classify the Civil War. To classify it as a social revolution that fits the English and French models is to misclassify and misunderstand it.

Far from fitting a social revolution model, the Civil War best fits a "separatist revolution" model applicable to the 1776 American Revolution, the 1967 Nigerian Civil War, the current Sudanese, Chad, Eritrean, Irish, and East Pakistani secessionist rebellions and a great number of "territorial culture group" (defined in a later section) conflicts in present and past societies.

When Mr. Moore looked at the American Civil War with the eyes of an economic determinist accustomed to, and prepared to, see only social revolutions or economic interest group conflicts—the American Revolution, he asserted, "at bottom. . .was a fight between commercial interests in England and America"—he distorted past reality beyond recognition.

Unlike separatist civil wars, the main antagonists in social revolutions *want to preserve the existing political community.* They fight to control their community because they want to bring about, or prevent, radical change in its political or economic or social or cultural subsystems. To classify a civil war as "belonging" to or "fitting" a

---

30. In my judgment, no necessary connection exists between Marx's social theory at its highest level of generality and his lower-level propositions that all history is "the history of class struggles" and that, in all societies at all times, economic attributes are the primary bases of group consciousness and group conflicts. His lower level propositions strongly tend to be economic determinist in character. In my judgment, the economic determinist strain in Marx has powerfully handicapped efforts to develop his brilliant general orientation into a powerful empirical theory of the development of human society in general and specific societies in particular.

social revolution model, therefore, we must *credibly* identify some specific group powerful enough to have initiated and led a "revolutionary offensive" that produced civil war. Once we recognize that no such group existed in the North prior to 1861, Mr. Moore's explanation of Civil War causation becomes demonstrably invalid.

When we place the word "black" before the word "slave", Mr. Moore's explanation cracks up on the hard rock of antebellum reality. During the past decade, historians increasingly have come to *admit* (used advisedly) that antiblack racism became pervasive in American society after 1819 and that the concept, "antislavery attitudes," encompasses an extraordinarily diverse set of attitudes ranging from abolitionism based on the full equality of all human beings, to antiarrogant slaveholderism, to anti-subhuman-black-slavism. Thus racism made it possible for Northerners simultaneously to be "antislavery" in some general sense *and intensely opposed to the abolition of black slavery in the South.*[31] Had a *genuinely scientific* (rather than a *nominally scientific*) historiography existed in the United States, the enormous volume of research on antebellum politics would long ago have demonstrated that antiblack racism became increasingly virulent and widespread in the North after 1819. Had we attained that advanced state, it seems improbable that Mr. Moore would have claimed that Northern politicians caused the Civil War because they were fated to

---

31. For an overview and summary of the relevant literature, and an important contribution to our better understanding of antiblack racism, see James A. Rawley, *Race and Politics* (Philadelphia: J.B. Lippincott Company, 1969), pp. 257-274 and *passim.* Mr. Rawley's explanation of Civil War causation, however, seems to me to be contradicted by the very evidence he cited concerning the extent and intensity of Northern racism. Convinced that Northerners would do nothing to free black slaves, he had to attribute secession to *misperceptions* widely shared among Southerners that "Black Republicans" *aimed* "to subvert race relations by introducing emancipation, equality, and amalgamation." *Ibid.,* 274. Particularly in view of intense Northern racism, that claim seems untenable. At best, however, it can only relate to developments in the late 1850s, long after the secessionist movement had crystallized. Moreover, I do not think that even a handful of leading Southern secessionists really believed that the Lincoln Administration would introduce "emancipation, equality, and amalgamation" and, because of *that belief,* launched The War for Southern Independence.

lead "the last revolutionary offensive on the part of what one may legitimately call urban or bourgeois capitalist democracy."[32]

As I have argued in my earlier essay on Middle Period historiography, we never have had a genuinely scientific historiography. Alas, myself included, we therefore have never *systematically and responsibly* studied political behavior during the "Middle Period."[33] My research on public opinion and Civil War causation has convinced me,[34] however, that after we have made the series of intensive studies required to reconstruct and explain "scientifically" *the politics of antiblack racism* from 1819 to 1861, specialists will strongly tend to accept this claim:

Had Northerners held a referendum in November, 1860, solely on a proposition requiring the Federal government to require the Southern state governments to abolish slavery by some form of legislative action, probably no more than 2 percent, almost certainly no more than 5 percent, of the Northern electorate would have voted "Aye."[35]

Other specialists may now dispute that claim. Or they may dismiss it

---

32. One of my colleagues, Theodore Hershberg, is doing some important research designed to yield the "hard data" required for any credible assessment of possible changes in the economic and social status of free Negroes during the mid-nineteenth century in the North. Even his preliminary results seem most impressive to me; his study promises to be of major significance. His work reinforces my conviction that the politics of antiblack racism, combined with the impact of immigration, urbanization and industrialization, resulted in a sharp deterioration in the condition of Northern blacks after 1819. Sharp deterioration in the condition of Northern blacks and a "revolutionary offensive" to free Southern black slaves seem so patently contradictory that I cannot believe that Mr. Moore would maintain that they could have simultaneously existed.

33. See pp. 209-223 above.

34. For a variety of reasons, only a small part of that research has appeared in published form. For references to those publications, and for my general orientation, see my essay "An Approach to the Scientific Study of Past Public Opinion," pp. 105-159 above. Experience has led me to shun predictions about the actual publication of "research in progress." It seems useful to note, however, that the statement in the text is based on research that began in the 1950s and, with considerable interruptions, has subsequently continued.

35. It would be absurd for me to try to support that claim in a footnote. I make it for two reasons: 1) I believe it to be true; 2) so that its implications, if true, will be considered by historians who offer explanations about Northern public opinion as a significant determinant of Civil War causation.

as "iffy," intrinsically impossible to confirm or disconfirm.[36] What seems beyond dispute, however, is that *prior* to the outbreak of war, no *politically significant* Northern group existed that advocated action by the Federal government to *compel* Southerners to abolish slavery. We can better understand that phenomenon when we recognize that, over a century later, Mr. Moore's assertion (supported neither by theory nor empirical evidence) that the institutions of Southern black slavery and "competitive democratic capitalism" could not coexist in the same society is tragically (and daily) refuted in the Republic of South Africa (and other "competitive democratic capitalist" societies). True, apartheid is not quite black slavery; neither, for that matter, was the state of near-peonage that millions of black Americans endured for long decades after 1865 when "modern capitalist democracy" was much more developed in the United States than it had been prior to 1861. What else do those phenomena represent, however, but hereditary legal privilege and hereditary legal subordination?

A committed economic determinist for whom social structures and ideologies are primarily a function of economic group structures, Mr. Moore failed to recognize that racism permitted (and still permits) Americans, North and South, to espouse and believe in, *legal* equality of rights and opportunities for white men, while defining blacks, *North* and South, as members of an "untouchable" caste outside white society and subject to a radically different set of rules.

Bluntly stated, to understand Mr. Moore's explanation of Civil War causation is to dismiss it as not worth serious consideration. I have seriously considered it only to indicate that something must be radically wrong with a historiographic system that permits it to be taken seriously.[37] To further support that argument, I proceed to assess Eugene Genovese's explanation.

---

36. On the indispensability of "contrary-to-fact conditionals" in historical explanations, see the incisive discussion in Ernest Nagel, *The Structure of Science: Problems in the Logic of Scientific Explanation* (New York: Harcourt, Brace and World, 1961), 68-73, 588-592.

37. Mr. Moore's bibliography testified to his amateur status and to his failure to familiarize himself with the *historiographic reviews* of the vast literature on Civil War causation. His short (and skewed) bibliography listed Howard K. Beale's pioneering 1946 essay and the collection of brief passages from primary and secondary sources edited by Kenneth Stampp in 1959. It showed no awareness,

B. Eugene Genovese's Explanation of Civil War Causation.   Unlike
Mr. Moore, Mr. Genovese recognized that the Civil War is best classified
as a separatist rebellion. And unlike Mr. Moore, to achieve his ambitious
goal of developing a credible explanation of the Civil War that would
exemplify and support *his* version of Marxian social theory, he
disdained superficial, so-called "secondary analysis" of secondary works
and committed himself to sustained, intensive empirical research. Like
Mr. Moore, however, because his version of Marxism is basically an
economic determinist theory of human behavior, he assumed that social
structure means economic group structure and that men's ideologies
primarily derive from their economic roles. Also like Mr. Moore, his
work was uninformed by a scientific style of analysis and research. As a
result, his separatist rebellion explanation is no more credible than the
social revolution explanation advanced by Mr. Moore.

1. Mr. Genovese's Explanation Summarized.   Contrary to Mr.
Moore, in a volume of essays published in 1965, Mr. Genovese argued
that we best understand what happened before armed conflict began if
we use Edward Channing's term and characterize the civil war between
Southerners and Northerners as "The War for Southern Independence."[38] He cheerfully acknowledged that his explanation was not

however, that Thomas J. Pressly had published the standard book on the subject
in 1954, that David Potter had published a major review essay in 1961, and that
several excellent, relevant review essays appeared in 1965 in *Writing Southern
History.* Another example: Mr. Moore felt entitled to dismiss the "whole
[Owsley] school of Southern historians" as having written "utter rubbish" about
the process of democratization of white society in the South. His bibliography
showed total innocence, however, about those works of Fletcher Green and
Charles Sydnor that effectively demonstrated the rapid advance of formal
democracy for whites by 1860. Given the nature of his claims, "inadequate"
seems to be a mild word to characterize his bibliography on Civil War causation.
From the comments of colleagues who specialize in other revolutions "explained"
by Mr. Moore, I would be inclined to think that "inadequate" does not uniquely
apply to his chapter on Civil War causation. See, *Social Origins of Dictatorship
and Democracy,* pp. 117, 532-534.

38. Eugene Genovese, *The Political Economy of Slavery* (New York: Vintage
Books, 1967) pp. 3-39, and *passim.* The book was first published in 1965,
although some essays contained in it had been published earlier. For Channing's
characterization of "The War for Southern Independence," see the illuminating
discussion in Thomas J. Pressly, *Americans Interpret Their Civil War* (Princeton,
N.J.: Princeton University Press, 1954), pp. 179-182.

original.[39] In essence, it had been first advanced by Karl Marx in 1861, although I view Mr. Genovese's version as, in some ways, more subtle and more "Marxian" than the original statement.[40]

In journalistic articles for the New York *Tribune* and *Die Presse* of Vienna in 1861, Marx explained the outbreak of "The North American Civil War." His basic hypothesis can be summarized by this quotation:

> A strict confinement of slavery within its old terrain, therefore, was bound according to economic law to lead to its gradual effacement, in the political sphere to annihilate the hegemony that the slave states exercised through the Senate, and finally to expose the slaveholding oligarchy within its own states to threatening perils from the side of the "poor whites." With the principle that any further extension of slave territories was to be prohibited by law, the Republicans therefore attacked the rule of the slaveholders at its root. The Republican election victory was accordingly bound to lead to the open struggle between North

39. In his introduction, Mr. Genovese wrote: "I have attempted to demonstrate that the material prerequisites for the slaveholders' power were giving way before internal and external pressures; that the social system was breaking on immanent contradictions; that the economy was proving incapable of adapting itself to reforms while slavery existed; that slavery was naturally generating territorial expansion; and that therefore secession and the risk of war were emerging as a rational course of action. I have, in other words, tried to rebuild the case on which a materialist interpretation of an irrepressible conflict may rest. In doing so, I realize that much of the argument is an extension and refinement of arguments presented as long as a century ago . . ." *Political Economy,* 9. I assume that "materialist interpretation" and "a century ago" referred to Karl Marx's explanation of Civil War causation.

40. Although Mr. Genovese properly criticized Marx's failure *to try* to understand the ideology of Southern slaveholders, his explanation of "The War for Southern Independence" basically derived from Marx's assumption, namely the slaveholders' desperate need to expand geographically to maintain their social system. Compare Genovese, *Political Economy,* 8-9, 13-39, 243-274, and his essay, "Marxian Interpretations of the Slave South," in Barton J. Bernstein, ed., *Towards a New Past* (New York: Random House, 1968), pp. 90-125, with Richard Enmale, ed., *The Civil War in the United States by Karl Marx and Frederick Engels* (2nd ed; New York: International Publishers, 1940), pp. 57-83. In his most recent book, Mr. Genovese noted that he stood by the "argument on the Old South" advanced in his *Political Economy.* I have taken that statement at face value. See his, *The World the Slaveholders Made* (New York: Vintage Books, 1971), pp. 95-96. The book was first published in 1969.

and South. . . [The slaveholders knew that the rapid development of the Northwest would lessen their ability to control the Federal Government. Given Lincoln's election] it was better to make the break now than to look on at the development of the Republican Party and the upsurge of the Northwest four years longer, and begin the struggle under more unfavorable conditions. The slaveholders' party therefore played *va banque!* [That is, staked all on a single card.—Ed.].[41]

As I have suggested, Mr. Genovese's version of Marx's explanation of Civil War causation was not a carbon copy. As Mr. Moore can be said to have combined Marx and the revisionists, Mr. Genovese can be said to have combined Marx and Ulrich B. Phillips and George Fitzhugh to present a much more sympathetic view than Marx did of the ideology of Southern slaveholders and the motives that impelled them to secede. Like Marx, however, Mr. Genovese treated Southern slaveholders as an essentially unified group who functioned as "the ruling class" in their section. Unlike Mr. Moore (and the revisionists), to Mr. Genovese, economic power necessarily equalled political power.[42] Also unlike Mr. Moore, according to Mr. Genovese, the slaveholders functioned as anything but capitalists in planters' clothing, they functioned as a *precapitalist, anticapitalist* ruling class.

In his various publications, Mr. Genovese has stated his explanation somewhat differently and somewhat contradictorily. But I think it can be accurately summarized as follows:[43]

1. Antebellum Southern society was ruled by a premodern, anticapitalist slaveholding class.

2. Unlike the social class that dominated Northern society and set its character and tone, the Southern slaveholding class did not function according to a capitalist set of values. As a group, members of that class failed to develop an acquisitive spirit as the core component of their world outlook, and rational profit-seeking and wealth accumulation as the driving force of their economic activity. Judged by the criterion of

41. Enmale, ed., *op. cit.,* pp. 69-70.

42. For example, see Genovese, *Political Economy,* pp. 7, 34-35, 243, 247-248, 269-270.

43. My summary of Mr. Genovese's explanation is based upon my understanding of the claims asserted in the different essays he brought together in his *Political Economy.*

maximum economic development, compared to Northern capitalists, a far greater degree of irrationality characterized both the production and consumption activities of Southern slaveholders.

3. Because their slave labor system created a civilization that inevitably produced far less efficient masters and workers than did the Northern civilization based on free labor, Southerners were inevitably doomed to fall further and further behind Northerners in economic power *and, therefore,* in political power.

4. Given the differences in Northern and Southern society that stemmed from their different labor systems, Northern capitalists and Southern slaveholders inevitably developed basic and irrepressible economic, political, social and moral conflicts. These conflicts could be fought out nonviolently within the American political system only as long as Southern economic development did not lag much behind Northern economic development. But a lasting state of equilibrium was impossible, given the intrinsically, irremediably irrational character of the Southern economic system. In the section dominated by Northern capitalists, economic development was qualitative and had no upward limits; in the section dominated by Southern slaveholders, economic development was quantitative and tended toward stagnation, the fatal flaw that doomed the slaveholders as a class. To quote rather than paraphrase Mr. Genovese:

> In the South this weakness proved fatal [Northern qualitative, Southern quantitative, economic development] for the slaveholders. They found themselves engaged in a growing conflict with Northern farmers and businessmen over such issues as tariffs, homesteads, internal improvements, *and the decisive question of the balance of political power in the Union* [emphasis added]. The slow pace of their economic progress, in contrast to the long strides of their rivals to the North, threatened to undermine their political parity and result in a Southern defeat on all major issues of the day. The qualitative leaps in the Northern economy manifested themselves in a rapidly increasing population, an expanding productive plant, and growing political, ideological, and social boldness. The slaveholders' voice grew shriller and harsher as they contemplated impending disaster and sought solace in complaints of Northern aggression and exploitation.[44]

---

44. *Ibid.,* 17-18.

5. Although Southern economic development increasingly lagged behind Northern economic development, the Southern slaveholding class could maintain its civilization as long as the slave system could be geographically expanded to occupy hitherto uncultivated land. The territorial expansionist drive of the slaveholders, therefore, stemmed from their correct assumption that the continued export of slaves from older settled areas to newly cultivated areas was the only way to maintain the viability of the Southern economy and the economic basis of the civilization they had created and valued. The planters required *unchallengeable* control of the national government, therefore, to insure that slavery not only could *legally* expand, but that it *did actually expand* to encompass an area substantially greater than that included within the Old South. That is, "if the men who made up the ruling class of the South were to continue to rule," they also had to control the national government to insure the geographic expansion of slavery *whenever* they deemed such expansion necessary. Among other reasons compelling them to obtain "room to expand," as a result of their wasteful, land-exhaustive form of agriculture, "The steady acquisition of new land *could alone* [emphasis added] guarantee the maintenance of that interregional slave trade which held the [slave] system together."[45]

6. It was rational for Southern slaveholders to try to force the national government to take actions that would insure the expansion of slavery beyond the Old South. Once they irrevocably lost their ability to do so, as the Republican victory in 1860 showed that they had, they correctly concluded that their society was doomed if Southerners remained within the existing American political community. They acted rationally, therefore, when, in a desperate effort to save their premodern civilization and themselves from social extinction, they used their political power in the South to bring about secession.

Much more Marxian than Marx in trying to understand and explain the behavior of slaveholders, Mr. Genovese, unlike Marx, did not abusively condemn either their ideology or them for acting in accord with its dictates. "What else would a Marxist expect them to believe or to have done?" in effect, was his rebuke to Marx. But his explanation

_____
45. *Ibid.*, 246-247.

of secession, as distinct from his moral judgment of slaveholders, differed in no significant way from the one Marx dashed off in his journalistic articles of 1861. To quote rather than paraphrase Mr. Genovese's explanation:

> When we understand that the slave South developed neither a strange form of capitalism nor an undefinable agrarianism but a special civilization built on the relationship of master to slave, we expose the root of its conflict with the North. The internal contradictions in the South and the external conflict with the North placed the slaveholders hopelessly on the defensive with little to look forward to except slow strangulation. Their only hope lay in a bold stroke to complete their political independence and to use it to provide an expansionist solution for their economic and social problems. The ideology and psychology of the proud slaveholding class made surrender or resignation to gradual defeat unthinkable, for its fate, in its own eyes at least, was the fate of everything worthwhile in Western civilization.[46]

Much later in his book, in effect, although not in so many words, Mr. Genovese claimed that he had demonstrated the validity of Marx's explanation of Civil War causation. In language that simply paraphrased Marx, he claimed that he had demonstrated that:

> The decision of most slaveholders to stake everything on a desperate gamble for a political independence that would have freed them to push their system southward emerges as a rational, if dangerous, course of action.

2. Mr. Genovese's explanation assessed. Mr. Moore's basic error was to misclassify and misunderstand the Civil War as a social revolution; Mr. Genovese's basic error was to misclassify and misunderstand the antebellum Southern mode of production as an economic system dominated by a precapitalist, anticapitalist, patriarchial, paternalistic quasi-aristocratic ruling class of slaveholding planters who, "in truth, grew into the closest thing to feudal lords imaginable in a nineteenth-century bourgeois republic."[47]

---

46. *Ibid.,* 35-36. The quotation below that paraphrases Marx's statement is from, *ibid.,* 254-255.
47. *Ibid.,* 23, 30-31; *World Slaveholders Made,* 95-97.

In my opinion, Mr. Genovese's description and analysis of antebellum Southern (and Northern) economic development is radically, irremediably erroneous. Moreover, his description and analysis of the distribution of political power in the South and North, as well as his description and analysis of Southern slaveholders as essentially constituting a unified "ruling class," is radically, irremediably erroneous. His explanation of Civil War causation, therefore, is untenable.

Mr. Genovese's analysis of the Southern mode of production may partly have derived from his having taken literally, and applied mechanically, an observation Marx made about the different forms of "co-operation in the labour process." In a famous passage, Marx distinguished between noncapitalistic and "capitalistic co-operation." In his words:

> The sporadic application of co-operation on a large scale in the ancient world, in the Middle Ages, and in Modern colonies, is based on *direct* relations of dominion and servitude, principally on slavery. The capitalistic form, on the contrary, presupposes from the outset the free wage labourer who sells his labour-power to capital.[48]

Read literally and applied mechanically, that observation might lead a doctrinaire Marxist to deduce this invariant proposition as applicable everywhere: *No free laborer, no capitalist.* As I read Marx, he did not mean to assert that, in modern societies (as distinct from "colonies") that had highly developed capitalist sectors, owners of the means of production could not be capitalists simply because they used slaves to maximize profits on capital and returns on entrepreneurial energies—particularly when they simultaneously engaged in economic activities that employed free wage laborers, as many Southern slaveholders did. If Marx did mean to be understood in that fashion, then in my opinion, his proposition should be rejected. It is then too narrow to help us understand the ethos and activities of slaveholders in the United States during the nineteenth century.

Contrary to Mr. Genovese, I believe that Lewis Gray's definition of

48. See T.B. Bottomore and Maximilien Rubel, eds., *Karl Marx: Selected Writings in Sociology and Social Philosophy* (New York: McGraw-Hill Book Company, 1964), pp. 119-120.

the concept, *plantation system,* is compatible with a nondoctrinaire Marxian approach to economic and social development. It powerfully helps us to understand the mode of production and society that developed in the South.

> The plantation was a capitalistic type of agricultural organization in which a considerable number of unfree laborers were employed under unified direction and control in the production of a staple crop . . . the [plantation] *system represented a capitalistic stage of agricultural development* [emphasis added] since the value of slaves, land, and equipment necessitated the investment of money capital, often of large amount and frequently borrowed, and there was a strong tendency for the planter to assume the attitude of the business man in testing success by ratio of net money income to capital invested. . . .[49]

Unlike Mr. Moore, Mr. Genovese scathingly rejected Gray's analysis of the Southern mode of production. Instead, he resurrected the magnolia-and-old-lace fantasies of Ulrich B. Phillips and George Fitzhugh to depict Southern slaveholders in an antihistorical, and therefore anti-Marxian, fashion. Mid-nineteenth century Southern slaveholders, he claimed, constituted a premodern, anticapitalist class whose members functioned as patriarchical heads in residence of extended families, white and black, living in organic plantation communities.

Marx's observations about the different forms of "co-operation in the labour process," of course, could not reasonably have been used by Mr. Genovese to create that fantasy world. That he viewed the Southern mode of production in those terms leads me to conclude that, basically, he drew more heavily upon Ulrich Phillips (and George Fitzhugh) for intellectual inspiration than on Karl Marx. That conclusion seems particularly reasonable when we consider that the epigraph for his first volume of essays is this revealing quotation from Phillips:

> Plantation slavery had in strictly business aspects at least as many drawbacks as it had attractions. But in the large it was less a business than a life; *it made fewer fortunes than it made men* [emphasis added—L. B.].

---

49. Lewis C. Gray, *History of Agriculture in the Southern United States to 1860* (New York: Peter Smith, 1941 printing, first published 1933), 1: 301-302.

To try to combine Phillips (and Fitzhugh) with Marx, as Mr. Genovese did, is a formula for intellectual disaster. But it is a formula that helps us to understand how he came to create, in his imagination, a world that the overwhelming majority of nineteenth-century Southern slave-holders never made in reality.[50]

To lend some credence to his attempt to resurrect Phillipsian and Fitzhughian visions of the antebellum Southern mode of production and society, Mr. Genovese had to try to destroy the solid empirical research of Lewis Gray, Kenneth Stampp, Paul Gates, *et al*–empirical research that had previously relegated such visions to the historical graveyard. But evidence had long been available, and in recent years has been growing at a rate even faster than the Southern economy grew from 1840 to 1860, to show that Mr. Genovese's attempt stood antebellum economic reality, South and North, on its head. To support that judgment in full detail would take a very long paper. For my purposes, relatively brief exposition must suffice.

Like Mr. Moore's argument, much of Mr. Genovese's structure of analysis and explanation collapses when we place the word "black" in front of the word "slave." Contrary to his assumptions, Southern slavery has to be viewed primarily as a matter of *race* rather than *class* because the notion cannot be taken seriously that, after 1800, whites could have been slaves (or even indentured servants) in the United States. *No black slaves, no slaves.* To fantasize as George Fitzhugh did that white "wage slavery" in the North was more economically (or psychically) exploitative than black "real slavery" in the South not only was ludicrous as a description of reality, it was ludicrous as an ideology justifying black slavery and formed no serious part of that ideology.

As a good Marxian theory of ideology might have helped Mr. Genovese to see if he had not been so captivated by Fitzhugh and Phillips, *given the long history of antiblack racism in the Anglo-American world,* the extraordinary profitability of black slavery to

---

50. Genovese, *Political Economy,* 1, for the quotation from Phillips. In passing, I merely note that Mr. Genovese offered no evidence to support his sweeping claims about the premodern, patriarchical character of the Southern slaveholders as a class. In effect, he simply asserted that they had the characteristics he ascribed to them, based upon his reading of Fitzhugh and Phillips. For his extravagant–and to me, incredible–praise of Fitzhugh as a social theorist, see his *World Slaveholders Made,* pp. 118-244.

slaveholders, and more indirectly and to a much lesser degree, to most Southern and Northern whites, produced a highly successful ideological justification of slavery. *Racism justified slavery, racism alone could have justified slavery in the United States during the nineteenth century.* From the viewpoint of Southern slaveholders, racism had two marvellous properties: 1) it permitted them to convince themselves that they were Good Men living in a Good Society (I agree with Mr. Genovese, but for entirely different reasons, that they were so convinced); 2) it effectively destroyed the possibility that nonslaveholders, North or South, might act to abolish black slavery.

Taking his stand on the quicksands that swallowed up Fitzhugh and Phillips, Mr. Genovese dismissed Lewis Gray's brilliant analysis of slaveholding planter capitalism, particularly the "strong tendency *for the planter to assume the attitude of the business man* [emphasis added] in testing success by ratio of net money income to capital invested...."[51] To support his argument that, judged by such capitalist criteria, the Southern mode of production was premodern, anticapitalist and irrational, Mr. Genovese emphasized the relatively low rates of industrialization and urbanization in the South compared to the North. Far from supporting his analysis, that "fact" demolishes it when we invoke the eminently capitalist principle of comparative advantage—an observation designed to emphasize that a scientific style of analysis leads researchers to recognize that "facts" are only *facts* within the conceptual framework of some relevant theory.

---

51. Gray, *Southern Agriculture,* 1:302. In addition to the solid support given to Gray's analysis by the massive researches of Kenneth Stampp and Paul Gates, see the impressive, comprehensive essay by Robert W. Fogel and Stanley L. Engerman, "The Economics of Slavery," in Robert W. Fogel and Stanley L. Engerman, eds., *The Reinterpretation of American Economic History* (New York: Harper and Row, 1971); the same authors' report, "The Relative Efficiency of Slavery: A Comparison of Northern and Southern Agriculture," (December 1970, mimeo); and three first-rate pieces by Morton Rothstein, "The Cotton South As A Dual economy," *Agricultural History,* XLI (October, 1967), 373-382; "The Ante-Bellum Plantation as a Business Enterprise," *Explorations in Entrepreneurial History/Second Series,* VI (1968), 128-133; "The Cotton Frontier of the Antebellum South: A Methodological Battleground," *Agricultural History,* XLIV (January, 1970), 149-165. The list could be extended at length. Without holding them responsible in any way for my views, it also seems appropriate to note that I have benefitted from recent discussions with Messrs. Fogel, Gates and Rothstein, and Robert Douglass, a graduate student at the University of Pennsylvania.

In essence, the principle of comparative advantage assumes that men who wish to engage in rational economic activity, given the various alternatives available to them, will choose those enterprises most likely to prove relatively most profitable in the long run, given *both* their own "resources" and those available to existing *or* potential competitors ("resources" refers to all "factors of production"). Suppose we invoke the principle of comparative advantage, take inventory of the *different* natural resources available to Northern and Southerners, consider the world market, recognize the relatively low state of technological development in all sectors of the American economy when we consider the different climatic and topographical conditions confronting Northerners and Southerners, appreciate that black slavery was the only form of labor that could have been used to operate large-scale agricultural activities anywhere in the United States, and calculate the economies of scale in agriculture available only on large slave plantations (to cite only a few of the relevant considerations). When we do that, we see that the relatively low rates of industrialization and urbanization in the South prior to 1861 were rational, fully in line with classical capitalist economic theory. As we would expect, therefore, and as recent studies demonstrate, far from lagging behind Northerners in economic development, *white* Southerners' "per capita income rose at least as rapidly as the national average" between 1840 and 1860.[52]

Other methodological errors aside, Mr. Genovese failed to analyze intensively and *compare systematically* Northern and Southern agriculture (to say nothing of the Northern and Southern economies as a whole). The fundamental characteristic of antebellum "agriculture," North and South, was that it *primarily* was a capitalistic system of land speculation and was only *secondarily* a system of commercial agriculture designed to provide annual returns from commodity production.[53] Given the combination of Southern staples and black slavery,

52. The quotation is from the summary statement of one of the "main findings" in Fogel and Engerman, "Economics of Slavery," in Fogel and Engerman, eds., *Reinterpretation of American Economic History,* 312.

53. By primarily a capitalist system of land speculation, I mean that most men engaged in agriculture expected that their capital would increase much more as a result of their buying land cheap and selling it dear, or holding on to land bought cheap while it rose in value, than from their annual returns from commodity production. To say that does not imply that Southern plantation

land speculators in the South had great advantages over land speculators in the North. As capitalist economic theory would predict, due to that and other economically rational considerations (rational both from the individual *and* regional point of view), population density in the South was markedly lower than in the North. To cite that "fact" to show that Southern economic development lagged behind that of the North because of the (alleged) "irrationalities" built into the Southern mode of production based on slave labor, constituted one of Mr. Genovese's major errors. That error testified to his lack of acquaintance with location theory—a body of theory indispensable for any study of economic development.

Given the *extremely high value per pound and durable nature* of Southern agricultural commodities compared to Northern agricultural commodities, transport costs formed an *extremely small* proportion of the wholesale price of Southern commodities. As a good economic theory of capitalist development would predict, therefore, and as history shows, large and small speculators in Southern land "feverishly" scrambled to acquire far more cheap land far from towns and cities than their resources permitted them to cultivate in any fashion, let alone cultivate intensively and expensively with the use of natural or artificial fertilizers. In more formal terms, given the small weight of

owners, for example, did not expect to profit from their farming operations and from the rise in value of their slaves; it only implies that taking advantage of rising land values seemed to them the quickest and surest way to fortune—or to increased fortune. My views on land speculation in American history were shaped by long conversations with, and close reading of, the two leading specialists, Paul Gates and James C. Malin. Allan Bogue has also labored to improve my understanding of the subject. For an interpretation building on the work of Gates and Malin, and works inspired by them, see Leslie E. Decker, "The Great Speculation: An Interpretation of Mid-Continent Pioneering," in David Ellis, ed., *The Frontier in American Development: Essays in Honor of Paul Wallace Gates* (Ithaca, N.Y.: Cornell University Press, 1969), pp. 357-380. A recent, first-rate guide to the voluminous literature on land speculation is found in Robert Swierenga, *Pioneers and Profits: Land Speculation on the Iowa Frontier* (Ames: Iowa State University Press, 1968), pp. XIX-XXVIII, 3-6, and *passim.* To appreciate the primary role of land speculation in the activities of Northern farmers, see Clarence H. Danhof, *Change In Agriculture: The Northern United States, 1820-1870* (Cambridge, Mass.: Harvard University Press, 1969), pp. 103-104, and *passim.*

transport costs in determining the price level of Southern staple products, speculators in the South acted on the rational assumption that they could maximize profits on their capital and entrepreneurial energy by acquiring "low rent land" whose market price (for various reasons) tended to lag significantly behind its "real" market value. (That statement, of course, neither asserts nor implies that *every* speculator—or most speculators—actually *operated* rationally.)[54]

Slaveowners enjoyed a particularly favorable position to engage in largescale land speculation—one reason so many great fortunes were made in the South before 1861.[55] (I view that fact as a revealing commentary on Mr. Genovese's acceptance of Phillips' ideological justification of slavery, "it made fewer fortunes than it made men.") Speculators in Northern lands found it extremely difficult to get free laborers to cultivate any part of their holdings and thus provide annual returns to help pay interest, tax, supervisory and other costs. As Allan Bogue has shown, to make large profits on capital invested in cheap land remote from markets, they had to buy low, sell high, and sell

---

54. I gained a better understanding of the factors that determine the location of agricultural production from my having minored in agricultural economics at Cornell University as part of my graduate program, as well as from an SSRC post-doctoral fellowship to study location theory at Harvard University under the aegis of Walter Isard. Mr. Isard, of course, is not to be held responsible for my current views but he first exposed me to the literature on location theory. For a clear exposition of the basic principles of the theory, see Edgar M. Hoover, *The Location of Economic Activity* (New York: McGraw-Hill Book Company, 1948); for a more technical analysis directly relevant to agriculture, see the chapter, "Agglomeration Analysis and Agricultural Location Theory," in Walter Isard, *Location and Space-Economy* (Cambridge, Mass.: M.I.T. Press, 1956), pp. 172-206. The classic work, of course, is von Thunen's *Isolated State*. See the edition, edited by Peter Hall and published by Pergamon Press in 1966. My impression is that American economic historians have tended to give insufficient attention to transportation factors in accounting for the development of American agriculture, particularly its land speculation component.

55. See Paul W. Gates, *The Farmer's Age: Agriculture 1815-1860* (New York: Holt, Rinehart and Winston, 1960), pp. 129-133, 146-152. Two excellent detailed case studies of especially capitalist-minded Northerners who went South to make their fortune as large slave plantation owners, land speculators, railroad stockholders, investors in municipal bonds, bankers, etc., are Rothstein, "Antebellum South," in *Agricultural History*, XLI (1967), 373-382, and his unpublished essay, "The Natchez 'Nabobs': Kinship and Friendship in an Economic Elite."

quickly; that is, they had to time their purchases and sales skillfully and luckily.[56] In contrast, slaveowners could *order* their slaves to go *whenever* and *wherever* they wanted them to go and do *whatever* they wanted done. When we appreciate the tremendous advantages slaveholding land speculators enjoyed compared to nonslaveholding land speculators, we better appreciate the *capitalist* economic rationality of the Southern mode of production, the dispersion of population in the Old South, the relatively low level of industrialization, and the rapid rise in the price of slaves, particularly during the 1840s and 1850s.

Suppose we brush away Fitzhugh's and Phillips's fantasies about organic slave plantation communities and look at the Southern mode of production as it really was. We then see that it is the crudest form of geographic determinism—that error to which American historians have been peculiarly vulnerable since Turner gave it classic expression in 1893—to claim that slaveholders required much more land than the Old South encompassed to insure the successful functioning of the Southern mode of production after 1860.[57] As Lewis Gray observed four decades ago:

> The belief . . . that in 1860 slavery in the South was on the point of being "strangled for lack of room to expand" is a wholly mistaken interpretation of actual conditions. The plantation system was not seriously limited by scarcity of land. It had utilized only a small fraction of the available land area. The most fertile and easily available soils may have been occupied, but there was an extensive area remaining, a considerable part of which has been brought into cultivation since 1860. Before the Civil War railways were rapidly opening up new fertile areas to plantation agriculture. Far from being a decrepit institution, the economic motives for the continuance of slavery from the viewpoint of the employer were never so strong as in the years just preceding the Civil War.[58]

56. To appreciate the qualities needed for successful speculative activity in Northern land, see the systematic study made by Allan Bogue, *From Prairie to Cornbelt* (Chicago: Quadrangle Books, 1968), pp. 43-46, and *passim*.

57. James C. Malin, more than any other historian, has focused attention on the devastating impact that geographic determinism has had on American historiography. See his *Essays on Historiography* (Lawrence, Kan.: private printing, 1948), pp. 1-44, and his *On the Nature of History* (Lawrence, Kan.: private printing, 1954), pp. 99-111.

58. Gray, *Southern Agriculture,* 1:476.

Put another way, had it not been for the Civil War, every reason exists to think that the per capita income of *white Southerners* would have continued to rise significantly for a long time after 1860, either measured in absolute terms or compared to the per capita income of white Northerners.[59]

On the basis of economic theory and the plethora of impressionistic evidence available in secondary sources, I have long been convinced of this proposition: Judged strictly from the viewpoint of "capitalist rationality," prior to 1861, directly and indirectly, investment of capital and entrepreneurial skill in large-scale southern plantations worked by black slaves was the most lucrative form of economic activity that *could generally* have been engaged in anywhere in the United States.[60] For "noneconomic" reasons, some capitalist-minded

---

59. See the discussion in Fogel and Engerman, "Economics of Slavery", in Fogel and Engerman, eds., *op. cit.* pp. 328-338.

60. My views crystallized during the 1951-1952 postdoctoral year I spent at Harvard learning about location theory from Walter Isard. Having done my dissertation under Paul Gates at Cornell on the responses of New York merchants and farmers to the Communication Revolution, a subject that required me to immerse myself in agricultural and economic history, and having minored in economic history and agricultural economics, I found Lewis Gray's analysis far more convincing than U.B. Phillips. (Actually, for a variety of reasons, even Gray seriously underestimated the rationality of the Southern mode of production for Southern whites in particular and white Americans in general). In 1952-1953, I gave a survey course in American history at Columbia and had to organize my ideas on the topic, "Northern and Southern Economies: Competitive or Complementary?" It seemed clear to me then, and seems even clearer now, that the economies were unusually complementary. On economic "grounds," for example, eastern and western agriculturalists were far more competitive with each other than with Southern agriculturalists. The only Southern *economic* groups that tended to suffer (at least relatively) from Northern competition were some types of businessmen in the seaports and nascent manufacturers. That factor *helps* to account for the shift of the "secessionist capital" from Columbia, S.C., in the 1830s and 1840s to Charleston, S.C. in the 1850s. Some of my findings on Eastern agrarian hostility to improvements in transportation—improvements which severely intensified the difficulties they experienced from Western competition—are summarized in my *Merchants, Farmers and Railroads: Railroad Regulation and New York Politics 1850-1887* (New York: Russell and Russell, 1969) 1-28, 80-83. The book was first published in 1955 by Harvard University Press.

men shunned that form of investment; others, *perhaps more capitalist-minded,* enthusiastically seized the opportunities and rewards it offered.

To gain wider credence, suppose I weaken that proposition to claim only this: The dominance in the Southern economy of its slaveholding sector is best understood and explained on rational economic grounds; it strongly tended to be very profitable for slaveholders as individuals and for white Southerners as a group.

Once either the strong or weak proposition is granted, we can readily understand the powerful—but far from exclusive role—that economic development played in transforming Southern ideology from the pathetic, defensive apologetics around the turn of the nineteenth century to the extraordinarily confident "slavery is a positive good" manifestoes of the 1840s and 1850s. Making "ingenious" use of racism to justify their argument that black slavery was right and good for all members of American (and world) society, black and white, North and South, we know that Southern ideologists brought such a revolution about. And the evidence overwhelmingly shows that no *significant* section of white Southern elite or mass opinion doubted that such a revolution had been brought about or believed, as Mr. Genovese claimed they believed, that the "internal contradictions in the South and the external conflict with the North placed the slaveholders hopelessly on the defensive with little to look forward to except slow strangulation."

No doubt a researcher can seem to support that claim, as Mr. Genovese did, "by haphazardly culling quotations from haphazard assortments of contemporary sources" (to quote my strictures on traditional historical methodology). But to see that Southern elites, as a group, did not misperceive the reality later reconstructed by Lewis Gray (and numerous other researchers) and confidently looked forward to a rosy economic future, we need only consider the implications of their triumphant proclamation in the 1850s that "Cotton is King."[61] Secession did not represent a desperate gamble on the part of men who thought that their society faced "strangulation" and doom. Precisely

61. See the numerous essays brought together in E.N. Elliott, ed., *Cotton Is King and Pro-Slavery Arguments* (Augusta, Ga., 1860).

because leading secessionists took the "Cotton is King" argument
seriously, they believed themselves to be invincible. Secession tended to
occur in an atmosphere of Jubilee and lighthearted gaiety, not
desperation and sense of impending doom.

To give some of the flavor of the "Cotton is King" argument, I
quote a contemporary assessment of the rosy economic present and still
rosier economic future. That assessment both supports, and is supported by, it should be noted, the massive secondary research recently
summarized and powerfully developed by Robert Fogel and Stanley
Engerman.

U.S. Senator James H. Hammond of South Carolina was a longtime
secessionist who had every reason to believe what he was saying because
he had personally enjoyed tremendous economic success. We have every
reason to believe that he knew what he was talking about because he
perfectly exemplified Gray's concept of the rational planter-capitalist
On October 29, 1858, at Barnwell Court House in South Carolina, he
delivered a lengthy, well-prepared speech designed to strengthen his
political position and increase his influence. It radiated confidence.
Given the speaker, the circumstances, the audience, and the contents,
that speech is an excellent indicator, not only of contemporary
economic realities, but of contemporary perceptions of economic
realities (a much more difficult phenomenon to measure).

> I confess that, for many years of my life, I believed that our only
> safety was the dissolution of the Union, and I openly avowed it. I
> should entertain and without hesitation express the same senti-
> ments now, but that the victories we have achieved and those that
> I think that we are about to achieve, have inspired me with the
> hope, I may say the belief, that we can fully sustain ourselves in
> the Union and control its action in all great affairs. . . . You must
> not suppose, for a moment, that I am opposed to the expansion
> of the area of African slavery. On the contrary, I believe that God
> created negroes for no other purpose than to be hewers of wood
> and drawers of water, that is to be slaves of the white
> race ... [but we ought to abandon the idea of geographic
> expansion because] the South, numbering twelve millions of
> people, *possesses already an imperial domain that can well
> support a hundred millions more* [emphasis added]. What does
> she need to seek beyond her borders, or what has she to fear?
> With such a sea coast and harbors; such rivers, mountains, and

plains; so full of all precious metals, so fertile in soil, so genial in climate, producing in such unparalleled abundance the most valuable agricultural staples of the world; capable of manufacturing to any extent; and possessing the best social and industrial systems that have ever yet been organized,—she might have sunk into sloth from excess of prosperity had she not been kept on the alert by the fierce assaults of an envious world. Assaults which, at one time alarming, it has been in fact scarcely more than wholesome exercise to repel; an exercise which has made us the most virtuous and one of the most enlightened and most powerful people who now flourish on the globe.[62]

It is a commentary upon the established historiographic system that *systematic, comparable, cumulative* studies have not yet been made of secessionist movements and secessionist groups from the 1820s to 1861. I cannot even make a guess, therefore, about the proportion of erstwhile secessionists who took Hammond's *political* position by the late 1850s. I quote his speech to illustrate the erroneous nature of Mr. Genovese's claim "that slavery needed room to expand but had none" and that "most slaveholders" therefore decided to "stake everything on a desperate gamble for a political independence that would have freed them to push their system southward. . . ." That claim not only makes erroneous assumptions about the *motives* of secessionists, it assumes a degree of political unity among Southern slaveholders that they never attained prior to the outbreak of war (or afterward either, for that matter).

As I have earlier noted, in addition to Mr. Genovese's erroneous assumptions about the Southern mode of production and economic

---

62. "Speech of the Hon. James Hammond, delivered at Barnwell, C.H., October 29, 1858" (Charleston, 1858), 11-15. As is well known, Hammond reversed his position after Lincoln's election and joined the stampede of South Carolinians who resigned from federal offices. What tends to be ignored, however, is that he strongly deprecated the stampede and his own participation in it. "I thought Magrath and all those fellows were great asses for resigning and have done it myself. It is an epidemic and very foolish. It reminds me of the Japan[e] se who when insulted rip up their own bowels." As quoted in, Robert C. Tucker, "James Henry Hammond, South Carolinian" (unpublished Ph.D., University of North Carolina, 1958), 477-478. As I observe later in the text, the genie of Southern nationalism that Hammond had done as much as any man to call forth in the 1830s was very hard to put back in the bottle once let out. But that is the subject for a series of books, not a footnote.

development, his explanation derived from his assumption that the slaveholders essentially constituted a unified "ruling class." To support that assumption, he offered no empirical evidence— perhaps because he thought that Marxian political theory entitled him to assume that the slaveholders *must* have functioned as the "ruling class" in the South.

Resisting the temptation to comment on the underdeveloped state of Marxian political theory (something long known to Marxists who have undertaken systematic political research),[63] I think it best simply to observe that Mr. Genovese's assumption had no basis in fact because of these—among other—considerations: 1) All during the antebellum period, slaveholders fiercely divided on party lines and the competing parties stood for drastically opposed principles and policies. 2) Unlike European (and other) ruling classes, the slaveholding *economic* class was highly heterogeneous in its social composition (e.g., religion, ethnicity, education). 3) By 1860, in almost all Southern states, all adult whites had attained equal political rights. 4) Within the South, political power was dispersed and dissipated by fierce intrasectional, interstate, and intrastate cleavages. 5) Within the South, nothing existed remotely like the central capital and/or court so important to the development and existence of ruling classes in other societies.

To say that Southern slaveholders did not constitute anything like a ruling class (except that they all "ruled" black slaves), is not to say, of course, that anything like a genuinely democratic political system existed in the South (or in the North either, for that matter). It is to say that no warrant exists for any researcher to mechanically invoke Marx's ruling class concept and vaguely formulated propositions. Such invocation cannot absolve scholars from engaging in systematic,

---

63. One of the greatest weaknesses in the Marxian approach to the study of society has been the relative inattention paid to the actual workings of political systems in specific societies. The "ruling class" concept remains at a primitive stage of development and is so casually invoked as to be worse than useless. Marxian "general propositions" about the distribution of power in societies tend to be unsupported by any systematic, empirical research; instead, Marx's scattered fragmentary observations tend to be taken as self-evident, requiring only concrete examples and plausible extension. A recent example is Ralph Miliband, *The State in Capitalist Society: An Analysis of the Western System of Power* (London: Weidenfeld and Nicolson, 1969).

empirical research focused on such hard questions as: 1) what was the distribution of political power in the United States; 2) who held disproportionate political power; 3) how did they acquire and hold on to (or lose) it; 4) what did they do with it?

Serious attempts to develop a credible explanation of Civil War causation cannot dodge such questions. Researchers, however, had long dodged them. The way was open for Mr. Genovese, therefore, to make the theoretical, conceptual, methodological and substantive mistakes evident in his analysis and description of slaveholders' political attitudes and positions in respect to the geographic expansion of slavery.

As a result of developments that began long before an alleged land-shortage could possibly have affected their political attitudes, by the late 1850s, it is possibly true that most slaveholders agreed that, *in principle,* the *federal government* should not *formally and officially* deny them the *nominal right* to bring their slaves to any area still in a territorial status. But even on that issue (and generally on all issues related to slaveholders' "rights"), throughout the antebellum period, slaveholders intensely divided on the *policies* to follow to secure their nominal right. More to the point for our present purpose, as I have quoted Hammond's speech to suggest, throughout the antebellum period, slaveholders intensely differed over policies related to the *desirability* of actually acquiring additional territory. What entitled Mr. Genovese, therefore, to assert flatly that "most slaveholders" were convinced long before secession actually occurred that unrestricted territorial expansion of slavery was imperative for them to continue to function as a "ruling class?"

To some extent, Mr. Genovese tried to support his assertion by using, a century later and in a scholarly monograph, the same impressionistic technique of haphazard quotation that Marx, based in London, had used to dash off his journalistic articles on "The North American Civil War."[64] But Mr. Genovese mainly tried to support his assertions by simply making another set of assertions. To wit, expansion had been imperative to the survival of slavery. "Individual southerners" (he really meant "Individual slaveholders" but treated the two terms as synonymous, a revealing indicator of his assumption that

---

64. See the quotations scattered throughout the chapter, "The Origins of Slavery Expansionism," in Genovese, *Political Economy,* pp. 243-270.

nonslaveholders counted for nothing in the South) who opposed that policy, therefore, failed to act the way that"the interests of their class and system required them to [act]...."[65] False consciousness, what historiographic crimes have been committed in thy name!

Less rhetorically put, my point is that when we read Mr. Genovese closely and critically, we see that to support his assertion about the position of "most slaveholders" on territorial expansion, he simply *declared* that: 1) slaveholders constituted a ruling class; 2) objective realities "dictated expansion if the men who made up the ruling class of the South were to continue to rule;" and 3) most slaveholders *therefore* must have favored the policy he said the logic of history required them to have favored.

Consider that Mr. Genovese's assumption about the objective reality of Southern economic development had no basis in fact. That error emphasizes for us—if emphasis were still needed—that it is fatal to adhere to an uncritical, doctrinaire version of Marxism that, at this late date, continues to invoke the radically subjective concept of false consciousness. That concept may appeal to scholars seeking absolution from the hard job of measuring attitude and opinion distribution by engaging in systematic empirical research informed by a genuinely scientific orientation. But the price of such absolution is that one forfeits the right to be taken seriously.[66]

Uncritical use of Marxian concepts and propositions was not the only source of Mr. Genovese's erroneous claims about the distribution of political power and the determinants of antebellum political attitudes and conflicts. Like Mr. Moore, he also uncritically accepted the traditional "balance of power" notion. Specifically, he claimed that slaveholders were doomed if the *number* of free states and free state congressmen became—and remained—significantly larger than the *number* of slave states and slave state congressmen. To quote Mr. Genovese:

---

65. *Ibid.*, 264.

66. For a devastating critique of researchers who impose *their own subjective view* of "class interests" on the human beings they purport to study, see Giovanni Sartori, "From the Sociology of Politics to Political Sociology," in Seymour M. Lipset, ed., *Politics and the Social Sciences* (New York: Oxford University Press, 1969), pp. 70-87.

The economic process propelling the slave South along expansionist paths had its political and social parallels, the most obvious being the need to re-establish parity in the Senate [after the balance of power was broken with the admission of California in 1850] or at least to guarantee enough voting strength in Washington to protect Southern interests. In an immediate political sense the demand for more slave-state Congressmen was among the important roots of expansion, but in a deeper sense it was merely a symptom of something more fundamental. Had the South not had a distinct and powerful ruling class at its helm, a decline of its political and economic power would have caused no greater alarm than it did in New England.[67]

Closely examined, the balance of power assumption makes sense only if we also assume that the inhabitants of the free states were united behind policies or programs designed either to abolish slavery or to injure slaveholders so seriously as somehow to bring about the disappearance of slavery. Moreover, it requires us to assume not only that the inhabitants of the "old" free states were united against the continued existence of slavery, but that the inhabitants of the "new" free states inevitably would take that same position and thereby fatally weaken the ability of slaveholders "to protect Southern interests." As one example is enough to show, neither assumption had any basis in fact.

The admission of California in 1850 did upset the exact numerical balance of free and slave states that had existed since 1812. But did its admission result in the diminution of the political power of slaveholders? Did it increase the likelihood that Northerners hostile to slavery would control the federal government and take actions designed to undermine the foundations of Southern slavery? No. The admission of California, like the earlier admission of free states in the Old Northwest, significantly *increased* the power of the Southern political elites who had strongly tended to dominate the Democratic party since Jackson's election in 1828, and through it, the national government. To quote Roy Nichols on California politics during the 1850s:

California had a politics all her own in which the local Democracy had been riding high, wide, and handsome. . . . Many persons were of Southern origin—so many in fact that the new region was

67. Genovese, *Political Economy*, pp. 247-248.

sometimes called Virginia's poorhouse; and they seized early leadership. The first legislature, in 1849, named a Tennessean, who had been a Congressman from Mississippi, to be one of the United States Senators; Dr. William M. Gwin went to Washington *and, with his Southern connections, became a prominent figure in the select circle of the Senate* [emphasis added].[68]

The admission of new free states actually increased the ability of Southern political elites to dominate the Democratic party and national government. Among other reasons, it did so because antiblack racism strengthened the Democratic factions in the West that tended to accept the leadership of militant "State Rights" Southern Democrats. At times, of course, some Western Democrats rebelled when particularly provoked by what might be called "the arrogance of slaveholders' power," crudely and repeatedly displayed. That observation is designed to suggest that, for reasons entirely opposite to those given by Mr. Genovese (and Mr. Moore and numerous other writers who have fostered the "balance of power" myth), the increased population of the Western free states did subtly work to diminish the power of the most aggressive faction of Southern Democrats. It did so by tending to make them overconfident, overarrogant, and overreaching. Here I refer to Southern Democrats *who were not secessionists.*

Secessionists who used the Democratic party to achieve their goals essentially tended to know what they were doing, I am convinced, when they made demands politically (and personally) outrageous to Western and Northeastern Democrats. The art of "radicalizing" latently hostile populations was not invented by "New Leftists" in the 1960s; Southern secessionists brilliantly practiced it from 1830 to 1861. Particularly during the campaign of 1860, they devoted themselves to the difficult task of electing a "Black Republican" to the Presidency of the United States. Had they not succeeded in their desperate efforts, it is possible that secession never would have occurred.

I make such sweeping claims, of course, simply to indicate the error in the traditional assumption that increased population in the Western free states necessarily threatened the political dominance enjoyed by slaveholding Democrats on the national level. To test those claims

---

68. Roy Nichols, *The Disruption of American Democracy* (New York: Macmillan Company, 1948), p. 90.

adequately would take massive collaborative, cumulative research. Such research, I trust, someday will be undertaken when adequate resources exist to develop credible explanations of Civil War causation. But for that happier state of affairs to come about, the existing historiographic system must be overthrown and replaced—which leads me now to examine David Donald's explanation of Civil War causation.

C. David Donald's Explanation of Civil War Causation. Mr. Donald's explanation of Civil War causation represents an updated variant of James G. Randall's version of the revisionist thesis. Like the "great teacher under whom it was once my privilege to study,"[69] Mr. Donald viewed it as a needless war. But contrary to another revisionist, Avery Craven, who asserted that the transformation of nonviolent conflict into violent conflict stemmed from the *failure* of the democratic process,[70] Mr. Donald asserted that it stemmed from the regrettably *successful* working of the democratic process. The tyranny of the majority, he asserted, defeated "conservative statesmanship."[71] Obviously, therefore, his explanation sharply differs from Mr. Moore's and directly contradicts Mr. Genovese's explanation that war inevitably came because *conservative* slaveholders inevitably tried to *preserve* their premodern civilization.

Unlike Mr. Moore and like Mr. Genovese, Mr. Donald did not rely on secondary analysis. He presented his explanation after long, massive research in antebellum history. Also like Mr. Genovese (who did graduate work under him), Mr. Donald's research was innocent of corruption by a scientific style of analysis. He stated assumptions as facts and impressionistically culled contemporary sources for quotations to support conclusions that required data secured by systematic methods. Having dismissed all explanations other than his own on the grounds that they had little basis in fact and avoided answering the very

69. J.G. Randall and David Donald, *The Civil War and Reconstruction* (2nd ed.; Boston: D.C. Health Company, 1961), V.

70. Craven, "The 1840's and the Democratic Process," *Journal of Southern History,* XVI (1950), 161-176.

71. For his explanation of Civil War causation, see David Donald, *Lincoln Reconsidered* (Vintage Books: New York, n.d., 2nd ed.), 19-36, 209-235; "The Proslavery Argument Reconsidered," *Journal of Southern History,* XXXVII (February, 1971), 3-18.

questions they posed, he blithely proceeded to present an explanation vulnerable on precisely those grounds. Critically examined, as I will try to show, his explanation can be seen to derive from an orientation to collective violence that Ted Gurr, in a recent overview of psychological theories of human aggression, dismissed in these terms: "Some psychological theories about the sources of agressive behavior can be disregarded at the outset. There is little support for pseudo-psychological assertions that most or all revolutionaries or conspirators are deviants, fools, or the maladjusted."[72]

1. Mr. Donald's explanation summarized.   Mr. Donald's version of the revisionist thesis is suggested by the title of his 1960 Harmsworth inaugural lecture at Oxford, "An Excess of Democracy: The American Civil War and the Social Process." To comprehend all his major claims, however, we also need to examine his 1955 essay, "Toward a Reconsideration of Abolitionists," and his 1970 presidential address to the Southern Historical Association, "The Pro-slavery Argument Reconsidered."

By the 1850s, Mr. Donald asserted, the American social process had produced "an excess of democracy." What Tocqueville had warned against had come about. The Civil War occurred because no conservative "attempts to curb the tyranny of the majority were successful; all went too strongly against the democratic current of the age." Quoting Walter Bagehot, the British elitist, and Henry James, the American expatriate to England, to support his claims, he asserted that by the middle of the nineteenth century, democratization had produced a society in which the American people "suffered from an excess of liberty . . . [and] were increasingly unable to arrive at reasoned, independent judgments upon the problems which faced their society."[73] Echoing the Toquevillian-inspired warnings against "authoritarian mass democracy" current in the 1950s,[74] he depicted the mass

72. Ted Robert Gurr, *Why Men Rebel* (Princeton, N.J.: Princeton University Press, 1971), p. 30.

73. Donald, *Lincoln Reconsidered,* pp. 228-235.

74. See, for example, the chapter, "Working-class Authoritarianism," in Seymour M. Lipset, *Political Man* (Anchor Books: Garden City, N.Y., 1963), 87-126. The book was first published in 1960 and neatly reflects the ideological temper of the 1950s and the "end-of-ideology" ideology that flourished during that decade.

of American people *in the 1850s* as conformists "huddling together in their loneliness," lacking conservative, authoritative leadership and seeking "only to escape their freedom." As a result, Americans characteristically suffered from "hysterical fears and paranoid suspicions. . . . Never was there a field so fertile before the propagandist, the agitator, the extremist."[75] The result of all that: *relatively minor conflicts* proved insoluble and the Civil War resulted. Because paraphrase fails to do justice to Mr. Donald's statement of the "needless war" thesis, I quote him at length:

> . . . [the] crises which afflicted the United States in the 1850s were not in themselves calamitous experiences. . . . When compared to crises which other nations have resolved without great discomfort, the true proportions of these exaggerated disturbances appear.
>
> But American society in the 1850's was singularly ill equipped *to meet any shocks, however weak* [emphasis added]. It was a society so new and so disorganized that its nerves were rawly exposed. It was, as Henry James noted, a land which had "no sovereign, no court, no personal loyalty, no aristocracy, no church, no clergy, no army, no diplomatic service, no country gentlemen, no palaces, no castles, nor manors, nor old country houses, nor parsonages, nor thatched cottages, nor ivied ruins; no cathedrals, nor abbeys, nor little Norman Churches, no great universities, nor public schools . . . ; no literature, no novels, no museums, no pictures, no political society"—in short *which had no resistance to strain* [emphasis added]. . . . The structure of the American political system impeded the appearance of conservative statesmanship, and the rapidity of the crises in the 1850's prevented conservatism from crystallizing. The crises themselves were not world-shaking, nor did they inevitably produce war. They were, however, the chisel strokes which revealed the fundamental flaws in the block of marble, flaws which stemmed from an excess of democracy.[76]

Mr. Donald depicted the American mob as leaderless. But he asserted that it was motivated to frenzied, destructive action by propagandists, agitators, extremists. They whipped up mass fears and tensions until the weak social and political structures cracked under the strain. Given the inherently weak state of American society, he claimed in effect,

---

75. Donald, *Lincoln Reconsidered*, pp. 229-230.
76. *Ibid.*, pp. 234-235.

extremists can primarily be said to have caused the Civil War. We better understand his explanation when we note that, *in 1955,* among all the different varieties of extremists, he gave abolitionists pride of place. Abolitionists did what they did, he claimed, because they personally suffered from hysterical fears and paranoid suspicions induced by their membership in a rapidly declining social class.

> As young men the fathers of abolitionists had been leaders of their communities and states; in their old age they were elbowed aside by the merchant prince, the manufacturing tycoon, the corporation lawyer. The bustling democracy of the 1830s passed them by; as the Reverend Ludovicus Weld lamented to his famous son [the abolitionist] Theodore: "I have . . . felt like a stranger in a strange land."[77]

Summarizing his composite portrait of abolitionist leadership, Mr. Donald characterized them—and their social dislocation and status deprivation—as follows:

> Descended from old and socially dominant Northeastern families, reared in a faith of aggressive piety and moral endeavor, educated for conservative leadership, these young men and women who reached maturity in the 1830's faced a strange and hostile world. Social and economic leadership was being transferred from the country to the city, from the farmer to the manufacturer, from the preacher to the corporation attorney. Too distinguished a family, too gentle an education, too nice a morality were handicaps in a bustling world of business. Expecting to lead, these young people found no followers. They were an elite without function, a displaced class in American society.[78]

Mr. Donald took some pains to deny the possibility that the members of the displaced class were genuinely motivated by any desire to alleviate the misery of any human beings other than themselves. What they resented:

> . . . was the transfer of leadership to the wrong groups in society, and their appeal for reform was a strident call for their own class to reexert its former social dominance. Some fought for prison reform; some for women's rights; some for world peace; but ultimately most came to make that natural identification between

77. *Ibid.,* p. 28.
78. *Ibid.,* p. 33.

moneyed aristocracy, textile-manufacturing, and Southern slave-grown cotton. An attack on slavery was their best, *if quite unconscious* [emphasis added], attack upon the new industrial system.[79]

They really cared nothing for the plight of the black slaves. To rebel against the allied "Lords of the Lash and the Lords of the Loom" gave some meaning to their otherwise empty lives, gave them a cause. After the Civil War began, therefore, they attacked Lincoln in terms that betrayed an "extraordinary and unprovoked violence of expression...."[80]

Why direct verbal violence against Lincoln? Mr. Donald dismissed the notion that the abolitionists genuinely believed that Lincoln's refusal to adopt militant policies designed to undermine the Confederacy was greatly prolonging the war, increasing the bloodshed, and endangering the prospects of victory over the slaveholding secessionists. On the contrary, like Mr. Genovese, he knew false consciousness when he saw it (although this time it was false consciousness of the Freudian rather than Marxian kind). Abolitionists virulently attacked Lincoln primarily because:

... by his effective actions against slavery he left the abolitionists without a cause. The freeing of the slaves ended the great crusade that had brought purpose and joy to the abolitionists. For them, Abraham Lincoln was not the Great Emancipator; he was the killer of the dream.[81]

Having in 1955 identified and explained the unconscious drives of Abolitionist extremists, having in 1960 explained the propensity of the American masses to suffer from "hysterical fears and paranoid suspicions," in 1970 Mr. Donald focused attention upon the proslavery extremists of the South. Earlier he had argued that no rational basis existed for the abolitionists' attacks upon slavery and Lincoln; now, he argued that no rational basis could have existed for the proslavery advocates' frenetic campaign to justify the South's peculiar institution. If we try to account for their campaign on rational grounds, he

---

79. *Ibid.*, pp. 34-35.
80. *Ibid.*, pp. 18-19, 35.
81. *Ibid.*, pp. 35-36.

asserted, "the reasons for its appearance remain puzzling."[82] As we might guess, the puzzle disappeared after he probed deeper into the psyches of proslavery extremists.

In *1970,* Mr. Donald failed to refer to his 1955 explanation of the appearance of Abolitionist extremists. The omission seems puzzling because he claimed to have solved the puzzle of the proslavery extremists by using the same theory, concepts and techniques used in his earlier essay. Making judiciously imaginative use of contemporary quotations, he presented capsule biographies of several leading pro-slavery advocates.[83] He then noted that he could "go on and on with other accounts of proslavery advocates. . . ." But that was unnecessary, he claimed, because:

> . . . the general pattern is clear. All were unhappy men who had severe personal problems relating to their place in Southern society. Though ambitious and hardworking, *all failed* [emphasis added] in the paths normally open to the enterprising in the South; planting, practicing law, and politics. Few of them had any large personal stake in the system which they defended. *Most looked back with longing to an earlier day of the Republic when men like themselves—their own ancestors—had been leaders in the South* [emphasis added].[84]

In the South, as in the North, according to Mr. Donald, the extremists who whipped up the irrational passions of the American mob did so because they themselves were severely disturbed persons whose psychopathological problems derived from their social disloca-tion and status deprivation. Pseudopsychology, what historiographic crimes have been committed in thy name!

2. Mr. Donald's explanation assessed.   During the 1950s, as is well known, Columbia University functioned as a center for the prolific propagation of theses about the propensity towards extremism of "downwardly mobile, displaced status groups" and the regrettable propensity toward authoritarianism of "the lower classes." To account for those theses and their flourishing state at Columbia is irrelevant for

---

82. Donald, "Proslavery Argument," pp. 3-4.
83. *Ibid.,* 9-12.
84. *Ibid.,* 12.

my purposes (and beyond my capacity). It is relevant to note, however, that they stemmed from status-anxiety and "mass man" theories, in part derived from the revival of Tocqueville and in part from Harold Lasswell's use of Freudian theory to explain the "psychopathology" of "radical agitators."[85]

Mr. Donald had studied under James G. Randall, one of the leading revisionists, and was teaching at Columbia during the 1950s. It seems reasonable to think, therefore, that those circumstances help account for his having heavily relied upon theses derived from Tocquevillian sociology and Freudian psychoanalysis to develop an updated variant of the needless-war-caused-by-fanatics-and-agitators explanation of Civil War causation.

I also worked at Columbia during the 1950s. But on personal and ideological grounds, I then had (and still have) an *extreme* aversion to the "radicals are crazies who suffer from lost status and/or sexual repression" orientation. (No doubt, Mr. Donald will know what that *really* means.) On the basis of my own work, moreover, I was convinced that Mr. Donald's explanation exemplified impressionistic and irresponsible historical research, fatally flawed by superficial, poor use of concepts and theories that he failed to understand and used faddishly.

In part, I include that autobiographical note to indicate that my assessment of Mr. Donald's explanation does not represent the view of a detached critic dispassionately examining it from a distant Olympian height. Mostly, however, it is to indicate that soon after going to another university in 1961, I set a student to work on a master's thesis explicitly designed to test Mr. Donald's claims about abolitionists in particular and the "status deprivation" thesis in general. Having completed his thesis on Michigan abolitionists, the student then moved to Columbia University to do a dissertation extending his study to include New York abolitionists. His findings have now been published in book form. They directly contradict and thoroughly discredit Mr. Donald's claims. In my opinion, they also *further* discredit the entire

---

85. See Harold D. Lasswell, *Psychopathology and Politics* (New York: Compass Books, 1966), paper. The book was first published in 1930 and directly and indirectly, in my judgment, played a major role in shaping what has come to be described as "elitist theories of democracy."

body of work relevant to radicals and radical movements that stems from the combined Tocquevillian-Freudian orientation.[86]

Far from abolitionist leaders being stranded in rural backwaters and traumatically deprived of social status, Gerald Sorin found that:

> Abolitionism tended to draw its leadership from urban areas and from the highly educated, moderately prosperous segments of society. The abolitionists leaders pursued the most influential occupations in their communities and were actively engaged in public service. They generally seem to have had higher status in their respective communities than their fathers had had in theirs. It was impossible to find more than three or four men whose economic, social, or personal dislocation might reasonably be said to have left them discernably insecure and frustrated.
>
> The New York abolitionist leaders were intensely and actively religious. They had been exposed to the revivalism of the era—a revivalism which was the "precedent condition to all ensuing crusades." They were motivated by a reawakened religious impulse, a strong sense of social justice, and the sincere belief that they were not only insuring their own freedom from guilt, but that they would affect society in such a way as to assure social justice for everyone.
>
> The leaders were concerned with the rights and civil liberties of the free Negro, and were concerned with the slave as a person as well as an abstract cause. . . . The abolitionists' intense religiosity, more than their psychological makeup, explains why they employed the terminology of sin and guilt. And their forcefulness in this area was a function of the frustration they suffered watching churches, parties, and ordinary citizens ignoring their pleas. . . . That there was desperation in their appeals is explained by the fact that the abolitionists believed that America had become corrupted by its worship of the bitch-goddess success, that she was sacrificing the ideals of her own revolution and her Christian integrity on the altar of materialism, and that the nation thus had adopted a value hierarchy which placed private

---

86. Compare Mr. Donald's two essays in *Lincoln Reconsidered* with Gerald Sorin, "The Historical Theory of Political Radicalism: Michigan Abolitionist Leaders as a Test Case", (Wayne State University, unpublished M.A. essay, 1964); "The Historical Theory of Political Radicalism: New York Abolitionist Leaders as a Test Case" (Columbia University, unpublished Ph.D., 1969); *The New York Abolitionists: A Case Study of Political Radicalism* (Westport, Conn.: Greenwood Press, 1971). See also Benson, *Jacksonian Democracy,* 110-114, 208-213.

property, union, wealth, and future power above emancipation.[87]

The contrast between the assertions tossed off by Mr. Donald and the findings of systematic research oriented towards a scientific style of analysis could hardly be more contradictory. Nor could they provide better evidence for my general critique of the established historiographic system exemplified by Mr. Donald. But to add more evidence and to reinforce my argument that something must be radically wrong with a scholarly system that handsomely rewards men who do work of the calibre Mr. Donald does, I turn now to his 1970 presidential address to the Southern Historical Association.

As the quotation on page 276 above shows, Mr. Donald asserted that the proslavery ideologues' behavior stemmed from traumatic experiences they had suffered because of downward social mobility. Unlike their ancestors who "had been leaders in the South," they had "all failed in the paths normally open to the enterprising in the South: planting, practicing law, and politics." To demonstrate that Mr. Donald, with impressive impartiality, misrepresented proslavery ideologists and secessionists as baldly and badly in 1970 as he had misrepresented abolitionists in 1955, I think it only necessary to assess his capsule biography of James H. Hammond. Before examining it in detail, because the whole adds up to much more than the sum of its parts, I quote it in full:

> Another South Carolinian will be our final example. The son of a Yankee schoolteacher who had wandered into upcountry Carolina, James Henry Hammond obviously had the brains but not the family connections required for success in the South. Neither in law nor in journalism could he make a name for himself, and he constantly felt that people were looking down at him. Then he met and married Catherine Fitzsimmons, daughter of a wealthy Charleston merchant and distiller, and promptly abandoning both his newspaper and his law practice, he removed to his wife's plantation, where he lived ostentatiously in an effort to ape the aristocrats of his state. Professor Frederick A. Porcher of the College of Charleston called Hammond "the only intelligent man I ever knew . . . whom I considered to be a 'purse proud man'; he evidently and palpably valued himself more on account of his

87. Sorin, *New York Abolitionists,* 119-120.

possessions than upon any of those intellectual powers for which the people admired him." Porcher may have exaggerated the extent of popular admiration for Hammond, for despite a constant lust for office, he succeeded only once in a popular election; to his other positions he was appointed. *Desperately ambitious, he sulked on his wife's plantation, becoming ever more passionate in his defense of the South and of slavery* [emphasis added].[88]

To understate the case, Mr. Donald's Hammond is not the Hammond described by his biographers. Mr. Donald wrote that he "obviously had the brains but not the family connections required for success in the South. Neither in law nor in journalism could he make a name for himself. . . ." Elizabeth Merritt's biography (1923) noted that in 1828, when Hammond was twenty years old, he gained admission to the bar in Columbia, South Carolina. Quoting his diary entry of April 19, 1836 (when he had gained great celebrity as a freshman member of the U.S. House of Representatives and was twenty-eight years old), she then wrote:

> He opened his law office there, "without a friend who could in the slightest advance my fortune & steeped to the lips in poverty. Without a name without a family connection," his practice was almost at once more lucrative and successful than he could have expected.[89]

Some failure. Some sense of failure.

South Carolina politics were too absorbing during 1829 and 1830, Dr. Merritt then observed, for Hammond to remain on the sidelines. "He threw himself into the nullification controversy and began his political career by starting in Columbia a newspaper called the Southern Times [first issue, January 29, 1830]." Did he again fail "to make a name for himself?" I quote Dr. Merritt:

> Even so early as this [1830] Hammond had the pleasantest confidential relations with the leaders of the nullification movement. [Governor] Hayne wrote to him privately predicting the happiest effects for the course he had laid out for his paper F.W. Pickens told him the secret of his authorship of the

88. Donald, in *Journal of Southern History*, 37:12.

89. Elizabeth Merritt, *James Henry Hammond: 1807-1864* (Baltimore: Johns Hopkins Press, 1923), pp. 12-13.

successful "Hampden" articles and was glad when Hammond said he would republish them in his paper. Even so prominent a man as Eldred Simkens, Sr., Calhoun's law partner, did not know, though he suspected, who Hampden was. Calhoun knew the good work Hammond was doing.[90]

Within a short time, Dr. Merritt continued, Hammond had "worked" his paper's circulation:

... up to two thousand subscribers, a very good circulation for the time and place.

A rumor [early in 1831] that Hammond contemplated leaving South Carolina distressed the State Rights leaders. McDuffie wrote praising the Times in high terms, calling it "all important in the present crisis" and "the ablest journal in the state." Governor Hamilton "earnestly implore[d] ... [him] not to think of leaving the Country [i.e., the state. L.B.]. He became more than ever high in the councils of the State Rights party.[91]

Hammond was then all of *twenty-three* years old. Some failure in journalism. Some sense of failure in journalism.

Having failed both in law and journalism and "constantly feeling that people were looking down at him," Mr. Donald continued, Hammond (fortunately) met and married a wealthy heiress and, "promptly abandoning both his newspaper and his law practice, he removed to his wife's plantation, where he lived ostentatiously in an effort to ape the aristocrats of his state." As the paragraph I quoted in full shows, Mr. Donald depicted Hammond as a "desperately ambitious" man who had failed in law and journalism, who also failed in planting and politics, and who "sulked on his wife's plantation, becoming ever more passionate in his defense of the South and of slavery." To coin a phrase, let us look at the record.

To my knowledge, the most detailed biography of Hammond yet written is a dissertation completed by Robert C. Tucker in 1958.[92] I am greatly tempted to quote page after page from it to show that Mr. Donald's presidential address, again to use delicate understatement, is not to be taken uncritically at face value. But brief paraphrase and quotation make the point. Planting first.

90. *Ibid.*, 13-14, 16.
91. *Ibid.*, 18.
92. See n. 62 above for full citation.

Late in November 1831, Hammond took possession of his wife's plantation. Prior to his having taken it over, the plantation had been badly operated and "brought an average income under the management of Mrs. Hammond's brother of only $775.00 per year, less than half of Hammond's own income [i.e., what his income had been as lawyer-editor]." Lacking agricultural experience, Hammond set about the job of "learning the business of planting."[93] How did he do?

In 1832, having kept meticulously detailed books, Hammond found that the plantation's gross income "was $12,483.45, and plantation expenses were $2,754.34, leaving a net income of $9,729.11. All things considered, the twenty-five year old planter had a right to be proud of his first year's record."[94]

During the winter of 1832-33, the nullification crisis reached its climax. Hammond "was appointed 'Aid de Camp to the Governor and Commander in Chief with the rank of Lieutenant Colonel in the Militia', and was charged with military arrangements in Barnwell District [i.e., his home district]."[95] Although the crisis ended in March, Hammond continued to play very active military, political and social roles during the year. But the "business of the plantation had to go on in spite of the various alarums and excursions." It went splendidly. "Total income from all plantation sources in 1833 was $14,099.37. Expenses amounted to $2,885.00, leaving a net income for the year of $11,214.37. Since eighty-two full hands had been employed in all activities, the income per hand was $136.76. The improvement over the showing in 1832 indicates that Hammond was mastering his new calling of planter."[96]

In 1834, the popular Hammond resisted pressure to run for the state legislature because he had set for himself the more ambitious goal of election to the U.S. House of Representatives. He easily won election to it, a subject about which I will have more to say later. But "the

---

93. Tucker, *op. cit.*, pp. 78-79, 84-85.

94. *Ibid.*, 102-103.

95. *Ibid.*, 132-133.

96. *Ibid.*, 156-174. The quotations are from pp 156 and 173, respectively. That Hammond's excellent showing resulted in high self-confidence and self-esteem is evident in his having decided to go into the risky business of horse-racing, "the sport of kings," with Pierce M. Butler, one of South Carolina's great planter-aristocrats. *Ibid.*, 173-174.

plantation again produced a good income in 1834 even though the
owner was away much of the time on political business." Specifically,
to give the capitalistic details, "the net income was $14,003.00 or
$162.67½ per full hand."[97] (I cannot suppress the temptation to call
attention to the lovingly precise, detailed calculations that testify to
Hammond's cost-accounting mentality—precisely detailed calculations
that alone are enough to testify to the imaginative quality of Mr.
Genovese's world of premodern, anticapitalistic slaveholders). Mr.
Tucker then observed:

> Each of the three years Hammond had been in complete charge
> of Silver Bluff plantation he had increased the net income and the
> income per hand employed. Nevertheless, he had found the land
> and Negroes his wife had inherited were equally poor.[98]

No need exists to recite Mr. Tucker's detailed account of the
capitalist-minded, energetic course of action Hammond pursued over
the years to remedy the defects he had found in his wife's plantation. I
simply note that, in every sense, it was highly rewarding to Hammond.
It bore not the slightest resemblance to Mr. Donald's account of how
Hammond functioned (nor to Mr. Genovese's account of how large
slaveholders functioned).

By 1860, Hammond was one of the great slaveowners of the South,
having been "successful as both a scientific and practical planter. . . ."
Having "acquired a fortune by marriage, he added to his possessions
until he was the master of over three hundred slaves and thousands of
acres of improved land."[99]

Politics next.

To lend credence to his thesis about the traumatic experiences that
frenetically drove men to become proslavery extremists and secessionists, Mr. Donald had to show that Hammond not only had failed in law,
journalism, and planting, but had also failed in politics. Thus he used
the quotation from Porcher's memoirs (the quotation is actually out of
context, its meaning is reversed, and Porcher of Charleston was
probably not well acquainted with Hammond) as a means to suggest
that Hammond had also failed in politics.

---

97. *Ibid.*, 191-218. The quotations are from pp. 207, 213, respectively.
98. *Ibid.*, 214.
99. *Ibid.*, 482-483.

Porcher may have exaggerated the extent of popular admiration for Hammond, for despite a constant lust for office, he succeeded only once in a popular election; to his other positions he was appointed. Desperately ambitious, he sulked on his wife's plantation, becoming ever more passionate in his defense of the South and of slavery.

Surprising is a mild word to describe Mr. Donald's performance in those two sentences. Surprising for a variety of reasons. One is that a Tory-minded historian such as Mr. Donald who deplored the excess of democracy in antebellum America and the defeat of conservatives by the American mob should not have regarded the failure of Hammond to win popular elections as evidence that something *was wrong with Hammond.*

Another reason to describe Mr. Donald's performance as surprising is less speculative. By any reasonable standard, Hammond actually had an extremely successful political career. Among other indications of his power and success, he *won election* (discussed below) as U.S. Representative, Brigadier General of the state militia, Trustee of South Carolina College, Governor, and U.S. Senator (in that order).[100] Moreover, he was convinced, and undoubtedly correctly so, that he would have enjoyed much greater power and success except for his having gratified other lusts than his "constant lust for office."

During his term as Governor, it was alleged (probably correctly), Hammond had seduced one of Wade Hampton's daughters. The immediate and long-term complications that resulted from the ensuing scandal seriously injured him politically and lessened his ability to gain all the public offices he wanted, when he wanted them. To quote Mr. Tucker, "Like many in political life, Hammond had aspirations to a United States Senatorship, but as time passed [i.e., after the scandal broke in 1844] he saw that his chances of achieving that high office were jeopardized by his indiscretion. In fact, it was not until 1857 that that coveted office came into his possession."[101]

But the reason that Mr. Donald's two sentence summary of Hammond's political career might best perhaps be described as astonishing is this: His summary distorted the antebellum South

---

100. *Ibid.*, 175-190, 219-255, 320-360, 409-478.
101. *Ibid.*, 424-427; see also Merritt, *op. cit.*, pp. 80-81.

Carolina political system. Hammond "succeeded only once in a popular election; to his other positions he was appointed." By whom, for example, was he "appointed," U.S. Senator? He was "appointed," of course, by the legislators of South Carolina. Who else could possibly have "appointed" him to that office? By whom was he "appointed" Governor? By the legislators of South Carolina, of course, because neither the governorship, nor almost any other office in South Carolina (except state legislator and U.S. Representative), *were subject to popular election.* It is astonishing that Mr. Donald used Hammond's election by the South Carolina legislature to such high offices as Governor and U.S. Senator to demonstrate his failure in politics and thereby explain his (allegedly) having "sulked on his wife's plantation, becoming ever more passionate in his defense of the South and of slavery." To quote a summary description of the antebellum political system in South Carolina:

> To a degree unequalled in the other southern states of the late antebellum period, the South Carolina legislature was the center of political life in the state, and through the legislature the planters exercised their control over state and local affairs. The Constitution of 1790 under which South Carolinians were governed for more than seventy years created a highly unified, centralized system of government almost entirely devoid of checks and balances. All real power rested in the legislature, which was "a sort of House of Commons in the extent of its power." Not only did the legislature have the usual lawmaking powers, but it also elected the governor, Presidential electors, United States senators, state judges, the secretary of state, commissioners of the treasury, the surveyor general, and most local officials. Thus, executive, judicial, and administrative functions of the state government were in the hands of the legislative branch.[102]

In addition to helping to discredit Mr. Donald's explanation of the proslavery activities of Hammond (and Southern "extremists" in general), that quotation generally helps to show the basic error in Mr. Donald's explanation of Civil War causation. For it shows that antebellum South Carolinians, neither socially nor politically suffered from an "excess of democracy" or "an excess of liberty."

---

102. Ralph A. Wooster, *The People In Power* (Knoxville: University of Tennessee Press, 1969), pp. 6-7.

For Mr. Donald's explanation to be credible, he had to show this condition to have existed: As a group, *conservative-minded* Americans—when *conservative* is not simply defined to mean men who favored policies Mr. Donald thought they should have favored—bore far less responsibility for the specific sequence of events and decisions that terminated in Civil War than did *democratic-minded* Americans (again reasonably defined and not caricatured).

As a group, South Carolinians, between 1819 and 1861, we can surely agree, had the least democratic institutions and were the least democratic-minded of any Americans identified by state. As a group, we can also surely agree, upper class (however defined) South Carolinians (particularly men from the coastal parishes and districts) probably suffered as little from excessive democratic-mindedness and possessed as much conservative-mindedness in respect to social, economic, cultural, and political institutions and issues, as any numerically significant group in the United States. Surely, then, according to Mr. Donald, we must find that as a group, upper class South Carolinians, particularly those who valued tradition, order, authority, established hierarchical religion, classical forms, and all other Henry Jamesian stigmata of conservative-mindedness, actively worked to develop a rational, nonviolent political solution to problems and issues agitating, and agitated by, democratic-minded Americans, North and South. Because all available relevant studies indicate that, as a group, upper class South Carolina conservatives engaged in precisely the opposite form of behavior required of them by Mr. Donald's explanation, it is so clearly contrary to fact as to preclude its being taken seriously.

What should be taken seriously about Mr. Donald's explanation, in my opinion, is its implications for historiography. Wittingly or otherwise, he permitted his deeply-held conservative ideology to distort terribly the reality of antebellum American life. As I have suggested, only someone genuinely contemptuous of genuine democracy and genuine liberty could have so distorted antebellum American society and politics as to have claimed that the Civil War occurred because the American people suffered from an "excess of democracy" and an "excess of liberty." But my main point here is not to criticize Mr. Donald for having permitted his ideological convictions to distort

American history, it is to criticize the historiographic system. As the historiographic system now functions, among other defects, it permits scholars to impose their ideological convictions on the past, unconstrained either by scientific methodology or by the sanction of effective penalties if exposed as ideological warriors masquerading in academic garb. (For example, Arthur Schlesinger, Jr.'s, *Age of Jackson* notoriously exemplified a publicist using history as a weapon to advance partisan and personal interests. But he received—and continues to receive—great rewards for that performance.)[103] To further develop my argument that the historiographic system does not provide effective constraints upon ideological predispositions, I now assess Eric Foner's explanation of Civil War causation.

D. Eric Foner's Explanation of Civil War Causation. In a sense, Mr. Foner summarized his explanation of Civil War causation in the title of his book: *Free Soil, Free Labor, Free Men: The Ideology of the Republican Party before the Civil War.*[104] Based on prodigious research in primary sources and thorough familiarity with secondary sources, his explanation, broadly-speaking, represents an original combination of some elements contained in Mr. Moore's explanation and some elements contained in Mr. Genovese's. And as I will suggest later, in contrast to the Tory conservative ideological view of antebellum

---

103. For a devastating analysis of Schlesinger's bias, see Bray Hammond, "Public Policy and National Banks," *Journal of Economic History* VI (May, 1946), 79-84. Mr. Schlesinger, of course, was following in the path blazed for him by George Bancroft and Claude G. Bowers, two Democratic publicists who used history as a blunt weapon to serve party and personal interests. In my judgment, the award of the Pulitzer Prize to Mr. Schlesinger for his *Age of Jackson* stands as a severe indictment of the established historiographic system. I do not call for an "expunging resolution" to erase that award from the records. I do call for a transformation of historiography that will make it unlikely that such mendacious performances will receive scholarly approbation.

104. Eric Foner, *Free Soil, Free Labor, Free Men* (New York: Oxford University Press, 1970). It seems relevant to note that I am greatly impressed by Mr. Foner's intelligence, industry, and thorough mastery of *traditional* historical methodology. I criticize his work to demonstrate the inadequacy of traditional historiography, as well as to emphasize my argument that the established historiographical system militates against brilliant young scholars becoming genuinely scientific historians.

American society that informed Mr. Donald's explanation, as Mr. Foner asserted his explanation, it can reasonably be described as informed by a "radical liberal" (my term, not his) ideological view of antebellum American society.

1. Mr. Foner's explanation summarized.   To summarize Mr. Foner's explanation accurately presents some difficulties. One difficulty is that, like Mr. Moore, he freely used the language of reification. Another is that when he used such terms as Northerners, Southerners, Republicans, Democrats, and the like, he frequently neglected to indicate the proportions of the populations encompassed by those broad terms that he believed actually held the attitudes, or took the positions, he ascribed to them. To illustrate that point, as well as help suggest the nature of his explanation, I quote two passages:

> The decision for civil war in 1860-61 can be resolved into two questions—why did the South secede, and why did the North refuse to let the South secede? As I have indicated, I believe secession should be viewed as a total and logical response by the South to the situation which confronted it in the election of Lincoln—logical in the sense that it was the only action consistent with its ideology. In the same way, *the Republicans' decision to maintain the Union was inherent in their ideology* [emphasis added].[105]

Actually, as the following passage suggests, Mr. Foner strongly tended to equate what he took to be *the Republican* ideology with what he took to be *the ideology of Northerners as a group:*

> The two decades before the Civil War witnessed the development of conflicting sectional ideologies, each viewing its own society as fundamentally well-ordered, and the other as both a negation of its most cherished values and a threat to its existence. The development of the two ideologies was in many ways interrelated: each grew in part as a response to the growth of the other. Thus, *as southerners* [emphasis added] were coming more and more consciously to insist on slavery as the very basis of civilized life, and to reject the materialism and lack of cohesion in northern society, *northerners* [emphasis added] came to view slavery as the antithesis of the good society, as well as a threat to

---

105. *Ibid.,* 316.

their own fundamental values and interests. The existing political system could not contain these two irreconcilable ideologies, and in the 1850's each national party—Whigs, Know-Nothings, and finally Democrats-disintegrated. And in the end the South seceded from the Union rather than accept the victory of a political party whose ideology threatened everything southerners most valued.[106]

The ambiguities inherent in those two passages (and in his book generally) can be pointed up by posing one question: Did Mr. Foner intend to assert that, by 1860, *all* (or even a majority) of *Southerners* consciously insisted that slavery was "the very basis of civilized life" and that *slaveholders* must not only have the legal right to bring their chattels to any part of the Union while it was in a territorial status, but that slavery must actually come to *exist* in all states and territories of the Union? Taken at face value, that is what he asserted. But I do not believe that he really intended to make that clearly untenable assertion. Given the ambiguities in Mr. Foner's formulations (a characteristic defect of historians), they require extensive reformulation. I cannot be certain, therefore, that my summary conveys precisely what he intended to assert. But I have tried to reformulate his assertions in terms that are logically consistent, accurately convey their essential nature, and avoid extravagances that discredit his explanation.

As I understand Mr. Foner's explanation, he claimed that, given the nature of the capitalist society that developed in the North (essentially "a society of small-scale capitalism"), a substantial majority of Northerners *inevitably* developed an ideology that required them *consciously* to adopt a program designed to abolish slavery in the South. Republicans—particularly the "radicals" such as William H. Seward who made up their party's vanguard—crystallized, developed, and most forcefully articulated the ideology that required the abolition of slavery. But to a greater or less extent, that ideology was shared by a substantial majority of Northerners—as demonstrated by the (alleged) fact that the Douglas Democrats "who commanded the support of most northern Democrats" by 1860 "shared a good many of the Republicans' attitudes towards the South."[107]

---

106. *Ibid.,* 9.
107. *Ibid.,* 305-306.

Contrary to Mr. Moore, however, who dismissed the containment thesis out of hand and argued that the Northern offensive against the South therefore inherently required the use of revolutionary violence, Mr. Foner viewed the Republican radicals as spearheading a *gradualist* (my term) social revolution. *Contrary to their intentions and expectations, it was transformed into a violent social revolution.* But its character was transformed because a substantial majority of Southerners *correctly* perceived the significance of Lincoln's election. (That claim is basic to his explanation; without it, his explanation logically collapses.) They speedily seceded before their capacity to guarantee the survival of their society increasingly diminished. Put another way, Mr. Foner viewed secession as a well-informed, highly rational decision by a substantial majority of Southerners to use *counterrevolutionary violence* to prevent the victory of the gradualist social revolution *unmistakably* signalled by Lincoln's election.

> Emancipation might come in a decade, it might take fifty years. But North and South alike knew that the election of 1860 had marked a turning point in the history of slavery in the United States. To remain in the Union, the South would have had to accept the verdict of "ultimate extinction" which Lincoln and the Republicans had passed on the peculiar institution.[108]

To convey the essential nature of Mr. Foner's explanation, however, it is critically important to emphasize that his claims went much beyond the "containment thesis" in its passive form, i.e., confine slavery to the Old South and, in time, its abolition would somehow come about without Northerners having to take positive action to interfere with its operation. He accepted the claim asserted by Mr. Genovese (and many others before him, of course) that slavery had "to expand or die."[109] But as the following quotation indicates, his version of the Northerners' antislavery ideology claimed that it inevitably required them to take positive action to speed that process and thereby insure containment's fatal impact upon slavery.

> As southerners viewed the Republican party's rise to power in one northern state after another, *and witnessed the increasingly anti-southern tone of the northern Democrats* [emphasis added],

---

108. *Ibid.,* 313-316.
109. *Ibid.,* 311-312.

they could hardly be blamed for feeling apprehensive about the future. Late in 1859, after a long talk with the moderate Unionist Senator from Virginia, R.M.T. Hunter, Senator James Dixon of Connecticut reported that the Virginian was deeply worried. "What seems to alarm Hunter is the *growth* of the Anti-slavery feeling at the North." Southerners did not believe that this anti-slavery sentiment would be satisfied with the prohibition of slavery in the territories, although even that would be bad enough. They also feared that a Republican administration would adopt the radicals' program of indirect action against slavery. This is why continued Democratic control of Congress was not very reassuring, for executive action [i.e., action taken by a Republican administration] could implement much of the radicals' program. *Slavery was notoriously weak in the states of Missouri, Maryland, and Delaware. With federal patronage, a successful emancipation movement there might well be organized. And what was more dangerous, Lincoln might successfully arouse the poor whites in other states against the slaveholders* [emphasis added].... [contemporary quotations then follow to that effect]. For many reasons, therefore, southerners believed that slavery would not be permanently safe under a Republican administration. [Followed by additional contemporary Republican statements designed to validate the correctness of the southerners' belief.] [110]

Mr. Foner did not assert that Southerners *misperceived* either the nature of "*the* Northern antislavery ideology" or the nature of the total ideology from which it inevitably derived. On the contrary, he asserted that "much of the messianic zeal which characterized political antislavery derived" from the Northern total ideology (particularly strong among Republicans but by no means restricted to them) that postulated "the superiority of the political, social, and economic institutions of the North, and [inspired] a desire to spread these to their ultimate limits [i.e., everywhere in the United States]."[111]

As I trust my summary has made clear, Mr. Foner's explanation of Civil War causation required him to assert that the Northern politicians most responsible for its coming envisioned, and acted to achieve, a gradualist social revolution; it did not require him to assert that they acted to achieve a violent social revolution of the classical type

---

110. *Ibid.*, 314-315.
111. *Ibid.*, 316.

292 TOWARD THE SCIENTIFIC STUDY OF HISTORY

exemplified by the English and French models. Unlike Mr. Moore's explanation, therefore, Mr. Foner's explanation cannot be dismissed out of hand. But as I will now try to show, its basic claims contradict antebellum reality.

2. *Mr. Foner's explanation assessed.* Mr. Foner's explanation went beyond the containment thesis in its passive form. It cannot be discredited, therefore, by my simply pointing again to the falsity of the assumption that slavery had "to expand or die." It would take a book in itself, however, to examine all of Mr. Foner's broad-ranging claims about the nature of American society in general, the nature of Northerners' society, total ideology, antislavery ideology, political system, and political behavior, in order to support my assessment that they strongly tend to be basically, irremediably wrong. It seems most economical, therefore, to focus on his claim that, prior to Lincoln's election, the dominant group of Republicans were firmly committed to a program of positive action designed to abolish slavery in the South and would inevitably have tried to implement such a program had secession not occurred.

Although Mr. Foner's claims went beyond the containment thesis, they rest on the same erroneous assumptions concerning the intrinsically weak—and rapidly weakening—nature of the Southern economy and society based on slave labor, compared to the Northern economy and society based on free labor. To illustrate that point concretely, I again quote this passage:

> Slavery was notoriously weak in the states of Missouri, Maryland, and Delaware. With federal patronage, a successful emancipation movement there might well be organized. And what was more dangerous, Lincoln might successfully arouse the poor whites in other states against the slaveholders.

In effect, although not precisely in so many words, Mr. Foner claimed that the weak state of the Southern economy, and the serious internal contradictions within Southern society stemming from that weakness, would motivate a Republican administration to adopt a "falling dominoes" strategy and thereby bring about the end of slavery.

Let us set aside the question of whether even an insignificant group of Republican leaders ever indulged in private pipedreams that envisioned their successfully proposing that their party adopt such a program. Let us also set aside the question of whether such a program had won political power for Republicans anywhere in the North. Instead, let us simply use Missouri to take a look at antebellum economic and political realities.

Was slavery so "notoriously weak" in Missouri that a Republican administration would have been induced to try to use "federal patronage" to organize "a successful emancipation movement there"? In 1830, there were 25,091 slaves in Missouri. By 1840, the number had more than doubled to 58,240; by 1850, they totalled 87,422. By 1860, the rate of increase had slowed. But it was still substantial for the number of slaves then totalled 114,931.

It is true, of course, that the percentage of slaves *in the total population* decreased after 1830. But had Mr. Foner tried to use that "fact" to support his claim, he would have committed an error similar to Mr. Genovese's use of the relatively low rates of Southern industrialization and urbanization to support his claim about the "fatal" weakness of slaveholders compared to their Northern "rivals."

Far from testifying to the weakness of slavery in Missouri, the post-1830 decline in the *percentage* of slaves paralleled that found throughout the South—even the lower South. As Lewis Gray observed: "In Kentucky and Missouri the course of change in percentage of slaves followed that of the lower South, increasing up to 1830 and thereafter declining. In Missouri this was due mainly to the heavy immigration of nonslaveholders after 1830."[112] But didn't the heavy migration of nonslaveholders into Missouri (and other states) testify to grave weakness in the slave sector of the Southern economy and the society dependent upon it? Another quotation from Gray shows how that assumption contradicts economic and social reality: "The fact that from 1840 to 1860 slavery was relatively declining [i.e., declining percentage of slaves in population] even in the lower South appears to have been due partly to the fact that in spite of the alleged discouraging influence of slavery on immigration [i.e., migration to it], *the lower South was a large gainer by net white immigration* [emphasis added]." (Another reason was that "the rate of natural increase for whites was

---

112. Gray, *Southern Agriculture*, 2:650-651.

higher than for slaves."[113] In short, no evidence exists that the presence of slaves in an area significantly retarded white migration to it. (All things considered, I think a strong case can be made that slaveholders' ability to develop new areas by slave labor significantly contributed to, rather than, diminished the migration of whites to most parts of the South.) What about the political realities? Was the white population of Missouri likely to respond favorably to a Republican administration that used "federal patronage" to organize an "emancipation movement?" To suggest the fanciful quality of that notion, I quote from a recent history of the Whig Party in Missouri:

> Prior to Taylor's election [to the presidency in 1848], sectional controversy played an unimportant role in Missouri politics. Just as *Communist, Papist,* or *appeaser* have spelled political ruin in other places and in other times, so both *abolitionist* and *nullifier* became politically fatal labels in Missouri. Either party would have been pleased to have attached one of those designations to the other, but such accusations were so far removed from reality that they had never adhered.[114]

Beginning in 1849, however, as a result of the national conflicts centering around slavery issues (e.g., Wilmot Proviso, Compromise of 1850, Kansas-Nebraska), "a politician's views on slavery became the primary determinant of his political success."[115] In that context, "soft on abolitionism" (my phrase) and not "strong or safe enough on slavery" (again my phrase) became extraordinarily potent weapons in Missouri politics. During the 1850s, they were used to advance partisan and personal interests in Missouri à la Joe McCarthy throughout the United States in a later frenzied period of American politics.

In 1860, Lincoln received 10 percent of the total vote in Missouri. Consider the attitudes toward abolitionism and slavery in Missouri during the 1850s. Can we then believe that the incumbent Lincoln administration would have adopted a program to strengthen the

---

113. *Ibid.,* 2:656-657.
114. John V. Mering, *The Whig Party in Missouri* (Columbia: University of Missouri Press, 1967), p. 166.
115. *Ibid.,* 167. For the politics of the slavery issue in Missouri after 1849, see *ibid.,* 167-211.

Republican party in Missouri by using "federal patronage" to organize an "emancipation movement"? For us to believe that, we would have to believe in a theory of American politics that would have required the Nixon administration in 1969 to have adopted an all-out integration program to undermine the bases of George Wallace's support in the Deep South!

As I have noted in respect to Mr. Moore's and Mr. Genovese's explanations, the theoretical and substantive structure of Mr. Foner's explanation strongly tends to collapse when we place the word "black" in front of the word "slave." The slaves were black. Virulent antiblack racism was endemic virtually everywhere in the North (even in areas where few blacks lived). Only a miniscule proportion of Northerners, therefore, could possibly have supported a political party that advocated a positive program to abolish slavery in the South—a terrifying development, anti-abolitionists declaimed, that would flood the North with "hordes" of "savage niggers" and bring unspeakable evils and disasters to whites.

Mr. Foner confused the tiny percentage of Republicans (to say nothing of all Northerners) who favored something like "real anti-slaveryism" (my term) with the more substantial percentage of Republicans (by no means a majority, we will eventually find) whose votes were significantly influenced by "anti-arrogant slaveholderism," "antiniggerism" (my terms), and similar *anti-abolitionist* forms of "antislavery."[116] To support my estimate of the percentage of Northerners who belonged to the different attitudinal categories historians have jumbled together under the vague concept, "anti-slavery," I quote from the New York *Times.*

Beginning late in November 1860, Henry Raymond, the *Times'* editor, wrote a series of public letters ostensibly addressed to W.L.

116. As I have argued in earlier essays, one of the most striking weaknesses in historiography has been the tendency of researchers to fail to define the concepts they use. "Antislavery" is a perfect example of how poorly defined concepts lead scholars to lump together radically different attitudes and opinions. Moreover, historians characteristically tend to ignore the consideration that cross-pressures operate and that the relative saliency and intensity of conflicting attitudes and opinions must be taken into account. For a concrete example of the need to deal with this problem, see my *Jacksonian Democracy: New York as a Test Case* (Princeton, N.J.: Princeton University Press, 1961), pp. 254-269.

Yancey, a leading secessionist. Raymond's letters seem particularly relevant for an assessment of Mr. Foner's claims because Mr. Foner, to support his basic thesis, had given very heavy weight to passages selected from an 1857 *Times* editorial.[117]

As Raymond depicted it, Calhoun had planted the seeds of secession. After his death, Yancey was the disciple who worked most zealously to bring the movement to fruition.

What then are your [Yancey's] reasons for urging a dissolution of the Union?

If I were to ask every disunionist in the South this question, nine-tenths of them would probably reply, the election of Lincoln and the triumph of the Republican party. But you know that in and of itself this constitutes no justification whatever. . . . [Lincoln's election was strictly constitutional and he has given firm assurances that he would not permit any infraction of Southern rights or trespass upon Southern interests.]

You fear that, whatever his personal opinions and purposes may be, he will be governed by the requirements of his party. But you have seen enough of public life to know that seeking power against a party in possession is one thing, and wielding it under all the responsibilities which it involves, is quite another. The Republican party will now have far more interest than any other in preventing renewals of the John Brown raid; in punishing every movement against the peace of a Southern State; in enforcing the laws, suppressing everything like resistance to their execution and securing that public tranquillity which rests upon justice and equal rights. You mistake the North in supposing that the election of Lincoln indicates any disposition on the part of the people to countenance any infraction of Southern rights. *They elected him because they did not believe he had the slightest sympathy with any such purposes,—and because they knew that the public welfare imperatively demanded a change in the spirit and tone of the Federal councils. And if the Republican Administration should tolerate the least invasion of Southern rights, the very first elections would deprive it of the support of every considerable Northern state* [emphasis added].[118]

To avoid the mistaken inference that Raymond thought that disunion-

---

117. Foner, *Free Soil, Free Labor, Free Men,* pp. 309-311. The discussion in those pages exemplifies another major defect in traditional historiography, namely the tendency to cite statements made years earlier, or years later, as evidence of attitudes and opinions (allegedly) held at a specified time.

ists regrettably misperceived Republicans' positions, it seems useful to note that he then went on to claim that "the real motive of the disunion movement" was to bring about the reopening of the African slave trade.

Why give weight to Raymond's unequivocal claim that neither the incoming Lincoln administration nor the great majority of Northerners would "countenance any infraction of Southern rights"? Because—among a large number of other reasons that might be cited—his claim is supported by the evidence that no significant group of Republican leaders even made a *serious political* issue of geographic restriction of slavery *in order to bring about its extinction.*

Antebellum economic realities made the "containment=ultimate extinction" equation nonsensical; or, at most, so distant a prospect (1900? 2000?) that it cannot be taken seriously as evidence of a political program to abolish slavery inspired by a "messianic zeal" to spread Northern liberal capitalist institutions "to their ultimate limits." It is always difficult, of course, to "prove" claims about the "real" motives that inspire American politicians to uncork a particular specimen of campaign claptrap. But consider the demagogic, opportunistic general character of the American political system by the 1850s and the particular political context in 1858. It then seems clear, for example, that when Lincoln invoked the containment thesis, and when Seward invoked the equally demagogic "Irrepressible Conflict" thesis, they did so primarily to defend themselves against impassioned abolitionist charges that they and other Republican leaders cared nothing about the *immorality* of slavery and *certainly advocated no program to abolish it in the South.*

In closely fought and critical elections, as in both Illinois and New York in 1858, a small percentage of *normally Republican* votes withheld from Republican candidates by various means (e.g., third party candidates, abstentions, activists' lowered enthusiasm) might have meant the difference between victory or defeat. The Liberty Party campaign that defeated Henry Clay in 1844 had dramatically shown politicians the devastating consequences for their careers that could

---

118. Raymond's letters to Yancey are conveniently reprinted in Augustus Maverick, *Henry J. Raymond and the New York Press for Thirty Years* (Hartford Conn., 1870), pp. 384-447.

result from opposition by "fanatical abolitionists." Viewed in context, as I will indicate below, Lincoln and Seward both had been recklessly demagogic in 1858. Once we recognize that, we can better appreciate the force of Raymond's dismissal of campaign rhetoric as a valid indicator of basic Republican attitudes and opinions.

Vulnerability to past campaign rhetoric has long seemed to me to be one of the most puzzling characteristics of American political historians. Most of them would not dream of taking seriously the claptrap freely indulged in by *contemporary* politicians who expect to gain (or hold) only a tiny percentage of votes when they casually toss it off and who, after the election is over, dismiss it as "just campaign—stuff." Yet sophisticated historians naively take *past* politicians' claptrap at face value.

Did Lincoln really call for a gradualist social revolution on June 16, 1858, when, during the course of his contest with Stephen Douglas for the Senatorship, he observed that arresting the "further spread" of slavery would "place it where the public mind shall rest in the belief that it is in the course of ultimate extinction...?" (Note the extraordinarily passive implications of that formulation, incidentally.) That question was answered long ago by Arthur C. Cole:

> Contemporary and later belief in Lincoln's abolitionist position seems to have rested largely upon the assumed meaning of his famous "House Divided" speech of June, 1858, which was interpreted as the proclamation of a crusade to eradicate slavery from the nation. *Lincoln consistently denied this interpretation and insisted that it was no more than a prophetic utterance of grave moral import* [emphasis added]. In the proper background of his antislavery views, Lincoln could not possibly have been convicted of the dread "abolition" heresy. Indeed, perhaps he never before his Presidency reached a more definite attitude than when at Peoria in 1854 he admitted his inability to offer any adequate immediate solution of the slavery problem: "If all earthly power were given me, I should not know what to do as to the existing institution."
>
> These were not the words of a man who would carry abolition doctrines—however moderate—into the White House.[119]

Even more plainly than Lincoln's "House Divided" speech, calculated political expediency dictated Seward's "Irrespressible Conflict" speech. As a result, it cannot sustain the ideological burden placed upon it by Mr. Foner (and many other historians).

In October 1858, Seward went all-out for the 1860 Republican presidential nomination. For him to have any chance of success, the New York Republican state ticket, badly beaten in 1857, had to win in 1858. But one faction of radical abolitionists (and prohibitionists) had nominated Gerrit Smith for governor to win support for their crusades and to put pressure on Republican leaders to take something like a real antislavery (and antiliquor) position. Given the political situation in New York, a good possibility existed that Smith's independent candidacy would result in the Democratic candidate winning election as governor. That would crush Seward's presidential ambitions. On the evening of October 25th, therefore, in the "burned-over district" of Western New York where antislavery was relatively strong—in other words, at a place *and time* calculated to do both the most good and least harm for the November 3rd election—Seward declaimed his "Irrepressible Conflict" set piece.[120] That it should be treated as

119. Robert W. Johannsen, ed., *The Lincoln-Douglas Debates of 1858* (New York: Oxford University Press, 1965), p. 14; Arthur C. Cole, "Lincoln's Election An Immediate Menace to Slavery in the States?", *American Historical Review*, XXXVI (July, 1931), 741-742, 740-767. A recent dissertation has underscored the argument that Lincoln's speech must be seen in the context of his campaign against Douglas. "Certainly the 'House-Divided' doctrine exposed Lincoln to a persistent Democratic change that he was dangerously radical when in truth this was not so. His... speech was more remarkable for conservatism than for radicalism because Lincoln did not demand abolition of slavery. He did not even declare that he desired slavery to be put in a course of 'ultimate extinction'.... Lincoln did not foresee Douglas' twisting the Biblical phrase to mean the alternatives of a divided union or a uniformity of custom. He saw only a crisis, not an irrepressible conflict." Ronald D. Rietvelt, "The Moral Issue of Slavery in American Politics, 1854-1860" (University of Illinois, unpublished Ph.D. dissertation, 1967), pp. 118-119 and 100-200.

120. The most detailed study of Seward's position is found in Walter G. Sharrow, "William Henry Seward: A Study in Nineteenth Century Politics and Nationalism, 1855-1861" (University of Rochester, unpublished Ph.D. dissertation, 1965), pp. 228-260. My views concerning Seward's (and Weed's) opportunism and demagogy are also based on my own study of New York State politics during the 1850s. To describe Seward as taking a "radical" position on slavery, or any other issue, during the late 1850s, in my judgment, is hopelessly to misunderstand the nature of the Republican Party that emerged after the nativist, anti-Catholic frenzy of the mid-1850s demolished the Whig Party in its old form. But again that's a topic for a book, not a footnote.

campaign demagogy, and, closely read, *carefully denied* that the Republicans would take positive action against slavery, becomes evident when we consider the claims and implications of a postelection editorial in the *Radical Abolitionist:*

> The Republican nomination [of Edwin Morgan for governor] was not enthusiastic—nor was it enthusiastically received. . . . Political editors put down the probable vote for Gerrit Smith at from 25 to 50,000. The lowest number, as it now appears, had it been cast as every body expected it would be, would have defeated Morgan. . . . [The Republicans took various actions to counteract Smith's candidacy.] One thing more was needed, and that was to persuade Abolitionists that the Republican party was about to take "radical" ground against slavery. Who should do this? No less a man than Senator Seward, the expectant of a Republican Nomination for the presidency (and whose prospects would be blasted in case of the defeat of Mr. Morgan) undertook this great task himself. At Rochester, in one of the most elaborate speeches of his life, he laid himself out, very obviously, for that sole purpose. . . . As soon as the polls were closed, the Republican presses set themselves at work, to explain away the Radical abolitionism of Governor Seward! It had done its work, and must now be got rid of as soon as possible. . . .
>
> Already the N.Y. Evening Post, explains Mr. Seward's Rochester speech, as merely a prediction, that, some time or other, or somehow or other, slavery in all the States will be done away, thus divesting it, altogether of its power as a political appeal. . . .
>
> The New York Tribune had preceded the Post in explaining away the Rochester speech of Mr. Seward. . . . [The Tribune was then quoted as follows:] "It shows what Mr. Seward contemplates is to give aid and comfort to that policy of emancipation in the Slave States of which, in his time, HENRY CLAY, was so conspicuous an advocate, and which now has its leading representatives among the gallant Free-Soilers of Missouri; *and that he does not in any manner desire that the pernicious institution should be removed by the unconstitutional interference of the Federal Government, as has been falsely charged upon him* [emphasis added—L.B.] ."
>
> So abolitionists who voted for Morgan, and the Republican party at the instance of Mr. Seward, instead of voting for GERRIT SMITH, are permitted to console themselves with the reflection that they have placed themselves on the same platform, in respect to slavery, with HENRY CLAY![121]

Should the *Radical Abolitionist's* interpretation be accepted? Of course. Why? Among numerous other reasons, because its interpretation perfectly fits *Seward's own description of his motives,* as defensively expressed in a letter to James Watson Webb, a conservative Republican editor in New York City, immediately after the election:

> I saw a reserve Republican power of 70,000 or 80,000 in [New York] state in the rural districts who had slept two years since the last Presidential Campaign, betraying the state to the Democratic party last year, needing to be aroused with a battle cry that they could respond to. I saw the invidious efforts of the Ultras undoing the confidence of this mass in the Republican party . . . local divines threatening to disgust the people and to result in such a diminution of zeal as would lose our ticket here in the country where alone it could be saved.[122]

North and South, to quote a recent biographer of Seward, "Public reaction to the speech was immense and varied."[123] According to that biographer (basically favorable to Seward), he was surprised by the national furore—a furore that later contributed to his loss of the presidential nomination in 1860. That the "Irrepressible Conflict" speech, like the "House Divided" speech, cannot validly be used as an indication of Northern determination to abolish slavery by positive action needs little additional comment other than to quote his biographer's summary analysis of Seward's performance in the 1858 campaign:

> The 1858 elections in New York demonstrated the vital relationship between state and national politics. A Republican defeat might well have eliminated Seward from further contention. His activity in the campaign indicated that he realized the immediate political necessity of countering the effect of Gerrit Smith's candidacy and defeating the state Democrats. To accomplish the former, he merely reiterated a position which he had long proclaimed. He pursued the latter objective by employing the

---

121. *Radical Abolitionist,* December, 1958, pp. 34-35. Morgan won by about 17,000 votes; Smith received about 6,000. Among other things that made the election close, the Republican Party in New York was well on its way to serving as a notoriously corrupt instrument for the benefit of railroads and other large-scale corporations. See Sharrow, *op. cit.,* pp. 262-264, 285-288.

122. For Seward's letter to Webb, see Nichols, *op. cit.,* pp. 218-219.

123. Sharrow, *op. cit.,* p. 243.

new technique of characterizing the northern Democrats as active leaders of the slave forces. He must have been aware of the distortion involved in the argument, but he was willing to present the charges for partisan goals. Although he explicitly assured his audiences [at Rochester and in a later speech] that the triumph of freedom would be gradual, peaceful and constitutional, his failure to go beyond assurances furthered his radical image. His ambiguity allowed misinterpretation of his true position. Although he was surprised at the nation-wide reaction to the speeches, the radical stance assisted the Republican cause in the state campaign.[124]

Whether genuinely surprised, or whether he had acted on the realistic assumption that nothing mattered later if Morgan lost (my assessment of his performance), Seward definitely had not sounded the trumpets for a crusade to end slavery by positive government action. He had demagogically used the "ultimate extinction" notion simply to appeal to a tiny percentage of New York voters strongly committed to real antislavery whose votes were crucial to his presidential ambitions.

Why did Mr. Foner (like so many other historians) show such vulnerability to campaign rhetoric and take Lincoln's and Seward's demagogy at face value? Not at all, in my judgment, because of personal deficiencies. On the contrary, I have criticized his explanation to illustrate and support my general argument. To wit: Working within the limitations of the present historiographic system, researchers inevitably have failed to develop an adequate methodology to study either the formation and distribution of past attitudes and opinions, or their *impact* upon past political behavior and government decisions.

Unconstrained by a rigorous methodology, it is only "natural" that researchers' ideological convictions distort their perceptions of past reality. It was only natural, therefore, that the radical liberal ideology that shaped Mr. Foner's treatment of antebellum American society should have mistakenly led him to see the majority of Northern whites as committed to a gradualist social revolution designed to secure freedom for black slaves.[125]

---

124. *Ibid.,* p. 247.

125. In my judgment, little basis exists for Mr. Foner's roseate view of Northern society as "a society of small-scale capitalism" whose political elites identified with, and were dominated by, "the aspirations of the farmers, small entrepreneurs, and craftsmen. . . ." Foner, *op. cit.,* pp. 316, 11-39

Such misperceptions, in my judgment, also tend to derive from another basic defect of the present historiographic system. Working within its framework, researchers strongly tend to shy away from the hard job of developing good general theoretical and analytical models for the study of revolutions and rebellions. Lacking such models, Mr. Foner viewed the outbreak of Civil War as primarily due to ideological conflicts *between substantial majorities* of Northerners and Southerners. The theory of revolution implicit in that view understandably has a certain attractiveness from the perspective of a historian whose book can be (sympathetically) described as informed by a radical liberal democratic ideology. That majoritarian theory of revolution dooms us to failure, however, when we set ourselves the immensely hard job of first trying to identify who caused the Civil War, and then go on to try to explain why they wanted to, and were able to, take actions that resulted in its occurrence.

E. Can Researchers Ever Develop Credible Explanations of Civil War Causation?   To borrow a phrase from Mr. Donald, I could "go on and on" to show that: 1) no extant explanation of Civil War causation is credible; 2) no significant progress has been made in the methodology (broadly conceived) that historians have used while trying to develop such explanations. Suppose those claims are granted. It could then be argued that credible explanations of Civil War causation have not been developed because credible explanations of *past complex phenomena can never be developed*. In effect, in 1965, Kenneth Stampp took that position in a book of readings and documents on *The Causes of the Civil War.*

> . . . in spite of all the attention given to the Civil War, historians seem nearly as far from agreement about its causes as were the partisans who tried to explain it a century ago. . . . It may then be asked whether there was any point to the enormous effort that has gone into the various attempts to find the causes of the Civil War. If after a century the debate is still inconclusive, would not the historian be wise to abandon his search for causes and confine himself to cataloguing facts and compiling statistics? Is it not all the more discouraging to find, as the documents in this book indicate, that twentieth-century historians often merely go back to interpretations advanced by partisans while the war was still in

progress? I think not. *Because the century of historical inquiry, if it leaves the causes of the Civil War in doubt, has nevertheless been extremely illuminating* [emphasis added]. Uncertainty about the war's causes has driven historians back to the sources time and time again, with the result that we have gradually enlarged our knowledge and deepened our understanding of our greatest national crisis. Hence, I find the prospect of a continuing debate, however much it may annoy those who find it disagreeable to live with uncertainties, the best promise that research and writing in this period of American history will continue to have vitality.[126]

Mr. Stampp's version of the "no credible explanation possible" argument is, in my judgment, self-contradictory, self-deluding and evasive. Self-contradictory because historians cannot have "gradually enlarged our knowledge and deepened our understanding" of why the Civil War occurred if, after a century of research, they remain "nearly as far from agreement about its causes as were the partisans who tried to explain it a century ago" and *"often merely go back* [emphasis added] to interpretations advanced by partisans while the war was still in progress." Self-deluding and evasive because it invokes pseudo-psychology *à la* David Donald to put down critics who cite the recurrent cycles of wheel-spinning revisionism in Civil War historiography as evidence that something *must* be radically wrong with the established historiographic system.

In 1968 the late David Potter presented a more elegant version of the argument presented by Mr. Stampp (and numerous others).

The last three decades [i.e., since 1940] have witnessed considerable advances in the historical understanding of many of the developments which preceded the Civil War, but it can hardly be said that they have brought us visibly closer to the point at which a jury of historians seems likely to arrive at a verdict which will settle the controversy as to causes. Indeed some of the most fundamental issues in the controversy, namely those turning upon the significance of the slavery question, have been reactivated and seem now to have given new dimensions to the whole dispute.[127]

126. Kenneth M. Stampp, ed., *The Causes of the Civil War* (Englewood Cliffs, N.J.: Prentice-Hall, 1965), pp. 1-4. I have spliced together quotations from two pages but they are in context.

127. David M. Potter, *The South and The Sectional Conflict* (Baton Rouge: Louisiana State University Press, 1968), p. 89.

After a lengthy analysis of the post-1940 literature, Mr. Potter concluded:

> The literature on all the varied questions which impinge directly or indirectly upon the Civil War is so vast that it almost defies the effort to view it together in any one focus. Perhaps the most pervasive quality which it all has in common is that it continues to be explicitly or implicitly controversial. . . . The irony of this disagreement lies in the fact that it persists in the face of vastly increased factual knowledge and constantly intensified scholarly research. The discrepancy, indeed, is great enough to make apparent a reality about history which is seldom so self-evident as it is here: namely, that factual mastery of the data alone does not necessarily lead to agreement upon broad questions of historical truth. It certainly narrows the alternatives between which controversy continues to rage, and this narrowing of alternatives is itself an important proof of objective progress. But within the alternatives the determination of truth *depends more perhaps upon basic philosophical assumptions which are applied in interpreting the data than upon the data themselves* [emphasis added]. Data, in this sense, are but the raw materials for historical interpretation and not the determinants of the interpretive process. This is why the heavily researched field of the coming of the Civil War still remains, *and seems likely ever to remain* [emphasis added], subject to what we call reinterpretation—by which we mean *the application of individual philosophical views to the record of the past* [emphasis added].[128]

The full implications of that conception of historiography were clearly spelled out in Martin Duberman's laudatory review of Mr. Potter's book.

---

128. *Ibid.*, 146-147.

129. *New York Times Book Review*, January 12, 1969, p 16. That no basis exists for the contention that by its very nature, human behavior, past and present, defies scientific study has been brilliantly demonstrated by Ernest Nagel in *Structure of Science*, pp. 447-606. Of course, Mr. Nagel's arguments derive from his definition of science as something radically different than the curious notion that "the practice of scientific method consists in the use in all inquiries of some special set of techniques (such as the techniques of measurement employed in physical science), *irrespective of the subject matter or the problem under investigation* [emphasis added]. Such an interpretation of the dictum [the conclusions of science . . . are the products of scientific method] is a caricature of its intent, and in any event the dictum on that interpretation is preposterous." *Ibid.*, pp. 12-13, and VII-IX, pp. 1-28.

To read him [Mr. Potter] is to become aware of a truth that only
, the greatest historians have been able to show us: that the chief
lesson to be derived from a study of the past is that it holds no
simple lesson, *and that the historian's main responsibility is to
prevent anyone from claiming that it does* [emphasis added].¹²⁹

In other words, unless historians equate "scientific" with "simple
lesson"—clearly, a nonsensical equation—Mr. Potter's critique of Civil
War historiography had demonstrated that nothing could ever be done
to develop *scientific* explanations of past complex phenomena. At their
very best, historians can only hope to function in ways that *prevent* the
acceptance of pseudo-explanations that contradict existential reality.
Phenomena such as the occurrence of the Civil War inevitably must be
explained differently by individual researchers who do not hold similar
ideologies about human nature and the Good Society.

Critically examined, that conception of historiography could not be
more fatalistic or pessimistic. No exercise of intelligence, no amount of
work, no passionate desire to try to find the truth, nothing can alter
Historian's Fate. Doomed to spend their lives as ideological warriors,
historians primarily use past human behavior as a battleground to fight
out contemporary ideological conflicts.

I have long rejected that "subjective relativist" theory of historical
inquiry as both self-fulfilling and illogical. If bias inevitably, significantly distorts historical research, why fight it? Why not candidly
avow one's biases and let the reader (somehow) make his own choice
among different historians' different interpretations of the same
phenomenon? Moreover, subjective relativists simply assume that no
methodology can ever be developed to *effectively* constrain scholars
from permitting their personal philosophies to determine, *significantly
and decisively,* their efforts to reconstruct past human behavior. That
assumption is illogical unless one is prepared to go further and assert
that social science in general, not merely scientific history in particular,
is an impossible dream. But that position is so clearly untenable that
subjective relativists strongly tend to shy away from taking it.¹³⁰

130. See Benson, *Jacksonian Democracy,* pp. 288-289, and n.l. For a critique
that demolished the logical foundations of subjective relativism, see Nagel,
Structure of Science, pp. 576-582, and his essay, "Relativism and Some Problems
of Working Historians," in Sidney Hook. ed., *Philosophy and History* (New York:
New York University Press, 1963), pp. 76-91. See also my essay, "On 'The Logic
of Historical Narration,' " in *ibid.,* 32-42.

In my judgment, the subjective relativist theory of historical inquiry has no serious claim to serious attention. I view its vogue as best understood as simultaneously a product of, and indicator of, the terrible disillusionment Western intellectuals experienced after World War I and the rise of totalitarianism shattered nineteenth-century liberal illusions of assured, far-reaching social progress, achieved relatively easily and painlessly.

Contrary to Mr. Stampp and Mr. Potter, I believe that when we critically examine Civil War historiography we should draw this conclusion: Researchers have failed to develop a credible explanation of its occurrence, not because the task is beyond Man's powers, but because that task is beyond the powers of men working within the confines of the established historiographic and social scientific systems. Having expressed that judgment, I will now try to support it by suggesting how we might do better in the future than we have done in the past.

2. A Tentative Explanation of Civil War Causation

One of the most persistent myths about Civil War historiography is that a vast body of work exists that focuses on the problem of developing credible explanations of the war's occurrence. That is a delusion. To use Mr. Potter's term, a vast body of work exists that *impinges* on Civil War causation. But to my knowledge, not a single study has been published whose author tried to: 1) focus attention directly on the problem of developing a systematic, responsible explanation; 2) present a clearly-stated, logically-consistent explanation; 3) present systematic empirical data, and inferences logically derived from those data, to support that explanation. Two examples make the point.

Analyzing the relevant literature since 1940, Mr. Potter characterized Allan Nevins' massive six volumes, *The Ordeal of the Union, The Emergence of Lincoln, The War for the Union,* as "the first modern full-scale narrative of the period from 1850 to 1861." He then made these revealing comments:

... it stands today as the only great overall narrative based upon modern research. But for the examination of historiographical trends, it is pertinent here to concentrate upon *the rather brief and infrequent passages in which Nevins offers observations on the causative aspects of his theme* [emphasis added] ... he rejected the older simplistic idea that slavery in the strict sense of the chattel servitude of Negroes, was the crux of the controversy, and he offered instead the hypothesis that "the main root of the conflict (and there were minor roots) was the problem of slavery *with its complementary problem of race-adjustment*. ... It was a war over slavery *and* the future position of the Negro race in North America."

Nevins' striking observation is valid or not, according to the level of meaning at which one reads it [emphasis added].[131]

That last sentence succinctly points up the basic ambiguities in the "brief and infrequent passages" in which Mr. Nevins had actually offered "observations on the causative aspects of his theme." As Thomas J. Pressly had earlier observed, because Mr. Nevins' scattered explanatory claims were vaguely formulated, subject to different readings, and self-contradictory, historians quarreled heatedly over *what* he said, to say nothing of their quarrels over the validity of what *they* claimed he had said.[132]

Avery Craven provides perhaps an even better example that Civil War historiography fails to satisfy the most elementary criterion for credible explanations, namely *clarity of statement*. More than any other modern historian, he is associated with work that *impinges* on "the coming of the Civil War." And yet, in the preface to his last major book, *The Growth of Southern Nationalism*—a book that summarized several decades of his research—he protested that *he had never tried to advance or support an explanation of its occurrence.*

... when an author has worked his way through a mass of materials dealing with events so complex and involved as those leading to civil war, he is under obligation to give his *larger impressions* [emphasis added] of how such a tragedy came about. For that reason the concluding chapter of this book takes its present form. It is not intended to be a discussion of the *causes* [original emphasis] of the Civil War. It is only an attempt to state a few general impressions as to how events got into such shape

131. Potter, *Sectional Conflict*, pp. 103-105.
132. Pressly, *op. cit.*, pp. 310-323.

that they could not be handled by the democratic process. That some people cannot see this difference between such an effort and one attempting to state *causes* [original emphasis], the author from previous experiences well knows.[133]

To underscore his disavowal, his bibliography contained this note:

Avery Craven, *The Coming of the Civil War* (New York, 1942), also covers the general period but makes no effort to study the causes of the coming struggle.[134]

Need anything more be said?

In addition to the failure of historians to formulate and present their hypotheses about Civil War causation clearly and explicitly, they have failed to develop and use a standard general analytic model of internal war (discussed below) to guide their research. Predictably, therefore, when historians publish work impinging on Civil War causation, they strongly tend to deal with different aspects of the same event, different events, and different sequences of events. Different and contradictory (real or apparent) explanations, therefore, strongly tend *not* to produce direct, decisive confrontations of opposing claims; confrontations that would facilitate confirmation of one claim and disconfirmation of others. As the melancholy record shows, that is a formula for scholarly chaos and endless cycles of wheel-spinning revisionism, not the *progressive revisionism characteristic of scientific disciplines.*[135]

Thus far, I have focused attention on Civil War historiography as the product of the established historiographic system. Viewed in larger perspective, however, its deficiencies are best attributed to radical defects in the social scientific system in general.

A. Typologies, analytic models, theories of internal war. As Harry Eckstein has usefully defined intrasocietal violent political conflict or

133. Craven, Chapters IX-X, and the last chapter, "Some Generalizations."
134. *Ibid.,* p. 413.
135. That argument was developed in a paper that Thomas J. Pressly and I gave at a session of the 1956 convention of the American Historical Association, "Can Differences in Interpretations of the Causes of the American Civil War be Resolved Objectively?" The paper was mimeographed, widely distributed, and severely criticized by the three commentators, David Donald, David M. Potter, T. Harry Williams. For whatever it is worth, I am more convinced than ever of the validity of the basic argument developed in that paper.

internal war, the concept is broadly inclusive. It refers to "any resort to violence within a political order to change its constitution, rulers or policies."[136] For obvious reasons, especially since World War II, social scientists have been intensely interested in trying to develop good general theories of internal war. But they have made little progress. Summarily expressed, that was the conclusion of Jesse Orlansky, the author of a recent, comprehensive evaluation of the state of research on internal war. That evaluation, it deserves emphasis, was commissioned by the Department of Defense, an agency not likely to regard the state of research on internal war as a mere *academic* problem. To quote Mr. Orlansky:

> The crucial conceptual issues about internal war are still in the pretheoretical stage. Satisfactory theories of internal war have neither been compiled nor evaluated. . . . In brief, our knowledge is broad and our understanding is shallow.[137]

Viewed in larger perspective, therefore, I think it reasonable to assert that the failure to develop credible explanations of Civil War causation derives mainly from the combined effects of three factors:

1. The historiographic system has failed to develop and support a critical mass of scientifically trained historians committed to long term research focused *directly* on the problem of Civil War causation (explanations almost invariably are *by-products* of research focused on other problems, e.g., biographies).

2. Social scientists have failed to develop; a) a widely used, good *typology* of internal wars; b) a widely-used, good general *analytic model* of internal war; c) good general *theories* or *sets of propositions* applicable to internal wars.

3. The existing social scientific system provides neither the organization structure nor the long-term financial support necessary to develop credible explanations of specific instances of internal wars. It tends to inhibit, therefore, the cumulative development of good typologies,

---

136. Harry Eckstein, "On the Etiology of Internal Wars," *History and Theory,* IV (1965), 133.

137. I have spliced together, but in context, statements that are many pages apart. See Jesse Orlansky, *The State of Research on Internal War* (Arlington,.Va.: Institute for Defense Analysis, 1970), pp. 13, 101.

analytic models and theories for the fruitful study of internal war in general.

To try to support those assertions adequately would require a long book. Rather than try to support them summarily, I think it more useful first to sketch a general typology, analytic model and theory and then apply them to provide a tentative explanation of Civil War causation.

1. A typology of internal wars.   Intrasocietal political conflicts can be divided into two main types: 1) "rules of the game" or nonviolent conflict; 2) violent conflict or internal war. According to the primary *target* of the group (or groups) most responsible for the "decision" to use violence to bring about change, internal wars can be divided into three main types: 1) *coup d'etats,* or attempts to change an Administration; 2) *social revolutions,* or attempts to change a Regime or a Society; 3) *separatist revolutions,* or attempts to change the boundaries of a Political Community (or create a new one).[138]

As is true of any typology, of course, those categories are best viewed as ideal types. Only analytically can they be rigorously distinguished from one another. Specific internal wars tend to represent some mixture of types, with one or the other target predominating at different stages of development (discussed below), or among different groups at the same stage, or even among members of the same group at the same stage.

For example, I think that much of the scholarly controversy over the American Revolution centers around the problem of determining which target (Regime, Society or Community) was the primary and which was the secondary target of which group(s) of actors. To resolve that controversy, of course, presupposes that some reasonably good estimates can first be made of the relative power of the diverse groups of Americans responsible for the Revolution's occurrence. Having done that, researchers could then try to make reasonably good estimates of the primary and secondary targets of those groups.

When the typology identified above is concretely applied, another real-life consideration must be taken into account. An internal war

---

138. For a review of the different—and conflicting—typologies that have been suggested, see *ibid.,* pp. 49-66.

might have been caused primarily by a group whose members wanted to bring about a separatist revolution. After large-scale, sustained violence had occurred, however, other groups might have been inspired or sufficiently strengthened to transform it into a social revolution. Here the War for Southern Independence can serve as a classic case both of how internal wars can be transformed in character and how scholars (e.g., Barrington Moore, Eric Foner) can mistakenly transpose consequences and causation.

My basic point is that typologies cannot be used literally and mechanically in empirical research. Different categories of the genus, *internal war,* are mutually exclusive analytically, not empirically. Moreover, each of the three categories identified above actually represents a high level of generality. For example, to provide the most useful analytical and theoretical framework for studies of particular instances of the broad category, *separatist revolutions,* it can be further subdivided: 1) *national-imperial revolutions* (e.g., the sixteenth-century Dutch "Great Revolt" within the Spanish Empire); 2) *colonial-imperial revolutions* (e.g., the 1776 American Revolution within the British Empire); 3) *secessionist-national revolutions* (e.g., the 1861 War for Southern Independence, the 1967 Biafran rebellion within Nigeria, the current East Pakistani or Bengali revolt within Pakistan.)

2. A general analytic model for the study of internal war.   Several years ago, Lawrence Stone severely criticized the all-inclusive definition of internal war quoted above (e.g., sporadic riots differ greatly from sustained, large-scale revolutionary violence).[139] His criticisms, I trust, are met by the analytic model summarized below and outlined more fully in Appendix I.

The model has two main parts, a *narrative framework* and an *analytic framework.* The narrative framework, or chronicle of events, requires researchers to *identify explicitly* the sequence of decisions that culminated in the *terminal decision* (e.g., Lincoln's proclamation on April 15, 1861). The analytic framework requires researchers to: 1) *identify* the actors mainly responsible for each decision; 2) explain their *power* to take the actions that resulted in a specified decision; 3) explain their

139. Lawrence Stone, "Theories of Revolution," *World Politics* XVIII (January, 1966), 160-162.

motives for taking those actions; 4) explain the *impact* of specified actions upon subsequent actions and decisions included within the narrative framework.

I place heavy emphasis upon the requirement that researchers explicitly identify the actors responsible for specified decisions primarily for two reasons: 1) causal claims that fail to identify who (allegedly) took specified actions that (allegedly) had specified results are too vague and ambiguous to be empirically confirmed—or disconfirmed; 2) *general laws* (or propositions) relevant to a general class of human phenomena must be stated in probabilistic terms; invariant laws, if true, must be trivial. Credible explanations of the occurrence of a particular instance of a general class of phenomena, therefore, must identify *who* caused it to happen. After all, even if the odds are 3 to 1 that, given specified "structural conditions," a separatist civil war will occur, it need *not* have occurred in all cases when those conditions are satisfied. To explain credibly why it actually *did* occur, we need to determine who took what actions, why they were able to, and why they wanted to.

To meet Mr. Stone's criticisms of the broad definition of internal war, in the proposed model, specific instances are differentiated, not only by the type of change they are designed to produce (i.e., administration, regime, society, political community), *but by their stage of development.* For example, some groups who try to bring about a secessionist-national revolution may only reach the "sporadic spontaneous riot" stage and then fade away; others may go through a succession of stages, identified by a *combination of greater continuity, planning and violence,* to reach full term and "give birth to a new nation." While taking due account of Mr. Stone's criticisms, therefore, in designing the analytical model, I tried to preserve the great utility of Harry Eckstein's broad definition of internal war. (It is useful because it widens the number and range of cases and links them together as indicators of *malfunctioning* political systems. *Malfunctioning* denotes no value judgment in favor of the status quo. My use of that term, therefore, should not be caricatured to place me on *that* side of the barricades.) To meet the requirements of the model's narrative framework, researchers must classify decisions (broadly conceived) as occurring within different stages of revolutionary development, as well as identify *turning points* toward, *or away from*, fully developed revolution.

Adoption of the proposed typology and analytic model (or more adequate ones that may be developed), in my judgment, would remedy one of the great weaknesses now handicapping studies of internal wars, past and present. To repeat and generalize my earlier observations about research focused on the Civil War, at present, researchers who try to explain the occurrence of the same internal war are guided neither by a standard typology nor a general analytic model appropriately adapted to a particular category of internal war. The result is that different explanations strongly tend *not* to produce decisive confrontations of rival claims. Moreover, the absence of a general analytic model seriously handicaps comparative studies of different internal wars, and the development of theoretical propositions about internal war at different levels of generality.

3. An underdeveloped general theory of separatist revolutions. Good typologies and analytic models do not automatically provide good answers to good questions about internal wars (or any other phenomena). They do help to develop and make explicit a logically-related set of good questions that researchers can then try to answer systematically and responsibly. To answer good questions systematically and responsibly, however, we must develop some reasonably credible and relevant general theory or set of theoretical propositions. To focus attention on that problem, not to imply that I have solved it, I restate what I fondly view as a logically coherent, if underdeveloped, general theory of separatist movements and separatist revolutions. (An earlier statement of the theory, and a fuller definition of its key concept, *territorial culture group*, is found on pp. 207-208 above.)[140]

140. In its earliest form, the theory was first publicly advanced at a session of the 1968 Southern Historical Association convention (and "published" and distributed widely in mimeographed form). Prodded by Lawrence Stone to formulate it more adequately, I reformulated it in 1969 and, in the fullness of time, it appeared in 1971 in Billias and Grob, eds., *American History*, reprinted in this volume. See p. 208 above. The version presented in this paper seems to me to be an improvement. It seems safe to "predict," however, that this version is far from the last word on the subject. My primary objective is to focus attention on

Given a political community that includes two or more relatively sizeable territorial culture groups (geographically distinct groups with "visibly" distinct ideational or cultural patterns), then: The more strongly the members of each culture group value its patterns, the greater the interaction between (or among) members of different groups, the more strongly they tend to perceive their own group's cultural patterns to be competing for dominance with those of other groups. In such a political community: The more inclusive the suffrage and the greater the extent and intensity of mass participation in the electoral process (e.g., the United States after 1828), the more centralized the political system and the more concentrated and greater the symbolic and real power of a single executive (e.g., the strong American presidency created by the Constitution and developed strongly under General-President Jackson), the greater the tendency for latent hostilities to become manifest and for political cleavages to develop along "visible" geographic fault lines. Under those conditions, the more irresponsible the political system and culture, the more intense the struggle for personal power among continually fluctuating groups of political elites and would-be elites, the greater the tendency for secessionist movements to develop and secessionist revolts to occur (e.g., pre-1861 Southern secessionists, contemporary East Pakistani secessionists).

Having sketched a general theory of separatist revolutions, I now briefly apply it to The War for Southern Independence. Of course, my

the problem of developing an adequate general theory of separatist internal wars, not to pretend that I have solved a very difficult problem whose solution requires drastic reorganization of the existing social scientific system.

During the course of revising this essay for publication, I learned of a recent book that also focuses attention on territorial group conflicts. Written by a political scientist, it uses the term, territorial *interest* group, rather than territorial *culture* group. My preference for the latter term, I should like to think, derives from better motives than pride of authorship. The connotations of "interest group" are significantly narrower than those of "culture group." Put another way, my concept stresses life-style and ideological conflicts rather than stratification conflicts, although I recognize, of course, that the latter can play important roles in reinforcing and developing, culture group cohesiveness. For a panoramic overview that emphasizes the territorial bases of group conflict, see Ivo D. Duchacek, *Comparative Federalism: The Territorial Dimension of Politics* (New York: Holt, Rinehart and Winston, 1970).

purpose in doing so is neither to try to demonstrate the credibility of my tentative explanation of Civil War causation nor the validity of the general theory I have sketched. My more modest and realistic purpose is to illustrate empirically and specifically what otherwise would remain an abstract and general argument.[141]

4. A tentative explanation of The War for Southern Independence as the victory of the "Southern Revolutionary Nationalist Party" formed during the presidential succession crisis of the 1830s.   "Was the Civil War inevitable?" An old historiographic chestnut that no one should ever have tried to crack. Literally, everything that happened in the past had to have happened. It happened, therefore, it had to happen, is the appropriate, trivial answer to the trivial question, "Was the Civil War inevitable?" Buried in that question, struggling to get out, of course, is a better set of questions: "Who caused the Civil War to occur and why?" And implicit in that vague, ambiguous set of questions are a number of more precise questions; they become explicit when we apply the analytic model sketched above to the problem of Civil War causation. Rather than spell them out in detail, I summarily pose and answer two of them in general terms:

1) What conditions made it likely that a group would form who wanted to create a new nation in the Old South and who were prepared, if necessary, to use revolutionary violence to achieve their goal?

2) Who were the Southern secessionists, why did they succeed, what were their motives?

It seems as certain as anything can be in human affairs that the gradual abolition of black slavery in the North after 1790 and its flourishing state of development in the South after 1815 (particularly after 1833) constituted a *necessary* condition for The War for Southern

---

141. It would be absurd to try to "demonstrate'. the credibility of my tentative explanation at this time and in this form. I advance it to suggest how general theories can be used to generate hypotheses about a specific internal war. The basic argument of the essay, of course, is that credible explanations of Civil War causation must follow, not precede, the "overthrow" of the existing historiographic (and social scientific) system. The job of credibly explaining Civil War causation is not beyond the powers of Man. But I think that it is beyond the powers of men burdened by the fetters of the present historiographic and social scientific systems.

Independence. It was a *sufficient* condition, however, only to insure the existence of a small group of elite Southerners passionately determined to bring about secession from a political community whose Constitution or Administration *officially, publicly* forbade black slavery in some geographic areas. To forbid—*officially, publicly*—slavery in the North, and later in parts of the West, was to stigmatize it. Inevitably, some Southerners whose social roles derived from the existence of a social system based upon slavery perceived its stigmatization as intolerably threatening to their honor and self-esteem. To a greater or lesser degree, it was also perceived as threatening to the honor and self-esteem of *all white* Southerners (as French Canadians today generally resent the dominance of the English language—and the English—in Canada, as Ukranians generally resent Russian dominance in the Soviet Union, Croats generally resent Serbian dominance in Yugoslavia, and the like).

That some significant proportion of Southern elites should have come to view the stigmatization of slavery as literally intolerable becomes even more understandable if we make this assumption: Particularly in respect to members of the master class, antebellum Southern society tended to develop individuals with *authoritarian* personality traits more strongly than it did individuals with *reconciling* personality traits. That assumption seems reasonable, particularly when we consider the functional requirements of a society in which white master-black slave relationships were dominant, as well as consider Kenneth Boulding's definition of the two personality types:

> The . . . [authoritarian personality] has a very large core of particular values that he identifies with his person. Consequently, he is not interested in reconciliation but only in imposing his will and his values on others; the existence of differing values he regards as a threat to his person rather than as an opportunity for mutual learning. By contrast, the reconciling personality identifies his person not with any particular set of values or doctrines, but with a learning process, a search for truth, and an interest in, and concern for, the welfare of others.[142]

Given the nature of antebellum Southern society, the abolition of slavery in the North, and the increasing profitability and growth of

---

142. Kenneth Boulding, *Conflict and Defense: A General Theory* (New York: Harper Torchbooks, 1963), 312-313.

slavery after the post-1815 period of readjustment, it seems reasonable to "predict" that a significant group of elite Southerners would exist who: 1) possessed markedly authoritarian personalities; 2) experienced considerable personal success; 3) felt official, public stigmatization of slavery to be intolerably threatening to their honor and self-esteem; 4) acted with a reasonable degree of (but not perfect) rationality, therefore, to bring about secession from the American political community in order to create a new nation and political system "whose corner-stone rest [ed] upon the great truth, that the negro is not equal to the white man; that slavery—subordination to the superior race—is his natural and normal condition"[143]

Over time, who were the secessionists, what did they do to achieve their goal, why did they succeed? A second set of conditions greatly increased the *probability*, both that a dedicated group of Southern secessionists would form, and that the movement they set in motion would succeed. Summarily described, that set of conditions can be identified as the Constitutional revolution of 1787-1788 and the radically defective political system it created. Given the heterogeneous, decentralized, libertarian, and *relatively* prosperous nature of American society, it was radically defective even during the 1790s; as American society developed in the nineteenth century, it became increasingly defective.

As everyone knows, the Founding Fathers desperately wanted to prevent the creation of political parties. Contrary to received opinion that hails them as demigods, history plainly shows (to me, at any rate) that their Constitution was an intellectual and political disaster. Given the nature of American society in the late eighteenth century and its reasonably predictable evolution in the nineteenth, the governmental system created by the new constitution was almost certain to, and did actually, produce: 1) an incredibly irresponsible party system; 2) an extraordinarily disastrous concentration of real and symbolic power in

---

143. The "corner-stone" quotation, of course, is from the famous speech of Alexander Stephens in March, 1861, justifying the Confederate Constitution. To assume, as I do, that the structure of antebellum Southern society was conducive to the development of authoritarian individuals is neither to claim that a majority of Southern elites were of that type nor to adopt a superior moral stance. Given the nature of antebellum society, a low incidence of authoritarian personalities among Southern elites—and would-be elites—seems highly unlikely to me.

the Presidential *office*. (In my judgment, history plainly shows that the American presidency is the most defective major institution in any "developed" political system. An institution designed to *concentrate* power, it directly conflicts with other institutions designed to *disperse* power—a formula conducive to political schizophrenia, not political integration.) Both developments contributed greatly to the formation of Northern and Southern territorial culture groups. Both made it far more likely that some political actors would successfully try to exacerbate, rather than reduce, tensions between Southerners and Northerners.

Given the evolution of American society after 1790, among the more radical defects of the American political system, first place must go to the cluster of features that facilitated the highly disproportionate concentration of national political power in a heterogeneous *coalition* of Southern political elites. That concentration of power particularly contributed to the formation of a Southern secessionist group. Among other reasons, it did so because, as late as the early 1830s, Southern elites strongly tended to be ideologically defensive about their society. During the 1820s and early 1830s, difficult economic readjustments still were being made in the South, largely as a result of the shift away from traditional staple products to cotton and the tremendous quantitative and geographic expansion of cotton production after 1815.

During the nullification crisis (itself largely a product of personal and partisan struggles for political power on national, state, and local levels that resulted in "Southernism" emerging as a potent political weapon), predictably enough inspired by a few Southern *intellectuals* such as Thomas Cooper and Nathaniel Beverly Tucker, a very small number of Southern political elites converted to Southern nationalism. (James H. Hammond serves as the classic example.)[144] After the

---

144. At some future date, I hope to publish the results of my research on the critical role of Southern intellectuals in the development of Southern nationalism. Here I simply call attention to it in order to emphasize the major role that cultural leaders strongly tend to play in developing separatist and nationalist movements. For an excellent illustration of my general proposition, see the discussion of the leading role played by Breton intellectuals in Jack Reece, "Anti-France: The Search for the Breton Nation (1898-1948)" (Stanford University, Ph.D., 1971).

nullification crisis passed in 1832-1833, with the Old Southern Republican anticentralization position increasingly dominant on the national level, the Presidential succession crisis of 1833-1836 created the basis for a powerful *coalition* of Southern *"provincials,"* (i.e., men who viewed the State as the primary political community or "country" and out-of-staters as "foreigners"), *sectionalists* and *nationalists.* (The three groups are analytically distinct, but in practice, as a theory of separatist revolutions would predict, the lines between them blurred and shifted. As almost invariably occurs during the early stages of a separatist revolution, individuals wavered and oscillated in their commitment to Southern Nationalism. Separatists strongly tend to experience genuine "identity crises," a consideration that helps us to understand not only the oscillation of the Southern Nationalists but their passion.)

Obviously, I use the terms "revolutionary" and "party" in a very loose sense, but I think it instructive to say that, in 1835-1836, a tiny group of Southern nationalists formed the "Southern Revolutionary Nationalist Party" that ultimately brought about secession in 1860-1861.[145] (Throughout the entire period, they were unwittingly aided by the ineptness, opportunism, and demagogy of Northern politicians, exemplified in various ways and degrees by Martin Van Buren, William Seward, Abraham Lincoln. But those "bad politicians" are best viewed not as "bad men" or "bad statesmen"; they are best viewed as the "inevitable" products of a radically defective political system.)

Determined to heighten Southern national consciousness, the South-

---

145. "Circle" more than "party" in some ways better suggests the highly informal, undisciplined, competitive nature of the relationships among men involved in the secessionist *movements.* "Party" does have the great advantage of emphasizing that political organization and political conflict are the main weapons of men who work to transform *latent social groups* into *manifest conscious social groups.* Marx's stress on political organization and conflict as instruments to stimulate and heighten group consciousness seems to me to be one of his greatest, if regrettably underdeveloped, theoretical insights. See the brilliant passage on the lack of class consciousness among French peasants during the mid-nineteenth century in his "Eighteenth Brumaire of Louis Bonaparte," reprinted in Lewis S. Feuer, ed., *Basic Writings on Politics and Philosophy: Karl Marx and Friedrich Engels* (Garden City, N.Y.: Doubleday Anchor Books, 1959), pp. 338-339.

ern Nationalists joined other disaffected Southern political elites in fierce opposition to the election of a Northerner, Martin Van Buren, to the presidency (as the Virginia Dynasty had successfully resisted the election of a Northern president in 1816 and thereby helped bring about the first real sectional crisis, the Missouri Controversy). In December 1835, during the course of the presidential conflict and tremendously aided by it, literally coached by Thomas Cooper and cheered on by Nathaniel Beverly Tucker, James H. Hammond accidentally stumbled on the issue of trying to prevent Congress from receiving or routinely disposing of antislavery petitions. Accidentally discovered by Hammond as a result of his inexperience and ignorance of legislative procedures, what came to be known as the "Gag Rule" issue was consciously used to heighten sectional antagonisms and Southern national consciousness. If a small group of Northern abolitionists had not existed, Southern nationalists, sectionalists and provincials would have had to create them—as, in fact, they did.[146]

As long as abolitionists concentrated upon trying to arouse intensely racist Northerners to force Southerners to right the wrongs done to black slaves, they were doomed to remain a tiny sect, politically impotent, their lives literally endangered in the North. But the fight over the Gag Rule on petitions, deliberately initiated by a loose coalition of disaffected Southern elites as a tactical maneuver in the larger strategy of the presidential succession crisis, transformed the "anti-slavery crusade".

Nicely illustrating action-reaction propositions about how conflicts escalate until they culminate in large-scale violence, to the mutual benefit of Northern abolitionists and Southern secessionists, the antislavery crusade became, as some leading actors on both sides hoped

146. Had the American academic world in particular, and American society in general, been less tormented during the last few years, by this time a number of my students and I might have achieved our goal of publishing a systematic, intensive study of the Gag Rule decision (a project that has occupied my attention, on and off, since 1961). It may be useful to note that the project has not been abandoned, that in the fullness of time it should culminate in at least one book on the Gag Rule, and that the statements in the text are not casual impressions, but are based upon a great deal of intensive research by myself and a number of students, particularly Robert Cort, H. Michael Neiditch, Lawrence Simon.

and other contemporaries feared that it would, no longer an impotent struggle for the rights of black slaves, but a basic conflict over the rights, principles, honor and self-esteem of Northern and Southern *white citizens.*

That conflict manifested itself in a variety of forms from 1835 to 1861. Understandably enough, to justify breaking away from the political community for which their forefathers "fought and died," most secessionists probably convinced themselves, erroneously, that their society was in "mortal danger" from Northern aggressors. Moreover, apart from misperceptions of reality, for tactical reasons, Southern secessionists, sectionalists and provincials demanded that extremely "bold action" be taken to meet the danger posed by Northern aggressors "on the threshold." In turn, either out of conviction or expediency, some Northerners took the position that, unless "the North" took extremely bold action, a real danger existed that slavery would not only expand in the West but would be reinstituted in the North.

Predictably, the conflict deliberately stimulated by Southern Nationalists after 1830, particularly after 1835, had irrational aspects, involved serious misperceptions of reality, and increasingly was conducted in frenetic and hyperemotional fashion. But it was not basically irrational or pathological. It was not created by hysterical paranoids. It was not the product of an "excess of democracy". It was deeply-rooted in the objective reality of men's need for self-esteem. It was the type of conflict likely to develop in bicultural or multicultural political communities. In one form or another, its counterpart can be found today in large numbers of nation-states.

Once aroused, conflicts over the self-esteem and honor of members of territorial culture groups take on a life of their own; *that particular genie* is particularly hard to put back in the bottle. In accounting for the ultimate success of the Southern Nationalists, however, I think that the greatest weight must be given to the extraordinarily irresponsible, extraordinarily defective character of the American political system during the antebellum decades. (Only historians contemptuous of genuine democracy would view its defects as produced by a democratic political system. Its defects directly stem from the elitism of the Founding Fathers who, trying to devise a system to prevent democracy in a society whose charter myth was the Declaration of Independence, instead created one that worked irresponsibly and badly—with results tragically evident today in the fires burning in the hamlets of Vietnam and the ghettoes of America.) And as Calhoun brilliantly observed in his theoretical works written during the 1840s, the most radically defective part of that system was the exalted role given to the indivisible presidency in a society that contained territorial culture groups with a strong latent propensity for conflict.

To support my hypothesis that the direct and indirect effects of the strong Jacksonian presidency, by no means exclusively *but more than any other determinant,* account for the success of the Southern secessionist movement, I think it instructive to *glance* (used advisedly) at Switzerland in 1847-1848 and Yugoslavia and Pakistan today. It is instructive to do so because all three societies are multinational and contain distinct territorial culture groups.

In 1847, preceded by centuries of intense conflict and violence, civil war briefly broke out in Switzerland among different territorial culture groups. But this time civil war resulted in the adoption of the federal constitution of 1848. The Swiss "Founding Fathers" consciously looked to American experience for guidance and took over bicameralism. But their version of federalism *consciously, radically* differed from the American model in respect to the executive branch of government. Unlike the Americans in 1787, the Swiss deliberately designed their collegial presidency to give the different territorial culture groups in their political community a significant share of real and symbolic power on the federal level. Specialists strongly agree that the remarkable post-1848 stability and effectiveness of the Swiss federal system, as well as the post-1848 diminution of territorial culture group conflicts, owes much to the collegial presidency created *in conscious revulsion against the American presidency.*[147]

147. Far from pretending to possess any expert knowledge about the Swiss case, I explicitly avow that my "knowledge" of it is superficial, derives strictly from secondary sources in English, and my "claims" are very tentative. Again, that is precisely the point. Systematic comparative research requires sustained, effective, collaborative "team research," something alien to the historiographic ethos and difficult to achieve in the social scientific fields relevant to studies of internal wars. But as I observe in the text, the consensus of expert opinion about the Swiss case is so striking that I feel justified in using it for the purposes of this

One case, of course, a general law does not make. But contemporary developments in Yugoslavia and Pakistan (and other countries such as Canada, Ireland, Belgium, Nigeria, etc.) seem to me to support strongly the line of argument sketched above. For example, as a logical part of the massive decentralization program that the Yugoslavs have consciously devised and implemented during the last two decades, in 1970, after long study and debate by Yugoslav political leaders and social scientists, President Tito proposed a constitutional amendment for adoption in 1971. It provides that, after his retirement (the comparison with Washington's Farewell Address is instructive—and chastening for Americans), a collegial presidency will come into being that goes much further than the Swiss model to foster national cohesion by insuring equality of representation of different territorial cultural groups included within a single political community.

To quote from Tito's letter proposing the change:

> With a view to a consistent organization of the federation as a community of equal peoples and nationalities and so as to insure the influence and responsibility of the republics and provinces in the discharge of the functions of the federation it is necessary that a Presidency of the S[ocialist] F[ederal] R[epublic of] Y[ugoslavia] be instituted as an autonomous constitutional organ of the federation composed of an equal number of representatives

paper. Among the numerous secondary sources I have read, I have depended most heavily upon the following: Kenneth D. McRae, "The Constitutional Protection of Linguistic Rights in Bilingual and Multilingual States," in Allan Gottlieb, ed., *Human Rights, Federalism, and Minorities* (Toronto: Canadian Institute of International Affairs, 1970), 211-227; Kenneth D. McRae, *Switzerland: Example of Cultural Coexistence* (Toronto: Canadian Institute of International Affairs, 1964); George A. Codding, *The Federal Government of Switzerland* (Princeton, N.J.: D. Van Nostrand, 1961); Myron L. Tripp, *The Swiss and United States Federal Constitutional Systems: A Comparative Study* (Paris, 1940); William E. Rappard, "Pennsylvania and Switzerland: The American Origins of the Swiss constitution," in *University of Pennsylvania Bicentennial Conference Studies in Political Science and Sociology* (Philadelphia: University of Pennsylvania Press, 1941), pp. 49-121; Hans Kohn, *Nationalism and Liberty: The Swiss Example* (London: , 1956); E.J. Bonjour, *et al, A Short History of Switzerland* (Oxford: Oxford University Press, 1952); Herbert J. Spiro, *Government by Constitution: The Political Systems of Democracy* (New York: Random House, 1959); Carl J. Friedrich, *Trends of Federalism in Theory and Practice* (New York: Frederich A. Praeger, 1968).

of each republic and a corresponding number of representatives of each province.[148]

The Yugoslav case provides particularly strong support for my argument when we contrast it to the tragic developments now occurring in Pakistan. Yugoslavia and Pakistan obviously differ in important respects. (Any two countries differ in important respects.) But they share one fundamental characteristic; they include distinct territorial groups in a single political community. Contrary to what I regard as the "lessons of history" and the principles of good theory, particularly in recent years, the dominant West Pakistani group has used the power of the strong, nearly-dictatorial President (a West Pakistani general) to resist East Pakistani demands for autonomy. Given the general theory sketched above, we could have predicted what the newspapers have daily reported, a startling rise of East Pakistani (or Bengali) nationalism.[149] To an extraordinary extent, theoretically-oriented historians familiar with the course of events during the "Great Secession Winter of 1860-61", during the winter and spring of 1970-71, experienced a sense of *déjà vu* when they read the daily newspaper reports on Pakistan.[150] Similar contemporary developments in a variety of other countries

148. "President Tito's Letter to the Federal Assembly," [Yugoslavia] *Review of International Affairs,* December 20, 1970, pp. 15-17. Without assigning them any responsibility for my views, I wish to thank Dr. Mladen Soic, Director of the Yugoslavia Information Center, Dr. Bruner of the Embassy of Yugoslavia, and Bogdan Denitch of Columbia University, for improving my understanding of developments in Yugoslavia and providing me with relevant documents. From my conversations with them and from my reading, I have the strong impression that the Yugoslavs are consciously making a massive effort to integrate social scientific theories and empirical research and apply them to the complex problems they face in developing a political system appropriate for their society. The process that resulted in President Tito's letter to the Federal Assembly, and the subsequent discussion of it, appear to justify a "policy science approach" to the conduct of human affairs. I am in no position, of course, to evaluate the Yugoslav solutions to their practical problems of existence. Their general procedures, however, seem to me to be superior to those by which social science is used in the United States to try to solve practical problems of social existence.

149. For incisive analyses of developments in Pakistan, see Selig S. Harrison, "Nehru's Plan for Peace," *New Republic,* (June 19, 1971), 17-22; Aijaz Ahmad, "The Bloody Surgery of Pakistan," *The Nation,* (June 28, 1971), 815-819.

(e.g., Ireland, Canada) could readily be cited. Despite surface differences, they are so strikingly similar in their fundamental character and point so strongly in the same direction, that I think it reasonable to claim that they support my general theory and my hypothesis about the success of the Southern Nationalists after 1830, particularly after 1835-1836.

To restate that hypothesis in summary form:

A small group of Southern Nationalists ultimately succeeded in bringing about secession. They succeeded largely because the American political system, particularly the Presidency, developed in a way favorable to their cause. Among other defects, its irresponsible character, its built-in propensity to stimulate sectional cleavages, its incitement to demagogy, its powerful inducements to and rich rewards for individual and group opportunism and amorality, its antidemocratic exaltation of "strong Presidents," its glorification of the cult of "the virile personality," all strengthened the ability of Southern Nationalists (and sectionalists and provincials) to initiate and intensify political conflicts over the self-esteem and honor of members of the two main territorial cultural groups that distinctly evolved after 1790—a development in itself strongly stimulated by the defects of the American political system. No group worked more consciously and more effectively than the Southern Nationalists to speed that process. Who caused the Civil War? Living in a bicultural society with a radically defective political system, the Southern Nationalists, much more than any other group, caused it to occur by working unyieldingly, intensively, rationally, effectively, to achieve what later came to be known as "The Lost Cause."

---

150. Analogies are always tricky; analogies based on superficial knowledge border on the irresponsible. But I find it difficult to refrain from observing that the course of events in Pakistan today underscores the brilliance of Calhoun's propositions about the dual presidency and concurrent majority in bicultural or multicultural body politics. Comparison of events in the United States and Switzerland from 1847 to-date, as well as developments in many other societies in the nineteenth and twentieth centuries, support the general theories Calhoun developed to try to avert civil war in the United States. (Need it be said that my observation does not place me on Calhoun's side in respect to the preservation of black slavery?)

3. A Modest Proposal to Reorient and Reorganize the Established Historiographic and Social Science Systems

Thus far I have focused attention on the failure of historians to develop a credible explanation of Civil War causation. That failure, I have suggested, is best viewed as an indicator of the deficiencies of the historiographic and social scientific systems rather than the deficiencies of individual historians.

What can be done to reorient and reorganize those systems?[151] A hard question. I have no comprehensive, easy answer to it. But to provide a basis for discussion and debate, it seems useful to suggest a tentative answer. Toward that end, I sketch a modest proposal designed to develop good theories of internal war and credible explanations of the occurrence of specific internal wars. That proposal, I am inclined to think, has larger implications and applications.

As noted earlier, Harry Eckstein's broad definition of internal war widens its range, greatly increases the number of cases, and links them together as indicators of malfunctioning political systems. It seems desirable to expand that definition. Internal war, or another term for the same concept, *intrasocietal political violence,* can be viewed as one category of a still broader concept, *intrasocietal violence.*

As I conceive the concept, *intrasocietal violence,* it derives from the assumption that no such thing exists as an *innate* human instinct for aggression, hostility or violence. Aggressors are made, not born (except

---

151. In recent years, non-historians have again increasingly come to recognize that systematic historical studies are indispensable to the development of good general theories. As a result, they have bravely—and innocently—tried to use "secondary analysis" of secondary works to fill what they regard as the void left by historians; in a few cases, they even have tried to use primary sources. Predictably, the results have tended to be less than satisfactory. The Leonard-esque aspiration only diverts attention from the need to develop mechanisms to provide for the rational and integrated division of labor between social scientists who specialize in specified aspects of present human behavior and those who specialize in specified aspects of past human behavior.

An overall critique of the established social scientific system, and a sweeping proposal to change it, is found in Sam D. Sieber, in collaboration with Paul F. Lazarsfeld, "Reforming the University—The Role of the Research Center" (Bureau of Applied Social Science Research, Columbia U., 1970, mimeo).

perhaps for individuals who suffer from brain or other organic defects). Granted that assumption, it follows that intrasocietal violence, from sporadic anomic violence to fullscale revolutions, *indicates that something is wrong with the society in which it occurs.* Violence threatens life, a condition contrary to human reason and human welfare for it contradicts the very purpose of social existence. It should be viewed and treated, therefore, as a symptom of *societal* rather than *individual* disorder.[152]

My general orientation also assumes that it is the "function" of the men who control the *public* political system ("public" may avoid disputes over the term "political system") to create the conditions necessary for the members of a society to live together peaceably. Given that orientation, intrasocietal violence can then serve as an excellent indicator of the functioning and stage of development of a political system. Contrary to Marx's unfortunate tendency to overreact against Hegel and dismiss *the State* as mere epiphenomenon, I view the political system as the *primary* subsystem of any society. In final analysis, the men who control its political system are the men ultimately responsible for the wellbeing of *all* the members of a body politic.

Given that general orientation, I think it reasonable to assert this proposition:

In any society, the greater the malfunctioning of its political system or the more underdeveloped its political system, the greater the incidence of intrasocietal violence (over some reasonable period of time).

Among other advantages, that proposition enables us to assess the American political system and American society more realistically than if we narrowly focus our attention on *political* violence. Such narrow focus ignores the remarkably high incidence of *nonpolitical* violence in American society long after its economy was highly developed.

Put still another way, I suggest that the problem of internal war is best viewed and studied as part of the larger problem of intrasocietal

---

152. For a succinct, penetrating statement of the utility of treating violence as an indicator of societal malfunctioning, see Lewis A. Coser, "Some Social Functions of Violence," *Annals of the American Academy of Political and Social Science,* CCCLXIV (March, 1966), 12-15.

violence. And at the risk of seeming to succumb to grandiosity, I think that the best perspective to adopt is to view the problem of intrasocietal violence as part of the still larger problem, *violence in human society.* When we expand the problem in that way, I believe, we place ourselves in a better position to develop solutions for its component parts, i.e., we are then in a better position to study different types of violence on different levels of aggregation. Among other advantages, expanding the conceptual framework in which internal war is studied permits us to make more effective use of the *method of controlled inquiry.*

As Ernest Nagel has effectively argued, in principle, controlled inquiry can serve as the *functional equivalent* in the social sciences of controlled experiment in the natural sciences.[153] The method becomes particularly useful when our general orientation permits us to view internal war *as a product of the same basic condition that produces other types of violence in human societies,* namely the malfunctioning of the overall system in which human beings are interdependent and interact. Research designs can then provide more effectively for "control" cases, thereby helping us remedy a serious methodological defect in studies of internal war. To quote Mr. Orlansky's critique again, "One of the most significant flaws in almost all studies of internal wars is the absence of controls."[154]

Given the present conceptual framework for the study of internal war, we can compare societies that experience specified types and stages of internal war with societies that either experience other types and stages of internal war or do *not* significantly experience any type or stage over relatively long periods. When we expand our conceptual framework to encompass all types of intrasocietal violence, however, we significantly expand our capacity to make comparisons. We can then also compare societies that experience specified types of internal war with those that experience *other types of intrasocietal violence,* as well as with those that experience *relatively little intrasocietal violence* of any type. Thus the expanded conceptual framework would permit us to compare, for example, the incidence of all types of *intrasocietal violence* in Switzerland and the United States over a long time period,

153. Nagel, *Structure of Science,* pp. 450-459.
154. Orlansky, *Research on Internal War,* pp. 110.

say 1789 to 1971. Such a comparative study is far more useful for the purpose of theory-building than the type of study we can make if we restrict our attention to the incidence of internal war, particularly civil war, in the two societies from 1789 to 1971.

Suppose we go even further and expand our conceptual framework to include *intersocietal,* as well as intrasocietal, violence. We can then engage in comparative studies not only likely to help us develop propositions about the causal relationships among conflicts on different levels of aggregation, but likely to help us develop fruitful concepts and theories to explain conflicts of any particular type, on any particular level of aggregation.[155]

The expanded conceptual framework has other significant advantages. For example, if generally adopted, it would tend to stimulate and facilitate effective interaction and collaboration among scholars who specialize in the study of internal war, scholars who specialize in the study of other types of intrasocietal violence (e.g., suicide, anomic violence, crime), and scholars who specialize in the study of intersocietal violence. Moreover, the larger conceptual framework significantly improves the chances that social scientists will be able to develop the organizational structure, as well as secure the financial support, required for *serious* attempts to generate and develop good theories of internal war and other types of violence in human society.

In my judgment, the argument sketched above supports the following proposition.

To date, scholars who study human violence (in any of its protean forms) have not had anything remotely like the organizational structure and financial support required to crack intellectual problems that probably are as difficult to crack as the atom or the genetic code. Pessimists may claim that those problems are intractable. But that *claim* cannot now be tested empirically. It cannot be tested because those problems *must* be intractable, given: 1) the traditional and extraordinarily fragmented organizational structure of the social sciences in particular and the academic world in general; 2) the pathetically

---

155. For an excellent analysis and exposition of the subject identified in its title, see the important book by Adam Przeworski and Henry Teune, *The Logic of Comparative Social Inquiry* (New York: John Wiley and Sons—Interscience, 1970).

inadequate financial resources now available to individuals, brave enough—perhaps, foolish enough—to tackle problems whose solutions require the functional equivalents of the natural science national laboratories such as Oak Ridge or Brookhaven. If we want to do serious intellectual work on the problems of internal war, intrasocietal violence and intersocietal violence, it seems reasonable, therefore, to propose the creation of a Violence Research Institute, based on the organizational model of the national laboratories.

Aside from providing a model for the serious conduct of social scientific research that would focus on major problems of human existence—I view present efforts as earnest, but not serious—the goal of the proposed Institute would be to develop good general theories about the causes, consequences, and control of violence for "the benefit of Humane Life", the primary goal of the seventeenth-century "natural philosophers" who set the Scientific Revolution irrepressibly in motion. To achieve that goal, it seems reasonable to think, the proposed Institute should have these characteristics:

1. It should be established on a long term basis. For significant progress to be made, a minimum of 20 years would seem to be a realistic perspective.

2. It should receive relatively large-scale *and assured* financial support, say one billion dollars over the first 20 year period (the approximate cost of the *preliminary* work on the SST).

3. Scholars should be able to associate themselves with the Institute in a wide range of roles: from fulltime, lifetime career personnel to once a month participants in seminars conducted under its auspices, or seminars "spun-off" from it and conducted by interested scholars at a number of colleges and universities.

4. It should be completely autonomous of existing academic institutions; its directors should be free to decide who they wish to have participate in its work and in what roles.

5. It should not replace—or threaten to replace—any existing center, institute, or program at any institution. It should be unique, therefore, in its comprehensiveness, scale of operations, and freedom from those parochial institutional concerns that make the American academic world the last major institutional relic of the nineteenth-century ethos of cutthroat competition and atomistic liberalism.

6. It should be multidisciplinary from the start, for functional rather than honorific (or "political") reasons. Only an intrinsically multidisciplinary organization can bring together, and effectively integrate, specialists equipped with the extraordinary range of interests, training and skills required to grapple seriously with the overall problem of human violence, and the subproblems it encompasses.

As Shakespeare had one of his characters sardonically observe, any man "can call spirits from the vasty deep". But will they come? That is the billion dollar question. More precisely, what likelihood exists that any existing agency will respond favorably to a call for the establishment of a Violence Research Institute? Alas, little or none. Why then call?

Among other reasons, it seems useful to call for such an Institute in order to set in motion a process that eventually may indeed culminate in its establishment—or the establishment of something like it. In the short run, however, my proposal primarily is designed to stimulate thought and debate on what can be done, on a more practical scale, to reorient and reorganize ongoing activities conducted within the framework of existing institutions.

In one sense, my main argument is that the deficiencies in the established historigraphic and social science systems do not mainly stem from lack of adequate financial support, they mainly stem from adherence to tradition and unwillingness to break free from the familiar institutional, disciplinary and departmental fetters that bind scholars to the past. Only a "revolutionary offensive" can strike off those fetters. And revolutionary offensives only get under way and succeed when ancient regimes no longer are propped-up by traditional ideologies and traditional authorities who once commanded, but no longer deserve, attention or respect.

Specifically, what can be done? One very modest example may economically serve to make the larger point.

In recent years, the directors of the graduate program in my department have scrapped the traditional concept that specialized fields of historical study must be defined exclusively by some fixed combination of geographical and chronological criteria (e.g., Modern European History, Recent American History from 1877 to the Present). Instead, students are now required to take at *least* one field of a "theoretical and/or comparative type", and a "regional-national field" specifically designed *according to the individual student's research needs and professional objectives.* A student interested in the general problem of intrasocietal violence, therefore, *might create* a field, "theories of internal war", that requires considerable intensive work *outside* the History Department. Given that theoretical interest and field, *within* the History Department, the student might then concentrate on selected aspects of American history from the mid-eighteenth century to the mid-nineteenth century.

Preliminary results of the experiment have been encouraging. Forced to break out of old routines, students and faculty have been able to view in a new perspective problems that had seemed old and stale, as well as identify new and interesting problems that had hitherto been obscured in the murky light of tradition.

Whether our particular experiment eventually turns out to be successful is not the real point. The real point is that the established historiographic system (like the established social science system) requires radical reorientation and reorganization for historians to achieve their professed goals. One way to begin that process, I have suggested, is to focus attention on large-scale problems that seriously affect human welfare (e.g., violence) and try to develop organizational structures and training programs more appropriate to their solution than those that presently exist.

To fail to be dissatisfied with the present systems, to clutch tightly to traditional and familiar ways, to stand pat, is a formula for Mandarins who think that to study the past and present one must be backward looking and essentially satisfied with the status quo. At this stage in scholarly development, I am convinced, to call for further progress requires us to call for radical change.

Appendix

A GENERAL ANALYTICAL MODEL FOR
EXPLANATIONS OF INTERNAL WAR
CAUSATION

I. Narrative framework (or chronicle of events) of *overall decision*
    (e.g., American Civil War), adapted to specific characteristics of
    political system in which internal war occurs.

   A. Identification of sequence of decisions that constitute the
       overall decision.

       1. *Main* decisions (arranged in *stages*, identified by *turning
           points*)

           a. *Decisions*

               1. D_1 – Initial decision (e.g., Missouri Compromises,
                   1819-1821)

               2. D_2 – (e.g., Tariff of 1824)

               3. D_3 – Dn (e.g., Tariff of 1828, Gag Rule on
                   Slavery Petitions, Wilmot Proviso, Kansas-
                   Nebraska S.C. Secession)

               4. D_t – Terminal decision (e.g., Lincoln's proclama-
                   tion calling forth "the militia of the several
                   states of the Union . . .", April 15, 1861)

           b. *Stages* (number and type vary according to internal
               war studied)

               1. Initial stage (e.g., 1819-1835, Missouri Com-
                   promise to Gag Rule)

2. Second stage (e.g., 1835-1846, Gag Rule to Wilmot Proviso)

3. Third stage (e.g., 1846-1854, Wilmot Proviso to Kansas-Nebraska)

4. Fourth stage (e.g., 1854-1860, Kansas-Nebraska to 1860 election)

5. Terminal stage (e.g., 1860-1861, S.C. Secession to Lincoln's Proclamation)

2. Subordinate decisions that constitute each main decision (arranged in stages identified by turning points)

   a. Decisions

   1. D_1 — (e.g., Tallmadge resolution, Feb. 13, 1819)

   2. D_2 — Dn

   3. D_t — (e.g., Monroe's Proclamation of Missouri as a state, August 10, 1821)

   b. Stages (as in Ab above)

II. Analytic framework to explain sequence of decisions

   A. Explicit identification of the decision explained.

   1. Overall decision

   2. A specific main decision of overall decision

   3. A specific subordinate decision of a specific main decision

B. *Predecisional* background of decision explained (references to phenomena prior to any D_1, relevant to explanation of sequence D_1 to D_t; can be taken as "given" and does not require "explanation," thus avoiding infinite regress back to Garden of Eden).

C. Identification of actors who play significant roles in the decision specified for explanation. (Distinguish among actors within formal decision-making organizations and those outside it.)

   1. Main antagonists

   2. Allies of each set of main antagonists in rank order of relative importance (i.e., relative power of each allied group to affect decision outcome)

   3. Others.

D. Explanation of relative power of actors.

   1. Main dimensions of concept of relative power

      a. Whose will prevailed or came closest to prevailing (i.e., whose position on issue adopted)

      b. Whose purposeful actions contributed most to creating situations that influenced decision outcome (i.e., purposely acted to shape events rather than benefitted from events not of their making)

   2. Power-convertible resources (examples, not exhaustive list)

      a. General position in society (e.g., group membership, legal and extra-legal rank, rights, privileges)

   b. General character (e.g., intelligence, integrity or lack of it)

   c. Particular position of competence relevant to decision (e.g., skill, information, experience)

   d. Particular characteristics relevant to decision (e.g., intensity, persistence, personality)

   e. Numbers, i.e., proportion of group in population

3. Actions (examples, not exhaustive list)

   a. Strategy

   b. Tactics

   c. Organization

   d. Persuasion

     1) Physical force (e.g.. duels)
     2) Arguments (e.g.. "constitutional")
     3) Inducements (e.g., favors, bribes)
     4) Nonphysical pressures (e.g., economic pressures, political pressures)

4. Historical situation that influenced relative power of actors at time of decision (i.e., phenomena occurring independently of actors' actions)

   a. Domestic phenomena (e.g., transportation revolution, religious revivals, migration and immigration)

   b. Foreign phenomena (e.g., abolition of slavery in British West Indies, Mexican revolutions, "no-popery" movements in Europe)

5. "General laws or propositions" relevant to men's relative power in specific situations (probabilistic laws)

6. Explanation arranged by type of analyst (see E 2 below)

E. Explanation of relative importance and characteristics of motives or goals

   1. Dimensions of concept, "relative importance of characteristics of goals"

      a. Time perspective and scope of goals

      b. Rank order of importance

      c. Level of consciousness

      d. Openness of public avowal

   2. Goals assigned to specific actors by different types of analysts

      a. Self-avowed goals

         1) Publicly avowed
         2) Nonpublicly avowed

      b. Goals assigned by contemporaries

         1) Publicly assigned

            a) Friends or allies
            b) Enemies or antagonists
            c) Expert "neutral" observers

    2) Nonpublicly assigned

        a) Friends or allies
        b) Enemies or antagonists
        c) Expert "neutral" observers

  c. Goals assigned by historians

    1) Historians classified by attitudes towards specified groups of actors

3. Categories of "conscious goals" or "ends in view" assigned to actors (examples)

  a. Self-esteem or honor
  b. Prestige (individual)
  c. Status (group)
  d. Material interests
  e. Ideological goals (e.g., preserve slavery)
  f. Moral goals or norms (e.g., Christian brotherhood, natural rights)
  g. Political power to attain goals, a-f
  h. Political power "for its own sake"

4. Identification of habitual patterns of behavior or psychological dispositions influencing actors' choice of goals

5. Compatibility of goals, habitual patterns, psychological dispositions in respect to specific action

  a. Compatible (all "point" to one course of action)
  b. Cross-pressure (some "point" to one course of action, others to contradictory course of action)

6. Identification of relative importance of goals, habitual patterns, psychological dispositions

7. Explanation of relative importance of goals, habitual patterns, psychological dispositions, as determinants of behavior of specified actors in specified decision, making use of relevant "general laws or propositions"

8. Explanations of *origins and development* of goals, habitual patterns, psychological dispositions, making use of relevant "general laws or propositions"

    a. General social environment and historical development
    b. Specific group environment and historical development
    c. Personal environment and historical development

F. Impact of a specified decision on a subsequent decision or subsequent decisions

    1. Time span (terms vary according to type of decision and circumstances; distinctions tend to be arbitrary)

        a. Short-run
        b. Middle-run
        c. Long-run

    2. Type of impact (terms vary according to type of decision and circumstances; distinctions tend to be arbitrary)

        a. Direct
        b. Direct-indirect (direct impact on one set of actors, indirect impact on another set—or sets—of actors)
        c. Indirect

INDEX of NAMES

341

INDEX of SUBJECTS